As We Forgive Our Debtors

Bankruptcy and Consumer Credit in America

As We Forgive Our Debtors

Bankruptcy and Consumer Credit in America

Teresa A. Sullivan

Elizabeth Warren

Jay Lawrence Westbrook

BeardBooks

Washington, D.C.

Library of Congress Cataloging-in-Publication Data

Sullivan, Teresa A., 1949–
As we forgive our debtors : bankruptcy and consumer credit in America / Teresa A. Sullivan, Elizabeth Warren, Jay Lawrence Westbrook.

p. cm.
Originally published: New York : Oxford University Press, 1989.
Includes bibliographical references and index.
ISBN 1-893122-15-8 (pbk.)
1. Bankruptcy–United States. 2. Consumer credit–United States. 3. Finance, Personal–United States. I. Warren, Elizabeth. II. Westbrook, Jay Lawrence. III. Title.
HG3766.S79 1999
332.7'5'0973–dc21 99-16954
CIP

Printed in the United States of America

For H.D.L., who got me into this.
T.A.S.

For B.H.M., who encourages me.
E.W.

For loving my More-Than-Me
Mom, Dad, Polly.
J.L.W.

Preface to the 1999 Reprint Edition

When *As We Forgive Our Debtors* was first published in 1989, non-business bankruptcies had risen to nearly 581,000 and bankruptcy as a social issue was beginning to gain attention. By 1991, with the country again in a recession and with widespread industrial restructuring and downsizing, non-business bankruptcies rose to more than 811,000. In the 1992 Presidential campaigns, the bankruptcy numbers were taken as an important social indicator, albeit an indicator subject to differing interpretations depending upon political party.

The number of bankruptcies did not drop, despite the return of prosperity. Downsizing became part of the common lexicon and credit card marketing exploded. Non-business bankruptcies first reached the million-mark in 1996 and by 1998 more than 1,442,000 bankruptcies were filed. Congress chartered a national commission to examine bankruptcy reform, and numerous bills were introduced to change the bankruptcy system.

The sheer increase in scale of bankruptcies naturally attracted the attention of additional researchers, and the findings from *As We Forgive* have been part of the ensuing debate. A number of the findings developed here have remained remarkably robust. Since being confirmed by other studies, some of our results have made the complete circuit from controversial finding to conventional wisdom. Among the findings that so far seem robust:

- The proportion of bankruptcy filers who are women filing bankruptcy alone has increased.

- Bankrupt debtors come from a wide cross-section of the occupational distribution; blue-collar, white-collar, and service occupations are represented among the debtors.

- Despite their occupational status, bankrupt debtors are, on average reporting incomes well below the national average. These low earnings often result from a period of income interruption.

- Most bankrupt debtors are carrying debt loads that are two to three times the size of their incomes – in some cases, even larger. Many of these debts are unsecured, short-term liabilities.

- Bankrupt debtors have very modest assets, although a substantial fraction of them are homeowners.

- Given the low incomes and assets of the debtors, the effect of state exemption laws is difficult to discern in most cases.

- Roughly two of every three debtors who attempt Chapter 13 repayment plans do not complete their plans.

- Job loss, divorce, illness and injury appear to be implicated in many bankruptcies.

- Credit cards appear to be involved in a large number of bankruptcies.

- There are relatively few people filing a repeat bankruptcy, although there are a number of debtors who re-file in a different chapter (with out having received a discharge) shortly after their original filing.

A number of subsequent studies have confirmed all or part of these findings, or have generally eliminated competing hypotheses.

Some of our findings have sparked the interest of policy-makers. Our finding that a large number of "non-business" bankruptcies are filed by current or former entrepreneurs has helped stimulate interest in providing a chapter of bankruptcy for small businesses. Efforts to improve the collection of child support, to change credit card lending, and to change some of the internal processes within the bankruptcy courts all found support within these pages.

On the other hand, much of the national debate continues to focus on the numbers of debtors, as if controlling the numbers will somehow make the underlying financial problems disappear. Much of the debate seems to assume that the increased numbers of bankruptcies constitute prima facie evidence that the bankruptcy system is being abused. If the system is being abused, goes the argument, then unworthy or undeserving people must be cheating the rest of us by declaring bankruptcy. From this perspective, the new task of bankruptcy policy is separating the worthy from the unworthy. As was the case with welfare, some method of means-testing is the policy solution that is often proposed.

Our finding that most debtors cannot repay their debts has been largely ignored in the means-test debate, although some more recent studies confirm that the debtors still cannot repay more than a fraction of their debt, even with considerable sacrifice lasting many years. A great deal of Congressional effort has continued to focus on closing loopholes whose actual use was quite limited, while continuing to make bankruptcy law more complex. It has sometimes seemed as if the mere complexity of the Bankruptcy Code was an effort to reduce access to the bankruptcy courts.

Although perhaps frustrated with what seemed to us a misunderstanding of key findings, we were extremely gratified by the reception that the first edition of *As We Forgive* received. The American Bar Association honored us with a Silver Gavel Award in 1990, and the book was named a finalist in the Distinguished Scholarly Contribution competition of the American Sociological Association. To have earned distinction in two disciplines was a great satisfaction. We greatly enjoyed the opportunity to discuss our ideas with audiences in law schools and sociology departments all over the country. We also appreciated the opportunity to address professional audiences in the American Association of Law Schools, the American Sociological Association, the Law and Society Association, and the Population Association of America.

Our work also found an audience – often a critical one – within the bankruptcy bench and bar and among law policy wonks. The authors have at various times addressed bankruptcy judges, bankruptcy court clerks, and Chapter 13 trustees, and each of these audiences helped us to understand further what our data meant, or in some cases to clarify what the data did not mean or the issues on which the evidence remains ambiguous. We have been invited to give testimony before the National Commission on Bankruptcy Reform, before various committees in Congress, and to state legislatures.

Moreover, we found that the book opened doors to many interesting audiences and other professionals whom we might otherwise never have met. We were invited to address consumer credit lenders, consumer credit counselors, faculty who teach family finance courses, adult Sunday School classes, and even an insolvency support group.

We met faculty from schools of business, departments of economics, human ecology, and anthropology, and social work faculty who were interested in our work and shared details of their work. None of us has previously been involved in a project that generated so many diverse and interdisciplinary contacts.

Because bankruptcy continues to be an important issue in the United States, we have conducted a second study of consumer bankruptcy. It was conducted with cases filed in 1991 in the three states studied in *As We Forgive,* but also in the state of California and in two of the three districts in Tennessee. We have used the results from this study to update our findings from *As We Forgive* in a lengthy article (Teresa A. Sullivan, Elizabeth Warren, and Jay Lawrence Westbrook, "Consumer Debtors Ten Years Later: A Financial Comparison of Consumer Bankrupts 1981-1991," American Bankruptcy Law Journal 68,2 (Spring 1994): 121-154).

We have also used the new data to develop a second book-length treatment. This book, called *The Fragile Middle Class* (Yale University Press, 2000) differs from *As We Forgive* because we use the data not to study the internal workings of bankruptcy, but to look outward to the larger population from whom the bankrupt debtors were drawn. In *The Fragile Middle Class,* we attempt to discern how and why some people end up in bankruptcy courts. Once again, we try to look beyond the numbers to identify the causes. Much of what we conclude supports the findings we first reported in *As We Forgive.*

We would like to thank Susan Pannell, the acquisitions editor at Beard Books, for giving us this opportunity to bring *As We Forgive* to a new audience. We thanked our families in the initial preface, and we echo it here; our spouses and children have been wonderfully supportive of us even when it seemed apparent that doing empirical work in bankruptcy should be viewed as a symptom of something more serious than a mere scholarly pursuit. Winona Schroeder helped us in getting this reprint edition to publication, and we thank her for her frequent and valuable services. We thank again our learned colleagues who provided advice and argument, and we thank again the original donors who supported this work. We hope that this new edition will help additional readers puzzle out what lies beyond the bankruptcy numbers.

– TAS
– EW
– JLW

Preface

We feel singularly fortunate in the combination of unlikely circumstances that made it possible for us to do the multidisciplinary study that is the Consumer Bankruptcy Project. Our improbable good luck began with the coming together of three people with the background and interest to do a reasonably sophisticated study of consumer bankruptcy, including socioeconomic comparisons of bankrupt debtors with Americans generally. A fair number of law professors have done empirical studies, but all too often with little or no help from social scientists trained in survey research and statistical inference. On the other hand, despite devoting enormous resources to the study of income levels and sources, social scientists have largely ignored problems of debt. This neglect might stem from unfamiliarity with the complexities of debt collection in American law and practice. Our team of two law professors and a demographer arose from the happy circumstance of personal and professional relationships that threw us together. We learned about common interests, but more importantly we came to be fascinated by the things that the other person knew and could do.

Our good fortune extended through seven years of gathering and studying a quarter million pieces of information about consumer bankrupts and their creditors. For almost two years, hundreds of enthusiastic bankruptcy law students helped us to code all that information into a computer. All the material was coded twice to ensure the highest possible degree of accuracy in the data. We then had the help of a number of outstanding graduate students in two more years of very complex computer analysis of the data. With assistance from so many talented students in two different disciplines, we feel confident that our data provide a useful picture of consumer bankruptcy cases from 1981, when our cases were filed, until 1985, by which time most of them had been closed. For reasons explained in Chapter Two, we are also reasonably sure that the essentials of our findings would not be greatly different for cases filed in the late 1980s.

In describing what we have found in the bankruptcy files and in comparing that information with evidence we marshaled from national samples, we have followed a few conventions to simplify the reader's task. Figures reported in the text have been rounded; for example, dollar amounts were rounded to the nearest hundred dollars. Dollar values in the tables have been rounded to the nearest dollar. Other values in the tables are usually reported to two decimal places. Our criterion level for tests of significance has been $p \leq 0.05$. "Code" refers to the Bankruptcy Code, originally the Bankruptcy Reform Act of 1978. In bankruptcy, debtors file in Chapter 7, Chapter 11, or Chapter 13. For clarity, we refer to the chapters within our book as Chapter One, Chapter Two, and so on.

Our most important analyses are reported, at least in summary form, in both tables and text. Less important findings often appear only in the book's notes. We doublechecked many of the results by using different statistical techniques, but we have limited the techniques reported in the text to the most familiar ones. Above all, we have tried to keep all of the text accessible to an educated lay reader, explaining both the legal and the statistical issues as simply and yet as correctly as possible. We have also included a number of portraits of people in bankruptcy, both debtors and creditors. Although the names of debtors and of most creditors are pseudonyms, there are no "composite" cases: Each case description represents an actual case in our sample.

This book by no means exhausts the information in our files, but it does present what we believe to be the most important themes. A preliminary version of Chapter Three appeared in *American Bankruptcy Law Journal,* and a version of Chapter Thirteen appeared in *Law and Social Inquiry.*

For all of the good fortune that has accompanied us, we are indebted to a large number of people and institutions. Having become experts in the cataloguing of debts, we are happy to acknowledge our own.

We are especially grateful to the bankruptcy court personnel, bankruptcy judges, trustees, and practitioners who were so generous with their time and knowledge. Our confidentiality agreements prevent us from listing their names, but we thank them for their candor and insight. Without their help, this study would not have been possible.

Given the inherent challenges of multidisciplinary work, we needed the help of many of our colleagues. Among those quick to offer support were Professor Mark Yudof, dean of The University of Texas Law School, Professor Dudley L. Poston, former director of the Population Research Center at The University of Texas, and his successor Dr. Frank D. Bean. We received valuable criticisms from Professors Harley L. Browning, Julius G. Getman, Richard Lempert, Lynn LoPucki, Stewart Macauley, Richard Markovits, Raymond T. Nimmer, Lawrence E. Raffalovich, Alan Schwartz, William Whitford, Mark Warr, and Harold Wolf.

A number of professional audiences provided useful feedback: the National Conference of Bankruptcy Judges, the Federal Judicial Center Regional Workshop of Bankruptcy Judges, The National Association of Chapter 13 Trustees, the American Sociological Association, the Debtor/Creditor Section of the Association of American Law Schools, the Law and Society Association, the Society for the Study of Social Problems, The University of Texas Annual Bankruptcy Conference, the Federal Judicial Center National Conference for Bankruptcy Clerks, the Legal Studies Workshop of the University of Iowa School of Law, the Brooklyn Law School Faculty Forum, the Los Angeles Demographic Forum, the Population Studies Laboratory at the University of Southern California, the Population Studies Institute at the University of Colorado, the Department of Sociology at the University of Massachusetts, Amherst, the Faculty Colloquium Series at The University of Texas School of Law, the Women's Studies Research Seminar at The University of Texas, and the Law Faculty Seminar of the University of Pennsylvania.

We are grateful to an entire phalanx of research assistants. Hangon Kim, Catherine Nicholson, Kimberly Winick, Audrey Singer, and Barbara Zsembik traveled with us on hectic out-of-town collection trips to copy the cases to bring back for our student coders. More than a hundred law students at the University of Houston and The University of Texas spent hours learning the details of bankruptcy files and code books so that they could record the data from the files to produce our database. Jesse Castillo organized the files to produce more efficient coding. Catherine Nicholson took over the management of the student coders during the project's most intense time. She was a critical asset, working long hours to bring the database to completion. We are grateful not only for her remarkable competence, but also for the grace and good spirit she always brought to the job.

Douglas Forbes was our principal research assistant throughout the preparation of the book. He used his many talents with the computer and his unfailing good cheer to help us complete the data analysis. His long hours and his willingness to deal with the frustrations of a monstrous database were exemplary, and we thank him for his intelligence, insight, and professionalism.

Lloyd Potter and Starling Pullum provided valuable computer consulting. Pat Floyd gave tireless clerical assistance through multiple drafts of every chapter. Connie Nicholson kept our grant accounts straight and steered us safely through many bureaucratic tangles. Dr. Terri LeClercq gave valuable editing assistance as we neared the final draft.

We were generously supported in this project by NSF Grant SES-8310173, and we acknowledge the helpful advice of the NSF Law and Social Sciences Program Director, Dr. Felice Levine. Any opinions, findings, conclusions, and recommendations expressed in this publication are those of the authors and do not necessarily reflect the views of the National Science Foundation or any other sponsor. We are also grateful to the following for research grants that sustained and enriched the project at critical junctures: the American Bar Foundation, the Texas Bar Foundation, the University Research Institute of The University of Texas at Austin, the Policy Research Institute of the Lyndon Baines Johnson School for Public Affairs at The University of Texas at Austin, the Law School Foundation of the University of Houston, the Law School

Foundation of The University of Texas, the Public Policy Initiative Fund of The University of Pennsylvania, and the John M. Olin Foundation grant to the Institute for Law and Economics of the University of Pennsylvania. Additional research assistance was provided through the National Institute of Child Health and Human Development (NICHD) Training Grant #HD07081-12 and NICHD Center grant #HD06160-18.

Finally, we offer special thanks to our patient and helpful families. This project disrupted far too many evening meals, vacations, ball games, promised pick-up times, and much more. It became part of the woof and warp of family life, with project, co-authors, and families inextricably linked in surviving everything from a car accident to the arrival of a new baby. Polly Westbrook helped us collect data in Texas and in Illinois, worked to straighten out data in Austin, and served as a much-needed audience for early drafts. Bruce H. Mann has a special understanding of the joys and frustrations of interdisciplinary work, and he provided critical support over the life of the project. Douglas Laycock edited the penultimate draft and gave us much valuable advice. Joel Westbrook and Amelia Warren helped us survive a crisis with mislabeled files, spending tedious hours recataloguing and refiling. Alexander Warren and Joseph Peter Laycock helped locate files and collate manuscripts. John Patrick Laycock is too small to have helped, but cooperating in a normal pregnancy and being a good baby earn him heartfelt thanks. We wrote in Chapter Five about the entrepreneurs who put their whole families to work, and this project taught us that research is another form of entrepreneurship. For us it was more of a family business than we had ever intended.

Austin, Texas T.A.S.
Philadelphia, Pennsylvania E.W.
January 1989 J.L.W.

Contents

1

Introduction

Bankrupt. The single word is a body blow, like "Dead."

Financial death overtook more than 400,000 American consumers who filed for bankruptcy in 1986.[1] The number has more than doubled in less than a decade. Concern is mounting about what these numbers mean for the American economy and what they say about our national character.

In this book you will meet some of the growing army of Americans who have been in bankruptcy, heroes and scoundrels and ordinary people: the single woman in Illinois struggling to support six children on her part-time job; the Texas couple who tried bankruptcy once and liked it so much they ran up more than a year's income in credit card debt and did it again; the Pennsylvania couple fighting to keep their home after the husband lost his job because of an injury; the Dallas couple that put everything they owned into a can't-miss business—to open at the 1980 Moscow Olympics. You will also meet some of their creditors, both victims and fools: the recently divorced wife whose husband tried bankruptcy to evade the divorce settlement; the friend who poured perhaps $100,000 into an Illinois couple's failing business; the giant corporations that gave an unemployed salesman four MasterCards and three VISAs.

In addition to reading about the people in bankruptcy, you will learn about the pathology of the 600 billion dollar consumer credit system that is both the driving engine of the American economy and a source of deep concern. In the 1970s and 1980s, our society has increased its private debt—along with its government's deficit—to one record high after another. From 1980 to 1987, consumer debt grew from 300 to 600 billion dollars. The dramatic growth in consumer bankruptcies has paralleled this great increase in personal liabilities.[2] Such parallel growth should not be surprising, because there is necessarily a close link between debt and legal action. The granting of credit ultimately rests upon the promise of the state to enforce debts. As Henry Clay pointed out almost 150 years ago, the state has always qualified that promise by restricting how far it will coerce people to pay.[3] For example, the state will not exact a pound of flesh, even if the debtor promised it. Bankruptcy is the ultimate limitation on the state's willingness to force its citizens to pay private debts. Thus, it is integral to the enormous financial and legal system that starts with a credit application and sometimes ends in a repossession, a lawsuit against the debtor, or bankruptcy.

The moral and cultural origins of bankruptcy are found in the Biblical "jubilees," a forgiveness of debt every seven years. Bankruptcy has been part of our own legal heritage since Elizabethan times, and the U.S. Constitution expressly grants to the federal government the power to make bankruptcy laws.[4] What has changed recently is the far greater use of these laws by both individuals and businesses. Bankruptcy has not become routine, but it has become commonplace. During the 1980s, Braniff, Continental, LTV, Johns Manville, Texaco, and many other old and famous businesses have joined millions of individuals in seeking protection in bankruptcy court.

Bankruptcy is a remarkable phenomenon. It is financial death and financial rebirth. Bankruptcy laws literally make debts vanish. When a judge signs a paper titled "Discharge," debts legally disappear. This is the fate of billions of dollars of debt discharged in bankruptcy every year.[5] Hundreds of thousands of debtors are released from their obligations, free to earn and spend as they choose.

Bankruptcy is a powerful phenomenon. But curiously enough, given our information-hungry society, it is one about which we have little hard information.[6] The government records to the last tenth of an inch how much snow fell in Hingham, Massachusetts, in 1984, and the yield per acre of planted wheat in Deercreek, Oklahoma, in 1987. But nowhere does the government publish data on how much debt was discharged in bankruptcy, on how much the incomes or assets were of debtors who filed for bankruptcy, on which creditors bore what losses in bankruptcy, or on whether the consumers and businesses who filed bankruptcy survived and prospered or continued to struggle. The government reports the raw numbers of filings, notes the bankruptcy chapter in which the petitioners filed, and makes a halfhearted effort to sort out the business from the consumer filings. Beyond that, the government—and the rest of us—have no idea what happens in bankruptcy. Although bankruptcy touches the lives of several million people every year—debtors, their families, their employers and co-workers, and their creditors—what we know about them comes from little more than an occasional newspaper article or office gossip about "somebody my brother knew."

This book is based on the Consumer Bankruptcy Project, the largest study of consumer bankruptcy ever undertaken. It required collection of more than a quarter of a million pieces of information from a sample of 2400 bankruptcy petitioners whose cases began in 1981 and for the most part ended by 1985. Thousands of bankruptcy judges, lawyers, and clerks have seen the events that are told through these data. An even greater number of debtors and creditors have lived through some part of the process. But the view of each actor is idiosyncratic, and the closeness of a view narrows its perspective. We wrote this book to shed light on a bankruptcy system that is largely unknown to the public.

The preparation of this book entailed a complete data analysis, only a small fraction of which is represented in the various tables that follow. Indeed, the book is not an almanac of indigestible numbers. It is about human beings who declare bankruptcy and about the creditors they drag into the process with them. We talk about those people in bankruptcy that we have encountered, although we have changed their names to protect their privacy. We try not to let the statistics about debtors and creditors obscure the very real pain, anger, deceit, fear, and relief that color each bankruptcy file.

Bankruptcy Debates

Although the public's knowledge about bankruptcy has been limited, in the 1980s bankruptcy finally became a subject for widespread public debate, no longer limited to a small cadre of experts and to the silent people who were processed through bankruptcy courts. Business bankruptcies such as Johns Manville and A. H. Robins made the headlines, while editorials thundered that the massive increase in consumer bankruptcies demonstrated the moral breakdown of society and threatened the consumer credit system.

This public attention followed on the heels of the 1978 Bankruptcy Code (the Code), the most complete rewriting of bankruptcy law in American history. While the Code was mostly the handiwork of experts, House and Senate committees determined its final form. By a twist of congressional procedure and political horsetrading, the House version had been written in the House Judiciary Subcommittee on Civil Rights, of all places, and the generosity of its consumer provisions seemed to many to reflect its bleeding-heart liberal origins. After the adoption of the Code, and coincident with the advent of lawyer advertising and a series of economic shocks, the number of business and consumer bankruptcies rose sharply. Many commentators were quick to blame the increase on the new Code's liberality and to demand re-reform.

A vigorous debate arose over the effects of the new Code and the place and purpose of bankruptcy law in American life. Large-scale lobbying efforts besought state legislators to restrict the Code's effects. Almost before the ink on the Code was dry, bills were introduced in Congress to curb the Code's impact.

The consumer credit industry, in reaction to some 1978 Code provisions and to the rise in bankruptcies, funded a study by the Krannert School of Business at Purdue University. The study covered Chapter 7 (liquidation) cases filed in 1981, the same year that we began our study. The report asserted that $1.1 billion of debt a year that could have been paid was being discharged by debtors in bankruptcy and that almost a third of the people in bankruptcy could have repaid "a significant part" of their debts.[7] Discounting the country's economic problems, other academics joined in the claim that the new Bankruptcy Code had caused the great rise in filings by making bankruptcy too easy.[8]

These assertions challenged a central premise of bankruptcy law—that bankruptcy is used by honest debtors in serious financial trouble. Many voices now assert that increased filings "prove" that bankruptcy has become a haven for middle-class sharpies who bathe in the cleansing waters of bankruptcy rather than pay debts they are quite able to pay. The image of the bankrupt who is shrewder, not poorer, than the rest of us threatens to become the central stereotype in many discussions of bankruptcy policy.

The purpose of bankruptcy law, properly used rather than abused, is to serve as a financial hospital for people sick with debt. If hospital admissions rise dramatically, there are at least two explanations for the increase. It may be that doctors have started admitting patients who are not seriously ill and who could be treated as outpatients. Or the crowded hospital wards may simply reflect a breakdown of health in the community. If the hospital population suddenly rose, no sensible person would close the hospital doors and announce that the problem had been solved. Instead, medical researchers would examine the patients to find out if they were really sick and, if so, why.

We viewed part of our task in just this way. In any particular bankruptcy case, the task of evaluating fault is impossible unless a judge calls the debtors into court and cross-examines their circumstances and prospects at length. But across a large sample of bankruptcy cases, we could estimate whether the debtors were abusing the bankruptcy system or whether their financial collapse left them little prospect for repayment in or out of bankruptcy.

Aside from addressing such questions about debtors, we break new ground by devoting considerable attention to the position of creditors in bankruptcy. Debtors have been the focus of almost all prior studies and of the policy debates. Yet there is always a creditor on the other end of any debt. We examine which creditors face the most risk in bankruptcy. We assess the different circumstances facing different lenders, including credit card issuers, taxing authorities, banks, finance companies, ex-spouses, doctors, credit unions, and accident victims. We compare those who are in the business of extending credit (like finance companies) with those who never wanted to be creditors (like accident victims). We identify the creditors who lent to higher income debtors and those who lent to people with much lower earnings. We determine which creditors insisted on collateral to protect themselves and which did not. We review how creditors' bankruptcy exposure reflects their lending decisions. By examining the diverse creditors who show up in the bankruptcy process, we can draw inferences about the lending practices that may have made some of them frequent visitors to the bankruptcy courts.

Our data depict a credit industry that is far from monolithic in its lending practices. If there are creditors eager to extend excessive loans without adequate credit checks, there are others in the industry anxious to reduce losses by more careful credit practices. This latter group will find much in our data to improve the credit system.

The bankruptcy system was legislated in a vacuum of fact. We test the arguments and the unspoken premises of the bankruptcy debates against hard data about how bankruptcy actually works.

Framing the Issues

Three central questions are woven throughout this book. Who are the debtors and the creditors in bankruptcy? What factors have contributed to the spectacular increases in consumer bankruptcy? How should these data affect the normative and policy decisions underlying the consumer bankruptcy laws? These issues recur as we analyze the data.

Perhaps the most frequently asked question about bankruptcy is "Who goes into bankruptcy?" Are bankrupt debtors an underclass of Americans, economically and socially marginal, hanging on the edge until something tips them into bankruptcy? Are they largely blue-collar workers or a broad mix of the middle class? Bankruptcy files contain a wealth of information about the debtors who file, and we present many different pictures of those who step up to the bankruptcy counter in the courthouse.

The next most common question is probably "What causes bankruptcy?" This is a far more treacherous issue. One answer is simple: Debt causes bankruptcy, especially debt that is very high in comparison to income. The data show that few people enter bankruptcy without fairly spectacular debts that dwarf their incomes, and in that sense debt is the culprit.

Yet being in financial trouble does not always lead to bankruptcy. If Joe, Jean, and Julius are all in deep financial trouble, Joe may go bankrupt, Jean may struggle to pay, and Julius may skip town. From one perspective, it can be said that Joe's bankruptcy was "caused" by his unwillingness to struggle as hard as Jean or to sneak out of town like Julius.

Nor is it the case that what causes bankruptcy is what causes lost repayment. Avoiding bankruptcy does not necessarily imply that a debtor will repay. Jean may struggle, but she may still fail to pay her debts and her creditors may give up on her. The creditors will likely never catch up with Julius. None of the three will have much of a credit rating, but none of their creditors will get paid. On the other hand, Jean may succeed in her efforts to repay her creditors, but the bankrupt Joe may repay his as well, because at least 30% of those in bankruptcy try repayment plans, and at least 20% of the rest bind themselves to repay some of their debt outside bankruptcy.

Questions about the factors that contribute to bankruptcy—and to its spectacular rise in the 1980s—are a central part of understanding both the bankruptcy and the consumer credit systems. In that more limited sense of cause, we look at what may have contributed to each debtor's financial collapse. We can never know the incident that triggered the decision to file for bankruptcy, rather than to struggle or to run, but we can know a fair amount about the circumstances of the debtors who decided bankruptcy was their best alternative. We look at layoffs, medical debts, low incomes, business failures, and credit junkies. We talk about one-income families and women trying to support their families alone. Even if such factors do not cause bankruptcy, they indicate the sources of financial trouble for these debtors.

We also examine the increasing fragility of the consumer credit system. We discuss the growth imperative that drives lenders to press for more and more consumer debt at the same time that job layoffs and other unexpected financial crises make debtors more vulnerable to economic collapse. We suggest that consumer bankruptcy is an economic and social safety valve that permits debtors to function in an economic system even after their financial collapse. Our objective is to determine what changes in the system as a whole have put so much greater pressure on that safety valve in the last decade.

The Moral Dimension

We have no illusion that bankruptcy policy is a function merely of facts. Bankruptcy raises profound moral issues as well as financial ones. It is a concept and an experience surrounded by moral ambiguity and filled with paradox.

People see bankruptcy through a lens of fault. Most people would be moved by the plight of a steelworker laid off after years of service, depleted of savings, unable to find a job, and worried to distraction about feeding a family. Few people would shed a tear for the family who charged vacations, waterbeds, and dinners at Antoine's, and then skipped off to bankruptcy court. The result is a pervasive ambivalence about bankruptcy. Rebirth and a fresh start lie at the heart of our national mystique and many of our religious beliefs. But we do not admire broken promises, and we fear those who would avoid hard work by taking advantage of our compassion. Most people envision one or the other stereotype of the typical bankrupt—the unemployed steelworker or the grasshopper hedonist—and their visceral reaction to the idea of bankruptcy is largely a function of the stereotype they hold.

The cases in our files suggest endless combinations of irresponsibility, misfortune, and fault. The issue of fault is not subject to statistical analysis, and our computer contains no moral data. Yet our data give some glimpses into the questions of fault. The data reveal whether the debtors might be able to pay and suggest whether they take bankruptcy from desperation or cleverness. Our data also show how many debtors seem to qualify for the label "credit card junkies" and how many are in bankruptcy with devastating medical expenses. Beyond glimpses, we cannot measure fault, but it affects everything we discuss, for it is central to the moral ambiguity of our subject. Thus, we often describe the people we have found in our bankruptcy study, in the midst of all the medians and standard deviations. Not only will these people put some much-needed flesh on the statistical skeleton, but, conversely, what we do not know about them will remind us all of the human complexity underlying the cold figures.

The question of fault is not limited to the debtors. Once again, people's reactions to bankruptcy's treatment of creditors is largely a function of stereotypes. If we think of a huge finance company that enticed the debtor with frequent letters about "the $2,000 that is waiting for you," we are apt to be unsympathetic to its bankruptcy losses. If we think of the accident victim or the family doctor or the defrauded widow as the typical creditor, we may be ready to lean on debtors very hard. Even among professional creditors, we feel differently about careful lenders than careless and greedy ones.

The question of when the law says "let go" to the creditor and when it says "pay" to the debtor is the central issue in consumer bankruptcy. Ultimately, this is a moral decision. Will we collectively permit a creditor to take a debtor's last crust of bread? Will we permit a debtor to live high and avoid legal obligations? The answer to both is no, but it is hard to find a line between the two that can be easily administered, cheaply enforced, and collectively endorsed.

Many active participants in the policy debates would like to avoid the moral dimension of bankruptcy. Simple economic models, with their criss-crossing curves and abstract logic, provide a seeming refuge from the difficult moral questions that pervade the bankruptcy debate. But the moral dimension of debtor–creditor law will not go away so easily. It can be denied, ignored, derided, and glossed over, but it does not go away.

Theories of Economics, Social Behavior, and Legal Systems

The bankruptcy policy debates have been deeply influenced by the law and economics movement, which holds that people respond to stimuli along lines generally predicted by economic models. Such models have been proposed to guide legislative action at both the state and federal level. Although no one would deny the relevance of economic analysis to the financial phenomenon of bankruptcy, the models used have generally been simplistic and untested. Amendments to the Bankruptcy Code and the debt collection laws of 34 states have been premised on how economically rational actors would behave if the laws included certain incentives and disincentives. Some proponents of the economic approach have asserted that the proper mix of incentives and disincentives would lower the rate of bankruptcy filing, a powerful promise that has attracted many supporters.

The incentive/disincentive approach rests on empirical assumptions, although they are seldom explicit. Our data enable us to explore these assumptions in some important respects and to test the predictions of some economic models of debtor behavior. Because bankruptcy policy has been profoundly influenced by economic modeling, a direct test of the dominant economic model should affect bankruptcy policymaking. And because other legal policies have been affected by similar economic models, the findings in bankruptcy should affect how those models are used elsewhere.

Besides studying economic incentives, we analyzed social and demographic characteristics of debtors. The bankruptcy files contain a variety of information about debtors, including facts about their occupations and recent income histories, their migration history, home ownership, consumption patterns, and so on. These data add a social dimension to the portrait of bankruptcy petitioners.

We also explore the impact of judges and lawyers on the practical implementation of bankruptcy. Statute writers generally presume that the laws will be neutrally, uniformly enforced. The unspoken assumption is that it is sufficient to pass the laws and hire the personnel to administer them. Compliance varies with the recalcitrance of the law's targets, such as bankrupt debtors or criminal offenders. The system's own functioning should not alter the consequences for the debtors or criminals.

Criminologists and other researchers have demonstrated how the functioning of the legal system often produces unintended and even counterproductive results.[9] Our data reveal examples of such system failures, along with some examples of legal reforms that have worked very much as intended. In particular, we have had the opportunity to study the influence of local legal cultures on a supposedly "uniform" national law. We have also used our data to test whether possible proposals for bankruptcy reform would work when applied to the real world. Our findings will intrigue those interested in bankruptcy and consumer credit and may be of value to those who study the operations of the legal system generally.

The Path Ahead

Throughout the data analysis we try to juggle several balls at once, and we no doubt drop a few. In the pages that follow we try to give the reader the facts as clearly and objectively as we can. We try to report the policy debates as they have developed. But we also explain our view of how the data should influence the debates and, ultimately, bankruptcy policies. And when we identify the moral questions, we give our views, identifying them as our own and acknowledging that others can draw different conclusions.

It is no sin to have prejudices. Such is the human condition. But we believe we have a duty to continue trying to escape them, and we have done our best to do so as we describe the data. Our conclusions, and this introduction, were written last, not first. This book began with the data, not with a series of desired results. No doubt the questions we asked and the way we framed them were influenced by our views. Yet repeatedly we have found ourselves surprised by the data and forced to rethink our own understanding of bankruptcy.

At an early point in this project, for example, the income figures made us believe that bankruptcy was being used almost exclusively by the lower middle class as a safety net from poverty. After some analysis we realized that the debtors were far more diverse in social class. Only their incomes were consistently lumped at the lower margins. Then again, we were incredulous when the computer announced that more than half our debtors owned their own homes. Wrestling with the implications of that discovery consumed many hours. So, within the inescapable limitations of our own understanding of the world, we finished feeling that our views were shaped by the data more than the data were shaped by our views.

The following chapter explains how this study was designed and executed. A fuller technical description of the study design is in the appendix. Chapter Two also introduces the bankruptcy system to readers unfamiliar with the bankruptcy laws. It describes in general terms what happens to a typical consumer debtor who declares bankruptcy.

The remainder of the book is divided into two parts: "The Debtors" and "The Creditors." We begin each chapter by presenting the facts about debtors and creditors that we think are interesting and instructive. We follow the description with an explanation of relevant issues in the bankruptcy debate, the inferences we draw from the data, and the implications of our findings for bankruptcy policy.

Chapters Three through Five begin with a picture of the human stories partly told in the bankruptcy files. We present an economic description of the debtors—their debts, income, assets. After comparing the debtors' financial circumstances with those of the general population, we analyze the debtors' occupations, industries, and occupational prestige, again comparing those in bankruptcy with those in the general population. We then combine this data to look at income information by occupational and industrial grouping. We examine the important clues these financial and social descriptions provide about who uses bankruptcy.

Chapters Six through Nine take a closer look at important subgroups in bankruptcy—the self-employed, the homeowners, the women, and the people with medical problems. We compare these subgroups with their counterparts in the general population and with other debtors in bankruptcy. The presence of these important subgroups suggests that different policy considerations—such as expanded exemptions for small businesses or changed restrictions on home foreclosures—might be an important part of a coherent bankruptcy policy. These subgroups link bankruptcy to larger social support systems, such as limited liability for businesses, publicly supported medical assistance, child support enforcement, and unemployment benefits.

Chapters Ten and Eleven explore the presence of possible abusers of the credit system: the "credit card junkies" who charge and charge with little apparent regard for their ability to repay; and the repeaters who use bankruptcy to wipe the slate clean as often as the law permits. In both cases we find some evidence of irresponsible debtors and irresponsible creditors.

In the final two chapters of the section on debtors, we examine two of the most difficult policy questions in consumer bankruptcy: Should the debtors in bankruptcy be required to pay more, and what kinds of economic models of consumer behavior can be used reliably to shape bankruptcy laws?

Part II, "The Creditors," opens with some additional explanations of bankruptcy practice for the nonspecialist and centers on payouts to creditors. The data analysis begins with basic descriptive information about creditors listed in bankruptcy. We consider which creditor groups are most exposed in bankruptcy. Chapter Fifteen discusses the basic division in lending—between consumer lending and commercial lending—and shows how much of the debt in individual bankruptcies is really business debt. In Chapter Sixteen we further subdivide the creditors, focusing on bankruptcy debt that was imposed on reluctant or involuntary creditors, such as hospital emergency rooms or the victims of automobile accidents. We consider arguments for special treatment of these subgroups of creditors.

Chapter Seventeen presents the largest group of creditors in bankruptcy—the professional creditors comprising the consumer credit industry. We examine how they are affected by bankruptcy and how they might reduce their bankruptcy losses. We look at the debtor–creditor balance from the perspective of credit extension practices that put creditors at greater or lesser risk for bankruptcy. We examine how bankruptcy losses may reflect weaknesses in the consumer credit system, and whether creditors are likely to make adjustments to minimize their losses.

The last chapter returns to themes that are addressed throughout: what the bankruptcy system says about the larger consumer credit system; whether we have a bankruptcy crisis or a consumer credit crisis or both; and what role bankruptcy has come to play in a highly complex credit and debt collection system. We also talk about some broader issues—problems that could arise in any policymaking context—about making laws with few data, about using simplistic models, and about facing uncomfortable moral decisions. We try to point out some of the implications of our data for bankruptcy policymakers, for the credit industry, for social scientists, for political theorists, for economists, and for all those who worry about debt and debt forgiveness.

Viewing the data as a whole, we come to some conclusions about the reasons for the startling increases in consumer bankruptcy filings in the 1980s. Although there are many contributing factors, we find that the two primary systemic factors have been the burgeoning of consumer credit that has arisen from the changing attitudes of both consumers and the credit industry, and increased volatility in the American economy.

The consumer credit industry has increased its profitability by relaxing its standards and extending credit to almost everyone, including millions of Americans who make relatively low incomes and have few assets. The most recent example is the massive merchandising of such all-purpose credit cards as MasterCard and Visa. In late 1981 there were 572.2 million credit cards outstanding, 2.5 for every man, women, and child in America; by 1987, the number had grown to 841.4 million.[10] If the industry has gone too far in encouraging this growth, it is also true that the "me generation" has been only too happy to take advantage of it.

At the same time, most credit has become impersonal, a matter of computer printouts and objective indicators such as income and payment record. Few creditors today base credit decisions on the personal characteristics that were so important to the neighborhood banker in a simpler time. Conversely, it was a lot harder to let down one's banker-neighbor, Mr. Reed, than it is to stiff a huge, impersonal Sears or Citibank.

Our enormous, but fragile, consumer credit structure is threatened by the economy's growing instability. The rapid creation of a worldwide marketplace has produced many benefits, but it also maximizes capitalism's capacity to achieve—and inflict—rapid change. Few Americans are safe from layoffs. Business bankruptcies have escalated, along with the inevitable "downsizing" of the bankrupt businesses' workforces. "Merger mania" is justified by dismissing redundant staff in the new, combined business and thus reducing costs. After more than 20 years of relative prosperity following World War II, a period in which Americans came to believe that jobs were safe and income predictable, managers began to join factory workers in the unemployment line. Now when that pink slip arrives, the debts that were only worrisome, a bit out of hand, may become insurmountable. In the 1970s and 1980s, the middle class risked default—and even bankruptcy—to a greater extent than at any time since the Depression. For 400,000 people a year, that risk became reality in a court of bankruptcy.

Now let us pull open the stately doors of the federal courthouse and enter the darkling world of bankruptcy.

Notes

1. The figure is for fiscal year 1986, ending June 30, because this is the way the government reports the statistics.

2. D. Stanley and M. Girth, Bankruptcy: Problem, Process, Reform (Washington: Brookings Institution, 1971), pp. 124–27. The true amount of increase in recent years over prior years is itself controversial. The highly touted initial "explosion" in bankruptcy filings following the adoption of the 1978 Bankruptcy Code was probably overstated for a variety of statistical reasons, which we discuss in Chapter Two. It is clear, however, that there has been substantial growth in both business and consumer bankruptcies during the 1980s.

3. 26th Cong., 1st Sess., Cong. Globe 846 (June 4, 1840 App.).

4. U.S. Constitution, Art. 1, Sec. 8 (1787).

5. Estimates of the amount of debt legally discharged in bankruptcy every year vary widely. A precise figure based on available data is unobtainable, because much of the debt listed in bankruptcy is ultimately repaid, one way or another. See Chapters Twelve and Seventeen. Nonetheless, it is clear that the amount discharged annually is in the billions.

6. It is noteworthy that bankruptcy data are not routinely available as part of the continuing policy debate. For examples of the multitude of areas on which the government gathers statistics, consult U.S. Census Bureau, Statistical Abstract, 1984, the 37-page index of which includes entries from "abortion" (p. 954) to "zoology, degrees conferred" (p. 991) but does not included "bankruptcy." The 33 sections of the volume

include separate sections of "Law Enforcement, Courts, and Prisons" and "Banking, Finance, and Insurance," and many sections are devoted to various types of economic data on industries, employment, prices, and poverty. By 1988, the Statistical Abstract contained two tables on bankruptcy. One listed the number of petitions filed, by type and chapter, between 1975 and 1986 (Table 837, p. 501). The other listed the numbers of bankruptcy petitions filed and pending from 1905 to 1986 (Table 838, p. 501). These data are included in the section "Business Enterprise."

7. Purdue University, Credit Research Center, Krannert Graduate School of Management, Consumer Bankruptcy Study (1982), Vol. 1, pp. 88–91 (hereafter cited as Purdue Study).

8. E.g., W. J. Boyes and R. L. Faith, Some Effects of the Bankruptcy Reform Act of 1978, 29 Journal of Law and Economics 139 (1986) (statistical study purporting to show that bankruptcy filings rose when the 1978 Bankruptcy Code went into effect); R. L. Peterson and K. Akoi, Bankruptcy Filings Before and After Implementation of the Bankruptcy Reform Law, 36 Journal of Economics and Business 95 (1984) (a macroeconomic study of bankruptcy filing rates and various exemption laws which the authors conclude shows that bankruptcies rise as a consequence of liberalization of federal bankruptcy laws); L. Shepard, Personal Failures and the Bankruptcy Reform Act of 1978, 27 Journal of Law and Economics 419 (1984) (a statistical study correlating various "government transfer payments" and bankruptcy filings; this study, the author concludes, shows a rise in bankruptcy filings related to the adoption of the debtor protections in the 1978 Code). Articles without statistical studies have also concluded that the rise in bankruptcy filings was brought about by changes in the laws. See, e.g., W. J. Woodward, Jr., and R. S. Woodward, Exemptions as an Incentive to Voluntary Bankruptcy: An Empirical Study, 88 Commercial Law Journal 309 (1983). Woodward and Woodward summarize the dominant views in the field, although they disagree with these widely accepted conclusions:

> The relationship between bankruptcy filings and provisions of the Reform Act is commonly expressed in terms of "incentive": attractive provisions of the Act are said to provide debtors with "incentives" to choose bankruptcy. More specifically, if the provisions of the bankruptcy law are made more attractive to debtors, more of them will select that option as a solution to their financial problems. A corollary of this idea is commonly used to deal with rising bankruptcy rates: make the law less attractive to debtors and less of them will choose bankruptcy. (*Id.*)

9. E.g., E. M. Schur, Labeling Deviant Behavior (New York: Harper and Row, 1971) (prisons become schools for crime); S. A. Hakim and G. Regent, Crime Spillover (Beverly Hills, CA: Sage, 1981) (enforcement of crime in one area drives crime to another geographic area without reducing the rate); H. L. Packer, The Limits of the Criminal Sanction (Stanford, CA: Stanford University Press, 1968) (criminalizing drugs leads to unintended consequences in the form of additional crimes).

10. Telephone conversation between H. Spencer Nilson, Nilson Report, and Ralph Gaebler, Biddle Law Library, University of Pennsylvania Law School, 9 May 1989.

2

The Basic Information—A Little Law and a Few Numbers

Lawyers have traditionally regarded bankruptcy as a rather obscure specialty. Now that both personal and business bankruptcies are making big news (and big money), more nonspecialists have decided to learn something about the process. Indeed, as bankruptcy filings have soared, many nonbankruptcy lawyers are representing their clients as creditors in bankruptcy courts for the first time. Nonlawyers, from financial vice presidents to local building contractors, have also been forced to learn about bankruptcy to survive in a rapidly changing financial landscape. What newcomers find is a through-the-looking-glass world: court actions can be stopped in their tracks, a contract is a contract only sometimes, and assets can be frozen and deals undone all over the United States in an instant.

In this chapter we describe the meager information about consumer bankruptcy that is available from government statistics and a few prior studies in the field. We briefly discuss the design of our study; sociologists and other social science experts will find greater detail about the study in the appendix. The second part of the chapter introduces the consumer bankruptcy process to the nonspecialist. The second part can be safely skipped by judges, lawyers, and academics already familiar with the Bankruptcy Code.

The Available Data

Much of what we think we know about bankruptcy comes from the data compiled by the Administrative Office of the Courts (the AO). Every bankruptcy court in the country regularly compiles data to transmit to the AO. Some of these data are published in an annual report, which details the number of bankruptcy filings, whether they were voluntary filings, in what chapter they were filed, and whether they were filed singly or jointly by a married couple. The AO report also classifies cases by whether they are business or nonbusiness bankruptcies. No other data are reported regularly, so that only the gross numbers and a few simple categories are known. Thus, for example, there is no information on how much debt is listed in bankruptcy each year or how many debtors complete their plans to repay debts.

Even the few data available are of limited use. To take one example, the basic AO information on business versus consumer bankruptcies is poorly compiled.[1] Each bankruptcy clerk classifies the local cases, and despite some AO efforts at standardization, we learned in our study that each clerk has a distinct and different method of interpreting the classifications.[2] Numerous other complexities of the cases make the basic AO distinctions largely meaningless to answer questions critical to basic bankruptcy policy.

In addition to the AO data, there have been about a half dozen economic studies since 1978, replete with mathematical equations and not-so-subtle conclusions (e.g., bankruptcy rises in areas with "substantial non-white populations").[3] Several studies purport to demonstrate that it was not economic conditions but the new Code that was the primary reason for the increase in bankruptcies.[4] One argues that the increase in government transfer payments, such as social security payments, was a reason.[5] These studies suffer from some common difficulties: They all rely on data collected at the district level, including dubious and ambiguous AO data; they all control only a few variables for which data are available; and their analysis explains little of the variance in bankruptcy filings. Most importantly, they infer causal relationships without examining a number of potentially relevant economic complexities.

About a half dozen microdata studies have focused on individual debtors who filed bankruptcy, rather than the gross statistics about number of cases filed and district-level unemployment rates. The landmark work is the major study of debtors in bankruptcy by David Stanley and Marjorie Girth.[6] The Stanley and Girth study had an ambitious reach that included studies of bankruptcy files, interviews of 400 bankrupt debtors, reviews of 398 business bankruptcies, and some discussions with debtors in trouble who did not declare bankruptcy. It has provided much of what is known about bankruptcy.

The Stanley and Girth study was groundbreaking, but it was conducted in 1964. It analyzed bankruptcy under a very different statutory regime, when few debtors chose Chapter 13 repayment and when bankruptcy advertisements were not in every Sunday newspaper. Since the Stanley and Girth study, new analytic questions frame the bankruptcy debates. The Stanley and Girth study gives an important picture of bankruptcy at a particular time, but it cannot inform arguments about how the system operates now or about how statutory changes have affected consumer behavior.

Several small studies have been done. The notable pioneer is Philip Shuchman, whose empirical studies examined certain demographic and economic variables to draw some inferences about who uses the bankruptcy system.[7] A number of other researchers have conducted single-district studies.[8] Many of the smaller studies are of the pre-1978 system, and they all suffer from narrow, possibly unrepresentative data bases.

In Chapter One we mentioned the study done at Purdue University's Krannert School of Business. This study was funded by the credit industry and widely distributed by a top-notch public relations firm.[9] In a detailed technical and policy analysis of that study we examined the data collection and analysis and concluded that the study was so flawed as to shed little light on bankrupt debtors.[10]

The most recent study is a 1986 survey of lawyers, judges, and trustees about the 1984 Amendments to the Bankruptcy Code, which we discuss shortly. The study has no direct information about debtors or creditors in the bankruptcy system. It focuses instead on the professionals' perception of changes in the system since 1984.

For an area full of financial and social consequences and heavily laden with potential for statistical analysis, there are remarkably few empirical studies of bankruptcy.

The Consumer Bankruptcy Project

The Consumer Bankruptcy Project is the largest study of consumer debtors undertaken in the United States. For this project, we gathered information from 1547 bankruptcy cases filed in 1981, of which 1529 cases are usable.[11] More than half—58%—of the sample consisted of joint bankruptcy filings by a husband and wife, so that we studied information from a total of 2409 individuals who had declared bankruptcy.

Unlike many other court forms, which contain little information about either the plaintiff or defendant other than the details of the dispute submitted to the court, debtors in bankruptcy answer a series of detailed questions about themselves, their families, and their complete financial circumstances.[12] Depending on the chapter in which they have filed, debtors must provide information that includes, among other things:

- Where (or if) they work
- How long they have worked there
- How much money they make
- How much they made last year
- Are they being sued
- How much they spend on rent each month
- To whom they owe money
- How long they have owed money
- Are they behind on any payments
- What kind of cars they own
- How old their children are
- How much their home is worth
- If they have tried to run a business
- Who co-signed their notes
- What debts they paid before bankruptcy

- Whether they make alimony payments
- Where they have lived for the past six years
- How much they have paid their lawyers

A debtor must swear to the accuracy of this information, on penalty of perjury. The bankruptcy forms are compiled in law offices with the assistance of a trained person, often after the debtors make several trips home for additional records. Someone in the law office usually types the forms and files them in the bankruptcy court, where they become part of the official record of the debtor's bankruptcy.

We decided to focus on the bankruptcy forms because more information is available in these forms than most people could explain in a half-hour interview. Moreover, the accuracy of the information is likely to be higher than it would be when people are trying to recall complex information and give immediate answers. A debtor who provides incorrect information in the bankruptcy forms risks either a denial of discharge or prosecution for perjury, an incentive that we believe made the forms more detailed and accurate than we could replicate in an interview.[13]

We drew a sample of all natural persons who had filed for bankruptcy under Chapters 7 and 13 of the Code, the chapters normally used by consumers. Only those petitions filed by corporations and partnerships and those filed in Chapter 11 were eliminated from the sample. We systematically sampled about 150 cases from each federal judicial district we studied.[14]

We studied the files of debtors choosing bankruptcy in ten different federal judicial districts—the three in Illinois, the three in Pennsylvania, and the four in Texas. Ideally, we would have liked to have studied all districts throughout the country, but that would have required millions of dollars and an army of helpers. We sacrificed greater regional variation by studying all the districts in each state, rather than ten districts scattered around the country. This approach gave us the advantage of studying debtors governed by the same state laws—all Pennsylvania debtors, for example—who seemed to represent very different local bankruptcy systems. For example, we knew that less than 3% of the debtors in the Middle District of Pennsylvania (Harrisburg) tried to do a "pay back" bankruptcy, whereas over 41% of the debtors in the Eastern District (Philadelphia) proposed a "pay back" plan. By studying all three Pennsylvania districts we could examine a variety of factors that might explain these differing approaches to bankruptcy within the same state.

We selected Texas, Illinois, and Pennsylvania because they varied in interesting ways that we believed might be important to bankruptcy outcomes. These three states represent a wide variation in the amount of a debtor's property that they exempt from seizure by creditors, from the generous exemptions in Texas to the small exemptions in Illinois (the details are discussed later in this chapter). All three states have diverse economies with both agricultural and nonagricultural employment, big-city industries, and small-town businesses. In 1981, the sample gave use the booming Sunbelt and the decaying Rustbelt, characterizations that make ironic reading as fortunes reverse themselves. The unemployment rate was considerably higher in Illinois and Pennsylvania than in Texas (8.5% and 8.4% versus 5.3%), but in all three states there were large-scale economic dislocations that contributed to the plight of some debtors. We chose populous states for our study. In 1981 these three states accounted for 13% of all nonbusiness bankruptcy filings, and for that reason alone, they are significant in considering variations in consumer bankruptcy. Finally, one district from each of the three states had been part of earlier studies, giving us a basis for comparison.

We studied all the cases filed in a single year, 1981. This gave us the advantage of correcting for any seasonal bias, such as a post-Christmas rush. It had the necessary disadvantage of giving us only a snapshot of bankruptcy—what happened in a single year. We actually collected the data from the courthouses between 1983 and 1986, by which time most Chapter 7 cases were closed and the payment plans in Chapter 13 were either well under way or already in trouble. Because bankruptcy cases may be in court for months or years before being completed and because the clerks frequently are slow to file papers, a time lag between the initial petition and the closing of a case is inevitable. By studying 1981 cases we had the advantage of studying cases that were new enough to reflect current bankruptcy filings and old enough to be complete.

Since 1981, there have been some significant changes in the bankruptcy system, which, as we are keenly aware, could jeopardize the generalizability of our study. In 1982, the U.S. Supreme Court declared the jurisdictional basis of the bankruptcy system unconstitutional. To correct the jurisdictional deficiencies, Congress passed the 1984 amendments to the Code, which included a number of amendments to the consumer provisions as well. These amendments, which we discuss in more detail later in this chapter, had the overall intention of making bankruptcy less available and less generous to consumers.[15]

An obvious question is whether our findings about 1981 cases remain accurate after these amendments. We believe they do, because we looked for basic data about who chooses bankruptcy and how the system operates. The somewhat greater financial restrictions on debtors after the 1984 Code are unlikely to have a dramatic impact on such basic questions. Our interviews with judges, trustees, and attorneys confirm this opinion.

Moreover, we believe these data have continuing validity because we are able to use them to test a key hypothesis that underlies the 1984 amendments. The amendments assume that the debtors' decisions to enter bankruptcy or which chapter to choose once in bankruptcy could be predictably affected by certain statutory incentives. Our data contradict these assumptions, which suggests that the statutory incentives in the 1984 amendments had little impact. We discuss this analysis in Chapter Thirteen.

Further confirmation of the viability of these data comes from the only major study focusing on the impact of the 1984 amendments. The American Bankruptcy Institute, a not-for-profit, nonpartisan organization that serves as a national clearinghouse for information about bankruptcy, surveyed bankruptcy judges, trustees, estate administrators, and attorneys to determine their beliefs about the effects of the 1984 amendments.[16] The researchers concluded that the amendments had produced remarkably little change in the consumer bankruptcy process.

Our data base includes about 158 pieces of information from 1547 bankruptcy cases from ten judicial districts—nearly a quarter of a million pieces of information about the debtors in bankruptcy. This gives us information about debtors' assets, income, debts, employment, migration history, and so on. Moreover, this sample gives us data on the 23,426 creditors listed in these files, including the type of creditor, how much each creditor was owed, and whether the creditor had some collateral that it could use to satisfy the loan.[17]

An Introduction to the Consumer Bankruptcy Process

At the heart of all bankruptcy law, for individuals and for businesses, is the discharge of debts and other legal obligations, the "fresh start." The notion of beginning anew, of rebirth, lies near the center of our restless, westward-moving culture and is also the central proposition of its dominant religions. Whether a bankrupt debtor, given more time, can pay in full or can pay little or nothing, the relaxation of strict legal obligations is the indispensable centerpiece of American bankruptcy law.

At the same time, bankruptcy law is a supercollection device for creditors. Indeed, American bankruptcy law arose from two separate bodies of English law, one designed to protect debtors and the other to aid creditors.[18] As we discuss later, ordinary debt collection law has serious flaws from a creditor's point of view. Its two most important weaknesses are that it is purely state law, making collection across the country very difficult; and it is competitive, with every creditor for itself. Bankruptcy law immediately captures all the debtor's assets in one country-wide net after a single filing. It also restrains actions by any individual creditor, permitting creditors to act collectively, often through a trustee, to preserve asset values and to ensure a fair distribution.

Bankruptcy law in many ways is the rest of the law upside down and backward. In part this is true because of its two most fundamental policies. The fresh start for debtors, a chance for a person in financial collapse to begin anew, is an appealing idea—until one confronts the inevitable fact that it permits people to walk away from their obligations and to break their promises. Protecting each creditor from other creditors to achieve the fairest collective result is also an attractive idea, but the concrete effect is that creditors are barred from taking action to protect themselves, a right that the rest of the law enshrines and vindicates.

What follows here is a very brief description of the consumer bankruptcy process. Because the discussion of the law is brief and intended for the nonspecialist, it is necessarily simplified, sometimes to the edge of distortion. A bankruptcy specialist who chooses to read this legal introduction will have to resist the temptation to bang the table and demand "What about the exception to the exception in section 523(a)(7)?" Such a specialist can safely turn to the next chapter. The only new information for these readers are a few summary statistics about bankrupt debtors, which we have gathered in a note.[19] For the nonspecialist reader, we hope it goes without saying that our legal discussion is not a "how to" manual for bankruptcy.

The Road to Bankruptcy

As elementary as it may sound, we start with the difference between going broke and going bankrupt. They are the same only in Monopoly. We often say "He'll bankrupt himself" when we really mean he'll go broke if he continues spending. Being broke means not being able to pay your debts and, often but not always, not having any assets left. Being bankrupt means filing a petition in federal court under Title 11 of the U.S. Code, asking for the protection of the bankruptcy laws.

The road between being broke and being bankrupt is often a long one. Many people struggle for a long time with their debts before they decide to seek bankruptcy protection. Ironically, many debtors wait too long to file for bankruptcy. Suppose a hypothetical Mr. Smith resists going into bankruptcy despite falling badly behind in his payments. He may be fired when his boss grows tired of too many collection calls at work. If Smith is then forced to file for bankruptcy with no job and bad prospects, his creditors are not likely to be paid anything. If he had gone into bankruptcy while he still had a job, he could have tried a bankruptcy payment plan or at least could have paid some of his creditors. An earlier filing would have stopped the calls and might have saved his job, giving Smith a better postbankruptcy position and perhaps a chance to attempt some repayment.

During the time of a debtor's prebankruptcy financial travail, there will be growing pressure from informal collection efforts as well as formal collection actions under state law. The informal actions will include a barrage of phone calls and letters that demand payment, threaten legal action, and warn of a ruined credit rating. These efforts will sometimes escalate to calls to friends and relatives and visits to the debtor's employer, as well as a host of other devices collection agencies and credit departments have developed. Creditors attempting to collect a debt are subject to ordinary laws restricting people's behavior, such as prohibitions against assault and trespassing. Debt collection agencies are subject to even greater constraints, such as limits on the hours they may make telephone calls (nothing after 10 P.M.) and restrictions against threatening legal actions they do not intend to pursue. Nonetheless, the lives of many debtors are filled with insistent demands for immediate debt repayment during the months preceding the bankruptcy filing.

State collection laws provide creditors with the means to try to collect their debts through the court system. Legal remedies begin when, after a period of nonpayment, a debtor faces foreclosures and repossessions by creditors with liens. Unsecured creditors, having no collateral to seize, may file lawsuits. In the typical debt suit, where the debtor has no real defense, the court enters a judgment against the debtor, a judicial ruling that the debt is owed and may be collected using formal legal means. Creditors who have obtained judgments then try to collect. It is important to emphasize that in our legal system virtually the only legal way to collect a judgment is by having a sheriff or marshal seize the debtors' property. With very few exceptions, notably alimony and child support, a creditor cannot imprison a debtor. The creditor is entitled to neither a pound of flesh nor years of indentured service. Our system works differently from the ancient Roman collection procedures, for instance, where it was possible for the creditors to carve up not only the debtors' assets but the debtors as well.[20]

The secured creditor, having bargained for and received a property interest in the form of a lien at the very start of the loan transaction, has a great advantage. The lien permits the creditor to foreclose or repossess and to pay itself from the proceeds of selling the collateral. If the collateral is worth at least as much as the debt, the secured creditor will be paid in full. If not, the secured creditor will have to "sue and seize" for the remainder, just like an unsecured creditor.

On the other hand, the unsecured creditor with a judgment has a real problem with collection. Many debtors have few assets that would bring much at a sheriff's auction, and often their assets are exempt from creditor seizure. (State exemption law is discussed later.) The best chance for most creditors is to garnish the debtor's wages. Garnishment requires securing a court order directed to the debtor's employer requiring that part of each paycheck be paid to the creditor in satisfaction of its judgment. Sometimes a creditor can get a similar court order to garnish a debtor's bank account, demanding that the cash be paid over to the creditor. Even garnishment, however, is limited by both state and federal law, and some states prohibit any wage garnishment.

The effectiveness of property seizure and garnishment often is the leverage they give creditors rather than the dollars they produce. Debtors facing a mortgage foreclosure, repossession of the family car, or a wage garnishment may sell other property, borrow from family, and let other debts slide in a scramble to keep something they value.

Faced with lawsuits and perhaps garnishments, and even more immediately with informal pressure in person and by phone, a debtor may decide to seek bankruptcy help. Debtors often hear of bankruptcy from a friend who had a friend who used it, or they see an ad in the Sunday newspaper: "Debt Relief—call Pauline Reed, Attorney at Law." However it happens, the debtor gets an appointment with Pauline Reed, Esquire, and usually begins the bankruptcy process sitting in a spare but pleasant waiting room for a two o'clock appointment with Ms. Reed, or, often, Ms. Reed's legal assistant.

The law permits debtors to file bankruptcy without attorneys in a *pro se* ("for himself") petition. In fact, few consumer debtors take this route. In our review of 1529 cases, we found only 62 *pro se* petitions. Most of them were in one district,[21] and the nonlawyer "clinic" advising these debtors was later closed down. Notwithstanding the number of $12.95 books that advise people about how to do their own bankruptcies, (and auto repairs, if it is really an all-purpose manual), most people find the laws too complex and the forms too intimidating to tackle without a lawyer. Despite the problems they may have paying lawyers' fees, they are right. Filing your own bankruptcy is just like performing your own brain surgery.

The data show that 1466 of our 1529 debtors consulted an attorney who filed their bankruptcies. This means 1466 debtors had to find the money for two things: attorneys' fees and filing fees. The filing fees are a standard $60 for everyone, and the courts do not waive them just because the applicants are poor—no filing fee, no bankruptcy. A debtor can ask to pay the filing fee in installments, usually $20 each, but the courts will approve only if the *attorney* has not been paid anything in connection with the filing and agrees to defer payment until after the court fees are paid. The courts make sure that they are paid first and that the attorney has a keen interest in seeing that they are paid.

Because most attorneys insist on being paid in advance, the debtor must find some money for fees and filing before bankruptcy is possible. Some people are literally saving up for their bankruptcies. This is the opening paradox in an experience full of paradox.

The typical case in our sample was a husband and wife, one petition filed jointly. They paid their attorney an average of $500, with fees ranging from a low of $60 to a high of $5,000. Some debtors come up with the filing fee by skipping their other payments, such as the monthly mortgage payment, knowing that bankruptcy will forestall a foreclosure. Others dig deep and borrow from Mom or the guys at work. We talk about other options later. For now, we simply note that bankruptcy may be a tool for people in financial trouble—but the very poorest probably cannot afford it. Not even legal aid, for which these debtors may or may not be eligible, is likely to provide much help. In general, there are not enough legal aid services available, and bankruptcy is too complex a specialty for most overworked legal aid attorneys to tackle. Virtually all debtors in bankruptcy must somehow find the money to pay the lawyer and for filing fees.

Filing Powerful Papers

During the initial interview with their attorneys, the debtors should learn their first bit of bankruptcy law: Anyone can go bankrupt. There are no threshold requirements that the debtors be insolvent (debts greater than value of assets) or be unable to pay their bills by some measure or other. There are some limitations on using one type of bankruptcy procedure or the other, but in general everyone has a right to go bankrupt.

The debtors will provide the attorney copious information about their affairs. The attorney, or, more likely, a secretary or paralegal, will fill out the appropriate bankruptcy forms. The debtor husband and wife and the attorney will sign the forms, with the debtors certifying the accuracy of the information on penalty of perjury. Either the attorney or an office clerk usually takes the forms and $60 to the bankruptcy filing office.

Down at the filing office, which is usually in the federal courthouse, a clerk quickly glances over the forms to see that the critical information (debtors' names, lawyer's name) is listed and takes the $60 fee. The clerk stamps the papers "FILED" and notes the date, hour, and minute. Although, to our knowledge, no one ever hears a drumroll or a crash of cymbals, the instant the clerk's stamp hits the paper, the world of the debtors, the debtors' family, creditors, co-debtors, and employers has forever changed. The debtors have just filed bankruptcy (although they may be tied up in traffic on their way home from the attorney's office by now), and the legal consequences of what has happened are immediate and dramatic.

At the instant that a debtor or a debtor couple files for bankruptcy, a whistle blows to stop all collection efforts. The legal term is "automatic stay." From the moment of filing, there are to be no debt collection efforts against these debtors. No phone calls. No letters. No bills. If the loan company is about to sell a car it has repossessed from the debtors, it must stop. If the bank's attorney is in court and about to move for a judgment against the debtors for failure to pay on a promissory note, the attorney must stop. If the sheriff is about to move the debtors' furniture out into the street because the rent has not been paid, the sheriff has to stop. If an employer is about to deduct money from the debtors' wages under a garnishment order, the employer must stop. For many debtors, this is the most visible impact of filing bankruptcy. At least for a time, the postfiling period brings the debtors a blessed quiet, an end to the cacophony of collection.

If a creditor or the sheriff acts before getting notice of the bankruptcy, whatever was done—repossession, sale of property at auction, or whatever—is void and will be undone. If someone tries to collect after getting word of the bankruptcy filing, formally or informally, that person is in contempt of court and faces a fine or jail.

The filing also has a powerful legal effect on the debtors. As a legal matter, the debtors no longer own any property. A new legal entity is born: the bankruptcy estate. All the debtor's property owned before the filing now belongs to the bankruptcy estate. Some property may be reclaimed by the debtors later in the course of the bankruptcy, and debtors actually retain possession of all of their property at the start. But they are no longer entitled to dispose of their goods without the approval of the court. Debtors need court approval to sell their homes, close their bank accounts, or even pay some bills. The whistle blows for everyone.

The reason for stopping all collection activities and preventing the debtors from disposing of any assets is straightforward: The court as referee needs a chance to stop the action, lock all the doors and windows so none of the debtors' assets mysteriously disappear, and figure out what is happening. The system demands that no quick and clever creditors take anything away and that no debtors hand anything out. From this point until the case is resolved, whatever the debtors owned is under the jurisdiction of the court.

It may take a little while for the word to filter out that the debtors are in bankruptcy. The debtors may tell ("My lawyer said you'd better not call us anymore because we've filed for bankruptcy"). The lawyer may tell ("Your Honor, this case against my clients must be stayed because they have just filed for bankruptcy"). And the bankruptcy court in good time will tell everyone by sending out a formal notice to every creditor the debtors list ["NOTICE" The above listed person(s) . . ."]. The court will also send notices automatically to certain creditors, such as the Internal Revenue Service and other taxing authorities, even if they are not on the debtors' list. In this notification the court will explain who has filed, how much the debtors list as owing to this creditor, and where the creditor should file a claim against the debtors if the creditor wants to be paid from whatever money the bankruptcy raises.

The Critical Bankruptcy Choice: Chapter 7 or Chapter 13?

How the case proceeds from this point depends on the kind of bankruptcy filing the debtors have made. A single person or a family in financial trouble usually has two alternatives: Chapter 7 or Chapter 13. A Chapter 7 is a relatively quick option that may pay something to the creditors and gives the debtors a discharge and a fresh start in about four months. In a Chapter 13 the debtors will try to make some repayment over the next three to five years. Chapter 7 debtors give up their nonexempt assets and keep all their future income; Chapter 13 debtors keep all their assets but promise repayment from their future income.

The choice between filing a Chapter 7 "liquidation" bankruptcy and a Chapter 13 "payment plan" bankruptcy is the most fundamental decision bankrupt debtors make. Debtors are largely free to choose either "deal." In Chapter 7, the debtors give up all the assets not legally sheltered from creditor seizure. In exchange, they receive a discharge, a legal release from all preexisting debts (with a few exceptions, discussed later). The sale of all nonexempt assets gives liquidation bankruptcy its name. The proceeds will be distributed to the creditors. The discharge from debt is the financial fresh start that is one of bankruptcy's central functions.

Chapter 13 of the Bankruptcy Code offers the debtors virtually the opposite deal. In Chapter 13 the law permits them to keep all property, exempt and nonexempt, in exchange for their promise to pay all or some specified part of their debts under a three- to five-year payment plan approved by the court. The remainder of the debt will be discharged. Unlike Chapter 7, Chapter 13 is limited to consumer debtors. Only an individual human being or married couple, not a corporation or partnership, can file Chapter 13. Furthermore, it is limited to people with fairly modest debts. An individual may not file in

Chapter 13 with secured debts greater than $350,000 or unsecured debts over $100,000.[22] People with larger debts—notable recent examples include Clint Murchison and John Connally—must use Chapter 11 bankruptcy if they want to avoid Chapter 7.

Chapter 11 is primarily for business reorganizations by corporations and partnerships, but it can be used by individuals as well. Chapter 11 is like Chapter 13 in that its primary function is formulation of a payout plan as an alternative to liquidation under Chapter 7. Generally, Chapter 13 is more desirable for most debtors, if they are eligible for it. Congress recently adopted a new payout chapter, Chapter 12, which is a kind of super-Chapter 13 for family farmers only, enabling them to reap most of the benefits of Chapter 13 even though their debts are too great to qualify for that chapter.

Chapters 7 and 13 have very different legal and financial consequences that may affect the debtor for years to come. Congress and the credit community are also vitally interested in the choices debtors make between chapters and are eager to influence those choices. This basic choice is a central focus of our discussion of consumer debtors in bankruptcy.

The Typical Chapter 7

Within a few weeks of filing, Chapter 7 debtors must appear at the federal courthouse to submit themselves for examination at a "section 341 meeting" (section 341 of the Bankruptcy Code mandates this meeting). For most debtors, this is the most searching part of the bankruptcy process. This meeting usually determines whether the bankruptcy process will sail along routinely or grind up both time and money as it works through this case in careful detail.

At this meeting, debtors often meet their trustee in bankruptcy. The trustee usually is a local lawyer who specializes in bankruptcy and who has volunteered for a panel of trustees available for appointment in Chapter 7 cases. The panel is selected by a federal official called a U.S. Trustee, who has a variety of administrative and watchdog functions in bankruptcy but is seldom heavily involved in individual consumer bankruptcy cases. The Chapter 7 trustee selected for a particular case has a number of administrative responsibilities. Where there are nonexempt assets to be sold, the trustee conducts the sales and distributes the proceeds to the creditors. The trustee receives a small fee in routine cases but is in line for much larger fees as a percentage of the estate in big cases.

The players at the 341 meeting are the debtors, the debtors' attorney, the bankruptcy clerk, the trustee, and any or all of the people to whom the debtors owe money. The debtors are sworn in and asked to submit to questions from anyone assembled. The debtors' attorney will advise them, trying to help them present a clear picture of their financial circumstances. If the proceedings take a particularly nasty turn—for example, if someone claims that the debtors engaged in some criminal behavior—the attorney may need to protect the debtors from self-incrimination.

In most courthouses, the clerk of the court or the trustee officiates. Typically, several 341 meetings are held on a given day, the corridors of the courthouse crowded with waiting debtors, creditors, and lawyers. The clerk swears in each debtor, records the proceedings on a tape recorder, notes who shows up, and sometimes summarizes anything unusual that happened at the meeting in a note to be kept in the files. The trustee often asks questions to determine whether all the debtors' assets are accounted for and to probe for any suspicious prebankruptcy conduct.

Although the 341 meeting is designed to be somewhat adversarial, many are thoroughly routine. For typical debtors (a low income, few assets, no unusual transactions), the examination is likely to be cursory. Often no creditor bothers to appear. At the close of the 341 meeting, the trustee is usually satisfied that the debtors have revealed their assets and have done nothing fraudulent, so the liquidation begins.

At the 341 meeting the questions often focus on the debtors' claim of exempt assets, assets the debtors get to keep. No creditor is entitled to the clothes off a debtor's back, but beyond that bare essential, state laws vary widely in what they permit a bankrupt debtor to keep. Exemptions are often the key issue, because many debtors claim all their assets are exempt, leaving nothing for liquidation and distribution among their creditors. Although in most cases the debtors' exemption claim (made on a document in the original filing) passes without question, a particularly attractive asset or a particularly fed-up creditor or a particularly aggressive trustee may trigger an exemption fight.

THE EXEMPTIONS—WHAT CHAPTER 7 DEBTORS CAN AND CANNOT KEEP

Exemption rules involve an interaction between state and federal law. Even though the Constitution in 1789 expressly gave Congress the power to make bankruptcy laws, Congress has consistently deferred to local law and custom in framing bankruptcy statutes. Indeed, for the first hundred years of our history, Congress was not able to fashion a generally acceptable federal bankruptcy statute, and the subject of debtors and creditors was left largely to state law. In the nineteenth century Congress adopted four bankruptcy laws, but the first three were unsuccessful and were repealed shortly after passage. Not until 1898 did Congress pass a bankruptcy law that worked and remained in place. Even then, it incorporated state rules in many respects, notably with respect to property exempt from the claims of creditors.

During the nineteenth century, with no federal laws to protect debtors, state governments moved to protect debtors from losing everything to their creditors. The state laws arose first in the West, where a populist tradition flourished and many debtors fleeing from their eastern creditors tried to fashion their own fresh start on the prairies. In Texas, for example, there was a strong Spanish heritage of exempting the family homestead from creditor claims. In time, nearly all state laws provided some protection for the family home. The amount of protection varied widely, as did the provisions for exempting other property from creditor seizure. Bibles, farm tools, household goods, and milk cows were among the items that early debtors could keep even if their creditors proved a debt in a court of law and sent the sheriff out to collect.

In the twentieth century most states made some effort to update their exemption laws, permitting debtors to keep property deemed essential to contemporary life. Provisions were added to permit debtors to keep modern necessities such as automobiles, although some courts had anticipated legislative action by ruling that where an old law said "horse and carriage," a car could be substituted. As time went on, pension rights and the value of life insurance policies were added to the exemption lists in a number of states. Many states also decided that a creditor should not be able to take all of a debtors' wages, so those states prohibited or restricted wage garnishment. Although patterns are evident, state exemption laws are generally marked by enormous diversity and wide variations in generosity. What a California debtor can keep, for example, differs dramatically from what an Alabama debtor can save.

One conceptual consistency in the various exemption schemes is that most exemptions are specified by both category and amount. For example, stocks and bonds are unlikely to be exempt, but a state might exempt the debtor's work tools up to a specified value.

The diversity among state exemption schemes is preserved in the federal bankruptcy laws. The Bankruptcy Act of 1898 permitted the bankrupt debtors to keep whatever state law allowed them. The federal law simply left to the states the toughest normative and practical debt collection decision: how much goes to the creditors and how much stays with the debtor.

The hodgepodge created by absorbing the state laws into the federal system was widely criticized. The Bankruptcy Reform Act of 1978 (the new Code) created a uniform set of federal bankruptcy exemptions, but a last-minute political compromise permitted wide local variation to persist. The new Code permits debtors either to choose these federal exemptions or to rely on the state exemptions to protect some property, but it also allows the states to "opt out" of the federal scheme, thus leaving bankrupt debtors with only state exemptions—just as the 1898 Code had provided. By 1988, 35 states had taken advantage of this opportunity.[23] Congress once again sidestepped a sticky political issue by leaving the decision to the state legislatures.

EXEMPTIONS IN THE SAMPLE STATES

The best way to explain exemption law is by using examples, and the three states in our study are excellent examples. We chose them in large part because they reflected widely divergent points on the continuum of state exemption laws. This summary hits only the highlights, but it gives some idea of the law in each state we studied.

In Pennsylvania in 1981, debtors could choose between the federal exemptions and the Pennsylvania state exemptions. Among the things that an individual debtor in bankruptcy could keep under the federal provision was up to

$7,500 in equity in a home, all household items worth less than $200 each, up to $1,200 in equity in an automobile, and $400 in other property—money in the bank or more equity in the car, for example. There were also provisions protecting life insurance policies, pension rights, and other entitlements. These federal provisions were rather flexible, so that, for example, someone who did not own a home could use that exemption amount on other property. (The statute has since been amended so that the federal exemption protects less, a move we discuss later in greater detail.) A husband and wife could "stack" their exemptions, giving them a $15,000 homestead exemption plus doubled exemptions in items such as household goods and cars.

In Pennsylvania, these federal exemptions looked pretty good. The Pennsylvania state exemptions permitted debtors to keep only their clothing, a few items such as a family Bible and a sewing machine, and $300 in undesignated goods. Debtors could forestall creditor attachment on their home only if the home was owned by a married couple and only one of them owed the debt in question.[24] Because Pennsylvania had not opted out, its debtors could take either the federal or the state exemptions. Pennsylvania's option was not much of a choice, and only a handful of Pennsylvania debtors in our sample (6%) decided to take the Pennsylvania exemptions.

In Texas, the bankrupt debtors faced a much better option. Texas also permitted federal exemptions, but the state exemptions had a more generous impact for many debtors. Texas permitted most debtors to keep unlimited value in a homestead. A family, usually a married couple or a single parent, could also keep up to $30,000 worth of a laundry list of items, including an unlimited number of cars and pickup trucks. An individual in most cases got the same homestead protection and a $15,000 exemption on other goods.

Nonetheless, even in Texas the effect of categorizing as exempt only certain types of property necessitated important choices. For example, Texas did not exempt cash or cash equivalents, but the available federal exemptions permitted some cash to be exempted. The result was that some Texas debtors took the federal exemptions to exempt cash or, quite often, a tax refund they had coming. A majority (54%) of Texas debtors took Texas exemptions, while the remainder found that the federal exceptions fit their circumstances better. The choice between federal exemptions and generous state exemptions gave Texas one of the strongest debtor protection arrangements in the country.

The Illinois debtors who filed bankruptcy in 1981 were at the other end of the spectrum. Because Illinois had opted out, federal exemptions were unavailable. If debtors owned a home, up to $10,000 in home equity could be exempted. For a head of household, a maximum $3,000 exemption was available for all furniture, household goods, clothing, cars, books, and the like. For an individual, the exemption dropped to $1,000 worth of goods. Illinois has made some changes since the time this sample was drawn, but its exemptions remain among the lowest in the country.

Texas is often counted among the more politically conservative states, yet Texas amended its exemption laws several times since 1981 to make them even more generous to debtors. For example, in 1987 Texas made retirement funds, including individual IRAs and Keogh plans, completely exempt from the claims of creditors, with no limit on their value. Illinois, generally considered more liberal, has grown a bit more generous, but it remains a Scrooge compared to Texas. In politics, as elsewhere, bankruptcy is often upside down.

After debtors have claimed all their exemptions, they are required by law to hand over their nonexempt property to the trustee in bankruptcy. In fact, our files show that debtors sometimes claim values in excess of the statutory limits or items that are not protected, but neither a creditor nor the trustee objects, so the debtors keep the goods. The data here are not entirely clear, but it is fair to say that debtors in our sample often escaped bankruptcy with somewhat more of their property than the law allows. The principal reason is that the goods in question often are simply not valuable enough to be worth fighting over even if they exceed the available exemptions.

One important asset, the debtor's current paycheck, needs no exemption claim. In Chapter 7, wages earned after the bankruptcy petition is filed are not included in the debtor's bankruptcy estate but are part of the fresh start. Along with the silencing effect of the automatic stay, the arrival of the first paycheck free of garnishment and other creditor threats is one of the earliest and most important benefits of Chapter 7 bankruptcy.

CLOSING OUT THE CHAPTER 7

Assuming no challenge to the debtors' exemption claims and that the section 341 meeting has passed without incident, the debtors now just wait for the papers to work their way through the bankruptcy filing system, when they will be finished with the process. In many courts the debtors will return to the courthouse several weeks after the 341 hearing. This time they will be ushered into the courtroom to see the bankruptcy judge for the first—and probably the last—time. At the hearing will be a crowd of debtors, all being discharged at once. The judge may give a little lecture—the serious side-effects of financial profligacy or how bankruptcy will protect the debtor, depending on the judge's inclination. Debtors usually rise en masse and are declared discharged from their debts. After a recent change in the law, in many districts there is no discharge hearing and no appearance before the judge; the discharge arrives in the mail. Either way, after the discharge the debtors are free of liability on the debts they listed in their bankruptcies. They will get a certificate of discharge, rather like a diploma from a defensive driving course.

At this point the debtors' fresh start has begun, but not everything in the debtors' lives has improved. For one thing, they no longer have the option to declare Chapter 7 bankruptcy. For the next few years these debtors must exercise special caution. No matter how pressing or unexpected the debts, they are barred from another Chapter 7 discharge for six more years.

Another change in the debtors' lives is that they have been legally declared bankrupt. Bankruptcy is a matter of public record, which can remain on the debtors' credit record for up to ten years. Among those who look at these records on a daily basis are credit reporting agencies, which, in turn, pass the information to future creditors who subscribe to their services. Although no substantial empirical work has been done on postbankruptcy credit, bankrupt persons probably have less access to conventional credit than most people. Of course, they can get credit from "Harry, The No-Hassle Credit Man," at Harry's special prices, and eventually they may be able to reclaim a decent credit rating.

POSTBANKRUPTCY FINANCES: NOT ENTIRELY DEBT-FREE

The Chapter 7 bankruptcy just described is the plain vanilla bankruptcy. Most debtors have one variation that is important to the narrative: some of their debts are secured.

Most consumer debtors owe money "on" something that secures payment of a debt. The collateral is often a home, a car, appliances, or other household goods. About 86% of the debtors in our sample owed money to at least one secured creditor. Many debtors have several such loans. On average, the debtors in the bankruptcy sample owed 15 different creditors, of whom 3 were secured creditors. The secured debts tend to be on big-ticket items, and they constitute a large proportion of the typical debtors' debts.

If the debtors do not pay, the secured creditor has a right to repossess. The secured creditor's lien overrides state exemption laws, so the home mortgage lender can foreclose even if the debtors are left without a home; the car lender can repossess even if cars are exempt at state law. The secured creditor's rights are also recognized in bankruptcy, so the bankrupt debtors are faced with a choice: either continue paying on the secured loans despite bankruptcy, or give up the collateral. A third option, "redeeming" the collateral by paying the creditor its full market value, is theoretically available, but few bankrupt debtors can afford such a cash payment.[25] Those debtors who do not have cash can keep the collateral in exchange for continued payments, but only if their secured creditors agree. Creditors are often willing to oblige in exchange for a renewed promise to pay.

Many debtors elect to continue payments on some or all of their secured loans. Some of them formalize the arrangement by signing a "reaffirmation agreement," but we have found indications that many debtors continue paying, the creditor acquiesces, and no formal agreement is ever signed or filed with the court. Either way, the debtors have used bankruptcy to wash away the unsecured debts, but they are not completely debt-free: They may still have substantial debt burdens. After bankruptcy, the debtor trying to hold on to property subject to a security interest must pay to the last dollar or the secured creditor can take it away.

Creditors may insist on a formal, legally enforceable agreement to repay after bankruptcy. A reaffirmation agreement, signed by the debtors and approved by the court, binds the debtor to repay notwithstanding the bankruptcy discharge. Secured creditors often get such an agreement in return for letting the debtor keep the collateral. Although there is no similar leverage for an unsecured creditor to obtain a reaffirmation, some creditors are able to get them anyway. Debtors sometimes sign reaffirmation agreements out of guilt, friendship, intimidation, or confusion. *Any* creditor, secured or unsecured, who gets a reaffirmation before the discharge hearing has a legal right to collect after bankruptcy.

Reaffirmation agreements have been a source of enormous controversy. If debtors sign enough reaffirmations, secured or unsecured, the promised fresh start is likely to grow stale. Reaffirmations also permit one creditor to jump ahead of all the others. But they generate some cash repayment for the creditors, and they may represent what the debtor wants to do. The credit community argues that they are too hard to get and some bankruptcy analysts argue that they are too easy to get. Formal reaffirmations in bankruptcy occur with some frequency. About 19% of all Chapter 7 debtors in our sample reaffirmed one or more of their debts. Since then, the 1984 amendments to the Bankruptcy Code have made reaffirmations easier to obtain.

Even debtors who do not sign a reaffirmation agreement and who return the collateral on their secured loans find their postbankruptcy lives can be burdened with debt. The debtor's worse case occurs if creditors object to discharge. The fresh start is for the unfortunate but honest debtor. Someone who has engaged in fraud or other egregiously wrongful conduct may be denied a discharge in whole or in part. Complete denial of discharge, leaving the debtors with every one of the debts they brought in, is reserved for the most serious kind of misconduct related to the bankruptcy. For example, a complete denial could result from lying to the bankruptcy court, concealing assets, or destroying property during the year before bankruptcy. In other cases, the fraud or other misconduct relates to a specific debt and will lead to denial of discharge of that one debt only. A common ground for nondischarge of a single debt is dishonesty in a credit application, which renders that one debt nondischargeable.

Certain types of debts may be nondischargeable for policy reasons not directly related to debtor misconduct. For example, Uncle Sam protects himself as usual by making recent unpaid taxes, such as income taxes for the last three years, nondischargeable. Other public policies are served by refusing discharge of debts for alimony and child support and for education loans.

A finding that the debtors will get no discharge on some or all of their debts is the biggest disaster in a Chapter 7, so it is entitled to full judicial attention. If a credible charge has been made, the judge will schedule a trial, and a parade of witnesses and documents will begin. But this is where it pays to know the law. If the debtors' case suggests a discharge problem, then the debtors may choose Chapter 13, where the discharge rules are more lenient. Even if the debtor stays in Chapter 7, a creditor will not bother with an objection to discharge unless the amount at stake is large enough to be worth suing over. Out-of-court settlement of an objection to discharge may serve as the basis for a reaffirmation, especially in the case of an unsecured debt. Few of the debtors we studied ever litigated their right to a Chapter 7 discharge, but we could not count the objections to discharge that were discussed but never filed.

WRAPPING UP THE CHAPTER 7

The entire Chapter 7 process takes roughly four months for most debtors—a little more if the courts are crowded or the attorney is casual, a little less if everyone is organized.[26] Typically, debtors see their attorneys three times: at the initial interview, at the 341 meeting, and at the discharge hearing. The debtors have gathered more detailed financial information than most people are accustomed to putting together all at once, but they are unlikely to have been questioned or challenged on any of it. Agreements with secured creditors or with unsecured creditors who get reaffirmation agreements are likely to be worked out quietly in the courthouse halls between the debtors' attorney and counsel for the creditor. Some debtors will see a creditor or two at the 341 meeting; many will not. The debtors may get a glimpse of the judge in the final discharge hearing, but many debtors are excused even from that contact with the court nowadays.

What most debtors have been through probably seems more like a routine tax audit than a courtroom scene from Perry Mason. There are lots of forms and an enormous number of detailed questions to answer. Legal questions crop up unexpectedly from time to time, for example, when the attorney asks if some of the furniture could be reclassified as "tools of the trade," but a genuinely adversarial process is rare. If the debtors want a Chapter 7, they are likely to get it with little dispute.

Having said that, there has been a change since 1981 that may have made life tougher for some Chapter 7 debtors. Congress has added a provision permitting the bankruptcy judge to dismiss a Chapter 7 case for "substantial abuse" of the bankruptcy process. This provision, interestingly enough, applies only to cases that involve primarily consumer debt, as opposed to business debts. A standard as vague as "substantial abuse" has inevitably been applied in very different ways in different parts of the country, and the fact that only the judge or the U.S. Trustee can raise the question (no creditor is allowed to move for dismissal on this ground) means even greater diversity in application. With a few notable exceptions, it seems to be applied primarily to debtors who come into bankruptcy with substantial incomes. As we will see, this means very few debtors need be concerned about it, because most have very low incomes. For the great mass of debtors, Chapter 7 remains a readily available alternative means to deal with debt problems.

The Chapter 13 Alternative

The debtors who decide to file in Chapter 13 have taken the second of the two "deals" the law offers to the financially distressed. They will try to pay some or all of their debts in monthly installments, usually over a three-year period. In exchange, they can keep all assets. In particular, the debtors may keep property subject to liens, often with a restructured loan permitting a lower monthly payment than the original loan. This feature of Chapter 13 may be what convinces some debtors to try to make payments rather than simply take the Chapter 7 discharge. Or the debtors may hope a better credit rating will result or that Chapter 13 is less stigmatizing than Chapter 7. Or the debtors may simply believe they are morally obliged to keep trying to pay something on their debts. We explore these motivations for Chapter 13 cases throughout the analysis of the data.

After filing, the Chapter 13 debtors will also be scheduled for a 341 meeting. At this meeting there will be all the same players as in Chapter 7 (debtors' attorney, clerk, trustee in bankruptcy, and any interested creditors), but the focus of the examination will be different. The trustee and the creditors still want to know something about the debtors' property, because the debtors must agree to make payments in Chapter 13 at least equal to the value of the nonexempt property they keep (this requirement is discussed below). But the focus of the 341 meeting is on the repayment plan the debtors propose.

CHAPTER 13 PLAN REQUIREMENTS

When an individual or a couple files for Chapter 13, they fill out the same basic property, income, and debt schedules as the Chapter 7 debtors. They also furnish a detailed budget plan for their expenses and debt repayment over the next three to five years. The debtors list all their household income, including the incomes of both spouses even if only one spouse files for bankruptcy. They also list all regular expenses: rent payments, utilities, union dues, child support, entertainment, and so on. The difference between their income and fixed expenses is the amount from which they propose to repay their creditors.

Approval of a Chapter 13 plan does not require the agreement of the creditors. If the debtors propose payments in Chapter 13 within the requirements of the statute, the court approves the plan regardless of the creditors' views. On the other hand, Chapter 13 sets minimum amounts a plan must pay. For secured creditors, the minimum payment must at least match the value of the collateral, plus interest, but the payment may be made over a longer time. Certain unsecured creditors with special priorities (such as tax authorities, former spouses, and children with support orders) receive payment in full. For the rest of the unsecured creditors, the minimum amount that must be paid equals the debtors' remaining disposable income, after paying necessary living expenses and the secured and priority debt payments.

The home mortgage lender enjoys special protection in Chapter 13. Mortgage payments cannot be rescheduled for lower payments over a longer time. Instead, a mortgage lender is entitled to full repayment exactly according to the original mortgage agreement, or the mortgage lender can foreclose. Congress was persuaded that this special protection was necessary to encourage home mortgage financing at the lowest cost.

Chapter 13 debtors have one option to constrain the strict enforcement of a home mortgage: The debtors can make up missed payments, even if the lender is ready to foreclose immediately. If the debtors were in arrears on the home mortgage when they filed Chapter 13, they may propose to repay the arrearage under the plan while keeping current on the remaining regular payments. If the debtors keep up with both payments—the regular payments and the catch-up on the arrearages—the creditor cannot foreclose. If they pay off the delinquent payments in full under the plan, the debtors emerge from the Chapter 13 with the mortgage intact and living in their homes as if no payments had ever been missed.

Once the debtors and trustees have budgeted money to make monthly payments on the reworked secured claims, to make the home mortgage payments and cure any arrearages, and to pay off the priority claims in full, the remainder of the debtors' money is available to pay the unsecured creditors. The unsecured creditors are to be paid on a pro rata basis according to the size of each claim and how much money the debtor has left to apply to debts. The law provides no guaranteed minimum. The debtor might propose to pay the unsecured creditors ten cents on the dollar or to pay in full.

As we indicated earlier, debtors must propose to pay at least as much as the creditors would have gotten in a Chapter 7. Two hypothetical families, the Smiths and the Joneses, illustrate the main points. Each family owes unsecured creditors $10,000 and proposes to pay their creditors 25% of what they are owed in a three-year Chapter 13 payment plan. All of the Smiths' property is exempt, so if they file Chapter 7, the creditors get nothing because there would be nothing for the trustee to sell. By contrast, the Joneses own a beach house, not exempt under state or federal law, worth $5,000 more than the mortgage on it. If the Joneses filed Chapter 7, the trustee would sell the beach house and the Joneses' creditors would get $5,000, 50% of what they are owed (ignoring the trustee's fee and expenses). The Smiths' plan could be confirmed by the court, because 25% in Chapter 13 is much better than nothing in Chapter 7. The Joneses could not get their plan confirmed because the creditors would get 50% in a Chapter 7 liquidation whereas the Joneses are offering only 25% in their Chapter 13 plan. The result is that debtors who own little nonexempt property can propose to pay anything, even a token 1% of their debts, and still meet this test. Conversely, debtors with a fair amount of nonexempt property either lose that property in Chapter 7 or pay the equivalent of the value of their property to their creditors in Chapter 13.

The original statutory scheme adopted in 1978 had no other requirement for the amount of payment to unsecured creditors in Chapter 13. This created a real problem for the courts. Because most consumer debtors have little or no property beyond their exemptions, most of them could propose as little as 1% in payment in Chapter 13 and meet this test. Most courts responded by applying an additional "good faith" test. The statute required that the debtors propose a plan in good faith. Most courts interpreted this to mean that the debtors had to make some repayment even if there would have been none in Chapter 7. The amount required varied tremendously from district to district and from case to case. In 1984 Congress amended the payment requirements to require that debtors devote all of their "disposable income" to plan repayments. If debtors in Chapter 13 have money beyond their necessary living expenses, they must use it to pay off their debts.

It is not clear that the addition of the disposable income test has significantly changed the practical operation of Chapter 13. Many courts continue to apply a good faith test in addition to the new disposable income test. Under either test, much the same inquiry must be made about the "reasonableness" of each of the claimed expenses as a way to determine the income available to the creditors.

Notwithstanding the limited legal requirements for what debtors must pay in a Chapter 13, the debtors in our sample promised to make fairly substantial repayments. They typically promised to repay 51%, which was generally well above the strict legal requirements. A substantial portion of the debtors—36%—promise complete repayment of *all* their debts.[27] These debtors plan to use Chapter 13 to prevent their creditors from moving against them one at a time in a state court, but they promise that they will repay them, each and every one, in full.

The Chapter 13 repayment amounts vary greatly from debtor to debtor and from district to district. Yet our figures make it clear that most debtors do not seek to pay only the bare minimum required by the statute. Instead, Chapter 13 is treated by many attorneys and clients as a method for substantial repayment.

The trustee for Chapter 13 has very different duties from the trustee in a Chapter 7. In Chapter 13, the trustee's main job will be to collect the debtors' weekly or monthly payments and to disburse them to the creditors according to the court-approved plan. Consequently, a considerable portion of the trustee's time at the 341 meeting is spent questioning the debtors' plan. What happens if either husband or wife gets laid off work? Have the debtors provided enough for utilities and medical expenses? Have they remembered to include expenses for children's schoolbooks and lunches? The trustee's questions are oriented toward whether the debtors really can make the plan payments (or, in a few cases, whether the debtors could pay more). After the hearing, the clerk schedules a confirmation hearing at which the trustee makes a recommendation to the court about the debtors' plan.

WAITING FOR THE REAL FIGURES ON REPAYMENT

During the weeks before the court date, two critical things happen. The first is that the creditors must file their claims. Each creditor must send a form to the court stating the amount the debtors owe along with a copy of whatever billing records the creditor has. If the debtor and creditor agree on the amount owed, that becomes the claim, and it is then paid according to the plan proposal. If they differ, the parties will usually work out an agreement informally. Often the Chapter 13 trustee, rather than the debtor, contests a creditors' claim because one function of the trustee is to police the claims process. Very rarely, a dispute over a claim cannot be resolved and the parties must litigate in the bankruptcy court, where the judge will fix the amount due.

Creditors must file by a certain date after receiving notification of the bankruptcy—usually within a couple of months. Once the time for filing has elapsed, the trustee knows who will get how much of each distribution. Some debtors get lucky during this period because their creditors fail to file claims. These debts will be discharged if the debtors can make their other payments to the creditors who file claims. Thus it is not clear how much the debtors actually have to pay under their plan, even if they have promised to pay 100%, until the claims are filed and the amounts owed are settled.

The second important thing that happens before the confirmation hearing is that the debtors must begin making payments. This requirement was unclear before the 1984 amendments, and different judges imposed different rules. But most of the debtors in our sample districts were required to begin payments before they went to court for plan confirmation. The whole process has now been regularized, and debtors now must start making payments within 30 days of filing—even though the plan ordinarily has not yet been confirmed. The trustee often holds those payments and pays only certain secured claims, such as the house payment and car payment, pending confirmation.

Although a three-year payment period is standard, debtors have the option to propose a plan lasting up to five years. A family might propose a four- or five-year plan if they have a car loan they want to repay in smaller payments over a longer time or a big arrearage on a home to erase before the end of their bankruptcy. Any payment period greater than three years must be approved by the court, and five years is the legal maximum.

CONFIRMING THE PLAN

Once the trustee has a firm count of the number and size of filed claims, the trustee is ready for the debtors to go to the bankruptcy court. The bankruptcy judge holds a hearing to determine whether the debtors have proposed a plan that meets the legal requirements of the Bankruptcy Code and shows some reasonable likelihood of success. What happens to Chapter 13 debtors at this hearing varies sharply from one judge's court to another.

In most courts the trustee, who has by now become familiar with the case, recommends that the court confirm or deny the plan. Some judges follow that recommendation without further inquiry. Others take the debtors through a close examination of proposed expenses and income and confirm a plan only when the judge is satisfied that the debtors can meet the promised repayments.

Whether the judge actively questions the debtors or not, the plan is likely tailored to the judge's views. Trustees quickly learn a judge's guidelines for confirming a plan, and most bankruptcy attorneys know what a judge in their area will and will not accept. Debtors who propose payments that are unusually low or high relative to their income are usually advised to change their plans long before they enter the courtroom.

By the time of a confirmation hearing, most cases will meet the judge's informal guidelines. In our sample, judges confirmed 81% of the proposed plans. Most of the remaining plans were from debtors already in trouble after missing their postfiling payments.

LIVING WITH A CHAPTER 13 PLAN

The pleasure of having a plan confirmed is frequently short-lived. After confirmation, the debtors must live with the plan for three to five years. Some judges immediately order a debtor's employer to pay a certain percentage of the debtor's wages directly to the trustee for distribution to creditors. Others sign such an order but leave it in the file until and unless the debtor falls behind in plan payments. Other courts simply wait to see if debtors can pay and take action when a trustee or creditor complains.

Many Chapter 13 trustees are now specialists, so-called standing trustees. (They even have a national association and annual meetings.) These trustees have computerized their offices to receive, record, and disburse payments with maximum efficiency. In a large urban district, millions of dollars collected from bankrupt debtors flow each year through each trustee's office. In return for their services, the trustees receive a percentage—usually about 6%—of each payment.

The debtors who are able to make their plan payments in full go back to court at the completion of their plans for a discharge from any unpaid portion of their debts. For example, a family that promises to pay 60% of their unsecured debts over three years returns to the court a final time when they have completed all their payments. The debtors then receive a discharge from the remaining 40% of debts that they have not paid. Because a discharge is not granted until the end of the payment process, debtors who make some payments in Chapter 13 and then default remain fully liable for *all* the debts owed before bankruptcy.

The debtors who get a discharge are released from prebankruptcy debts, but like their Chapter 7 counterparts, they are restricted from going into Chapter 7 for six years. Only debtors who pay in full remain eligible for a Chapter 7 bankruptcy discharge during the ensuing six years.[28] Most credit agencies will identify all Chapter 13 debtors, regardless of their payment success, as having taken bankruptcy.

The fresh start for Chapter 13 debtors is much more comprehensive than for Chapter 7 debtors. The Chapter 13 discharge does not make exceptions for fraudulently incurred debts or educational loans or any other special classification of debtor misbehavior or protected creditor status. The only exceptions to the discharge are taxes (which are paid in full under the plan), alimony, child support, and, of course, the home mortgage and any other secured claims with remaining payments, which must be paid if the debtor wants to keep the property. All other debts are discharged.

The three- to five-year period between plan confirmation and a discharge hearing provides plenty of opportunities for debtors to slip. If the family encounters an unexpected financial crisis—a job layoff or unexpected medical expenses—they can ask the court to suspend payments for a time. If the problem appears to be long term, they can ask the court to modify the plan, giving them a different (and presumably smaller) payment plan. These options are available to all debtors in trouble, but few ask for them. By the time the plan is confirmed or shortly afterward, the debtors have usually paid their attorney. Additional legal help to modify their plans is likely to cost more money. Some trustees will suggest these alternatives, but their resources to advise debtors are necessarily limited.

Most debtors who have trouble simply stop making their Chapter 13 plan payments. Some trustees act as vigorous collection agents, hiring telephone collectors to work over the debtors like any debt collection agency, but more forcefully, since trustees are subject to far fewer legal constraints than those imposed on a private collection agency. Others send a few perfunctory letters, but not much more. In either case, a trustee who sees no results may simply move to have the debtors' Chapter 13 dismissed. Sometimes a creditor who has been monitoring repayments may call to urge the trustee to move for a dismissal. Other creditors, especially secured creditors with collateral to repossess, go to court themselves to ask the judge to dismiss the case. If the debtors fail to explain their lapses satisfactorily and to reassure the court that they can do better, the debtors are out of Chapter 13.

Usually several months elapse before the debtors' failure to make payments is entered in their files. Once the trustee notifies the court that the debtors are in arrears, it may be several more months before the trustee moves to have the case dismissed. Trustees differ in aggressiveness, and debtors differ in their responses. Debtors who talk with the trustee and make a few sporadic payments last longer than debtors who do not. Trustees who run a tight ship move to dismiss cases sooner. And creditors can influence the outcome by complaining loudly to the trustee or filing for dismissal in court.

Dismissal carries serious consequences for Chapter 13 debtors. However a dismissal comes about—if the court refuses to confirm a plan or if the plan is confirmed but the debtors do not make their payments—the debtors lose all protection of the bankruptcy court. The creditors can resume state court actions, garnishee wages, repossess, or do anything else that state collection law permits. The money for the bankruptcy has bought some delay, but little else.

Debtors in trouble may avoid dismissal by converting their case to Chapter 7 and discharging their debts. In that case, the creditors keep whatever the debtors have already paid and reduce the debts accordingly, and a Chapter 7 proceeds with property turnover, sale, and distribution. No permanent benefits carry over from the Chapter 13, and the debtors usually must pay their lawyer another fee.

After Bankruptcy

The legal story is usually over the for the Chapter 7 or Chapter 13 debtors when the discharge is finally granted. These people are largely on their own, although the law will intervene if a discharged creditor tries to collect. Also, employers are forbidden to discriminate against the debtors, and governmental agencies cannot base any action on a debtor's status as a former bankrupt. But that exhausts the protection. Creditors can cut off future credit, credit agencies can report the bankruptcy filing for ten years, and people can refuse to do business with a bankrupt person for as long as they want.

Describing the situation of the postbankruptcy debtors is a little like describing the half full/half empty glass of water. Most debtors have improved their financial situation, often dramatically so. But debtors who got a discharge sometimes face a large number of secured loans and reaffirmations that persist after the filing, making the fresh start a little stale and leaving the debtor to wrestle with some of the same old creditors. Chapter 13 debtors who filed and failed are back where they started, along with any Chapter 7 debtors who are denied a discharge. Bankruptcy is an improvement for many, but not a panacea.

Conclusion

The fundamentals of consumer bankruptcy law are simple. Chapter 7 offers a fresh start to financially distressed people who do not have much property to give up or who are willing to surrender their nonexempt property to put their financial debacle behind them. Chapter 13 offers an opportunity for people who want to pay to do so, giving them needed time.

These simple policies are anything but simple to implement. Debtors and their attorneys are faced with many sensitive and difficult choices, yet the debtors are usually hard pressed to come up with a $600 attorney's fee, an amount that hardly permits a lawyer to do an imitation of Oliver Wendell Holmes. At the same time, these small consumer bankruptcy cases number in the hundreds of thousands and their effects on the consumer credit system could constitute an important social and economic problem. One of the central tensions in consumer bankruptcy law is between the statute's complexities and the small amounts at stake in any one case. Another is the need for a bankruptcy system that is fair to individuals in financial trouble while it limits any seriously negative impact on the larger credit system, issues we address in subsequent chapters.

Notes

1. We have been unable to locate technical reviews of the quality of AO data. Changes are made in AO data reports without public explanation or technical documentation. During the intense congressional debates on bankruptcy in 1977, data series on bankruptcy were stopped without notice, so that during a critical phase of the debates, less rather than more information was made available. A data tape of the information reported in the Annual Reports was withdrawn from research use, and because it was done by the judicial branch, it was beyond the reach of the Freedom of Information Act. In lieu of published technical information, a loose, almost underground

network of scholars doing empirical legal research has sprung up to pass on "tips" about the data.

The impact of eliminating or reclassifying data without further explanation is more than just an academic's nightmare. The dramatic rise in bankruptcy filings following the adoption of the new Bankruptcy Code has been widely heralded as proving both the depth of an economic recession and the breakdown in the moral fiber of Americans, but it may be largely a statistical artifact: Part of the 1981 "jump" in the number of bankruptcy filings apparently was due to the AO's initial decision to count husband–wife petitions as two bankruptcies. Thus a powerful and widely cited statistic that was used extensively as a lever to amend the Bankruptcy Code in 1984 may have been little more than a statistical manipulation.

A knowledgeable bankruptcy practitioner can immediately spot problems in the AO's data categories. "Petitions filed" may or may not include cases that are reopened, a situation that some clerks reported to be increasing in frequency. Even the information that a case was filed in Chapter 7 may mislead if substantial numbers of cases are filed in Chapter 7 or Chapter 13 but convert to another chapter and are shown in subsequent years as "pending" or "terminated" in those chapters.

The AO data cause persistent problems for those trying to segregate the business cases from the consumer cases, an important distinction since knowing the number of individuals who filed bankruptcy and the number of businesses that went bust is critical to other analyses of bankruptcy. The category "business 7" includes everything from the demise of Braniff to the failure of a small Amway distributor. The category of "business 13" must mean that the Chapter 13 debtor was in business sometime before filing, because Chapter 13 filings are limited by law to natural persons and denied to corporations. The "joint business 7," which might at first blush suggest the failure of a small, incorporated business and the personal bankruptcy of its owner, must instead refer to the filing by a husband and wife, at least one of whom owned a business.

2. There appear to be no effective standardized procedures to guide the local clerks who must decide when a petition represents a "business 7" or a "business 13" petition rather than a nonbusiness equivalent. Although one clerk told us that some guidelines existed for classifying cases as "business" or "nonbusiness," we saw a variety of procedures in use. The cases that were relatively easy to identify had docket sheets that used a corporate name or listed individuals with a "doing business as" (dba) designation. The harder cases involved the "formerly doing business as" designation or were filed by a self-employed entrepreneur who had not designated dba. Some clerks asked the attorney to make the "business–nonbusiness" designation; others looked through the filing papers themselves. Some clerks declared a filing to be a "business case" if the petitioner's employer had declared bankruptcy. It is important to emphasize that no clerk seeks to introduce ambiguities into the statistics; the ambiguities are already there. Those responsible for compiling the data have not provided adequate instructions for resolving them, and clerks in different localities make a variety of decisions about what cases constitute business bankruptcies. What this means for analyses that rely on AO data to study nonbusiness or business bankruptcies is anyone's guess. The "asset" and "no asset" classification of cases presents analogous problems.

3. L. Shepard, Personal Failures and the Bankruptcy Reform Act of 1978, 27 Journal of Law and Economics 419 (1984).

4. W. Boyes and R. Faith, Some Effects of the Bankruptcy Reform Act of 1978, 29 Journal of Law and Economics 139 (1986); Shepard, 1984.

5. *Id.*

6. D. Stanley and M. Girth, Bankruptcy: Problem, Process, Reform (Washington: Brookings Institution, 1971).

7. P. Shuchman, Theory and Reality in Bankruptcy: The Spherical Chicken, 41 Law and Contemporary Problems 66 (1977); P. Shuchman, New Jersey Debtors 1982–83: An Empirical Study, 15 Seton Hall Law Review 541 (1985); P. Shuchman, The Average Bankrupt: A Description and Analysis of 753 Personal Bankruptcy Filings in Nine States, 1983 Commercial Law League 288; P. Shuchman and T. Rhorer, Personal Bankruptcy Data for Opt-Out Hearings and Other Purposes, 56 American Bankruptcy Law Journal 1 (1982).

8. R. Dolphin, An analysis of economic and personal factors leading to consumer bankruptcy. Occasional Paper no. 15 (East Lansing, MI: Bureau of Business and Economic Research, Michigan State University, 1965); A. F. Brimmer. Economic Implications of Personal Bankruptcies, 35 Personal Finance Law Quarterly Report 187 (1981); S. N. Subrin and J. Rugheimer, A Statistical Study of Bankruptcy in Massachusetts With Emphasis on the Bankruptcy Bar and an Examination of the Proposed Bankruptcy Acts, 50 American Bankruptcy Law Journal 137 (1976) (1505 debtors who filed in 1969–70 in Massachusetts).

9. The Purdue Study, which cost about $350,000, was funded by grants from the credit industry. The credit industry also hired Ogilvy and Mather, a prestigious ad agency, to publicize the results of the study and make certain that members of Congress were aware of the Purdue Study findings. E. Warren, Reducing Bankruptcy Protection for Consumers: A Response, 72 Georgetown Law Journal 1333, 1333–34 (1984).

10. T. A. Sullivan, E. Warren, and J. L. Westbrook, Limiting Access to Bankruptcy Discharge: An Analysis of the Creditors' Data, 1983 Wisconsin Law Review 1091. The Purdue Study attempted to estimate how much could be repaid to creditors if Chapter 7 petitioners were forced to enter a Chapter 13-like arrangement under which they paid creditors everything they earned in excess of the poverty level (plus a mortgage payment, if the petitioner were a homeowner). Their estimates of repayment were based on holding petitioners to the poverty level for five years, while all their additional income was turned over to the court for distribution to their creditors. We criticized the study for recommending Chapter 13-type plans without studying them. Throughout the study, we found mistakes of law and method. We criticized the selection of the sample, questionnaire design, and data analysis. For example, business debts were excluded from the "payback" formula without explanation of how they were identified and excluded; family incomes were used to calculate payback sums even if a petitioner were filing singly and other family income were not subject to court jurisdiction.

11. The cases that could not be used usually contained no information that could be coded. This might have resulted from "skeleton" filings that the lawyer intended to supplement but never did, perhaps because the client never returned. Or the later papers could have been misfiled. Whenever any data were available, they were coded, even if other data were missing. Missing value codes were developed for all variables.

12. The Chapter 7 forms are standardized. There is no prescribed format for Chapter 13. In our study, we came across four stationers' forms used to file Chapter 13. This is an inconvenience, because the information is differently arranged on each form, although the forms call for the same type of information.

13. Earlier studies suggest three problems in interviewing bankrupt debtors: high refusal rates, location difficulties, and inaccurate or misleading responses. The Purdue Study permitted interviewers to choose debtors to be interviewed during selected time

periods. Even though interviewers were given the possibility of selecting friendly interviewees, 1050 of the 2249 debtors approached refused to be interviewed. Among those who agreed to be interviewed, another 24% refused to authorize the release of their credit records. In all, only two-fifths of the debtors Purdue approached gave the information upon which the Purdue Study based its conclusions. Purdue University, Credit Research Center, Krannert Graduate School of Management, Consumer Bankruptcy Study (1982), vol. 1, pp. 25–26. We discuss the likely biases resulting from this response rate in Sullivan, Warren, and Westbrook, Limiting Access, p. 1110 n. 30.

The Brookings researchers intended to interview only 400 debtors, just 25% of the sample of 1675 debtors whose files they examined. It turned out to be so difficult to locate debtors and to obtain interviews that they could not get 400 interviews from the original sample. As a result, they drew a further "interview" sample of 1921 (for a total of 3596 potential interviewees), from which they managed to get enough further interviews to obtain the 400 total interviews they wanted. (It is not possible to tell from the report how many of the 400 interviews came from the original sample of 1675.) The report noted that the persons interviewed "were more stable, better satisfied, and in better financial condition than those who had disappeared or who refused to be interviewed." Stanley and Girth, Bankruptcy, p. 41 n. 1 and pp. 224–25.

The difficulties of locating bankruptcy petitioners were illustrated in another study, in which about 27% of the sample could not be located using the addresses in court records. When located, nearly one-third of those contacted in person or by mail and 29% of those contacted by telephone denied ever having been in bankruptcy. N. Bradburn and S. Sudman, Improving Interview Method and Questionnaire Design (San Francisco: Jossey-Bass, 1979), pp. 7, 81.

Although some important information is lost by using filed forms rather than interviews, we concluded that data compiled from the debtors' bankruptcy forms yield more reliable financial information about people in bankruptcy.

14. See the appendix, "Data and Methods."

15. In 1986 Congress added a new Chapter 12 to deal with the problems of failing family farms. These amendments had virtually no effects on the consumer bankruptcy system.

16. American Bankruptcy Institute, Perception and Reality: American Bankruptcy Institute Survey on Selected Provisions of the 1984 Amendments to the Bankruptcy Code (Washington: ABI, 1987).

17. See the appendix.

18. Historically, "bankruptcy" was involuntary, a creditors' collection device to divide all of a debtor's property equally among the creditors. "Insolvency" was a voluntary action designed to relieve debtors, so that a debtor who gave all his property to the court was discharged from debtors' prison—not excused from the payment of his debt. Insolvency and bankruptcy were brought together in a series of short-lived acts through the nineteenth century, until finally the first long-lived bankruptcy law was passed in 1898. That law survived until it was replaced by the current 1978 Bankruptcy Code. For more discussion and a list of sources, see T. A. Sullivan, E. Warren, and J. L. Westbrook, Limiting Access to Bankruptcy Discharge: An Analysis of the Creditors' Data, 1983 Wisconsin Law Review 1091.

19. For readers familiar with the consumer bankruptcy process, we summarize here the data covered in this chapter. In our review of 1529 cases, we found only 62 *pro se* petitions. More than half our sample was part of a joint bankruptcy filing, husband and wife. The attorney fees ranged from a low of $60 to a high of $5,000 with a mean

of $500. Pennsylvania's choice between federal and state exemptions was not much of a choice. Only a handful of debtors in our sample (6%) decided to take the Pennsylvania exemptions. About 54% of Texas debtors ended up with the state exemptions, while the remaining 46% chose federal exemptions. About 87% of the debtors in our sample owed money to at least one secured creditor. Many debtors have several such loans. On average, the debtors in the bankruptcy sample owed 15 different creditors, of whom 3 were secured creditors. Formal reaffirmations in bankruptcy occur with some frequency. About 19% of the Chapter 7 debtors in our sample reaffirmed one or more of their debts. The Chapter 13 debtors in our sample promised to make fairly substantial repayments. The mean repayment promised was 51%, which was generally well above the strict legal requirements. A substantial portion of the Chapter 13 debtors—36%—promise complete repayment of *all* their debts. Judges confirmed 81% of the proposed plans. Several of these points are discussed in connection with fuller explanations of the data in appropriate chapters later in the book.

20. "If the debtor be insolvent to serve creditors, let his body be cut in pieces on the third market day. It may be cut into more or fewer pieces with impunity. Or, if his creditors consent to it, let him be sold to foreigners beyond the Tiber." *Twelve Tables,* Table III, 6 (c. 450 B.C.).

21. The *pro se* cases were in the Eastern District of Texas, where a self-styled clinic helped the debtors fill out their own bankruptcy forms for an undisclosed fee.

22. Chapter 13 also requires that the debtors have "regular income," although that requirement has been very generously construed to include, for example, unemployment benefits.

23. The following states have enacted legislation prohibiting debtors filing bankruptcy in these states from using the federal exemptions: Alabama, Alaska, Arizona, Arkansas, California, Colorado, Delaware, Florida, Georgia, Idaho, Illinois, Indiana, Iowa, Kansas, Kentucky, Louisiana, Maine, Maryland, Missouri, Montana, Nebraska, Nevada, New Hampshire, New York, North Carolina, North Dakota, Ohio, Oklahoma, Oregon, South Dakota, Tennessee, Utah, Virginia, West Virginia, and Wyoming. Collier on Bankruptcy ¶522.02 (15th ed., 1987). With some exceptions, the states opting out of the federal exemption scheme generally permit debtors to keep fewer assets than the federal exemptions would permit.

24. 42 Pa. C.S.A. (Pennsylvania Commonwealth Statutes Annotated) 8123, 8124 (1970). Tenancy by the entirety, the doctrine that protects a spouse's interest in a homestead from the debts of the other spouse, is granted by Pennsylvania case law in *Patterson v. Hopkins,* 247 Pa. Super. 163, 371 A.2d 1378 (1977). For information on exemption levels in Illinois and Texas, see Tex. Prop. Code Ann. § 41.001 (Vernon 1984); Tex. Prop. Code Ann. §§ 42.001-.002 (Vernon 1984); Ill. Ann. Stat. ch. 110, §§ 12-901 *et seq.* (Smith-Hurd Supp. 1984–85); Ill. Ann. Stat. ch. 110, § 12-1001 (Smith-Hurd Supp. 1984–85); and Ill. Ann. Stat. ch. 110, § 12-1201 (Smith-Hurd Supp).

25. The Bankruptcy Code permits a debtor with a secured loan on certain personal property to redeem the collateral by paying its current value to the secured creditor. If, for example, a debtor owed $6,000 on a car actually worth only $4,500, the debtor in bankruptcy could, in effect, buy the secured creditor off for $4,500. The remainder of the $6,000 debt—$1,500—would be dealt with as unsecured debt and discharged. The hitch for most debtors is that they need all the cash up front to take advantage of this provision—an impossible requirement for most debtors in bankruptcy.

26. Four months is the median time elapsed from filing to discharge in a Chapter 7 in our sample. The mean time is 6.5 months. In many cases, however, the file was not completed until much later.

27. Of the 591 Chapter 13 cases in our total sample, the mean percentage of repayment proposed was 51% and the median was 45%. There were 117 cases for which we could not determine the promised percentage of repayment. Only 17 cases proposed payment of 1% or less.

28. There is a "hardship" exception, but it does not appear that it is often invoked. 11 U.S.C. § 727(a)(9).

I

THE DEBTORS

3

The People

The Consumer Bankruptcy Project is a systematic study of consumers in bankruptcy. The numbers generated in the study are critical to our story, for they inform the debate and identify inaccurate assumptions about debtors and creditors. At the heart of the bankruptcy process, though, are not numbers, but people who filed.

Before we begin a rigorous statistical analysis of these bankrupt debtors, we pause to look at some individuals among them. No debtor profile is entirely "typical" in any statistical sense. That is what the numbers are for. But all are "typical" in that each tells a story that recurs throughout our sample. These debtors provide a good introduction to the human stories that fill the bankruptcy files.

We introduce our debtors for another reason. The stories gleaned from the files remind us what we can and cannot tell about the people in bankruptcy. The files are rich with glimpses into the personal turmoil and stress that preceded the bankruptcy, but they often fall short of a full story of what happened to the debtor. Important facts about each debtor family are never captured within the manila folders in the bankruptcy clerk's office.

Throughout this chapter and those that follow, we have changed names and identifying details to protect debtors' privacy, even though the information is a matter of public record. For creditors, we have changed names but identified the business type, so that a fictitious doctor's name replaces a real doctor's name. We have not always changed the names of large companies. The stories are not composites; they are real stories from individual cases with the identifying details altered.

Douglas and Laura Mae Spice

Douglas and Laura Mae Spice moved four times in six years. The last move brought them to southern Illinois. Douglas Spice is employed as a laborer. He has worked for six months at a local firm. Laura Mae Spice has been a nurse's aide at a children's home for just over a year and a half. He made $11,000 in 1979 and $13,000 in 1980. She made $4,000 in each of the two years before filing Chapter 7 bankruptcy.

The Spices live in an apartment. They have two cars, a 12-year-old Rambler that does not run and a 15-year-old Ford that they drive to work. The Spices place a value of $400 on all their household goods, wearing apparel, jewelry, and other personal possessions. They report that they have no cash or savings.

Most of the debts the Spices list in bankruptcy were incurred in 1977, four years before bankruptcy, although some were incurred later. A look at the list of bills gives some idea of what happened to the Spices during the past few years. These are the debts listed on the Spices' forms:

Polyclinic	$ 900
Mt. Sinai Hospital	3,500
Dr. Wordt	15
Radiology	120
Dr. Travis	110
Dr. Winick	280
Clinic	337
Dr. Nicholson	158
Dr. Luna	60
MarketPlace Shopping	200
Mercy Hospital	1,145
Central Illinois Anesthesia	174
Illinois Department of Mental Health	20
Associates Finance	3,286
Central Illinois Light Co.	195
Medical Services	109
Morrison Clinic	330
Riverside City Hospital	115
May Avenue Hospital	451
Sears, Roebuck and Co.	473
Illinois Bell Telephone	326
Montgomery Ward Co.	830
Marsha Wexler, D.D.S.	28
Northside Clinic Association	679
Goode Health Center	700
General Telephone of Illinois	69
Johnson & Johnson	7
Carson Pirie Scott & Co.	40

Alexander's Sporting Goods	50
L. Mies Store	30
Dr. Wysanski	334
Dr. Peterson	78
Hendrickson Clinic	2,187
Dr. Laner	133

The number of medical debts and obligations to several different doctors, hospitals, and clinics indicates a serious illness in the family. The medical debts total $11,943, but most of the debts are relatively modest. This spread of small debts suggests that the Spices made substantial payments, that their insurance paid a substantial portion of most of the bills, or that they skip from doctor to doctor to avoid paying their bills. Most of the medical bills were incurred in 1977 and 1978, three to four years before their bankruptcy.

The Spices' list of unsecured debts amounts to $17,469. In addition, the Spices owe another finance company $2,515 secured by a lien on all the Spices' furniture, but this lien is invalid in bankruptcy. As we discuss later, in bankruptcy this loan is treated as unsecured, so that all of their debts, about $20,000, are unsecured. The Spices list their combined incomes for the year before bankruptcy at $17,000, well above the average in our sample. Yet their debts exceed one year of their combined incomes.

When the Spices filed for bankruptcy, the Central Illinois Light Company and a medical collection service had successfully sued the Spices and garnished both their wages, so their employers were required to pay a part of each paycheck to these creditors. After their bankruptcy filing had been made, the garnishment orders were lifted, and they once again collected a full paycheck.

In Chapter 7 the Spices discharged $19,984 in debt. They promised to pay their attorney $600, although at the time of filing he had not yet received any payment. They paid a $60 filing fee. Because they had few assets, they gave nothing up to the bankruptcy court, and after the bankruptcy their incomes were completely their own. There the file stops, although we would very much like to know what happened to them after bankruptcy. For example, did the medical problems recur? If so, did they have to come up with cash for all medical services? Bankruptcy substantially improved their immediate financial circumstances, but the questions about life after bankruptcy linger.

This case illustrates the trail of financial despair that we have found in so many bankruptcy files. We do not say that it is typical. For example, the attorney was not paid in advance, which is very unusual. It is also atypical for medical bills to be the primary problem; our data show that medical troubles may not be a common cause of bankruptcy at all. Mr. Spice's job is unusual as well; our average debtor had a higher prestige job. Nonetheless, the flat-broke Spices are an appropriate couple to begin our look at people in bankruptcy. Not only is their financial condition representative, but they are like many other debtors in having moved several times before bankruptcy and in having filed bankruptcy after several years of struggling to cope with a financial disaster.

Richard Dickinson White

Richard Dickinson White is an engineer for a railroad headquartered in St. Louis. In 1980 he made $32,000. He went into bankruptcy owing $2,912 in unsecured debts and $14,538 in secured debts. The secured debts included a $12,688 mortgage on a $16,000 home and a $1,850 lien on an eight-year-old Cadillac now worth $1,600.

The relatively modest debts coupled with a very stable income make White's filing puzzling. He filed a Chapter 7 bankruptcy, offering to give up any property in excess of his exemptions in return for a discharge on all his debts. But his file offers an irresistible clue to what triggered his bankruptcy filing.

In July 1980, Mr. White was divorced from his wife Patricia White. As part of the separation agreement, Mr. White had agreed to deed the house to his wife and to pay their outstanding debts. Mr. White was apparently no longer satisfied with this arrangement because seven months later he filed bankruptcy—listing exactly those debts he had agreed to repay as part of the divorce settlement. Mr. White simply gave up the Cadillac, and he told the bank to do whatever it wished with the house. Mr. White's discharge meant that all the joint creditors would now have to look to Mrs. White for repayment.

Mrs. White came to court to argue that Mr. White could not discharge these debts, because they were part of his alimony and support obligations, which cannot be discharged in bankruptcy. The judge disagreed, and Mr. White was discharged. But the judge added a line in his order that makes the reader wonder who got the last laugh: "The proper remedy for the wife in a case such as this is to petition the State Court for an increase in the amount of alimony or support that she is to receive from the debtor." In other words, Mr. White may get off the hook on the specific debts, but the judge advised Mrs. White to haul him back into state court to increase his support obligation, now that his financial circumstances had improved because he had discharged all that debt.

The effect of this bankruptcy is interesting to contemplate. It is probable that it had no effect at all. Unless Mrs. White also declared bankruptcy, there is no reason to believe that any creditor lost any money. Nor did bankruptcy do Mr. White much good. Even if he had not filed for bankruptcy, Mr. White never faced much risk for failing to pay on the mortgage obligation. If Mrs. White fell behind in the payments and the mortgage company asked Mr. White to pay, he could simply refuse. The mortgage company would probably foreclose on the house rather than bother with a lawsuit against him. Because sale of the home would probably yield considerably more than the mortgage value, he was unlikely to have to pay anything. He no longer lived in the home, and it would be Mrs. White's problem to find another place to live. Nor was Mr. White likely to pay much on the car even outside of bankruptcy. The repossession value was worth just about the amount of the outstanding loan. Once again, he could refuse to pay and the creditor would simply repossess the collateral to satisfy the loan. Mr. White's potential trouble with the divorce court will survive his Chapter 7 discharge. This means that Mr. White paid his attorney more than $1,000 to avoid less than $3,000 in unsecured debt. And if Mrs. White follows the judge's advice, Mr. White may not be through paying yet. Mr. White's case is an example of debtors trying to use bankruptcy strategically, even meanly, although it may also be an example of failure to achieve the desired results.

Fred and Winona Todd

Fred and Winona Todd both work full-time. Mr. Todd is a psychiatric aide in the state hospital, and Mrs. Todd is a manager at a state agency. The Todds live with their two teenaged children in their own home in central Pennsylvania. They have two cars, a 5-year-old Chevrolet and a 12-year-old Buick, and a modest amount of furniture and clothing.

The likely source of the Todds' financial problems is revealed in their statements of income. Both Mr. and Mrs. Todd changed jobs in the past year. The files do not reveal whether a time elapsed between jobs when either of them had no income. Even if they were both able to move immediately from one job to the next, however, there was an economic deterioration. Mrs. Todd managed a slight raise with her move; she increased her before-tax salary from $14,000 to $14,666. Mr. Todd, however, lost his job as a police officer, which caused his yearly income to drop from $18,000 to $9,648. Even if both were steadily employed, total family income dropped nearly 25% in one year.

Before they filed their bankruptcy, the Todds fell behind on their home mortgage. By the time they filed, they owed $967 in arrearages on a $45,000 mortgage. Their other debts were unsecured. They owed money to two banks (total: $6,471), two bank credit cards (total: $1,515), two stores (total: $1,822), a gasoline company ($196), the electric utility ($390), and a credit union ($1,500). Altogether the Todds owed their unsecured creditors $11,894, almost half their $24,000 income.

The Todds filed in Chapter 13. Their monthly budget of $1,319 seems very modest for a family of four—$305 for food, $20 for clothing, $5 for newspapers, magazines, and books (including schoolbooks), $10 for recreation. They also allocated $457 for their monthly mortgage payment. They planned to let the credit union where Mrs. Todd works continue to deduct $200 a month from her check to pay off the credit union's $1,500 loan.

The Todds had $130 per month that was not taken up by budgeted expenses. They proposed to give all this to the Trustee in Bankruptcy for three years. According to the Todds' plan, this amount would pay off the mortgage arrearage in full, pay the remaining attorney's fee ($500) in full, and pay the unsecured creditors 20% of what the Todds owed them. The plan allocated every dollar the Todds earned. There were no provisions for expenses exceeding their estimates, for any emergency expenses, or for any interruption in their income.

The Todds took a chance with their plan, but within a short time after filing it became clear that they had one stroke of very good luck: Their creditors were not particularly interested in them. The bankruptcy court had notified all their creditors that the Todds were in bankruptcy and that they would be making some repayment in Chapter 13. That notice instructed each creditor to send a statement of its claim to the bankruptcy court. When the creditors' statements arrived, the trustee would arrange proportional repayment. But four of the nine unsecured creditors did not bother to file a claim. The consequence was that these creditors' claims were discharged, and the Todds were not obligated to pay them anything.

The creditors who failed to file their claims were large companies such as American Express, Citibank MasterCard, Exxon, and the utility company. The amounts owed the nonfilers were not huge. American Express, for example, was owed $649, which means that it was scheduled for a $129.80 payment because the Todds had promised to pay 20% of each debt. On the other hand, J.C. Penney decided that it was worth filing for a $16.32 payment on its claim of $81.60.

The Todds made their payments as scheduled, and because the amount they owed had been diminished by nonfiling creditors, they completed their plan ahead of schedule. Two and a half years after they had filed bankruptcy, they had finished the payments they promised in the plan, discharged their remaining unsecured debt, and brought their home mortgage payments up to date. The Todds continued to own their home, their cars, and their furniture. They paid a bankruptcy filing fee of $60, paid an attorney $700 to handle their case, and paid trustee fees of $400. They paid the credit union in full, and the banks and stores now had 20% of their claims. The nonfiling creditors had nothing.

This case is an example of a Chapter 13 case that worked as Congress envisioned. The creditors almost certainly got more than they would have by a sellout in Chapter 7. The Todds got to keep their home by bringing the payments up to date, a result that probably pleased the mortgage holder as well, because most mortgage lenders want the debtors' interest payments, not their house. Aside from the success of this Chapter 13 plan, this case is instructive because it reveals one of the important patterns that we have found in the data: an income stream that is interrupted or reduced causes debt burdens that were merely difficult to become nearly impossible. A final point is that some readers may not be terribly happy with this case, feeling that the Todds should have been forced to sell their home, pay their debts, and move to an apartment. We will discuss that option in Chapter Seven.

Elaine Dover

Elaine Dover filed her Chapter 13 bankruptcy petition in downstate Illinois. Mr. Dover is not included in her petition. As she explains in her papers, she and her husband "are not yet separated but [he] contributes less than $200 a month" to the family. Her Chapter 13 plan proposes to pay 100% to her creditors.

Mrs. Dover's petition shows how hard her path to financial recuperation will be. She plans to support herself and her six children, ages 5 to 13, on a monthly income of $1,335. She receives wages of $758 as a factory inspector, another $377 from the Social Security Administration for the children, and the $200 her nearly ex-husband provides. Mrs. Dover plans to keep up with mortgage payments, meet her family's current expenses, and repay 100% of her debts. To do all this, she allocates only $100 a month to clothe a family of seven and $25 a month to cover their uninsured medical expenses.

Even with Mrs. Dover's tight budgeting, the numbers do not add up. Mrs. Dover's budget, modest as it may seem, shows her spending $1,357 each month to cover her current expenses and proposing to pay another $145 each month to her creditors above her current expenses—all from a monthly income of $1,335. Perhaps Mrs. Dover hopes to get more from her husband. Maybe she thinks she can work longer hours at the plant. The forms do not explain, and the numbers make no sense. Nevertheless, the court approved her plan.

Mrs. Dover's debts give only a glimpse into events in her life before bankruptcy. She owes $476 to a bank and $700 to the local True Value hardware store. She owes all her other unsecured debt ($2,300) to a hospital, a physician, a funeral home, and a cemetery. The official forms offer no further explanation.

Mrs. Dover's petition reveals the precariousness of her financial position before bankruptcy. Evidently her husband is completely disabled. He contributes $200 to her and their children from the $600 he collects each month from Social Security. He has no other earnings. Mrs. Dover explains that her own wages vary. She gets only 24 hours' notice when she will work, and her employer has called her an average of three days a week so far this year.

Although we can never know why any particular debtor made the final decision to file for bankruptcy, Mrs. Dover's bankruptcy file gives one strong clue. Throughout her troubles, she stayed current on her home mortgage payments of $250, but she fell behind on the payments on her four-year-old Chevy Blazer. In February, the bank repossessed her car. Mrs. Dover came up with the late payments, but the bank was evidently tired of dealing with her. The bank loan officer demanded that she pay the entire outstanding balance ($2,410) or the bank would sell the car to satisfy the loan. Before the bank could sell the car, Mrs. Dover filed bankruptcy. As Mrs. Dover's lawyer explains in her bankruptcy papers, she lives "a great distance from her job. She is currently borrowing an automobile from a friend, but must return the vehicle in the very near future. Without adequate transportation to work she will definitely lose her job." In Chapter 13, Mrs. Dover asked the court to make the bank give back the car, and she promised in her plan to make her payments in full.

At some point a deal might have been worked out with the bank, but by the time the debtor is in bankruptcy the swords are drawn. Neither party will yield, and the battle becomes one of technical legal points. For several months the bank and Mrs. Dover's attorney wrangled over the car, and in June she got it back. But she fell behind on her payments again, and the following March the bank was back in court to seek repossession of the car.

Mrs. Dover had a dismal record in Chapter 13. She made only a few payments under her plan. Her attorney complained that she had not shown up for meetings or answered his calls, and he eventually asked the court to let him withdraw from her case. The last papers in the file indicate that Mrs. Dover has not appeared to explain her lapses and that she faces having her case dismissed. Was she ill? Did the plant stop calling her for work? Was one of the kids sick or injured? Was she overwhelmed or irresponsible? The file is silent.

What did filing bankruptcy do for Mrs. Dover? She held onto her car for nearly nine months. She paid an attorney $200 (and evidently never paid the remaining $300 of his fee). She paid a court filing fee of $60. She made a few payments under her plan to her creditors. The things that are typical about Mrs. Dover's case are that she was in desperate economic trouble and that she proposed a completely unrealistic Chapter 13 payment plan that quickly failed, characteristics that are commonplace in the data. She apparently tried Chapter 13, rather than going for the Chapter 7 fresh start, because that was the only way she could keep the car she needed to get to work. In the end, Mrs. Dover lost the car and all her creditors were as free to pursue her for repayment as they had been before she filed. Bankruptcy for Mrs. Dover was a brief interlude in an ongoing struggle with little lasting economic impact.

John and Martha Fredrickson

John Fredrickson has worked in a Dallas consulting firm since 1980. His wife Martha worked for a big national company and also did some part-time consulting. In 1980, they earned $37,661. Relative to the rest of our sample, they are upper-income, wage-earning debtors, far out on the prosperity curve for most debtors in bankruptcy. The story of their Chapter 7 filing, however, has little to do with their current jobs.

The Fredricksons had a plan for a business that might make it big: Martha Fredrickson Cosmetics. In 1978 they formed a corporation, bought inventory, set up three subsidiaries to handle related travel and business consulting, hired an accountant to manage their business papers, and prepared for their opening shot in the field: introduction and sales at the 1980 Moscow Olympics—a ticket on the *Titanic*.

The Fredricksons had carefully incorporated all their businesses, a move most people believe will protect the owners from personal liability. But they learned that no one was willing to extend credit unless the Fredricksons agreed to be personally liable on the loans as well. When the business collapsed in 1980, the Fredricksons faced personal liability on debts totaling $461,720.

The unsecured debts alone totaled $332,639. A list of these debts gives some idea of the activities of the Fredricksons from 1978 to 1980, when virtually all these debts were incurred:

Accurate of Texas	$ 4,674
American Express	190
American Express	8,340
David Binder, CPA	550
Bio-Safety Research	2,400
Cannon Ball Rental	271
Cynthia Canter	396
Carren's Flowers	219
Central Freight	114
Central Trust Bank	925
Capital Corp.	50,000
Capital Corp.	1,232
Creditor Service Bureau	37
Dallas Transit System	86
Emery Freight	14
Equilease Corporation	1,450
Financial Collection Agency	72
Flower-A-Day Florists	44
Foster and Kleiser	1,923
Freeds Furniture	110
G. Liquor	1,715
Green Oaks Inn	149
Clerk, District Court of New York	475
J. L. White Co.	390
Kelly Associates	938
Kelly Services	102
Kwik Copy	156
Jeremy McPhail	550
Loew's Anatole Hotel	226
M. B. Kiser Air Conditioning	860
MESBIC Financial Corporation	107,170
Mahogany Magazine	1,400
Mana Products	300
Ohio State—Student Loan	500
Manufacturers Hanover Trust	25
Marine Midland Bank	350
Neiman Marcus	178
Olivetti Corp.	27
Orkin Pest Control	250
Peachtree Plaza Hotel	332
Pease Printing	565

David Quentin	45,850
RCA Service Company	100
Ramada Inn	557
Republic National Bank	10,600
Republic National Bank	8,000
S.P. Communications	542
Salesman's Opportunity Magazine	700
Sanger-Harris Department Store	234
Sears, Roebuck	90
Small Business Administration	72,000
Specialty Salesman Magazine	1,900
Stouffer's Greenway Plaza	892
Success Magazine	300
The Ice House	106
United Parcel	104
Sandra White, CPA	335
White, Mahomes & Bisco	24
Xerox Corp.	600

Their debts are a typical amalgam of those incurred by individual businesspeople. The Small Business Administration, some banks, private investors, and venture capital companies had made substantial loans. A host of suppliers extended credit. And the Fredricksons incurred some personal debts that are woven into the fabric of their obligations as well.

Besides their unsecured debts, the Fredricksons owed over $15,000 to state and local taxing authorities to pay their employee withholding taxes, sales taxes, and property taxes. Their remaining debt included a $111,000 mortgage on their home and a $3,000 lien on their car.

The business failed in early 1980, but it was late 1981 before the lawsuits against the Fredricksons began to catch up with them. They remained current on their home and car loans, and they made some payments on their other debts through August 1981. They faced collection suits from two of their creditors, and they had already paid $2,300 to an attorney to help them when they filed for bankruptcy.

Bankruptcy dramatically changed the Fredricksons' financial picture. They continued to live in their $190,000 home and make payments on the mortgage, and they kept their two-year-old Ford and continued the car payments. They also kept their modest amount of household goods and clothes. If they could hold off the tax authorities following bankruptcy and get those taxes paid, then they could keep all of their property. There is no account of whatever savings and time the Fredricksons had poured into the business while they operated it, but they gave up nothing more once they filed bankruptcy.

By filing bankruptcy, the Fredricksons discharged their unsecured debts completely. To keep their home and car, they had to continue payments on them. Tax obligations survive bankruptcy, so that they were obligated to pay

$15,000 plus interest. The student loan from Ohio State University also survives bankruptcy, so they continued to be liable for that $500 obligation. The Fredricksons reduced their total debt by over $330,000, and they left their future income and assets subject only to the tax claim, the educational loan, and the payments on the car and house, if they want to keep them.

If the Fredricksons had avoided bankruptcy, the annual interest payable at 18% on just their unsecured debts would have been $59,400—more than one and a half times their gross annual income. Even if interest were waived and no one instituted a lawsuit, the Fredricksons would have had to devote half of their gross income to their creditors for more than 26 years to pay off all their debts. After bankruptcy, the Fredricksons could enjoy an income in the upper 18% of all American families, a $190,000 home, a two-year-old car, and relatively few debts.[1] Although they could not pay any significant portion of their debts, they emerged from financial disaster living pretty well.

Their case is likely to invoke the mixed feelings characteristic of bankruptcy. Why should David Quentin, to take just one creditor on the Fredricksons' list, lose his $45,850, while the Fredricksons live the life of Riley? Yet it is clear that this family could never have paid any appreciable part of these debts. Furthermore, entrepreneurship—small business risk-taking—is a national ideal, as well as the greatest generator of new jobs in America. Do we want to make the penalties for losing so harsh that people will stop taking those risks? We will return to these issues when we discuss entrepreneurs in Chapter Six.

John Williams and Betty Sue Havco

John Williams Havco works at a high-tech company where he earns $21,504 per year. His income has been close to that amount for at least the past three years. His wife Betty Sue considers herself a housewife. The Havcos live in an apartment and apparently have no children at home.

The Havcos' creditors are a "Who's Who in Consumer Lending": three finance companies, three banks, five stores, two book services, and Encyclopedia Britannica. Their total unsecured, short-term debt is $25,331, about 120% of their annual gross income. They owe a total of $7,765 on their six Visa and MasterCard accounts alone.

Although the Havcos evidently have done a lot of shopping, they claim to own only a limited amount of household goods and clothing. They have a five-year-old Ford that is paid for and a two-year-old Ford that is subject to a lien for its full value. The Havcos' total assets (including their security deposit on their rent) amount to $3,031.

The Havcos' attorney included in their file a "Debt Listing Sheet" in which the Havcos recorded their monthly payments on each debt. The reason they filed bankruptcy becomes readily apparent. The monthly payments to which they were committed add up to $1,304. This amount is only slightly less than Mr. Havco's monthly take-home pay.

How the Havcos had managed such a huge monthly debt burden becomes clearer when they list how far behind they are on each payment. Except for the car payments, they average four months behind on every payment. A prudent guess is that the Havcos pay their creditors on a rotating basis: only a few get paid each month.

In Chapter 7, the Havcos discharged all their debt except one bank loan on their car. This debt for $4,726 they reaffirmed. Bankruptcy made a big difference in their monthly payments, which dropped from $1,304 (excluding rent) to $169.

The obvious point of this case is irresponsibility. The hard question is who was more irresponsible, the Havcos or the creditors who gave them six bankcards and all the rest of that credit.

Conclusion

This tiny sample of case studies presents just a few of the stories we read. The radio evangelist is not here, nor is the widow trying to pay off the debts of her husband's failed business. We did not write about the woman who filed her bankruptcy three months after the company she worked for filed its bankruptcy, or the man who went into bankruptcy and reaffirmed every debt he owed except one, which he discharged with a vengeance. These stories must wait to be told another day.

Yet even a few stories provide a picture of the recurring human side of the bankruptcy drama. The files for these people—and for many more in our sample—tell of heartache, revenge, optimism, disappointment, unavoidable disasters, and cavalier foolishness. They remind us that children and ex-spouses and friends are affected by bankruptcies that they did not file. They tell about a brief, but very intense time in the lives of people who are much like people we know—except that the bankrupt debtors are the losers in the great American game.

These cases preview many themes that will be elaborated in later chapters. Although Mrs. Dover and the Spices are working, their wages are low by national standards. The Todds have higher income, but it has dropped substantially from its earlier level. The statistical analyses will show that interrupted income streams are pervasive among the petitioners. The Fredricksons are failed entrepreneurs. Along with one-fifth of our sample who are self-employed, the Fredricksons' bankruptcy was part of the funeral rites for a family business. Many in our sample are like Mrs. Dover, the Todds, and the Fredricksons in trying to save their homes. Some, like the Havcos, seem to have used too much credit, and we will examine the extent to which our petitioners might be characterized as credit junkies. Most of our sample resemble the

Fredricksons, the Havcos, and the Spices in having far more in debts than they can reasonably pay.

These cases also remind us that economic issues—bankruptcy included—are intertwined with other aspects of social life. Mrs. Dover and Mr. White find themselves in bankruptcy following a marital disruption. The files suggest that for Mrs. Dover bankruptcy is a matter of necessity, while for Mr. White it may be a tactical maneuver. Mrs. Dover and the Spices report substantial medical expenses. In the national debate over medical costs, it is worth noting that bankruptcy may constitute the individual debtor's ultimate cost containment. These cases illustrate nicely the increased access of American women to employment and credit; four of the five women in this chapter are workers.

The cases in this chapter reveal some key choices that debtors must make in bankruptcy. The Todds' Chapter 13 succeeded, but Mrs. Dover's failed. The Spices and the Fredricksons entered bankruptcy after their creditors had started to pursue them in state court. We also see here some choices made by creditors. Some creditors initiate lawsuits and garnishments. Some are patient; Mrs. Dover's bank was not. Some of the Todds' creditors filed for repayment, while others passed up their chance. As we will note in the chapters on creditors, it is a dangerous oversimplification to assume that there is a single "creditors' position," for creditors have diverse interests in bankruptcy.

The files also leave much of each story untold. Is Mrs. Havco too lazy to take a job to help repay the Havcos' debts? Or was she ill and unable to work? Did Mrs. Dover keep her job? How did she take care of six children without a car and with so little money? Did Mr. White have to pay more support after he discharged the debts he had incurred with his ex-wife? The files do not tell.

We do not delude ourselves that we could ever learn enough from the bankruptcy files to know the justice of these cases. No sooner do we know one thing than another possibility, which might reverse what we believe to be a perfect outcome, suggests itself. If Mrs. Havco is healthy, do we want to know how Mr. Havco feels about her working? Is her age relevant? Does it matter whether she could get a job near home or what kind of job might be available? Even in individual cases, we never have enough facts to know for certain whether a debtor should be pushed into repayment or permitted a discharge with a minimum of fuss.

Decisions—and lawmaking—proceed with incomplete information. The details are smoothed out. The more deserving and the less deserving are sometimes mixed together. The justice is rough. But in a story about debtors in bankruptcy, it is useful to remember both the pathos and the foolishness, as well as the unanswered questions that should color any study of bankruptcy. We believe that a large dose of humility about this complexity and uncertainty will help us to interpret our results with appropriate caution.

With those admonitions fixed firmly in mind, we turn to statistical aggregates to describe the debtors in this study. While we can construct a profile of the statistical "average" debtor, we will also be interested in the variations among different groups of debtors. Since neither policy nor law can be based on the idiosyncrasies that each case reveals, we will instead seek the "slices" of data that best illuminate the backgrounds and circumstances of the debtors. And, before we are through, we will have a few more stories to tell.

Note

1. Calculated from data in U.S. Bureau of the Census, Current Population Reports, "Money Income of Households, Families, and Persons in the United States: 1981" (Washington: U.S. Government Printing Office, Series P-60, No. 137, March 1983), Table 14, p. 35.

4

A Financial Portrait of People in Bankruptcy

Most people have a general notion that debtors in bankruptcy face economic trouble, but little information is available to document their situations.[1] As a result, completely contradictory assumptions about the financial circumstances of debtors flourish side-by-side. In the rhetoric of policymaking debates, some speakers implicitly assume that all debtors are a poverty-stricken, chronically unemployed segment of the lower class; they never wonder how such people could have been approved for so much credit. Others argue that debtors in bankruptcy are not really so financially different from those who struggle to pay their bills, but they have made the clever decision to manipulate bankruptcy to avoid payment. What we found is that neither stereotype describes debtors of the 1980s.

Most individuals do not keep the elaborate financial records normally found in a business of any size: ledgers and journals, balance sheets, profit-and-loss statements. Many folks are doing pretty well just to keep the checkbook up to date and balanced. Bankrupt debtors may be even less well organized in that regard than the rest of us. Ironically, the decision to consider bankruptcy triggers a more thorough accounting of financial affairs than many people would otherwise ever make. As we outlined in Chapter Two, a person filing for bankruptcy must give a detailed and elaborate statement of assets and debts and of past and present income. These reports form the basis of our financial analysis of debtors in bankruptcy.

Financial Profile

We begin with the most basic information: the debtors' incomes, their assets, and their debts. Despite a wide range in the actual dollar amounts, almost all debtors are in deep financial trouble.

We report data from our common debtor sample (CDS). We eliminate 27 outliers, debtors with income, assets, or debts so far from typical that, in our judgment, including them would skew the whole picture.[2] We also eliminate files with too little information to make a sensible calculation about the debtor's financial circumstances.[3] This leaves us with a CDS of 1502, which we use for all data analyses unless we note otherwise.

There is enormous variation in the financial circumstances of our CDS debtors. Most have jobs of some kind, but many are unemployed. Most are wage earners, at least by the time they file bankruptcy, but a substantial proportion ran small businesses that had failed. Most have crushing burdens of debt in comparison with their incomes, but a few have debts that appear small compared with their incomes. In general, these people are far below the general population financially, but their financial profiles vary greatly.

Table 4.1 describes the basic financial circumstances for all the debtors in the CDS bankruptcy sample. Although the debtors must report many economic details, the key data can be summarized under the three overall headings: income, assets, and debts. We subdivided the total debt into its two component parts, secured debt and unsecured debt. For each column, we report the mean (the arithmetic average), the standard deviation (a measure of variation from the mean), the quartiles (the breakpoint between each quarter of the debtors), the number of debtors who give sufficiently complete information to permit an entry in the relevant column, and the number of debtors for whom information was missing.

Income

The first column of Table 4.1 describes the debtors' family incomes. This figure represents income from all sources. Where income was reported for both husbands and wives, the income reflects both,[4] as well as any income from transfer payments, child support payments, and other sources. The debtors' average (mean) income is $15,800, and their median income is $15,000. The mean income is derived by averaging all the family incomes together; the me-

TABLE 4.1. Distribution of Income, Assets, and Debts for Bankruptcy Petitioners[a]

Distribution	Family Income	Total Assets	Total Debt	Secured Debt	Unsecured Debt
Mean	$15,779	$29,355	$38,599	$23,034	$15,498
s.d.	9,609	40,034	54,815	38,566	31,268
25th percentile	9,448	2,988	9,737	1,600	3,826
Median	14,974	14,025	20,956	9,601	7,052
75th percentile	21,329	44,334	44,480	30,460	13,935
N	1,289	1,490	1,496	1,501	1,495
Missing	213	12	6	1	7

[a]Cases with extreme values on assets, total debt, or income are removed.

Source: Consumer Bankruptcy Project.

dian income is literally the income in the middle—half the debtors receive less and half receive more. The two measures of income diverge somewhat in this sample, which indicates that a few debtors scattered at the high end of the income range pull up the mean for the whole sample. Whenever the mean and median differ—a phenomenon that recurs throughout these data—it indicates that some debtors are outside the normal distribution pattern and that these debtors pull the average or mean up above the middle case. When that happens, it is important to have in mind both the mean case and the middle case, because each measure captures a portion of the true picture.

The government data we use for comparison with the national population are taken from the Current Population Survey, or CPS, conducted by the United States Census Bureau. The CPS is based on a monthly sample survey of 60,000 households in the United States. The CPS collects basic information about current employment, incomes, and other topics.[5] We use a sample of the sample to spare our computer.

We report the CPS data by families, which is the closest comparison we could make for the debtors in bankruptcy.[6] In 1981, the year our cases were filed, national median (middle) family income was $22,400,[7] expressed in 1981 dollars. National mean incomes were higher, at $25,800, the average being skewed upward by a relatively few people with very large incomes.[8] By contrast, both the mean and the median incomes of the bankrupt debtors were less than two-thirds of the national figures.

Income quartiles divide the bankruptcy sample into four groups. The lowest income quartile (the 25th percentile) is only $9,400. This means that one in four debtors in bankruptcy reports an income below $9,400. The highest quartile (the 75th percentile) of $21,300 indicates that the top quarter of the sample have household income in excess of $21,300. More than half of all the debtors are sandwiched between the 1981 federal poverty level, $9,300, and the 1981 median family income, $22,400.[9]

Although the debtors in bankruptcy represent a fairly well-defined group of lower middle-income Americans, there are substantial variations within that group. At the highest income level, 14% of the bankruptcy sample had incomes above the national mean family income ($25,800).[10] Although these debtors are not typical, their presence in bankruptcy makes it clear that the bankruptcy laws are not being used only by lower income people.

The lowest quartile of debtors in Table 4.1 shows a very different income picture. With incomes below $9,500, nearly all of the lowest quarter falls below the $9,300 federal poverty level for a nonfarm family of four in the study year.[11] This 25% of bankrupt debtors compares with 12.5% of families in the general population who were classified below the poverty level that same year.[12] A person in a bankrupt family is about twice as likely as other people to be classified below the poverty line.

The lower incomes of the debtors help explain their financial stress. But another piece of information puts the income data into context. The family income of bankrupt debtors is also spread among more people. In the United States in 1981, mean household size was 2.7. Mean family size among debtors in our sample was about 3.4, or nearly one person more.[13] Thus the already low incomes must stretch further. Because expenses rise with the number of people to be supported, the bankrupt debtors are in the worst possible squeeze: lower incomes supporting higher costs.

Assets

A complete picture of the debtors' financial positions also requires an idea of their assets. Someone with substantial assets is obviously better off than someone with the same income but no accumulated assets. The second column of Table 4.1 shows the asset information reported by the debtors.

The bankruptcy laws require debtors to list their assets and to estimate the current market value of each item. But just how much are the kitchen appliances worth? The bedroom furniture from Aunt Alice? Eight pairs of old socks? The bobtail cat? Many household items don't have clear valuations, and debtors are not expert appraisers.

Moreover, debtors have clear incentives to underreport their assets. State exemption laws limit how much debtors can keep, and debtors who seem to have little are less likely to attract the attention of their creditors for a closer scrutiny about repayment possibilities. No one is likely to come to the house to inventory the furniture or price the debtors' clothes. The debtor could use low values and "forget" to mention a few items, with no one likely to be wiser.

On the other hand, some items, such as cars and homes, are fairly easy to evaluate because there is a well-known resale market. Most bankruptcy judges and trustees are quick to examine these valuations and to flag anything out of line. These items often represent the bulk of value in a debtor's estate. Additionally, some debtors evaluate by original cost (the sofa cost $400 last year), even though the depreciated market value is much lower. Furthermore, the debtors sign their lists of assets and valuations under penalty of perjury, and their attorneys have some interest in keeping the debtors honest, if for no other reason than because attorneys do not want to litigate these matters in a flat-fee case. These counterincentives may suggest that the values reported are fairly accurate for most assets, especially large ones, and that some overstated values balance out some understated values.

Table 4.1 shows the overall mean assets for the debtors in bankruptcy. The mean is $29,400; the median is far lower at $14,000. The dollar amounts represent everything the debtors own, from their homes to their toothbrushes, with no deductions for outstanding mortgages or liens.

It is much harder to compare assets for the debtors in bankruptcy with the assets of the national population because in 1981 consumer asset information was not regularly collected by the government. Seven federal agencies do, however, jointly sponsor a special survey of consumer finances, including assets, every few years. The survey closest to our study year of 1981 was done in 1983.[14] The figures in the 1983 Survey of Consumer Finance exclude several assets, including all consumer durables such as cars and home furnishings, the cash value of life insurance, and pension benefits.[15] To make our figures comparable, we recomputed the debtors' assets, excluding the same items excluded by the Survey.

Of the families surveyed nationally, mean financial assets were $27,365, and mean home values were $56,133. Thus a homeowning family (60% of all families surveyed) with mean financial and home assets would have total assets over $83,000.[16] Although the bankruptcy sample had a nearly comparable proportion of homeowners, the bankrupt debtors had considerably lower asset value. The debtors' mean assets on the same basis, including homes, were far lower, at $24,700.[17] The debtors have only 30% of the assets of the hypothetical family, as indicated by the 1983 Survey.[18]

While the debtors' asset figures are relatively low, a reader might well ask "How can these people have any significant assets if they claim to be bankrupt?" There are four components to the answer to that question. The most important is that many of these assets are subject to liens, making much of this "wealth" only apparent, not real. The debtor who reports owning a car worth $10,000, while also indicating he owes $8,000 more on his car loan, in effect "owns" $2,000 worth of car and has only a contract to purchase $8,000 more car. But in our asset column in Table 4.1, the car adds the full $10,000. The debtor's net worth in the car's value will be $10,000 only if the debtor pays another $8,000. After depreciation, even the debtor who successfully completes repayment will probably never own $10,000 worth of car. The same distortion occurs with reports of home ownership, where a debtor lists a $45,000 home—and a $39,000 mortgage. For this reason, debts, especially debts secured by collateral, must be considered in determining wealth. Later in this section we discuss the debtors' secured debt and their "net worth," which link assets and debt on a debtor-by-debtor basis. The wide range of assets is matched by a wide range of debt, which leaves most debtors with relatively few assets to call their own. Until assets and debts are properly linked, "wealthier" debtors may be those at the bottom rather than the top of the asset range.

Three other facts put the debtors' asset figures into context. The first is that most of the "wealth" represented by these figures is the family home. Homes represent 64% of the total value of assets in our sample. In Chapter Seven we discuss homeowners in bankruptcy, including the central normative question: To what extent should general creditors be able to satisfy their debts by taking away a nonpaying debtor's home? The second important fact is that much of the value of these assets is owned by people in Chapter 13 trying to pay all or part of their debts. Chapter 13 debtors are only 39% of the debtors, but they own 54% of the assets. Finally, the assets in our sample are disproportionately owned by the self-employed. Although those who are currently self-employed constitute only 10% of our sample, their assets, including business assets like inventory and tools, represent 26% of the total assets in Table 4.1. In Chapter Six we analyze the financial situations of the currently self-employed along with those of an additional 10% of the sample who were formerly self-employed.

Even if we ignore all of these qualifications, the asset data show the debtors once again falling below most Americans, with assets typically about two-thirds lower than those reported for most families.

Debts

While debtors' incomes are low and their assets are even lower relative to other Americans, the debtors in bankruptcy show some extraordinary debt figures. Their debts are summarized in the third column of Table 4.1. These data show debtors with median total debts of nearly $21,000 and mean total debts nearly twice as high at $38,600.

Reports of debts tend to have a persistent bias: The amount of debt is frequently understated.[19] The most significant underreport of debt comes from the number of claims that are listed as "undetermined." Whenever a debtor knows something is owed but is unsure of the amount, the schedule lists the creditor's name and "undetermined" for the amount. We computed debt totals only from the amounts listed in the court petition. In this sample, 87 debtors—about 6% of the debtors—list one or more debts as "undetermined" in amount. These would have raised the debtors' total debt amounts, but we have no idea by how much.[20]

A second factor that causes debt to be underreported is that some debtors deliberately omit certain creditors, hoping that if they continue to pay without incident, the creditors will not learn of the bankruptcy. Although this is plainly a violation of the bankruptcy laws, we have evidence in the files that some debtors engaged in this behavior to conceal their bankruptcies from their home mortgage lenders. We discuss this phenomenon in the chapter on homeowners, but we note now that it causes debt totals to be sharply understated for some debtors by leaving out a large debt obligation.

Moreover, many debtors owe so much money and keep their records in such disarray that they forget to whom they owe money. Debtors are unlikely to make the mistake of listing debts they have paid, but they may forget to list some of the many debts they have not paid. Forgetfulness is more likely to yield underreported debt than overreported debt.

Finally, debtors often list debt in terms of the outstanding principal. Many creditors can (and do) legally claim past-due interest, late charges, collection costs, and the like. The debtor may have lost track of all these charges, even though they are legal obligations recognized in bankruptcy.

These factors tend to cause the amount of debt that petitioners carry into bankruptcy to be understated. As a consequence, the debtors' financial pictures look somewhat better than they otherwise would.

As with assets, our comparisons with national figures rely on the 1983 Survey. The Survey does not report total debt figures. Instead, it reports home mortgage debt and "consumer debt," which it defines as all open-ended debt (e.g., credit cards), installment debt (e.g., payments on a washing machine), and noninstallment debt (e.g., bank loans due in full on maturity). Table 4.1 reports all debt, so we recalculate our data using the Survey categories to make useful comparisons between the bankrupt debtors and the general population.

In the national population, the mean home mortgage was $27,100, whereas our debtors had mean mortgages of $29,083. Median mortgages showed a similar comparison. At the national median, families reported mortgages of $21,000, whereas our debtors' median mortgage value was $23,714. These data show that bankrupt homeowners carry mortgages of roughly the same size as those of most homeowning Americans.

It is nonmortgage consumer debt that shows vast differences between people generally and debtors in bankruptcy. Families across the nation had average nonmortgage consumer debts of $5,400, whereas the debtors in this sample averaged $20,600 per family, using the Survey definition of consumer debt. The more modest median debts show the same pattern: Median consumer debts were $2,400 nationally, in stark contrast with the median bankrupt debtor's burden of $10,800.[21]

Although debts of people in bankruptcy are generally much higher than are debts for the rest of us, they vary enormously within the sample. As shown in Table 4.1, the mean total debt is $38,600, with a standard deviation of $54,800—which shows an extremely broad range of indebtedness.

We have divided the debts into secured and unsecured debts, but we have no comparable classification of the national figures (as remarkable as that seems). Debtors in bankruptcy have far more secured debt than unsecured debt. Secured debts are owed to a creditor who has taken a lien on collateral: the home mortgages, the car loans, and the pay-no-money-now furniture and appliance purchases. In or out of bankruptcy, either the debtor pays or the creditor repossesses. At the mean, secured debts alone outrun the mean annual income for debtors, although the enormous standard deviation ($38,600) again suggests that some debtors inflate the mean by carrying debts that would make even the rich shudder.

Although unsecured debts are a smaller portion of the total debt load, they are remarkable because they indicate how much money debtors can borrow with a smile and a signature. The average bankrupt debtor had $15,500 of unsecured debt, about equal to the average debtor's yearly income. Fully half of our debtors have unsecured, mostly short-term debts of $7,000 or more. This figure is nearly half the annual median income of the debtors in bankruptcy.

An Interim Summary

The data from Table 4.1 provide a relatively complete financial picture of the debtors in bankruptcy. The most consistent pattern is the relationship between total debts on the one hand and income and assets on the other: At the mean, the 25th percentile, the median, and the 75th percentile, total debts exceed annual income. Similarly, debt dramatically exceeds assets—except at the top quartile, where they nearly match.

The aggregate description in Table 4.1 shows that few bankrupt debtors are affluent and many are poor. They earn about one-third less than most Americans. They support larger families, and they report two-thirds fewer assets than the general population. But they owe far more, nearly four times more in nonmortgage debt alone.

Analysis of Individuals' Circumstances

The income, asset, and debt comparisons in Table 4.1 describe aggregate patterns in our sample, but they do not indicate the relative position of any particular debtor, or even the average debtor. Having a high income or owning very valuable assets does not make a person financially invulnerable, as former Texas governor John Connally or heart surgeon Denton Cooley could testify from the bankruptcy courthouse. It is the relationship of the size of a person's debts to that person's income and assets that determines financial strength or weakness. The discussion that follows examines relative financial strength using variables constructed on a debtor-by-debtor basis.

Net Worth

The 1983 Consumer Survey was designed in large part to ascertain the net worth of individuals in the general population. As the Survey report notes, "Net worth is important both because it influences savings, consumption, and financial behavior and because it serves as an indicator of economic well-being."[22] Net worth is usually taken to mean what is left when a person's liabilities are subtracted from the total value of all assets. The Survey follows the general concept, although it omits automobiles and home furnishings from the calculation, which an accountant would point out somewhat understates aggregate net worth. But these items rapidly depreciate and they generally must be replaced if they are sold, which suggests that the government calculation is a sensible way to measure consumer net worth.[23] The Survey measure of net worth includes homes, cash, savings, stocks, investments, and similar assets.

One difficulty with the net worth figure is that it is a true measure of "wealth" only for those who have something to liquidate when they get into financial trouble. For the less affluent, squeezing $2,000 of value out of a home is tough to do even if the federal statistics say it is there because the house is valued at $60,000 and the mortgage is $58,000. The asset is ill-liquid, that is, it cannot be sold quickly. In addition, there are significant selling expenses, and the family will have to find another place to live—which means that net worth makes some people better off only on paper, especially in the lower financial reaches. Nonetheless, net worth provides some basis for comparing the economic circumstances of bankrupt debtors with the general population.

The national data show that a substantial portion of the general population has a small net worth. One-third of all the families surveyed showed a net worth of less than $5,000. This is no surprise to young couples starting out (with new mortgages, lots of purchases, and high hopes), and the federal statistics show a greater proportion of young people in the lowest net worth category. The remaining two-thirds of the population did better, reporting net worth ranging from $5,000 to above $500,000.

Tables 4.2 and 4.3 show the frustration of trying to use government statistics to understand people in serious financial trouble. Everyone with a net worth under $5,000 has been lumped together in the Survey tables. All those with small net worth and negative net worth are in a single category. This makes the comparison with bankrupt debtors much more difficult, because the net worth of most of the debtors is in the less than $5,000 category.[21]

More than three-quarters of the bankrupt debtors in Table 4.3 are insolvent; that is, they have a net worth of less than zero because their debts exceed the total value of there assets. If there were no exemption laws to protect some property from creditors, and if we made these debtors sell their clothes, kitchen utensils, and the cat, they still could not pay their debts. Another 5% of the debtors could sell everything right down to the skin and have less than $5,000 after they paid their debts. We do not have comparable figures for the general population, only the less than $5,000 net worth category. All we can conclude is that about one-third of the general population has a net worth of less than $5,000, while 84% of the debtors are worth less than that amount.

The mean net worth of bankrupt debtors is $−13,900, which is a long way from the mean net worth of $66,100 for the general population. The medians are closer together, but they still fall on different sides of the break-even point. The median bankrupt debtor has a negative net worth, $−8,100, while the median person in the general population has a positive net worth of $24,600.

But not all debtors are under water. Table 4.3 also shows that 16% of the

TABLE 4.2. Distribution of U.S. Families by Net Worth, Selected Years (percent except as noted)

	Current Dollars			Constant (1983) Dollars		
Net Worth (dollars)[a]	1970	1977	1983	1970	1977	1983
Less than 5,000	45	39	33	36	35	33
5,000–9,999	11	7	5	6	5	5
10,000–24,999	23	17	12	14	12	12
25,000–49,999	11	17	16	17	15	16
50,000–99,999	7	13	17	14	16	17
100,000–249,999	3	7	12	9	12	12
250,000–499,999	1	1	3	2	2	3
500,000 and above	[c]	[c]	2	1	[c]	2
Total[b]	100	100	100	100	100	100
Mean	$22,154	$31,039	$66,050	$56,781	$50,895	$66,050
Median	7,189	12,656	24,574	18,425	20,752	24,574

[a]Excludes major consumer durables such as automobiles and home furnishings as well as items mentioned in the text.

[b]Actual totals may not be 100% because of rounding.

[c]Less than 0.5%.

Source: Federal Reserve Bulletin, December 1984, p. 862.

TABLE 4.3. Range of Net Worth, by Employment Type, for Bankruptcy Petitioners[a,b]

	Employment Type					
	Current Wage Earner		Currently Self-Employed		Total Petitioners	
Range (dollars)	*N*	%[c]	*N*	%[c]	*N*	%[c]
Less than 5,000	1,136	85.2	119	77.3	1,255	84.4
−499,999 to −250,000	8	0.6	2	1.3	10	0.7
−249,999 to −100,000	18	1.4	22	14.3	40	2.7
−99,999 to −50,000	30	2.3	20	13.0	50	3.4
−49,999 to −25,000	94	7.1	21	13.6	115	7.7
−24,999 to −10,000	382	28.7	29	18.8	411	27.6
−9,999 to −5,000	342	25.7	9	5.8	351	23.6
−4,999 to −1	188	14.1	6	3.9	194	13.0
More than 5,000	197	14.8	35	22.7	232	15.6
0 to 4,999	74	5.6	10	6.5	84	5.4
5,000 to 9,999	60	4.5	7	4.5	67	4.5
10,000 to 24,999	81	6.1	10	6.5	91	6.1
25,000 to 49,999	37	2.8	8	5.2	45	3.0
50,000 to 99,999	19	1.4	8	5.2	27	1.8
100,000 to 249,999	0	0.0	2	1.3	2	0.1
250,000 to 499,999	0	0.0	0	0.0	0	0.0
Total (Missing = 15)	1,333	100.0	154	100.0	1,487	100.0
Mean	$−11,616		$−33,757		$−13,909	
Median	−7,861		−18,527		−8,132	

[a]Cases with extreme values on assets, total debt, or income are removed.

[b]Net worth is computed as assets (excluding household goods, cars, and boats) minus total debt.

[c]As a percentage of column total *N*.

Source: Consumer Bankruptcy Project.

debtors have a positive net worth over $5,000. The asset that produces net worth for debtors in either Chapter 7 or Chapter 13 is almost always the family home. Homeowners represent 94% of the debtors with a positive net worth greater than $5,000. In Chapter Seven we discuss the special circumstances of homeowners in bankruptcy and the debates about how they should be treated. For now we note that it is almost exclusively homeowner–debtors who show up on the right side of zero in a net worth table.

Once again, the reader might legitimately ask how there can be anybody in bankruptcy with a positive net worth, much less one greater than $5,000. As we indicated in Chapter Two, there is no requirement that a debtor show a negative net worth to declare bankruptcy. Instead, the Bankruptcy Code offers the debtor one of two propositions: keep your property in exchange for paying at least a portion of your debts in Chapter 13, or give up all your property over the exemption levels in exchange for a fresh start in Chapter 7.

More than three-quarters—76%—of the debtors in our sample with a positive net worth over $5,000 are in Chapter 13, trying to pay debts and keep property. The remaining 24% of these debtors are in Chapter 7, where they are subject to the very different exemption laws of the three states in our study. Exemption laws define the necessities a debtor can keep. In Chapter 7 bankruptcy, everything that exceeds the exemption level is sold for the benefit of creditors.[25]

Somewhat surprisingly, in light of very different exemption levels, there are not many differences in net worth by state. Texas debtors have greater mean assets than those in Illinois and Pennsylvania, and the difference is statistically significant. But when liabilities are subtracted from assets to produce net worth, Pennsylvanians' mean net worth is statistically different from Texans' net worth—Pennsylvanians are better off.[26] Texas debtors with *positive* net worth had significantly greater net worth than Illinois or Pennsylvania debtors with positive net worth. That is, when we look only at the relatively few debtors who have more assets than liabilities, the Texas debtors had an average net worth three times higher than the average in Illinois or Pennsylvania. We discuss the effects of state exemption laws in greater detail in Chapter Thirteen.

The net worth data give one more comparison in which the debtors in bankruptcy divide sharply from the general population. When assets and debts are matched for each family, as they are in the net worth calculation, we find most debtors are in terrible shape, but a few, mostly Chapter 13 debtors, look much better off. We will review these net worth data again with other financial data to determine how debtors might use these assets to pay their debts.

A Comparison of Debts with Income

In contemporary society, the relationship of income to debts is the most critical measure of financial condition. Some investment bankers making $200,000 live at the financial edge, and some clerks making $18,000 a year have comfortable, debt-free lives. Income compared with debt is particularly important in the context of financial collapse.

Because of the important financial information they reveal, we examine the debt/income ratios for each of the debtors in our sample.[27] We compute the ratios by dividing each debtor's reported debt by reported annual income, with both spouses' incomes combined for married couples. Because income is the denominator, a lower ratio indicates less indebtedness relative to income. A ratio of 1.0 means the debtor owes debts equal to one year's income; a ratio of 1.5 describes a debtor who owes debts equal to a year and a half's worth of income. A fraction less than 1.0 indicates that the debts equal less than one year's income, so that 0.5 would mean the debtor owes half a year's income in debts.

The calculation of debt/income ratios for the bankrupt debtors is subject to some inherent distortion. Income is the denominator in the ratio, and some debtors report zero income. Our computer, like your high school math teacher, will not let us divide by zero, so we have eliminated from this calculation all debtors with no income. The result is that 47 debtors who are among the worst off are not included in these statistics. Thus the reported statistics show better (lower) debt/income ratios than they would if the zero-income debtors could be included.

Another built-in bias also tends to improve the reported debt/income ratios for the debtors. As we noted earlier, bankrupt debtors consistently underreport debt. This necessarily reduces the debt/income ratios below their "true" level. That makes the report of debt/income ratios somewhat rosier than the reality.

We begin the computation of debt/income ratio by using all the income and all the debt reported in the bankruptcy files. Table 4.4 lists the basic data using all debt and all income in the total debt/income ratio. The mean total debt/income ratio is 3.2. At the mean, a family in our bankruptcy sample owed debts greater than three years and two months' worth of income. Once again, the mean is considerably larger than the median, suggesting that some extreme cases raise the report of the "typical" case. The median is 1.4, meaning that the middle family owes debts equal to almost one year and five months' worth of income. The standard deviation is 10.45, more than three times the size of the mean debt/income ratio. These numbers demonstrate that debt/income ratios cover a wide span, with some debtors owing less than a year's income while other debtors owe several years' income.

One variation in this analysis excludes home mortgages because of their unusual size and long repayment schedule. When we recalculate debt/income ratios with the mortgage debts eliminated, but all other debt and income still included, the debt/income ratios necessarily improve. The surprising finding is that short-term debts alone constitute a huge fraction of the debtors' in-

TABLE 4.4. Distribution of Total Debt/Income Ratio for Bankruptcy Petitioners[a]

Distribution	Total Debt/Income Ratio
Mean	3.20
s.d.	10.45
25th percentile	0.70
Median	1.41
75th percentile	2.60
N	1,241
Zero income	47
Missing	214

[a]Cases with extreme values on assets, total debt, or income are removed.

Source: Consumer Bankruptcy Project.

comes. For example, debtors in bankruptcy have mean nonmortgage debts of almost two years' worth of income. For the average-income family making $15,800 a year, that debt/income ratio would mean the family owes nonmortgage debts in excess of $31,000. This example gives some idea of the extraordinary financial burdens being borne by most bankrupt debtors. We discuss the debt/income ratios at greater length in subsequent chapters.

Debt/Income Ratios for the General Population

Government statisticians who concentrate on the economic condition of American consumers have gathered statistics on the debts and incomes of Americans on a debtor-by-debtor basis to create national data on debt/income ratios.[28] Other government agencies and financial journals have also begun to use debt/income ratios to describe more accurately financial trends for the general population. These data permit us to compare again the financial circumstances of bankrupt debtors with those of the general population.

Once again we turn to the 1983 Survey data from which government statisticians computed the debt/income ratios for a cross section of Americans. As before, the government study defines debt in a way that differs somewhat from everyday usage, so we reanalyze our data accordingly.[29] The government calculation creates a ratio of installment debt to income, a measure that omits several important sources of debt, including mortgage debt, tax debt, and tort debt.[30] These ratios are not a complete statement of the financial position either of debtors in bankruptcy or of the general population, but they do give a basis for comparison of relative debt burdens among the two groups.

Table 4.5 shows the debt/income ratios among the general population. Table 4.6 presents the ratios for debtors in our bankruptcy sample. As indicated, both sets of ratios are for nonmortgage, mostly short-term debt. Once again, most of the bankrupt debtors are jammed into a bracket containing only 5% of the general population, so that we cannot make more than a gross comparison. The federal survey shows only 5% of the general population has a debt/income ratio greater than 0.2; that is, only 5% of Americans owe at least 20% of a year's income in nonmortgage debt. The greater the ratio, the greater the burden of debt compared to income, so this 5% is the most financially pressed segment of the general population. By contrast, the bankruptcy data show that over 90% of those in bankruptcy have a debt/income ratio in excess of 0.2.

Only 5% of the general population has a consumer debt burden of 20% of income or worse, but the average (mean) burden of debt for the bankrupt debtors is 145% of their incomes—more than seven times greater. To make the point concretely, a person making $15,000 a year with a consumer debt burden like that of 95% of the population would have consumer debts under $3,000. The average bankrupt debtor with that income would owe almost $22,000 in consumer nonmortgage debt, as defined by the government. This is one of the largest differences between the debtors in bankruptcy and the general population.

TABLE 4.5. Ratio of Installment Debt Payments in 1983 to Family Income[a] in 1982, by Selected Family Characteristics (percentage distribution, selected groups)

	Ratio of Installment Debt to Income[b]				
Family Income[a] (dollars)	Total	No Debt	1–9%	10–19%	20% +
Less than 5,000	100%	84%	3%	3%	10%
5,000–7,499	100	79	7	4	10
7,500–9,999	100	65	14	12	9
10,000–14,999	100	66	14	13	7
15,000–19,999	100	56	21	17	6
20,000–24,999	100	51	27	18	5
25,000–29,999	100	50	31	16	3
30,000–39,999	100	44	45	10	1
40,000–49,999	100	42	47	9	2
50,000 and up	100	53	39	8	1
All families	100	59	25	11	5

[a]Family income before taxes.

[b]Covers homeowners with regular monthly payments including farm families and owners of mobile homes.

Source: Federal Reserve Bulletin, December 1984, p. 860, Table 4.

TABLE 4.6. Ratio of Debt[a] to Family Income, by Income Levels (percentage distributions), for Bankruptcy Petitioners[b]

Family Income (dollars)	Total	No Debt	1–9%	10–19%	20% +	N
Less than 5,000	100%	8.0%	1.1%	—	90.9%	88
5,000–7,499	100	2.2	3.4	1.1%	93.3	89
7,500–9,999	100	2.0	3.6	2.7	91.0	111
10,000–14,999	100	1.4	5.3	4.6	88.6	281
15,000–19,999	100	1.6	2.0	3.6	92.8	251
20,000–24,999	100	—	4.3	8.0	87.7	162
25,000–29,999	100	1.0	1.9	2.9	94.2	103
30,000–39,999	100	1.6	1.6	9.4	87.5	64
40,000–49,999	100	—	14.3	—	85.7	7
50,000 and up	100	—	—	—	100.0	8
All families	100	1.9	3.4	4.1	90.6	1,164

[a]See text. To the extent possible, the definition is comparable to Table 4.5.

[b]Cases with extreme values on assets, total debt, or income are removed.

Source: Consumer Bankruptcy Project.

Policy Implications

At the end of each chapter reporting data, we briefly consider what the numbers might have to do with bankruptcy policy. In the final chapter, we draw together the issues raised.

For statisticians, the numbers themselves are interesting. It is satisfying to know that the Grand Canyon is exactly 5320 feet deep at the lowest point and that the mean debt listed by consumers in bankruptcy is $38,599. But the figures we have just discussed, even at this first level of analysis, tell an important story. By all economic measures, when bankrupt debtors as a group are compared to the general population, their situations are grim. The debtors in bankruptcy earn much less and owe much more than most Americans. They have staggering debts in relation to their incomes. Their net worth, on average, is many thousands of dollars below zero. With incomes one-third lower, assets two-thirds lower, and consumer debts four times higher, the debtors in bankruptcy are those at the tail end of the financial curves for all Americans. The data show a segment of America in financial collapse.

We know that for many of our readers the conclusion that debtors in bankruptcy are in serious financial trouble will rank on a par with the conclusion that short people generally have short legs. But in the context of debates about the extraordinary rise in the use of bankruptcy and whether bankruptcy laws should be "tightened" and debtor protections withdrawn to prevent debtors from seeking the shelter of bankruptcy, the findings take on practical significance.

Those who argue that the system is shot through with abuse could make a plausible case if the only data available were anecdotes and raw statistics on numbers of filings. Our data suggest that such a conclusion will have to await a considerably more detailed inquiry—and that the answer may be much more complex than a simple slogan about bankruptcy abuse. In the chapters that follow we will continue to look for—and find—the sharpies, but this chapter shows that the central tendency is a group of people who are broke. The bankruptcy laws are generally serving the people they are designed to serve: people in serious, even hopeless financial trouble, who need either a fresh-start discharge from their debts or at least some protection from their creditors and a breathing spell while they try to repay.

Notes

1. The Brookings Study was based on cases closed in 1964, which means the cases were probably filed between 1960 and 1964. D. Stanley and M. Girth, Bankruptcy: Problem, Process, and Reform (Washington: Brookings Institution, 1971), p. 7. Because the Brookings Study cases are almost 30 years old, its findings about the financial distress of the bankruptcy filers could be dismissed if one assumed that the crafty middle class is responsible for the recent dramatic rise in filings.

2. Our CDS eliminates 6 debtors with incomes above $65,000, 5 debtors with assets above $500,000, and 17 debtors with debts in excess of $500,000. When a debtor is an outlier in any category, we eliminate the debtor from consideration in all three categories. In total, we eliminate 27 debtors (one debtor was an outlier in two categories). We eliminate less than 2% of our sample by culling these debtors.

Outliers are cases with such extreme values that they affect the estimation of statistics. See generally E. J. Kane, Economics Statistics and Econometrics (New York: Harper & Row, 1968), p. 255. Techniques for identifying and eliminating outliers can be found in J. Tukey, Exploratory Data Analysis (Reading, MA: Addison-Wesley, 1977), p. 44. Outliers badly distort the statistical reports. For example, the 17 debtors eliminated as outliers because of extreme debts raised the mean debt for all 1547 debtors by $12,100 *per debtor.* By eliminating these few we are able to speak more intelligibly about the means, although the variation between means and medians shows that the debts are still distributed well beyond the mean in a long tail consisting of a few debtors with very high debts.

The U.S. Census Bureau uses an editing practice that coincidentally has the same effect as eliminating outliers. All financial data in the Current Population Survey are "top-coded," which means that no financial information higher than a predetermined maximum will be reported. In 1981, that figure was $75,000. Anyone receiving $75,000 or more in any of several possible income categories was coded in the data tapes as receiving exactly $75,000. The reason for this practice is protection of the privacy of individuals who might otherwise be distinguishable by their replies to the questionnaires. The statistical effect is to limit somewhat the range of variation in incomes. In particular, the means are not inflated by adding in the high incomes of the occasional millionaire.

3. We drop 18 cases because the files contained virtually no useful data. In these cases there is a bankruptcy filing, but the basic forms are incomplete and there is no indication of an eventual discharge. We suspect that many of these files represent cases in which the debtor saw the attorney and the attorney filed a hasty petition, intending to amend it when more information was available. The debtor may not have come back, so that some papers were filed but the whole bankruptcy was effectively dropped. There would be no move to dismiss without a debtor or creditor interested in the process, and the papers could languish in the court filing offices until a general housecleaning. Some of these fragmentary files might represent filing errors on the part of the bankruptcy clerk's office. These 18 cases do not, however, include cases where only some data were missing. When there were enough data to give a sensible picture of the debtor's circumstances, we include the data, even if some facts were missing or the case was ultimately dismissed.

4. The bankruptcy laws require that in joint petitions both husband and wife list all income from all sources. Moreover, *all* Chapter 13 petitions, including those filed singly by only a husband or a wife, must include all sources of income for both spouses. This figure should include contributions to the family by other family members as well, but it would not include income that other family members kept for their own use. Income was not always reported among the self-employed, a fact that is discussed further in Chapter Five, note 5.

5. The CPS data are used, among other things, to indicate unemployment rates and to track family composition and age composition trends for shaping government policies. For example, CPS data are a primary source for the widely discussed facts that the United States is becoming a less agricultural nation and that jobs are growing at the fastest rate in the service industries.

6. The CPS data were weighted to represent the national population before we drew a random sample of 10% of the primary families and the primary individuals aged 21 or older. The primary family refers to a family that has no unrelated subfamilies living with it. The primary individual is an individual who is a householder but living without family members. For further information, see U.S. Bureau of the Census, Current Population Reports, "Characteristics of Households and Persons Receiving Selected Noncash Benefits: 1981" (Washington: U.S. Government Printing Office, Se-

ries P-60, No. 136, 1983), pp. 102–3 (hereafter "Households in 1981"). The CPS reports incomes both for families and for households. A report of family income will usually produce a higher average and median income than a report of household income. Intuitively, household income should be larger because it includes nonfamily members, but nonfamily households are usually small and have characteristics associated with lower incomes. Persons who are not living in families are more likely to be young (e.g., college roommates) or old (e.g., pensioners), or they are living in somewhat more unstable social situations. U.S. Bureau of the Census, Current Population Reports, "Money Income of Households, Families, and Persons in the United States: 1981" (Washington: U.S. Government Printing Office, Series P-60, No. 137, 1983), p. 2 (hereafter "1981 Money Incomes").

We have four possible comparisons to our debtors: mean and median incomes estimated either for families or for household. Which is correct? Means and medians we can easily calculate, and we routinely report both. But neither the "household" nor the "family" concept in the Current Population Survey is exactly comparable to the reporting unit in bankruptcy. The great majority of American households are composed only of family members. To the extent there is some difference for reporting purposes, we work on the assumption that the bankruptcy estate is more comparable to the "family" for several reasons.

First, the incomes reported in the bankruptcy papers never include unrelated individuals. The creditors have no claim on the resources of roommates, boarders, etc., unless they are co-debtors, but the law is much more likely to give creditors claims to the resources of other family members, especially spouses. Second, in Chapter 13 the standard forms require a petitioner to present a family budget, so that the entire family and not just the petitioner is involved at least indirectly in the payback plan. These are the reports compiled in our study. Further, even in Chapter 7 petitions that are filed by one individual, we found that income of a spouse was sometimes indicated, and we included these in our reports. Finally, obligations to ex-spouses and to children living in other households are still obligations in bankruptcy, even though the households have been reformulated. These factors lead us to conclude that the family unit is the more appropriate economic unit.

We recognize that because "family" income is higher we might be "stacking the deck" in the comparisons of debtors to the population generally, making the debtors appear relatively poorer. For those interested in tracking that comparison, we note the comparable household income figures in the footnotes.

7. The actual dollar value was $22,388. *Id.* Table 14, p. 35. National median *household* income was $19,074. *Id.* Table 3, p. 7.

8. *Id.*, Table 17, p. 47. National mean household income was $22,787. *Id.*, Table 3, p. 7. If we compare household incomes, the debtors' mean incomes are still 30% below the national mean ($22,800) and their median incomes are more than 20% lower than the national median income ($19,100).

9. Those readers who took college statistics will recall that in a normal distribution, the mean and the median are identical and 68% of the cases will lie within 1 standard deviation of the mean. In Table 4.1 the standard deviation for income is $9,600. Applied to our data, this would suggest a distribution in which about 34% of the debtors earn between $15,800 and $25,400 ($15,900 + $9,600) and about 34% earn between $6,200 ($15,800 − $9,600) and $15,800. Another 16% would earn less than $6,200, and the remaining 16% would earn more than $25,400. Income distributions, however, are rarely normal because a few high incomes will skew the distribution. The

national population shows a divergence between mean and median household income of $3,700, while the bankruptcy population shows a divergence of only $800. The smaller mean–median difference indicates that bankruptcy includes fewer people with unusually high incomes than does the general population because it is a few high-income people who cause the mean to exceed the median. Bankruptcy has a tighter cluster of incomes around the $15,000–$15,800 income level than the spread in the general population.

10. It may be useful to place the 1981 CPS income data in context. Income reports represent money income received before payment of personal income taxes and payroll deductions. See U.S. Bureau of the Census, Current Population Reports, "Money Income and Poverty Status of Families and Persons in the United State: 1986" (Washington: U.S. Government Printing Office, Series P-60, No. 157, 1987), p. 2. After adjusting for a 10.4% increase in consumer prices between 1980 and 1981, median family income declined by a statistically significant 3.5% from the 1980 figure, and median household income declined by 2.4%. This decline was experienced in the North–Central, South, and West regions of the country, although buying power remained constant in the North-East. *Id.*, pp. 1–2 and Table A. For comparison, it is helpful to know that in 1986 mean family income was $34,924, while median family income was $29,458. *Id.*, Table 2, p. 11. In terms of buying power, the 1986 median income stated in 1981 dollars would be $24,435. In other words, real median family income was up only $2,035. As a rule of thumb, the reader can "translate" our 1981 figures to 1986, adjusted for inflation, by multiplying the 1981 figures by 1.21 (calculated using the Consumer Price Index). U.S. Bureau of the Census, Statistical Abstract of the United States, 1988 (108th ed., Washington: U.S. Government Printing Office, 1987), Table 738, p. 450.

11. The exact figure, separately calculated, is 24%. The poverty figure is graduated by family size and residence. The conventional benchmark is for a family of four. U.S. Bureau of the Census, Current Population Statistics, "Characteristics of the Population Below the Poverty Level: 1981" (Washington: U.S. Government Printing Office, Series P-60, No. 138, 1983), p. 1 (hereafter "Poverty in 1981"). But using this benchmark could lead to some misclassification. For example, some of our single debtors should not be classified below poverty with a $9,300 income, whereas others with somewhat higher incomes but bigger families should be.

In Chapter 13 filings, it is possible to determine the number of economic dependents per debtor. For these cases we could compare family income with the poverty level graduated for family size. (We could not use the additional gradation that corrects for age of householder. In general, the poverty level is $400–$500 lower for families with an elderly householder. *Id.*, p. 181, Table A-2.) The Chapter 13 debtors are more likely than the national sample to be in poverty at family sizes between two and five persons.

TABLE 4.7. Family Size and Proportion of Households Below Poverty Level, for Chapter 13 Debtors and U.S. Households

Family Size	Proportion of Chapter 13 Debtors Below Poverty Level	*N*	Proportion of U.S. Households Below Poverty Level	*N*
1 person	14.1%	85	21.8%	19,354
2 persons	12.1	116	10.0	26,486
3 persons	15.2	105	10.7	14,617

TABLE 4.7 (*Continued*)

Family Size	Proportion of Chapter 13 Debtors Below Poverty Level	N	Proportion of U.S. Households Below Poverty Level	N
4 persons	11.2	134	10.7	12,868
5 persons	26.7	75	15.4	6,103
6 persons	16.7	36	17.5	2,480
7 or more persons	26.1	23	30.5	1,619

Source: Consumer Bankruptcy Project; "Households in 1981," Table 1, p. 7.

12. "Poverty in 1981," Table 1, p. 7.

13. Mean household size from "Households in 1981," p. 7. Only debtors in Chapter 13 are required to list all economic dependents, so our report of family size for all ten districts studied is based on the Chapter 13 debtors. The mean was 3.4 with a standard deviation of 1.7 and a median of 3.0. In the Western District of Texas, local rules require all debtors to give family size whether they are in Chapter 7 or Chapter 13. In that district the mean family size for Chapter 7 debtors was 3.3, not significantly different from the family size for the Chapter 13 debtors. For the 73 Chapter 7 cases in the Western District of Texas, the standard deviation was 1.2 and the median was 3.0. This suggests that the computed family size for Chapter 13 debtors is not different from the family size for Chapter 7 debtors.

14. Survey of Consumer Finances, 1983: First Report, Federal Reserve Bulletin (September 1984); Second Report, Federal Reserve Bulletin (December 1984).

15. Survey, Second Report, p. 861.

16. Survey, First Report, Tables 7 and 9.

17. The Survey figures are possibly higher than they would have been in a 1981 survey, given that period's inflation, which would affect real estate in particular. On the other hand, mean and median holdings of all financial assets and of liquid assets declined in constant dollars between 1977 and 1983 (Survey, First Report, p. 685). In addition, our asset figures are overstated. Among other things, our coding categories were so defined that we could not exclude all the items excluded by the Survey, including stocks and bonds, accounts receivable, and certain consumer durables. Thus we are including some assets not counted in the Survey. These potential problems of comparability do not affect our conclusion that bankrupt debtors have fewer assets.

18. As with so many other financial measures, the mean asset values exceed the median values because a few asset-laden people pull up the average. But bankrupt debtors suffer just as much in a comparison of medians. The data show a median total asset value (based on the criteria used in the Survey) of $9,500, whereas the Survey median for the general population was $41,261. Comparing medians, the bankrupt debtors have assets less than one-quarter the size of the general population (Survey, First Report, Tables 7 and 9). At the means or the medians, the bankrupt debtors have far less valuable assets than their counterparts in the general population.

19. Either underreporting or overreporting seems likely with other financial data. For example, see our discussion of assets on page 66. In a sample as large as ours, it is likely that these errors simply cancel each other out. Underreporting of debt is different because all the likely errors point in the same direction, underestimation.

20. We derived our figures from the debtors' schedules of debts, not from the

proofs of claim filed by creditors. Using the claims alone would have produced its own understatement bias, because many creditors do not file. The ideal would have been to look at both the schedules and the proofs of claim, but they are separately filed at many courthouses and both cost and the risk of inconsistency counseled consistent use of the debtors' schedules.

21. Survey, Second Report, Table T3, p. 859.

22. *Id.*, p. 861.

23. The Survey calculation also omits the cash value of life insurance, equity in small businesses and farms, and the present value of expected future benefits from pensions or social security (Survey, Second Report, 1983, p. 861). These omissions are not very important for us, because very few debtors reported assets of this sort. As to income, the Survey calculation compared the current year's assets with the previous year's income, which we replicated in the case of Chapter 7 debtors. For Chapter 13 debtors, we compared current income with current assets.

24. Because we overstate assets, we also overstate net worth in comparison with the Survey statistics. See note 17.

25. As we explained in Chapter Two, the differences among the three states are dramatic. The Texas debtors could keep an unlimited amount in a homestead and, if they were part of a family, they could keep up to $30,000 in personal goods. In Illinois, a debtor could keep only $10,000 in equity in a homestead and $3,000 in personal goods. In Pennsylvania, a debtor could keep even less at state law: $300 in personal goods, clothes, a Bible, a sewing machine, and possibly an interest in a home if only one spouse owed the outstanding debts. But Pennsylvania permitted debtors to take federal exemptions, which gave a married couple $15,800 to use on a home or personal goods, all their clothes, $2,400 on a car, and a few other items.

26.

TABLE 4.8. Distribution of Assets and Net Worth by State: Eligible Petitioners in Chapter 7[a,b]

Distribution	Texas	Illinois	Pennsylvania
Assets			
Mean	$28,050	$16,486	$17,855
s.d.	35,286	25,806	24,383
25th percentile	3,891	600	1,603
Median	13,450	2,368	7,283
75th percentile	44,895	21,075	26,707
N	333	294	256
Missing	0	0	3
Statistical tests			
F ratio: 17.77**			
Significant differences in state means:[c]	Texas > Illinois and Pennsylvania		
Net Worth			
Mean	$ – 26,693	$ – 20,743	$ – 17,579
s.d.	54,449	37,120	35,749
25th percentile	– 24,217	– 18,494	– 16,387
Median	– 13,101	– 9,330	– 9,738
75th percentile	– 6,417	– 5,273	– 5,248
N	332	294	256
Missing	1	0	3

TABLE 4.8 (*Continued*)

Distribution	Texas	Illinois	Pennsylvania
Statistical tests			
F ratio: 3.28*			
Significant differences in state means:[c]		Pennsylvania > Texas	

[a]Cases with extreme values on assets, total debt, or income are removed.

[b]Petitioners whose claim of home ownership could not be verified were removed for this analysis.

[c]Scheffe range test used for multiple comparison of means.

*$p \leq 0.05$

**$p \leq 0.01$

Source: Consumer Bankruptcy Project.

27. For members of families, income is added for the whole family, based on the information reported in the bankruptcy files. Debt is also compiled by family, so that the debt/income ratio describes the economic position of a whole family whenever that information is available.

28. Survey, First Report, pp. 27–35.

29. The survey calculations were based on monthly obligations and monthly income. Bankruptcy data are not reported by monthly figures, which forces us to use total debt and yearly income for each debtor. From the short-term nature of most of the obligations listed in both the federal data and the bankruptcy files, however, we believe the debt/income ratios are comparable. Nonetheless, insofar as some of these obligations are payable over more than one year, our figures will overstate the debtors' debt burdens compared to the government figures.

30. Government statisticians calculate a mortgage debt/income ratio, but their data are based on reports of monthly house payments, whereas our data are reported only on the basis of the total outstanding mortgage. Bankrupt debtors are not required in all cases to report monthly house payments or to indicate interest rates and taxes and insurance paid on a monthly basis, so there is no reliable way to compute the survey-defined monthly mortgage payment for the homeowning debtors in bankruptcy. The variables, including the presence or absence of tax and insurance escrows and varying interest rates and lengths of mortgages, prevent us from comparing the two mortgage ratios.

5

Debtors at Work: Occupations and Industries

Occupational health and safety laws protect working people. Securities laws protect investors. Lemon laws protect new car buyers. In each case, legislation is premised upon some notion of who makes up the target group, and that notion fundamentally affects the shape of the ensuing laws. Beyond the simple proposition that the bankruptcy laws protect people in economic trouble, there has been little information about the social class or classes served by these laws. In this chapter we develop a social profile of people who use the bankruptcy laws, informed by reports in their bankruptcy files.

As anyone who has ever tried to make small talk at a cocktail party knows, few facts communicate more about someone in an initial encounter than learning what kind of job the person holds. Emerson made the point: "Do your work and I shall know you."[1] Sociologists, after creating typologies of occupations and measuring occupational prestige, have found that occupation correlates with education, income, lifestyle, and social status.[2]

This chapter is devoted to understanding where the debtors fit into the workplace, the industries in which they work, and the jobs they do. This picture of the debtors at work is by no means a complete portrait of their lives. It does not reveal, for example, their ages, ethnic backgrounds, or family histories—data not available in the bankruptcy files. It does not directly include education or social status. Nonetheless, we believe that knowing about their jobs will reveal a great deal about where the bankruptcy petitioners stand in the social pecking order and better complete the picture of the people who use bankruptcy.

Discussions of bankruptcy often hint at various subgroups of typical bankruptcy filers, including the most repeated assertion that bankrupt debtors are largely blue-collar workers, often in declining industries.[3] What we found is that in the work they do, bankrupt debtors look surprisingly similar to the rest of us. Neither all, nor most, are unskilled laborers or clerical workers.

They are not concentrated in declining industries. They do not work at jobs with low prestige. They are pretty close to a cross section of America at work. There are some differences, mostly in the direction of somewhat lower paid and lower prestige jobs, but the striking point is that the differences are not very great.

In this chapter we must try to square the debtors' low earnings with the fact that they work in the same occupations and industries as most Americans. We find that many debtors in bankruptcy have recently encountered unemployment, layoffs, and other income interruptions that have changed their financial circumstances.

The Main Findings: What Bankrupt Debtors Do for a Living

The bankruptcy laws require debtors to give information about their occupations and current employers. We coded this information using standard government classifications. Among 1502 debtors, we have sufficiently detailed information to determine occupations for 1258 and industries for 1137.[4] The debtors lost to our analysis because of incomplete information are generally debtors with lower average incomes.[5]

Most of the discussion in this chapter covers all the debtors, wage earners and self-employed. The wage earners comprise the largest group in bankruptcy; about 90% of the debtors currently work for someone else. The currently self-employed—craftworkers, retailers, professionals, and other entrepreneurs—make up the remaining 10% of the sample. In the general population, the division between wage earners and self-employed is somewhat different, with 92% of the total population working for someone else while 7.3% are self-employed. Another 10% of our sample were once self-employed, although they are not now self-employed. In Chapter Six we focus specifically on the self-employed and the formerly self-employed.

The Unemployed

We start by analyzing the debtors who at the time they filed for bankruptcy did not practice any occupation in any industry: the unemployed. In analyzing unemployment, we considered only the "primary" debtor. In a single-debtor case, the primary debtor is simply the petitioner. In a joint husband-and-wife filing, we take the primary debtor to be the first-listed debtor. Based on our extensive reviews of the files, it seems nearly always true that the debtor who is listed first in a joint case is the historical primary wage earner for that family even if that person is currently unemployed.

Our figures for unemployment of the primary debtor on the date of bankruptcy are based for the most part on an explicit statement that the first-listed debtor is "unemployed." Of 1349 reporting cases, 111, just over 7%, explicitly report this.[6] It is likely that more unemployed debtors could be found among the 138 debtors who did not respond or responded ambiguously to the question asking for occupation. If all of them were in fact unemployed, the total unemployed proportion would be about 17% (249 of 1502 cases).[7]

We cannot be certain that all these debtors would meet the government's definition of unemployed, which is limited to people who are actively seeking employment.[8] Nonetheless, it is interesting to compare the 7% figure with unemployment rates generally in 1981. During 1981 the national unemployment rate was 7.6%. The annual unemployment rates in our sample states were 5.3% for Texas, 8.5% for Illinois, and 8.4% for Pennsylvania.[9] Our debtors' unemployment also varied by state. Debtors without work were 2.5% of the bankruptcy sample in Texas, 10.1% in Illinois, and 11.8% in Pennsylvania. The difference between the lower rate of nonworking debtors among Texans and the higher rates in Illinois and Pennsylvania was statistically significant ($p = 0.000$[10]).

If there is considerable unemployment among bankrupt debtors, the fact remains that most of them are employed at the time they file for bankruptcy. Between 83% and 93% of our debtors were employed at the time they filed for bankruptcy. Because the chronically unemployed find it very difficult to get credit, it is not at all surprising that these debtors mostly have jobs. These data show that bankruptcy, like credit itself, is used by working people.

Industries and Occupations

People's work can be analyzed along two dimensions: their industries and their occupations. Industry refers to the goods or services a firm produces. If you ask someone "What do you do?," that question frequently yields a response by industry: "I work for a law firm" or "I work for a chemical company" or "I work for the government." But equally often the answer is occupational instead: "I'm a lawyer" or "I'm in sales" or "I'm a secretary." Knowing both things about a person, occupation and industry, tells more than knowing either one alone. So we looked at our debtors by occupation and by industry and then we looked at both simultaneously, using classifications developed by the U.S. Census Bureau.[11] Our findings are set forth in the CDS columns of Table 5.1.

The debtors in our sample reflect the enormous diversity of the American workplace. We have no household maids, but two dentists. We have no doctors and no university professors, but no fewer than eight accountants. Of the employed and self-employed debtors, 11% are professional or technical workers, 9% are nonfarm laborers, 12% are "operatives" (semiskilled workers who, for example, run a machine in a factory), and another 12% are managers or administrators. The biggest occupational group is craftworkers (18%), although most are not at the highest skill levels.

By industry, the biggest group of bankrupt debtors work in the durable goods industries, 15%, but workers in retail stores are close behind at 14%. Those who render business services made up 9% of our sample, while about

Table 5.1. Industry and Occupation Distributions, Consumer Bankruptcy Sample (CDS) and National Sample (CPS)

Characteristic	CDS[a]		CPS[b]	
	N	%	*N*	%
Industry				
Agriculture	15	1.3%	181,684	3.2%
Mining	34	3.0	73,497	1.3
Construction	73	6.4	572,366	10.1
Durable manufacturing	169	14.9	989,172	17.5
Nondurable manufacturing	96	8.5	493,944	8.7
Transportation	124	10.9	431,324	7.6
Wholesale	30	2.6	288,576	5.1
Retail	158	13.9	617,315	10.9
Finance	48	4.2	304,379	5.4
Business services	98	8.6	235,874	4.2
Personal services	30	2.6	112,272	2.0
Entertainment	9	0.8	53,186	0.9
Professional services	122	10.7	843,803	14.9
Public administration	91	8.0	370,626	6.6
Military	39	3.4	81,087	1.4
Total	1,136	100.0	5,649,106	100.0
Index of dissimilarity = 17.0				
Occupation				
Professional-technical	138	11.1%	1,008,508	18.1%
Manager-administrator	149	12.0	957,065	17.2
Sales	90	7.3	351,126	6.3
Clerical	120	9.7	449,870	8.1
Crafts	222	17.9	1,113,412	20.0
Operatives except transport	151	12.2	589,543	10.6
Transport operatives	110	8.9	285,920	5.1
Nonfarm labor	109	8.8	218,446	3.9
Farmers/farm managers	6	0.5	102,884	1.8
Farm labor	5	0.4	45,819	0.8
Service workers	138	11.1	432,360	7.8
Private household	0	0.0	15,236	0.2
Total	1,238	100.0	5,570,188	100.0
Index of dissimilarity = 16.2				

[a]Cases with extreme values on assets, total debt, or income are removed. Percentages may not total 100% because of rounding errors.

[b]For details, see text and notes.

Source: Consumer Bankruptcy Project; March 1981 Current Population Survey.

8% work for federal, state, or local government. Our sample had tiny proportions from mining and entertainment and very few farm workers.

The Debtors Compared with the Rest of Us

These numbers impart the flavor of diversity, but they do not mean much without comparison with the general population. For that purpose, we turn again to the March 1981 Current Population Survey (CPS), from which we can develop an industrial profile of American workers. Table 5.1 presents the industrial profiles for both our sample of debtors and the entire labor force. The industrial groups in which the largest proportions of the general population are employed are durable goods manufacturing, professional services, and retail trade; the fewest Americans are employed in entertainment, mining, and the military.

The distribution of bankrupt debtors parallels the national distribution. Although the proportions and ordering vary, the most frequently listed industries—professional services, durable manufacturing, and retail trade—stay near the top, and the least frequently listed—entertainment, mining, and the military—stay near the bottom. The proportion of debtors in many of the largest industrial groups is very close to that of the entire population. The debtors in bankruptcy are underrepresented in professional services by an amount roughly balanced by their overrepresentation in transportation, business services, and government service. Nonetheless, professional services was the fourth highest industrial classification for the debtors, with about 11% being employed in this generally well-compensated industry. Thus, overall, the striking fact is that the differences in industrial classification are relatively small. Of course, we recognize that a "small" difference is partly a product of expectations: we expected the sample to look much more different from the general population.

We can do more than merely "eyeball" these similarities and differences. An index of dissimilarity can be used to summarize the distributional similarities for two groups. The index has a theoretical range from 0 (no difference at all) to 100 (no similarity at all). The score can be interpreted as the proportion of people in one group who would have to change characteristics—here, industries—to make the two groups look exactly alike.

The index of dissimilarity between the CPS sample and the bankrupt debtors shows that the bulk of the debtors work in pretty much the same industries as the rest of us. The index score is 17. This score indicates that only 17 of every 100 workers in the bankruptcy sample would have to change industries in order to mirror perfectly the distribution of the national population. The remaining 83 bankrupt debtors are distributed like the general population.[12]

In addition to examining the industries in which people are employed, the CPS also records the particular occupation each worker holds. By combining respondents within occupational groups, the CPS data give a profile of occupations of American workers. In this analysis, workers are separated into professional, clerical, laborer, service, and the other categories listed in Table 5.1, regardless of the industry in which they work. Thus the janitors who clean up office buildings are lumped with the janitors who clean up factory washrooms; the secretary in a textile plant is in the same category as the secretary in a law office. We used the same occupational codes to categorize the bankrupt debtors.

The occupations of most of the debtors in bankruptcy are similar to those of the general population. The greatest number of debtors are craftspeople, operatives, and managers, which are among the largest groups in the general population. Professional jobs account for about 18% of the general population and about 11% of the bankruptcy sample.

The index of dissimilarity confirms that the bankruptcy sample is not very different from the general population. The index score is 16. Bankrupt debtors include teachers and truck drivers, secretaries and nurses, barbers and clerks, just as the remainder of the population does. Bankrupt debtors have occupations somewhat lower in skill and average compensation levels, but once again the differences are not as great as we had expected. At this level of analysis, the data are inconsistent with the idea that the bankrupt debtors are drawn primarily from one occupational level or a few occupational groups.

Occupational Prestige

The Census Bureau classifies 12 major occupational groups from over 400 occupational specialties. These are the groups we use to classify our sample and the CPS sample. To describe the complexity of work in only 12 categories requires that each group cover a mix of jobs. Brain surgeons and dance instructors are both included among "professional, technical, and kindred" workers, and "managers and administrators" includes everyone from the chief executive officer of a multinational corporation to the manager of an apartment complex. We can provide a more finely tuned comparison of occupations by using occupational prestige scores.

Prestige scores have been developed from national surveys that ask the public to rate various occupations for prestige or social standing. The resulting scores have a theoretical range from 0 to 100 and a practical range from about 11 (street sweepers) to 84 (Supreme Court justices). Instead of using merely 12 broad categories, we are able to use dozens of rank scores. The prestige scores distinguish between brain surgeons and dance instructors and between CEOs and apartment managers.[13] This approach not only permits a more detailed comparison, but it also makes use of the fact that the social standing conferred by an occupation is highly correlated with its education and skill requirements.

When we compare the occupational prestige scores of the national sample with the bankruptcy sample, we find that the bankrupt debtors have lower prestige scores. As Table 5.2 indicates, the mean score for the bankrupt debtors is 37.7, compared with a mean of 41.6 for the CPS sample. The difference is

TABLE 5.2. Prestige by Industry, Consumer Bankruptcy Sample (CDS), and National Sample (CPS)

	Prestige Scores						
	CDS[a]			CPS[b]			
Industry	Mean	s.d.	*N*	Mean	s.d.	*N*	*t*-Value
Agriculture	33.7	11.5	13	34.9	10.5	181,684	0.36
Mining	35.6	11.7	33	37.1	12.0	73,497	0.73
Construction	36.7	11.4	68	38.6	10.6	572,084	1.36
Durable manufacturing	35.8	11.4	161	40.1	12.2	989,172	4.77**
Nondurable manufacturing	34.0	11.6	94	37.9	12.4	493,944	3.24**
Transportation	35.4	10.4	113	38.7	11.6	431,323	3.36**
Wholesale	37.5	10.1	27	40.0	10.8	288,576	1.26
Retail	36.2	10.5	146	36.7	12.0	617,315	0.69
Finance	45.6	12.1	46	48.4	12.5	304,378	1.55
Business services	39.0	10.9	90	38.0	11.7	235,874	−0.87
Personal services	31.3	11.4	30	32.2	13.2	112,271	0.43
Entertainment	38.8	12.4	8	40.2	12.2	53,185	0.30
Professional services	44.4	13.8	119	52.9	18.4	843,802	6.69**
Public administration	40.8	11.5	86	45.6	13.1	370,626	3.93**
Total	37.7	12.5	1034	41.6	14.3	5,567,737	10.03**

[a]Cases with extreme values on assets, total debt, or income are removed.

[b]For details, see text and notes.

$^{**}p \leq 0.01$

Source: Consumer Bankruptcy Project; March 1981 Current Population Survey.

statistically significant, so we could expect a difference about this large to be present in similar samples. Whether it is substantively significant is a question of judgment.

To give some idea of what these numbers mean, 42 is the prestige score for typists and stenographers, while 36 is the ranking of a metal rolling mill operator. Plumbers are at 34 and telephone installers and repairers receive a 35. Bookkeepers and cashiers rate a 41 and typesetters a 42. Ranked at 39, just between the general population and our bankrupt debtors, are cabinetmakers and telephone linemen and splicers. The bankrupt debtors averaged a little lower than this, while the remainder of the population averaged a little higher in occupational prestige.

Table 5.2 also permits a more refined comparison of the debtors and the general population. In Table 5.1 we compare the proportion of debtors with the proportion of the general population in each industry category. By using occupational prestige scores, we can examine the distribution of occupations within each industry. For example, we can distinguish within the education industry between a sample composed of higher prestige teachers and principals and a sample composed of lower prestige teachers' aides and maintenance workers.

Of the 14 industry groups, there are statistically significant differences in only five: durable goods manufacturing, nondurable manufacturing, transportation, public administration, and professional services. In nine industries, the occupational prestige rankings among the bankrupt debtors and the general population are indistinguishable.

The data on occupational prestige show the bankrupt debtors have lower average prestige, but the differences are relatively small. From the perspective of the workplace, the bulk of the debtors come right out of Middle America.

Jobs and Income

The findings in this chapter combine with those in the last to create a profound dissonance: The debtors in bankruptcy work alongside other Americans, in roughly the same industries and jobs, and with nearly the same general occupational prestige, yet they make a third less income. These findings are puzzling, because occupation and industry are normally highly correlated with income. There are exceptions, of course; clergymen are highly educated and are well respected, but except for a few televangelists, they receive relatively low incomes. Nonetheless, the rule for a cross section of Americans like our sample is that occupation and industry should closely match with income. In Table 5.3 we classify debtors by industry and income and again by occupation and income.

To take a specific example, Table 5.1 shows that the debtor sample and the CPS sample contain a similar proportion of retail store workers, about 14%. Table 5.2 shows that the debtors who are working at retail jobs have the same prestige as retail workers generally, about 36. Yet Table 5.3 shows that the retail workers in bankruptcy are making about 25% less per year year than their fellow retail workers in the general population.

These data show that the debtors in bankruptcy earn less than their counterparts in each industry and occupation. One explanation for these data is that bankrupt debtors are spread among the occupations and industries like other Americans, but within each subset they occupy the lowest paying jobs. The similarity of occupational prestige among the whole sample of bankrupt debtors and the general population tends to rebut that hypothesis. The indistinguishable occupational prestige in nine industries and the small differences in the remaining five makes the hypothesis of concentration in lowest paying jobs even harder to maintain. But we can also test it directly.

To determine whether debtors who deviate from the occupational and industrial mix of the general population are concentrated in the lowest paying jobs, we construct a statistical hypothetical, a process called "standardizing" the data. We can hypothetically take those 17 of 100 debtors reflected in the dissimilarity index and transfer them to other industries, as if our sample worked in the same mix of industries as the rest of the population. Then we can recompute the incomes of those 17 people, giving them a hypothetical income equal to the average *in our sample* for people in their "new" industries.

TABLE 5.3. Comparison of Mean Family Income Within Industry and Occupation, Consumer Bankruptcy Sample (CDS) and National Sample (CPS)

	CDS[a]			CPS[b]			
Characteristic	Mean	s.d.	*N*	Mean	s.d.	*N*	*t*-Value
Industry							
Agriculture	$12,260	8,959	9	$15,567	12,079	181,684	1.04
Mining	18,745	7,838	32	24,514	10,269	73,497	4.10**
Construction	16,801	8,124	54	24,150	14,568	572,366	6.58**
Durable manufacturing	17,894	9,330	153	25,778	13,379	989,172	10.42**
Nondurable manufacturing	16,788	9,000	83	25,704	14,313	493,944	8.97**
Transportation	20,515	10,299	114	25,796	13,002	431,323	5.45**
Wholesale	19,157	8,782	23	29,897	15,510	288,576	5.74**
Retail	15,144	9,460	126	20,324	13,695	617,315	6.12**
Finance	18,359	10,488	43	30,098	27,121	304,378	7.25**
Business services	15,793	9,328	86	23,216	14,880	235,874	7.33**
Personal services	13,075	1,617	20	19,399	16,530	112,271	2.37*
Entertainment	14,031	6,458	7	20,829	15,116	53,185	2.58*
Professional services	15,227	8,684	115	26,183	16,683	843,802	13.47**
Public administration	18,645	9,353	86	28,406	25,391	370,626	9.61**
Military	13,390	6,080	35	19,427	9,923	81,087	5.79**
Total	17,005	9,411	986	24,972	16,575	5,649,100	26.56**

Occupation							
Professional-technical	19,066	10,244	130	29,578	16,041	1,008,508	7.66**
Manager-administrator	18,962	10,551	114	32,821	24,819	957,065	13.96**
Sales	18,054	10,879	78	29,086	16,256	351,126	8.90**
Clerical	13,902	8,635	114	19,627	10,526	449,869	7.05**
Crafts	17,527	8,808	190	24,391	12,871	1,113,411	10.71**
Operatives except transport	15,890	7,750	135	20,707	11,148	589,542	6.45**
Transport operatives	19,669	10,969	101	20,976	9,893	285,920	1.19
Nonfarm labor	15,654	7,752	98	17,431	9,264	218,446	2.26*
Farming	9,413	11,203	4	16,726	13,725	102,883	1.13
Farm labor	9,931	11,154	4	12,057	7,411	45,818	0.33
Service labor	12,431	7,794	121	17,924	11,223	432,360	7.72**
Private household	[c]	[c]	0	4,988	2,133	15,235	
Total	16,694	9,505	1,089	25,054	16,638	5,570,183	29.00**

[a]Cases with extreme values on assets, total debt, or income are removed.

[b]For details, see text.

[c]Not applicable.

*$p \leq 0.05$

**$p \leq 0.01$

Source: Consumer Bankruptcy Project; March 1981 Current Population Survey.

Concretely, it is as if we took two people from say, retail sales and "moved" them to professional services and gave them the average salary of our debtors who really are in professional services. In that way, we can see what overall average income we would have if our debtors were in exactly the same industries as the national population.

When we directly standardize the data in this way, we find virtually no change in the debtors' mean income. (It actually decreases by $43.) In other words, the debtors in bankruptcy differ slightly in the industries in which they work, but changing industries alone would not raise their incomes. If they had had the same industrial distribution as the rest of us but were paid at the same rate as the other bankrupt debtors in each industry, their incomes would still have been much lower than ours.

We can also standardize the data on the other side of the comparison, for the general population. For example, we can take the CPS sample of the general population and hypothetically change enough of the people surveyed from one industry to another so that the CPS sample has the same mix of industries as the debtor sample. We give each person whom we "move" to a new industry the same average incomes as the other people in that industry in the general population. We get the same basic result. Changing the mix of the general population by industry to look like the bankruptcy sample leaves the general population with virtually the same income. (Actually, it goes down by about $170.)

Standardization can be done every which way. These first two results "move" debtors and members of the general population within their own groups. We can also take a debtor and "give" that debtor the same average income that the general population gets in the industry where the debtor works. When we do that with all the debtors, we find that they would have been making 99% of the salaries of workers in the general population, instead of one-third less.[14] Thus the data are conclusive: The debtors' lower incomes are not explained by the industries in which they work.

Beyond income, there is also a difference between the bankrupt debtors and the general population by occupations. The debtors could have the lowest paying occupations within each industry. Thus it seems sensible for us to run the same standardization tests to see if the occupational differences would explain the debtors' far lower incomes. We use the same approach as with industries. As we discussed earlier, debtors in bankruptcy had an occupational index of dissimilarity of about 16 compared with the general population. Once again, we hypothetically move enough bankrupt debtors (16 out of 100) to different occupational categories to make our sample look just like the CPS general population. Again we give these "moved" debtors the same average incomes as the other bankruptcy debtors in that occupation. We find that if debtors in bankruptcy had held the same occupations as the remainder of the population, they would have, on average, earned about $355 more, or about 2%. In other words, the differences between the bankrupt debtors' mix of occupations and that of the general population account for only $355 of their lower annual earnings. We can repeat for occupations all the standardizations just discussed for industries. Without belaboring the details, they also reveal that the debtors' occupations have little to do with their lower earnings.

Our final comparison of bankrupt debtors with the general population is a three-component decomposition of the difference in their earnings.[15] This technique assigns the dollar differences to three explanatory categories: differences in distribution among occupations and industries, differences in earnings for people with the same occupation and industry, and an interaction effect. This single test permits us to evaluate the relative effect of industrial and occupational composition differences and earnings differences within each industrial and occupational group. The interaction effect between occupation–industry and earnings is important to detect whether occupational–industrial differences might be canceling out part of the earnings differences or vice versa. Conversely, the two factors might be reinforcing each other.

This test confirms that occupational and industrial differences explain very little of the difference in earnings. Most of the income difference is unexplained by occupation and industry, and what is explained is largely canceled out by the interactions between occupation and industry.[16]

These tests leave only one conclusion: The jobs and workplaces in which our debtors work do not explain their lower incomes. The bankrupt debtors are working at much the same jobs, but they are making less than their co-workers in similar jobs in similar industries.

An Alternative Hypothesis: Income Interruption

As we explored the data on jobs and income, we developed an alternative hypothesis to explain the apparent anomaly of similar work at lower incomes. Although most of the debtors were employed at the time they filed for bankruptcy, we wondered if the explanation—or one important explanation—might be that they had suffered layoffs or had been shifted to lower paying jobs during the period of growing financial instability preceding bankruptcy. Perhaps the bankrupt debtors were being paid at similar, or only somewhat lower rates than their co-workers but had suffered an interruption in income during the two years before bankruptcy. This hypothesis had the advantage that it could plausibly explain the large gap we had found in two otherwise similar workforces. If a plumber makes $20,000 a year, a plumber laid off for four months would make only $14,300 (two-thirds of the yearly salary of a plumber), producing the one-third difference in income that the data showed between our debtors and the general population.

The possibility that debtors have experienced significant shifts in income is particularly important in a study of financial crisis. Debtors incur debt—and creditors extend credit—in light of a particular income level. The debt that would sink a clerk earning $11,500 a year might be moderate and responsible for an engineer making $30,000. The consequence is that everyone's financial position is very sensitive to a sharp change in income. Moreover, the debtor who has experienced an income interruption may have used credit during the no-income period to meet immediate needs, and a debt buildup during that time may cripple the debtor financially when work is again available.

Our hypothesis was that many debtors in our sample suffered income interruption before bankruptcy, and these interruptions explain a large part of the gap between their prebankruptcy incomes and those of the population generally. We tested this hypothesis in three ways. One was direct: We determined how many debtors were unemployed, and therefore without work-related income, at the time of bankruptcy. The other two were indirect: Job tenure would tell us how long a debtor has been employed at his or her present job, and income volatility, unusual swings in income, would suggest layoffs or job changes before bankruptcy. Because Chapter 7 debtors are required to report more income information, including annual income over the two years before bankruptcy, we limited our examination to them for all three tests, to keep the figures comparable.[17]

We explained earlier how we calculate the number of unemployed debtors. For this analysis, we include debtors who were probably unemployed, as well as those who explicitly reported themselves as unemployed. This gives us 112 unemployed primary debtors, about 14% of 829 Chapter 7 wage-earner cases.[18] At the start, then, we have a substantial group of Chapter 7 debtors who have suffered income interruption by virtue of unemployment.[19] For these 14% of the debtors, lower annual income and income interruption are undoubtedly connected and both are no doubt linked to their financial collapse.

Job Tenure

A second way to look for unstable work histories is in the debtors' reports of the length of time they have held their current jobs. Our discussion of tenure is qualified, because many debtors did not respond to this question.[20] As with unemployment, we look at primary debtors only.

It is very telling that the debtors in Chapter 7 bankruptcy were with their current employers for very short periods of time. The modal tenure—that is, the length of time on the job reported most frequently—was less than one year. The median job tenure was only one and a half years, which means that half of the sample had been on the job 18 months or less. By contrast, in January 1981, the median job tenure for all workers aged 16 or more was 3.2 years.[21] Thus the median for our sample was only half as many years as for the national labor force.

Not surprisingly, in the bankruptcy sample higher work-related incomes are positively associated with longer time on the job. Job tenure is significantly correlated with work-related income ($r = 0.178$, $p = 0.00$). As debtors stay on the job longer, their incomes rise. The relationship intensifies slightly when the correlation is controlled for industry ($r = 0.18$, $p = 0.00$) and the occupation of the debtors ($r = 0.19$, $p = 0.00$). These figures indicate that earnings rise the longer the debtor has been on the job regardless of the industry or the debtor's occupation.[22]

We also calculated a multiple regression equation combining industry, occupational prestige, and tenure to predict earnings in the year before bankruptcy, 1980.[23] This permits us to determine the extent to which tenure matters by examining the partial regression coefficient for tenure. This result is shown in Table 5.4, and the industry contrasts are drawn relative to the manufacture of durable goods.

These data confirm that tenure has a significant positive effect on earnings.

TABLE 5.4. Regression of Income Last Year on Job Variables[a,b]

	Regression Coefficients	
Characteristic	b[c]	B[d]
Job Variable		
Tenure	285	.207***
Prestige	143	.197***
Industry[e]		
Military	−1,291	−.025***
Agriculture	1,916	.015
Entertainment	502	.004
Personal services	−1,818	−.024**
Wholesale	4,109	.065
Mining	6,250	.112**
Finance	2,302	.047
Construction	5,295	.116**
Business services	2,092	.055*
Public administration	3,122	.090*
Nondurable manufacturing	4,087	.120**
Transportation	6,489	.203***
Retail	3,386	.110**
Professional services	702	.023
Constant	4,839	

Adjusted R^2: 0.11
F: 7.35***
N: 719

[a]Cases with extreme values on assets, total debt, or income are removed. Pairwise deletion of cases with missing variables.

[b]Current wage earners only.

[c]Unstandardized regression coefficients.

[d]Standardized regression coefficients.

[e]Reference category is durable manufacturing.

*$p \leq 0.05$

**$p \leq 0.01$

***$p \leq 0.001$

Source: Consumer Bankruptcy Project.

When we control for occupation and industry, each year of tenure would add $285 to a worker's wages. By comparison, one higher prestige point (which we use here as a proxy for occupation) is worth $143. This result indicates statistically that the low job tenure of debtors in bankruptcy is operating independently to reduce earnings.

Despite the very low time on the job of our debtors, it is possible that the tenure figures at least partly reflected higher pay for seniority or longevity, rather than the effects of layoffs and other job changes. To test this possibility, we recomputed the correlations, limiting the sample to those with at least one year of tenure. We then calculated again for people with at least two years on the current job, eliminating those who had suffered a layoff or termination in the two years before bankruptcy. The correlations dropped sharply when we removed those who suffered termination or interruption of employment in the two years before bankruptcy.[24] These results support the idea that income interruption is more important than seniority wage differentials in explaining the much lower incomes in our sample.

Income Volatility

These data suggest that more than half of the bankrupt debtors may have suffered unemployment during the two years before they filed for bankruptcy. Of course, some may have simply moved from one job to another, with no period of unemployment, but the combination of short job tenure and financial disaster strongly suggests that many of them suffered unemployment. Even among those who moved directly from one job to another, it seems likely that many may have moved to lower paying jobs to keep groceries on the table.

To explore the possibility that debtors may have suffered income interruption or sharp earning declines, we turn to the variations in their incomes during the two years before bankruptcy. As a gross indicator of income fluctuation, we compare the incomes of debtors in bankruptcy two years before filing with the incomes reported one year before filing. Of the 829 Chapter 7 wage earners, 650 had reported specified incomes for themselves or their spouses for both 1979 and 1980, the two calendar years preceding their bankruptcies. The figures that follow are based on these 650 cases. Because jobs were the principal means of support for these wage earners, we look only at work-related income, ignoring possible extra income such as rent from a boarder and safety net income such as disability or unemployment benefits.

Between 1979 and 1980, almost 80% of the debtors had experienced a change in income. Nearly 62% of the debtors had a change in income, up or down, of more than 10% from 1979 to 1980. Even for turbulent times, these figures portray highly volatile income streams, making a mismatch between debts and income likely.

As we had expected, a good number of people were "trapdoor" debtors, those who had suffered sudden and sharp losses in income. About 8% of the

Chapter 7 wage earners had their incomes cut in half between 1979 and 1980. About 14% had suffered an income collapse of at least one-third. Overall, almost a quarter of the debtors had lost 10% or more of their income from work during the two years before they filed. And debtors fell a long way if they fell at all: the mean decline in income was 37.2%. The average dollar decline was more than $5,000, against a median reported income of only $13,100 in the second year. These data expose a substantial subset of the bankruptcy debtors who had significant drops in income immediately preceding their bankruptcy filings.

To find that many bankrupt debtors suffered a big decline in income during the year before bankruptcy is hardly surprising, but the reader may be taken aback by what we found on the other side of the coin: the debtors who had gained in income between 1979 and 1980. There were more debtors whose income had risen than those who had lost ground, and the gains were even bigger than the losses. This was an utterly counterintuitive finding. When we first encountered this fact we kicked the computer three times, but it kept coming back with the same figures. Yet after we had looked at the rest of our data, including the unemployment and tenure numbers, we began to see the income-gainers as part of the larger picture of income volatility.

Just over half the Chapter 7 debtors had gained income from 1979 to 1980. The income rise was more than 10% for more than one-third of the debtors. Not only did a majority of our debtors have earnings increases in the year before filing bankruptcy, but the proportionate increases were substantial. The average debtor with increased income earned almost 70% more in 1980 than in 1979. These increases translated into an average absolute dollar increase of $3,500. Even the median increase was over $2,000.

What makes these facts intelligible is the average income for these "gainers" in 1979. The median gainer earned only $11,000 in 1979. This amount is well below the median for all Chapter 7 debtors, far below the national median, and only $1,700 above the 1981 poverty threshold. Their 1980 "gains" merely got them back to a median wage of $14,800, still well below that of the general population. These debtors had not achieved affluence; at best they had climbed back to the lower edge of the middle class.

These data are consistent with the hypothesis of income interruption due to unemployment or layoff. Income interruption is self-evident for the losers, especially the trapdoor losers. Some of the losers may have simply moved to lower paying jobs, but those who lost a third or more in earnings very likely suffered a period of no work at all. Very much the same probably is true of most of the gainers. The size of the increases, an average of almost 70% in one year, could rarely be attributable to a better paying job, even if one ignores the fact that these people are generally in terrible financial shape. Thus it seems probable that many gainers were in fact people who suffered unemployment or layoff during 1979, no doubt running up substantial bills in the process, and then returned to something closer to normal employment and earnings in 1980.

The tenure figures for gainers and losers are also consistent with these conclusions. The losers had far lower average tenure, which is consistent with the idea of recent unemployment. If we limit the calculations to those who gained or lost more than 10%, the losers had a median tenure of less than a year, while the gainers' median tenure was one year. These differences are consistent with a picture of losers who had suffered unemployment in 1980, versus gainers who were laid off or unemployed for all or part of 1979 but called back or reemployed by 1980.[25]

Even among the gainers who had as much as eight years of tenure, it is difficult to imagine that many of them got huge wage increases in a single year, especially when they filed for bankruptcy the next year. It is quite plausible, on the other hand, to imagine that their 1979 incomes were much lower than usual because of layoffs and work reductions and that their gains in 1980 were simply a return to their previous jobs and to something approaching their normal earnings.[26] The financial problems of the gainers then become understandable as a function of a drastic interruption in income two years before bankruptcy.

It appears likely, therefore, that many of the losers and gainers in income represent debtors who had suffered an abrupt shift in income through unemployment or layoff. If we take a 20% change in income as a strong indicator of income interruption, then 42% of the Chapter 7 wage earners had a serious loss of income during the two years before bankruptcy.

Pulling together the figures on unemployment, short tenure, and income volatility, a strong suggestion emerges that a majority of the Chapter 7 wage earners had interruptions in income and declines in earnings before bankruptcy. The consequence would be serious mismatches between income and debt. Both debtors and their creditors rely on a steady income in deciding on prudent levels of debt. The evidence strongly suggests that for many bankruptcy cases the disappointment of those expectations of income is a primary cause of financial collapse.

These data also suggest that there is often a lag between financial distress and the filing of a bankruptcy petition in court. Between 85% and 90% of these debtors were employed at the time they filed. A substantial proportion (the gainers) may have returned to something like their prior incomes at the very time they decided to give up the effort to pay their debts, debts that likely snowballed a year or two earlier.

The idea of a lag between financial disaster and filing for bankruptcy is consistent with what we learned in our interviews with judges, trustees, and lawyers. Many of those we interviewed suggested that debtors often delay filing until they have a new job. They painted a picture of a debtor who loses a job or is laid off for several months, postponing bill payment or paying only monthly minimums, buying on credit more than usual while hoping for reemployment. Creditors who push for repayment are told the debtor has no job. Finally, the debtor finds another job or is rehired. Shortly thereafter, the debtor is bombarded by creditors. So long as the debtor was unemployed, many creditors remained relatively quiet, evidently on the theory that there was little reason to expend resources on a debtor with virtually no prospect of repayment. But when the debtor returns to work, creditors begin to make calls, to threaten legal action, and sometimes to seek wage garnishments.

For a period of months after obtaining reemployment, the debtor may attempt to hold off creditors with some payment for each. Only after a period of renewed employment and increasing creditor pressure does the debtor finally face up to the reality that it is impossible to get far enough ahead to pay off these accumulated debts, especially as interest charges and late fees mount. Furthermore, the debtor has learned the hard way that continued employment is by no means certain and that payment of past bills will leave nothing for a nest egg if unemployment comes again. This is often, according to the interviews, the point at which a debtor seeks legal help and begins to consider bankruptcy.

In addition to this fairly typical picture, some judges and lawyers point to a very practical reason many debtors do not file bankruptcy until they have a new job: first they need money to pay the bankruptcy lawyer's fee. Many debtors are too poor for bankruptcy until they get a paycheck.

Thus it is likely that the key differences between those who show up in our files as gainers and those who show up as losers or as unemployed is only a question of timing. Those who wait a year or more after an income interruption will show a significant income gain when they return to work, but those who file bankruptcy immediately after a work interruption will show a loss in annual income immediately preceding the filing. The data suggest that different debtors may respond more quickly to income changes, but further analysis will have to await a study aimed specifically at that question.

These data do not suggest that everyone in bankruptcy has experienced major interruption in income. Although 42% of the debtors showed a difference of at least 20% in income between the first and second years before their filings, the other 58% reported swings of less than 20%. For a substantial number of debtors, incomes may have remained steady while other factors caused debts to swing wildly out of balance with income.

On the other hand, the very low job tenure of our debtors may indicate that the minority of debtors with stable income in the two years before bankruptcy include a fair number whose income slide began more than two years earlier and persisted throughout the prebankruptcy period. These debtors may have constant incomes for that period, but they may be carrying debts incurred on the basis of earlier, much higher incomes. Overall, it is fair to say not only that the debtors in bankruptcy have substantially lower incomes than Americans generally, but that many have had a long ride on an income roller coaster before their filing.

Statistics can carry us only so far. These income-interrupted debtors may have been fired for incompetence or misconduct. Or they may have been steady, competent workers who were struck by an economic thunderbolt, like the plant closings that swept Illinois in the early 1980s when J. I. Case, International Harvester, and similar companies in deep financial trouble laid off hundreds of workers. No doubt our sample contains examples of each. What we can say is that many of these debtors—and their creditors—suffered from a serious mismatch between income and debt because of unemployment or layoff.

Policy Implications

The analysis just completed goes beyond the almost tautological finding in Chapter Four that bankrupt people have financial problems, and that, in particular, they have low incomes and high debts. This chapter focuses on the occupations of the debtors and analyzes data that give us a better idea about who goes into bankruptcy and some insight into why they do so.

The most critical finding in this chapter is the similarity between debtors in bankruptcy and Americans generally. Bankrupt debtors are somewhat more likely to be unemployed, and their occupations and industries are not perfect matches for those of all other Americans. But debtors in bankruptcy generally work alongside other Americans. The differences between debtors in bankruptcy and most Americans are, for example, less than the occupational differences of men and women generally. Bankrupt debtors work in much the same industries holding much the same jobs as other Americans. By inference from that fact, they are likely to have much the same education, job training, and so forth.

These comparative data explode a number of myths. The debtors are not overwhelmingly blue collar, nor are they employed in marginal jobs. Yet at the other end of the spectrum of preconceptions, they are not in the best middle-class jobs. To anticipate a few myths in the making, the debtors are not concentrated in low-paying industries, or declining industries, or any other special niche we can identify.

The significance of this finding for bankruptcy policy is subtle but pervasive. As we indicated in the introduction, the image one holds of a typical bankrupt debtor has a profound influence on how that person sees the bankruptcy debate. It sets the normative tone for how bankruptcy policy should help/punish the innocent/blameworthy.

These data suggest that bankrupt debtors are our neighbors. They are not some distant and different "others" from whom we can distance ourselves. Their financial circumstances separate them from most people, but by some critical social measures they look like everyone else. The data will not support an overly sentimentalized view of these debtors as the poorest segment of society nor will it sustain a view of the slimy middle-class manipulator. Instead, these data show that, at the outset, the picture of debtors in bankruptcy should be a picture that looks very much like any other picture of people in the United States.

There is a peculiar problem in bankruptcy, however, that goes beyond the question of the images of the typical bankrupt debtor. Everyone with whom we speak about our research topic evidences some discomfort. Bankruptcy is an unpleasant subject for many, and discomfort may well be compounded by a concern that bankruptcy could someday happen to any one of us. All of us have a tendency to establish a distance between ourselves and the victims of various misfortunes. Was he mugged? He should have know better than to walk in that neighborhood at night. Was she raped? She should not have worn such provocative clothes.

This phenomenon, called "blaming the victim," serves as a psychological defense against the seemingly random occurrence of tragedy and trouble.[27] Everyone else can feel safe because, of course, everyone else is too careful to walk in dangerous neighborhoods and too discreet to wear daring clothing. There is a tendency to think of people who have fallen into bankruptcy either as belonging to a different social group (the very poor, the blue-collar workers) or as holding very different moral values (the middle-income sharpies). This makes their bankruptcies seem far away from anything a reasonable, middle-class American will ever have to face. Again, the data from this chapter suggest that the picture of debtors as some identifiable "other" who went to different schools (or did not go to school at all) and who work in other places (or do not work at all) simply will not wash.

The second key finding in this chapter relates the debtors' employment status to their economic circumstances. The finding that the debtors in bankruptcy earn, on average, about a third less than most working Americans has several possible explanations. These data show that the most obvious hypotheses—the debtors work in declining industries or generally low-paying jobs—are simply wrong. Instead, a high proportion of the files show strong evidence that an interruption in income preceded the bankruptcy filing. Obviously income interruption is not the cause of all bankruptcies, but it seems clear that it is a significant factor in many of them.

The implications of this finding for bankruptcy policy could be very important. Bankruptcy is part of a broad fabric of social support for people in economic trouble to the extent that it serves those who have suffered serious income interruption from layoffs, injury, or other causes. Just as unemployment insurance, food stamps, and free medical care are used in part to ameliorate the impact of job loss, bankruptcy may be viewed as part of the solution to problems caused by layoffs and other job losses.

The possibility that income interruption is a causal factor for a substantial number of bankruptcies suggests that economic volatility may make bankruptcy an important safety net even for the prudent. In that case, some policymakers may want to reconsider how hard the bankruptcy laws should push debtors who are trying to get back on their feet. It may also suggest that *both* debtors and creditors should reconsider the risks of credit in an increasingly volatile economy.

These data provide yet another perspective on the debtors in bankruptcy, one that highlights their similarity to other people and that suggests at least one reason some of the debtors get into the financial hole that leads them to declare bankruptcy.

Notes

1. R. W. Emerson, The Collected Works of Ralph Waldo Emerson (Cambridge: Belknap Press of Harvard University Press, 1979), Vol. II, p. 32.

2. P. M. Blau and O. D. Duncan, The American Occupational Structure (New York: Wiley, 1967); D. Treiman, Occupational Prestige in International Perspective (New York: Academic Press, 1977).

3. In its review of studies on bankruptcy, the commission on the Bankruptcy Laws of the United States noted:

> Almost all the studies reported that the majority of case debtors [*sic*] were blue collar workers, with variations ranging from "semi-skilled and unskilled" to "semi-skilled and skilled." Only Myers found the typical bankrupt to be either a white collar worker or a skilled worker. It seems clear that, in terms of the general population, blue collar workers, who in recent years have made up only slightly more than one-third of the working population, are substantially overrepresented. For some of the studies it seems clear that the unskilled and semi-skilled workers are equally overrepresented.

Commission on the Bankruptcy Laws of the United States, Report, (Washington: U.S. Government Printing Office, 1973), Part I, p. 43. Our findings are rather different, perhaps because we are using more refined measures of work than the white-collar–blue-collar or skill distinctions. It is also possible that there has been a change in the composition of bankrupt debtors since the Commission's review was completed.

4. Because of incomplete reports of occupations or industries or reports that are unclassifiable using the standard government categories, we lose about 260 debtors in the analysis of occupations and about 360 in the analysis of industries. The debtors we lose report lower average incomes. The two categories overlap, because we had only industry or occupation for some debtors and a small group of debtors reported neither. We had either a valid occupation report or a valid industry report for a total of 1304 debtors. The remaining 198 reported neither. We had a complete report, occupation and industry, from 1091 of the 1502 cases. We used all the cases reporting occupation, whether or not they reported industry, for occupational analysis and all industry-reporting cases for industry analysis. Where both occupation and industry are considered, we naturally could use only the cases reporting both.

5. There are two possible explanations for the fact that those who did not report on industry and occupation appear poorer than the rest. It is possible that they may have been making lower incomes because they were in more marginal industries and occupations, in which case our sample might truly look more dissimilar from the population as a whole than appears from our tables. On the other hand, it seems quite likely that the debtors who did not report occupation and industry were disproportionately the unemployed, who may have reported very low income or even zero income, yet could have been in mainstream jobs and industries until they got laid off. In that case, their omission would have little effect on comparability. It is our sense that these effects should at least balance, so that the "missing" cases would look roughly like those reporting by occupations and industries.

The combination of occupation, industry, or both with income data means we lost some additional cases in each category where income was not reported. For example, a total of 1091 cases reported occupation and industry, but only 991 of these cases also reported income and could be included when we looked at all three at the same time. For the various categories, the figures are: occupation reported, 1147 with reported income; industry reported, 1034 with reported income; occupation or industry or both reported 1306 with reported income; neither reported, 60 with reported income.

The cases that reported neither occupation nor industry but did report income had much lower mean income, $5,404 as compared with the cases that reported occupation or industry or both, with a mean income of $13,821. The cases that reported both had a slightly higher mean income of $14,993.

6. Of our 1502 cases, 128 had no report at all. Of the 1374 that did report, 15 of the cases reported nonemployment, such as "retired," and 10 cases reported something we could not classify, such as "employee."

7. A middle estimate of unemployment would be 9%, the figure we get when we add to the explicitly unemployed 28 nonreporting debtors who reported negligible income. These additional 28 debtors are probably unemployed. They consist of debtors who neither reported "unemployed" nor listed an occupation and who earned less than $1,000 in the year before bankruptcy. We infer that they were very likely unemployed.

8. According to the U.S. Bureau of Labor Statistics' definition, which is used to compute national unemployment statistics, a person is unemployed only if he or she is actively looking for work or awaiting the results of a recent job search. Some number of those in bankruptcy files who listed themselves as "unemployed" may not have been looking for outside work, such as housewives, some disabled or retired persons, and those who had simply given up on a job search. On the other hand, in only 15 of 1394 cases did a primary debtor report being disabled, retired, or "housewife" in lieu of occupation, so we doubt that very many primary debtors have been misclassified into our unemployed pool.

9. U.S. Bureau of the Census, Statistical Abstract of the United States, 1982–83 (103d ed., Washington: U.S. Government Printing Office, 1983), Table 628, p. 378.

10. Certain notations will be used consistently for the remainder of the book. We will always use *N* to indicate the number of cases in the analysis, and *p* to indicate the probability that a finding could have occurred by chance. The Pearson correlation coefficient, which has theoretical ranges from -1.00 to $+1.00$, is designated *r*. A positive *r* indicates that as one variable increases, so does the other. To use an example in the text, debtors with higher incomes also report longer job tenure. In the multivariate analyses reported in the tables, *F* indicates the values for the *F*-test, which is a measure of how well the model fits the data. Both *F*-tests and *t*-tests are used to test for significant differences. The multiple correlation coefficient, indicated by R^2, shows how much of the variance in the dependent variable can be explained by the statistical model.

11. The codes are available in U.S. Bureau of the Census, "Public Use Samples of Basic Records from the 1970 Census" (Washington: U.S. Government Printing Office, 1972), pp. 93–110). These codes were also used in the March 1981 CPS, which is our comparison.

12. By way of comparison, if we look at the occupations of working men and women and apply the index of dissimilarity, the index score would be 22. Out of every 100 men, 22 would have to change jobs for men and women to have the same occupational distribution. (In 1968 it was 44, which conveys some idea of how the occupational differences have narrowed.)

13. Treiman, Occupational Prestige, pp. 319–28.

14. The standardizations reported in the text are based on family income. We repeated the tests using personal income, with similar results, as follows:

TABLE 5.5. Direct Standardization of Family and Personal Income by Industry and Occupation, for CDS and CPS

	Family Income		Personal Income	
Variable	CPS	CDS	CPS	CDS
Industry				
Measured value	$24,972	$17,005	$16,945	$14,925
Standardized using CDS income	16,872	17,005	14,746	14,925
Standardized using CPS income	24,972	24,801	16,945	16,979
Occupation				
Measured value	25,054	16,694	16,967	14,629
Standardized using CDS income	16,953	16,694	14,666	14,629
Standardized using CPS income	25,054	23,480	16,967	16,026

Source: Consumer Bankruptcy Project; March 1981 Current Population Survey.

15. See E. Kitagawa, Components of a Difference Between Two Rates, 50 Journal of the American Statistical Association 1168–94 (December 1955).

16. The gap in mean family incomes between bankrupt debtors and the CPS sample is $7,856. Of this sum, the decomposition analysis shows that about $1,607, or 20%, can be attributed to the joint occupation–industry composition of the two samples. Another $7,905 is attributed to the earnings differences between similarly situated debtors and the national population.

The two figures add to more than the $7,856 difference we are trying to explain, because the interaction between occupation–industry and earnings cancels out to some extent. This interaction effect equals $ – 1,656. By holding first occupation–industry and then earnings rates constant, there is an "overcorrection" in our sum by $1,656. This overcorrection is the interaction effect, and it indicates that the workers with high earnings tend to be in the "best" occupations and industries—hardly a surprise. Practically speaking, the composition effect—the debtors' occupational and industrial distribution—has been washed out by the interaction effect. Again, we reach similar conclusions analyzing personal work-related income instead of family income.

17. As we noted before, there are considerable differences in the information the debtors must report in Chapter 7 and that required in Chapter 13. Only the Chapter 7 forms call for all the information we needed for this analysis, so we limit ourselves to Chapter 7 wage-earning debtors in the data that follow.

18. The text reports only wage earners. We also have one self-employed debtor who reported being unemployed. If the self-employed are added, we had 113 unemployed primary debtors, about 12% of 917 Chapter 7 cases. The unemployment rate is lower in our overall sample because it is lower among Chapter 13 petitioners. Only 18 Chapter 13 petitioners, or 3.1%, were unemployed.

19. In Chapter 7, the primary debtor is explicitly reported as "unemployed" in 93 cases. Following the protocol discussed earlier, we can identify another 20 cases that very likely represent an unemployed primary debtor. Although we added only these

20 cases from the 60 cases in which occupation was not reported, it is also possible that a number of the remaining 40 cases with no occupation reported represent people unemployed at the time of bankruptcy. See note 7.

20. Those who did not respond look like those who did in many respects. However, the nonresponders had much lower incomes and much higher unsecured debts. Those with missing tenure have significantly lower average incomes of $13,900 versus $17,100 for tenure reporters ($p = 0.00$). The unsecured debt totals are significantly higher at $17,700 and $13,600, respectively ($p = 0.02$). The groups do not differ significantly on a number of other variables. It seems likely that many nonreporters are unemployed or sporadically employed, which would be consistent with the inference of income interruption. It does not seem to us that these differences are likely to invalidate the conclusions about to be discussed. In fact, we suspect that our conclusions would be strengthened if these missing debtors had reported tenure—but we cannot be sure.

21. U.S. Bureau of Labor Statistics, "Job Tenure and Occupational Change, 1981," Bulletin 2162 (January 1983), Table 1, p. 1.

22. We analyzed the tenure data to determine whether there are interaction effects between tenure and industries or occupations that better explain debtors' low incomes. When we array industries by average tenure, we find no significant differences. Because the rather gross industry characteristics could mask differences in some subgroups, we analyzed separately industry groups in durable manufacturing, transportation, communication, and utilities. Again, there were no statistically significant differences in average tenure. The same was true of occupation. Tenure varies only weakly with occupation, and there is no significant difference in tenure among occupational groups. This reinforces the conclusion that tenure is a consistently important variable in explaining the bankrupt debtors' financial pictures in different occupations and different industries.

23. The partial regression coefficient shows the effect of tenure on earnings controlling for the effects of occupation, prestige, and industry. A coefficient of 100 would indicate that an extra year of tenure would add $100 to earnings, holding industry and prestige constant.

As we indicated earlier, even among our low-earning debtors there are still variations among occupations and industries in earnings. The white-collar petitioners earn more, on average, than the blue-collar petitioners, even if the scale and the gap are not the same as those in the general population. We tested the hypothesis that there is a differential rate of return to tenure in the different industries or occupations, suggesting, for example, that six years' tenure in manufacturing "pays off" more than six years' tenure in retail trade. We use a regression equation similar to that of Table 5.4 except we added interaction effects for each industry and tenure. None of the interaction effects are significant, and the explained variance does not change.

24. Both the zero-order and the partial correlation coefficient drop to 0.05 and lose statistical significance.

25. More than half of the losers had been on their present jobs less than a year, compared with 30% of the gainers. The gainers had a median tenure of two years, and a quarter of them had been working at the same job eight years or longer.

26. A debtor who had worked on the production line for International Harvester, for example, might describe himself as "Assembly-man, press operator—8 years," even if there had been more than one layoff and recall during that time.

27. W. Ryan, Blaming the Victim (New York: Vantage, 1976).

6

The Entrepreneurs

Thus far we have described our sample as a whole and its largest subgroup, wage earners. In this and the next five chapters, we consider identifiable groups of debtors who have more in common with each other than they do with the larger group. Not only are subgroups important to an accurate description of debtor behavior, but they sometimes have a powerful impact on bankruptcy policy. Some subgroups of debtors make a compelling case for special consideration. Bankruptcy laws are shot through with exceptions for special groups: homeowners, farmers, stockbrokers, people who own tools they use on their jobs, people with expensive medical devices, fishermen, jewelry wearers, tenants, landlords, married people, customers of commodity brokers, victims of drunk drivers, and people with pets—just to name a few.

Assumptions about subgroups shape many of the internal boundaries of bankruptcy law. Statutory exceptions for special groups in bankruptcy were passed without systematic data but with powerfully sympathetic (or horrific) anecdotes about this group or that group of people who deserve a break (or a kick in the pants).

With this chapter we begin a series of inquiries into seven important subgroups: entrepreneurs, homeowners, married couples, women alone, people with large medical debt, credit card junkies, and bankruptcy repeaters. In each chapter we discuss which bankruptcy policies, if any, are directed specifically to the subgroup and we present the economic circumstances we found in the subgroup in bankruptcy.

Entrepreneurs—The Risk Takers in the American Economy

The standard description of employment transformation in advanced industrial societies is that self-employment gradually disappears with the rise of large corporate employers. Family farms are replaced by agribusiness, small retail outlets are displaced by chain stores, and even self-employed professionals become employees of medical, engineering, and legal "professional corporations."

This shift in employment patterns alarms observers for whom the yeoman farmer and the small business owners are the mainstays of the community. Recent commentary about the decline of entrepreneurship in the United States has warned of declining rates of innovation and lower quality of goods and services. Some speculate that immigrants are the last bastion of entrepreneurship in the United States.

Two points about small businesses are uncontroversial: they hold a crucial place in the American economy, and they present tremendous financial risks for the owner. Small businesses provide many jobs that are the major producers of certain goods and services, but starting a small business is the financial equivalent of driving race cars or fighting oil-field fires. Big risks are associated with potentially big rewards for those who make it, but disaster awaits those who do not. In 1981, about half of all new small businesses had failed within their first five years, "failure" being defined by Dun & Bradstreet as bankruptcy and a consequent loss to creditors.[1] Most small businesses can get credit only when the owner agrees to personal liability, so it was no surprise to find small business owners in bankruptcy.

We come to the study of entrepreneurs from an odd perspective: our study is devoted to consumer bankruptcy. Entrepreneurs became important to the study only because they are a significant part of the sample of individual petitioners. An entrepreneur's bankruptcy is both a business and a consumer case.[2]

The self-employed in bankruptcy have features of both businesses and consumers in serious economic trouble. The plumber whose contracting business goes down the drain will have business debts (e.g., the bill at the plumbing supply house) along with consumer debts (e.g., a charge account at the local clothing store). Here we explore how such debtors differ from the self-employed who are not in bankruptcy and from the entire bankruptcy sample discussed in Chapter Five.

Business Trouble and Personal Bankruptcy

Although no business debtor is typical of the entire group, Jack Miller and his wife Pat illustrate several patterns we found within the data. They filed their Chapter 7 bankruptcy in March 1981 because of the failure of their business, Miller's Interstate Shell, located on the highway that runs through their small Illinois town.

The file suggests how a prospective entrepreneur might nurse a goal to own a business during years of work for a large organization. In 1971 Jack Miller retired from his job as an Illinois civil servant and started his own gas station. By 1978 or 1979 the business was in serious trouble, and in 1980 he closed it down. By that time Mr. Miller had already gone back to work as an auditor making about $15,000 a year. Pat Miller began selling jewelry at home parties in 1979, and she earned about $7,000 the year before they closed the gas station. Between them, they were making $22,000, an income much higher than the average in our sample ($15,800) and nearly as much as the average household in the nation. But their debts were far from average, more than $200,000 altogether, a large portion of which were business debts. They struggled with their debts and some lawsuits for almost two years after both had taken salaried jobs. Finally, the Millers sold some of the tools left in the garage to raise money for the bankruptcy lawyer's fee, and they filed for bankruptcy in early 1981.

The debts in the Millers' financial statement are a melange of consumer and business obligations; it is not always possible to separate them. Of a total $143,000 of unsecured debt, some debts are clearly personal, such as "Dr. Clive's medical bill" of $99. Others are clearly from the business, such as "novelties for station," $1,437. But many debts are ambiguous, such as several debts for "insurance" that might have been personal insurance or insurance on the gas station.

Above all, the origins of the Millers' debts are hard to determine because they paid off many of their original bills with new loans. They list three loans from the Central National Bank. One was a second mortgage on their home for $32,000. Although we cannot tell what debts might have been paid with this loan, we know that this $32,000 represented business debts because it is listed as "business consolidation loan." The other two loans were unsecured, for $21,000 and for $2,150. We cannot say for certain whether they were for business or personal purposes, although the larger one originated in 1978 when the business was apparently in serious trouble.

The Millers borrowed from family and friends as well. Between 1978 and 1980 they borrowed almost $10,000 from Fred Miller, and over a long period of time they borrowed almost $90,000 from Susan Edwina South. Ms. South also was a co-signer on still other notes of the Millers, so she got sued and had to pay when they did not. We do not know Ms. South's relationship with Jack and Pat Miller, nor do we know if the money went into the business, although it seems likely that much of it did. We will never know if Ms. South was outraged or heartbroken over the Millers' bankruptcy.

The Millers' assets were the usual mix of family furniture, television, stereo, washer and dryer. They had three cars and a John Deere tractor. They listed "misc. service station equipment." And they have a future source of income: a State of Illinois Civil Service Pension and Retirement Benefit Annuity worth $950 a month by the time of filing.

The file indicates how long the Millers will live with the consequences of their failed business. When they took out the business debt consolidation loan they gave the bank a second mortgage on their home. Their loans on the cars and tractor all exceed the values of the items by several thousand dollars. If the Millers want to keep any of this property, they will have to get the agreement of their secured creditors and pay off the liens in full.[3] Otherwise, they will begin their fresh start minus home, car, and tractor.

Human interest aside, the Millers' file illustrates several important points about the circumstances of bankrupt debtors whose businesses fail. We explore these issues more systematically with the data, but we do so remembering that the impact of the failure of a business is only partly reflected in the cold numbers.

Identifying Entrepreneurs

People in business for themselves made up about 7.3% of the nation's workers in 1981.[4] The proportion of self-employed in bankruptcy is substantially larger than the proportion of self-employed in the general population. The currently self-employed alone account for 10.4% of our sample of the debtors in bankruptcy, a percentage almost one and a half times greater than the self-employed in the general population. In addition, the bankruptcy files contain 144 former entrepreneurs such as the Millers, another 9.6% of the sample. Thus the entrepreneurs in our sample account for 20% of the individual debtors.

Debtors such as the Millers pose a classification problem for our study. Their bankruptcy was patently the result of the failure of a business, yet by the time of bankruptcy they had salaried jobs and were wage earners. We can identify them from their answers to a bankruptcy form question about former business activity.[5] These failed entrepreneurs are in bankruptcy to cope with the debts of their failed businesses, just like those who reported in their bankruptcy petitions that they were currently self-employed at the time of bankruptcy. When we look at the financial statistics of the former entrepreneurs—incomes, assets, debts, debt/income ratios, and the like—they generally look much more like the currently self-employed than like wage earners.[6] For these reasons, we generally include them in the self-employed category and exclude them from analyses involving "pure" wage earners.

Thus most of the discussion in this chapter includes both those who reported they were self-employed at the time of bankruptcy and those who reported they had been engaged in business previously. The principal exception is the analysis of occupations, industries, and incomes, because it is impossible to say whether the debtors' present jobs or their former businesses better define them financially or socially. For example, Mr. Miller had been an auditor for many years, then invested almost a decade of his life in managing a gas station, and then returned to his auditing job. It is hard to say which occupation—gas station manager or auditor—better defines him in terms of income comparisons or social status. Given these imponderables and given that our data are necessarily less clear with respect to former occupations than to current ones, we use current status to analyze the occupations, industries, and incomes of the debtors. For all other analyses, the formerly self-employed are combined with the currently self-employed, a group we designate "entrepreneurs."

Although entrepreneurs are a much larger portion of the bankruptcy sample than of the population generally, we believe our data actually undercount those who are in trouble because of a failing business. The files show people who give their occupations as "cooks" or "restaurant managers," suggesting wage employees, but listing significant debts for restaurant equipment and supplies. (At least we could not imagine that anyone's family had consumed $8,000 worth of fish batter.) Some files showed business equipment suppliers, commercial landlords, trade creditors, and "private investors" going after debtors who were listed as store clerks or truck drivers. But without a specific indication from the debtor of current or former self-employment, we left the debtor with the wage earners. Even on this restricted count, we can verify that one in five debtors in bankruptcy is a failing or failed entrepreneur.[7]

These data paint a vivid picture of the financial risks for the self-employed. If we combine those in business and those with a recently failed business, even our underestimate puts the proportion of self-employed in bankruptcy about three times higher than their proportion in the general population would suggest.

Occupations, Industries, and Incomes for the Currently Self-Employed

We begin our comparisons of the self-employed in bankruptcy with the self-employed in the general population by looking at jobs and income, replicating for this subgroup the analysis in the last chapter for the sample as a whole. We exclude the formerly self-employed from this one analysis because their current occupations and industries differ from those of their failed businesses.

The currently self-employed are a varied group who range from independent contractors cleaning houses and sweeping chimneys to high-tech entrepreneurs exploring silicon mysteries. The largest group of the self-employed in the CPS sample of the general population, over 19%, was in agriculture. The bankruptcy sample, however, included only 13 farmers from all three sample states. This is a notable result because agriculture is a substantial component of the economies of Illinois, Texas, and Pennsylvania. The low number in our sample may be explained by a combination of the realities of farming communities and our study design.

It is possible that in 1981 farmers avoided bankruptcy for social or economic reasons that cannot be discerned from bankruptcy files. One law professor involved in this study received many calls in the early 1980s from lawyers and academics concerned that the rural lawyers advising farmers were ill-informed about bankruptcy. A dearth of lawyers experienced in complex bankruptcies might explain why few farmers filed even if they were in trouble.

It is also possible that our omission of Chapter 11 cases eliminated many farmers. Debtors trying to save a business must use Chapter 11 rather than Chapter 13, if they owe $100,000 unsecured or $350,000 secured. Such large debts are not unusual for farmers, who must finance land, equipment, seed, fuel, and chemicals every year. The explanation for the low number of farmers in our sample will have to await a study aimed specifically at farmers in trouble. We can only note that farmers do not show up in the numbers we would expect, and their absence from the bankruptcy sample creates important statistical dissimilarities between the self-employed in bankruptcy and those in the general population.[8]

Another group with a smaller proportion in our bankruptcy sample than in the general population are the debtors in professional services. Although 9% of the self-employed nationally are in professional services, they account for only 3% of the self-employed in our bankruptcy sample. We have no reason to think that our study design excluded them unless their debts were too high for Chapter 13 and so they ended up in Chapter 11, outside our study's scope. Their smaller numbers in our sample may well reflect a lower propensity to file bankruptcy.[9]

Other groups were overrepresented. A quarter of the self-employed bankruptcy sample were in retail trade and another quarter were in business services, both groups proportionately larger than their counterpart groups in the national sample. Self-employed debtors in bankruptcy were in transportation, including many self-employed truck drivers, more often than the general population.

On some measures, the self-employed in bankruptcy look much more different from the general population than do the wage earners we analyzed earlier. The self-employed in bankruptcy are in a different mix of industries. Returning to the index of dissimilarity that we use to compare bankrupt wage earners with wage earners generally, the index for the self-employed in bankruptcy as compared to the self-employed in the general population is 31.6—almost double the comparable number for the wage earners.

There are fewer differences in occupations between the self-employed debtors and the national sample, but the data are potentially misleading in at least one respect. Large proportions of self-employed in and out of bankruptcy report themselves to be "managers or administrators" because they own their businesses. The manager/administrator classification so dominates both groups that further analysis is problematic. The index of dissimilarity on occupational groupings for the self-employed in bankruptcy and in the general population is 17—almost the same as the comparable figure for the whole sample. Because of the concentration of reported manager/administrator occupations, the self-employed tend to have relatively high prestige. The CPS sample of the self-employed had a mean prestige ranking of 44, compared with 41 for the self-employed debtors in bankruptcy. For the reasons just indicated, that ranking may be misleadingly high for both groups, and it is only somewhat higher than the mean for wage earners.

The debtors in professional services had significantly lower prestige than did professionals in the national sample (51 points versus 68). The debtors also had lower occupational prestige among professional and technical occupational specialties—53 points versus 66. These scores indicate that the national labor force contains relatively more of the well-compensated self-employed professionals such as physicians, accountants, and attorneys, whereas our sample is more likely to contain the self-employed dance instructors and private tutors. The differences in occupational prestige suggest that the self-employed in bankruptcy tend to be concentrated in the less prestigious and less well-compensated segments of these occupational groups. On the other hand, *higher* prestige for the bankrupt debtors in other occupations, such as craftworkers and transport operatives, helped bring the overall prestige ranking of the self-employed in and out of bankruptcy into closer alignment, perhaps because ownership is associated with more prestigious codes (e.g., truck drivers are more likely to be self-employed than are baggage handlers).

The currently self-employed in bankruptcy are like the bankrupt wage earners in that they make substantially lower incomes in comparison to non-bankrupts in the same industries and in similar types of jobs.[10] Indeed, the average incomes of self-employed and wage-earning debtors in our bankruptcy sample are statistically indistinguishable. The dollar differences at the means—$17,700 for the currently self-employed and $15,600 for current wage earners—appear substantial, but there is so much variance that the difference is not statistically significant.

Self-employed debtors report lower earnings in most industries than do the self-employed in the general population. There are large differences in professional services ($13,000) and retail trade ($10,000). There are two exceptions. Bankrupt debtors in the transportation industry earned $10,000 more than those in the general population, and the difference in incomes in business services was not statistically significant.[11]

When self-employed debtors are classified by occupations, their incomes are usually lower than their CPS counterparts in similar jobs. In the manager/administrator occupational group, the self-employed debtors report $10,000 a year less than the nearly $24,000 in the CPS national sample. Many other occupational groups also report lower incomes for the self-employed debtors in bankruptcy, although transport operatives' incomes just miss being significantly higher. To the extent that the bankrupt self-employed differ from other self-employed, they are concentrated in somewhat lower prestige jobs.

We repeat the statistical decompositions we did with the wage earners to determine whether industrial or occupational composition differences account for the lower incomes of the self-employed. We found that the composition of industry and occupation accounted for some income differences, but that bankrupt wage earners simply earn less—less in each industry and less at each job. Our analysis of self-employed debtors suggests a similar pattern. They work in much the same industries and occupations (with somewhat larger variation), but they earn considerably less from their businesses.[12]

These data show us that the self-employed debtors in bankruptcy—like all bankrupt debtors—are not terribly different from the rest of us. While the self-employed bankrupts are somewhat lower on the totem pole, it is not just chimney sweeps or housecleaners who go into bankruptcy.

Balance Sheets for Entrepreneurs —The Bad News Gets Worse

When we turn to the balance sheets of entrepreneurs in bankruptcy, we once again include the formerly self-employed, whose assets and debts look so much like those of the currently self-employed precisely because both groups are in bankruptcy after the failure of a business. Table 6.1 is therefore divided between pure wage earners and those who were "ever self-employed," that is, the currently self-employed plus the formerly self-employed as previously defined. If the reports of the balance sheets for all debtors in bankruptcy were bad, the balance sheets for the self-employed are much worse. Table 6.1 shows the differences between the self-employed and the wage earners in bankruptcy.

The comparison of assets in Table 6.1 shows that the self-employed report substantially greater assets than the wage-earning group. This is not to say that all self-employed debtors have enormous assets. One-quarter have assets valued at less than $9,000, but another quarter have assets in excess of $72,000. The lowest quarter of wage-earning debtors, by contrast, have assets under $2,200, and the highest quarter of wage earners have assets in excess of $38,000, substantially less than the median asset level for the self-employed.

TABLE 6.1. Distribution of Assets and Debts, Pure Wage Earners and Ever Self-Employed[a]

Distribution	Assets	Total Debt	Secured Debt	Unsecured Debt
Pure Wage Earners				
Mean	$22,835	$ 26,753	$16,850	$ 9,827
s.d.	27,249	31,660	23,824	17,121
25th percentile	2,196	8,715	2,068	3,475
Median	10,595	16,953	8,010	6,063
75th percentile	37,942	35,750	25,275	10,577
N	1,192	1,196	1,202	1,195
Missing	10	6	0	7
Ever Self-Employed				
Mean	$55,434	$ 85,824	$47,897	$38,087
s.d.	64,843	90,656	66,517	55,445
25th percentile	8,985	24,931	6,362	7,966
Median	40,592	53,193	25,976	19,039
75th percentile	71,727	109,899	59,000	46,305
N	298	300	299	300
Missing	2	0	1	0
Statistical Test				
t-value	−8.49**	−11.12**	−7.95**	−8.72**

[a]Cases with extreme values on assets, total debt, or income are removed.

**$p \leq 0.01$

Source: Consumer Bankruptcy Project.

The range of assets in both groups is enormous, but it is far greater for the self-employed. The differences are statistically significant with a very high level of probability.

This difference probably reflects the types of assets the two groups own. Wage-earning debtors own homes, cars, household goods, and occasionally an unusual item, such as a boat or an anticipated tax refund. The self-employed claim these same items, but they also claim inventories, accounts receivable, business machinery, tools, merchandise display cases, calculators, computers, and other items acquired to operate a business. The specialized goods owned by the self-employed are producer goods, not consumption goods or financial assets.

The good news of higher assets for entrepreneurs is offset by the bad news of the debts incurred to pay for them. The debt structures for all debtors in bankruptcy were staggering, but for the self-employed the debts took on truly monstrous proportions. The mean debt is $26,800 for wage earners, but it is $85,800 for the self-employed—a threefold difference in mean total debt. The pattern of much higher debt for the self-employed persists at every quartile and for both secured and unsecured debts. One in four of the self-employed report debts greater than $109,900. In almost every comparison, the self-employed in bankruptcy are in worse financial shape than the wage earners.

The self-employed have much higher debts than the wage earners, but they have very similar incomes. It follows that they are far more heavily burdened by their debts. To make this assertion confidently, however, we must look not merely at grouped data for the self-employed and wage earners, but at a comparison of individual debts with incomes, as we did in Chapter Twc. The results of this analysis are reported in Table 6.2.

TABLE 6.2. Distribution of Debt/Income Ratios for Pure Wage Earners and Ever Self-Employed[a]

	Debt/Income Ratio	
Distribution	Pure Wage Earners	Ever Self-Employed
Mean	2.5	7.1
s.d.	8.8	16.3
25th percentile	0.7	1.4
Median	1.3	2.7
75th percentile	2.3	7.5
N	1,049	194
Missing	155	106
Statistical Test		
t-value	−3.88**	

[a]Cases with extreme values on assets, total debt, or income are removed.

**$p \leq 0.01$

Source: Consumer Bankruptcy Project.

The bad news for entrepreneurs in bankruptcy is confirmed in Table 6.2. At the mean debt/income ratio of 7.1, a self-employed debtor would owe debts greater than seven years' income. By contrast, the wage earner at the mean would owe debts equal to less than three years' income. As usual, the means are inflated by extreme cases, but the medians also differ sharply: 2.7 for the self-employed and 1.3 for the wage earners.[13]

The net worth comparison of assets and debts for individuals shows much the same picture. Table 6.3 shows that the mean net worth for the pure wage earners is $-7,900, whereas those who were ever self-employed have a mean net worth more than three times worse at $-37,700. The medians of $-7,400 for wage earners and $-17,000 for the self-employed show the same pattern. The self-employed show a broader range, although even the highest quartile do not report positive net worth. Overall, however, the high assets of the self-employed match even higher debts, and they are in even more serious financial trouble than wage earners when they file for bankruptcy.

These data show that the bankrupt self-employed and the wage earners have similar incomes, but every other financial measure shows the self-employed two to three times deeper in trouble than the wage earners. Comparing the balance sheets of the wage earners and the self-employed in bankruptcy is a little like describing a lake that is 20 feet deep and one that is 50 feet deep. To someone who cannot swim the difference is academic. Nonetheless, the huge debts of the self-employed put a whole segment of individual bankruptcy into a special perspective.

The self-employed debtors—the individual human beings, not just corporations or limited liability partnerships—are on the hook for debts far beyond the range that could be paid from any realistic salary or by the small austerities of simple living and avoiding credit purchases. Most small businesses need a

TABLE 6.3. Distribution of Net Worth for Current Wage Earners and Self-Employed[a]

Distribution	Net Worth: Pure Wage Earners	Net Worth: Ever Self-Employed
Mean	− 7,937	−37,736
s.d.	26,531	71,993
25th percentile	−13,511	−51,305
Median	− 7,450	−16,980
75th percentile	− 1,713	− 4,100
N	1,189	289
Missing	13	2
Statistical Test		
t-value	7.03**	

[a]Cases with extreme values on assets, total debt, or income are removed.

$**p \leq 0.01$

Source: Consumer Bankruptcy Project.

high debt level just to keep goods on the shelves or trucks on the road. And small businesses become the center of the family's life. One imagines every conversation with the Millers came around somehow to "the station." The Millers borrowed and borrowed to keep Millers' Service Station alive. Incorporating the station did not matter, because the Millers guaranteed its loans or borrowed on their personal assets. When the business died in 1979, it left the Millers with six-figure debts, their home encumbered by business obligations it would take years to pay, and virtually all their other assets wiped out.

What do debtors do when their businesses fail? Some, like Mr. Miller, take salaried jobs. But others, those who continue to describe themselves as self-employed even at the time of filing, try to make their living from the ruins. They can try to reorganize their businesses in Chapter 13 or Chapter 11, paying off some debts from business revenues over the next three to five years. Others may declare Chapter 7, discharge their debt, and start again, searching for new credit and investment sources that are likely to be harder to find the second time around.

Sorting Out Business Debt

The individual debt loads that the self-employed carry into bankruptcy add up to a staggering portion of the overall debt listed in individual bankruptcy. The 156 currently self-employed debtors in our sample account for 25% of the total debt in these individual bankruptcies, even though they constitute only 10% of the cases.[14] The formerly self-employed add another 144 debtors, another 20% of the total debt listed. This means that the ever self-employed are 20% of the total sample, but they are responsible for 45% of the debt listed in bankruptcy.

For most statistical analyses we eliminate 27 outliers from our sample, because their extreme financial positions distort the data (see the appendix). They deserve mention here because 14 are self-employed and 6 more are failed entrepreneurs. If we include the outliers in the total count of individuals and debt in the bankruptcy sample, the proportion of debt carried by the entrepreneurs climbs even higher. In the full sample of 1529 debtors, the 320 small business debtors—the self-employed and the failed entrepreneurs—account for *more than half* of the entire debt in the sample: 21% of the cases had 56% of the debt. The self-employed are responsible for more than two and a half times as much debt as their numbers would suggest.

As the description of the Millers' case indicated, in a small business case we cannot sort out business debt from consumer debt. Sometimes a debt will be listed plainly as "business debt consolidation" or the nature of the debt will reveal its purpose, but often debts are simply noted by amount and creditor, and we are left to guess their origin.

Even doctor bills and shoe purchases, clearly consumer debts, may have a business origin. When the debtor and often the debtor's whole family are putting all their time and energies into a business that begins to sink, family members often stop taking a salary. They may take from the business only enough cash for unavoidable personal purchases, thus personal credit purchases rise: everything is charged, billed later, put on account, or otherwise purchased without dipping into the business cash flow. The Millers listed 12 creditors who seem to be typical creditors on personal debt—doctors, a local department store, the Disney book club. They had three Visa cards, evidently all charged to the limits. Whether the Millers always carried high personal debt or whether they used personal credit to stave off closing their business is something the files do not tell. For the Millers, and for every other debtor connected to a small business, even consumer debts are a part of the business picture.

These data show that aggregated reports about individual bankruptcies conceal the disproportionate debt burdens of the self-employed and the formerly self-employed. The debt carried by entrepreneurs represents over half of all debt listed in individual bankruptcies. A huge part of the *consumer* bankruptcy story is *business* bankruptcy debt.

Policy Implications

Wage earners with consumer debts that outstrip their incomes are the stereotypical individual debtors. Then there are the big corporations that make the news when they go bankrupt. Chapter 7 and Chapter 13 are written for the people, and Chapter 7 and Chapter 11 are for the corporations. If pressed, anyone would acknowledge that individuals in bankruptcy must include some failed entrepreneurs, but they are not the debtors who seem to spring to mind in most discussions.

One important implication of finding a substantial portion of entrepreneurs in bankruptcy is that many generalizations about the individuals who file for bankruptcy are necessarily misleading.[15] The fallacy of misplaced aggregation results from performing statistical operations on numbers that are not comparable. In this case, two discrete groups, wage earners and entrepreneurs, have been combined to produce statistics that fairly describe neither group.[16] Assuming that all individuals in bankruptcy are overspending wage earners paints a much more alarming picture of the number of wage earners who declare bankruptcy and the amount of debt loss they inflict on the consumer credit system. Such an assumption is a distortion that can lead to unwarranted results, such as more restrictive bankruptcy policies.

Discovery of a substantial number of entrepreneurs in bankruptcy also raises a serious question about whether the current bankruptcy system serves a significant portion of the population that badly needs it. Exemption law presents one example of inattention to small business failures. As we discussed in Chapter Two, under current bankruptcy provisions debtors can keep property specified as exempt under state laws or, in some cases, under the federal exemptions. These protections, however, were written with an idealized debtor in mind, one who is not self-employed.

Consequently, the Chapter 7 debtor can keep future wages, but not the property to produce them. In states that have not opted out of the federal exemptions, Chapter 7 debtors can keep some goods subject to nonpossessory, nonpurchase money security interest, but only if the goods are intended for personal or family use—no business goods need apply. Household pets and family furniture, personal medical aids, and family insurance receive a special nod. Tools of the trade receive protection, but only to $750 in value under the federal exemption. Most state exemption laws are similarly focused on the wage-earning debtor. The only entrepreneurs to receive regular congressional attention are the farmers. They now have a separate chapter in bankruptcy and no longer need to struggle to make bankruptcy protection designed for wage earners fit their special needs.

In Chapter 13 debtors keep all their property. But many entrepreneurs are ineligible for Chapter 13. If debts exceed certain limits, the debtor must choose the more expensive, difficult route of a Chapter 11 over a Chapter 13. Entrepreneurs who are deeply enough in debt will face a business-type reorganization when their personal guarantees forced them into bankruptcy. If the debtor can stay in Chapter 13 while the business is in deep trouble and the debtor has no other job, it will be hard to meet the Chapter 13 requirement to show "regular income." It will also be hard to meet plan payments. For a variety of reasons, the details of which are beyond the current discussion, the requirements of Chapter 11 may also be hard for small businesses to meet, and the benefits for individual proprietors will be fewer than for a corporation.

The 1984 amendments did introduce some special treatment for small business debtors, but primarily as exceptions to the tougher treatment of consumers.[17] These exceptions reflected neither a systematic approach to the problems of entrepreneurs, nor an acknowledgment of their difficult circumstances.

The current focus on wage earners is an ironic shift from earlier state debtor–creditor laws and the turn of the century bankruptcy debates. Once the prototype debtors were failed merchants who needed to file bankruptcy to start new businesses and farmers who needed to keep their draught horses and plows for another planting season. Then wage earning replaced family businesses and farms as the means of livelihood for most Americans. The advent of "wage-earner plans" in the 1930s and efforts to "modernize" debtors' property exemptions altered the implicit assumption about who needed bankruptcy protection. Although wage earners remain the largest group in individual bankruptcy, the self-employed represent an important subset, one that brings to bankruptcy more than half the total debt and that requires some special treatment.

In 1986 Congress took a first step toward special treatment for individual debtors in business. A new chapter of the Bankruptcy Code was adopted, Chapter 12. Limited to farmers, it is essentially a "super" Chapter 13, with much higher debt limits and a variety of provisions designed to help farmers reorganize and keep their farms. The problems it addresses are not limited to farmers but characterize many small businesses in trouble. Eventually Congress may decide to let other entrepreneurs enjoy its benefits.[18]

The possibility of simplified reorganization plans for owners of small businesses deserves attention for businesses other than the family farm. It may be that many other self-employed debtors need a chance to reorganize their debts and attempt repayment without being shut down by their creditors. Just as farmers were not adequately served by the existing dichotomy between personal and big business bankruptcy, these entrepreneurs may not be well served either.[19]

Entrepreneurs in bankruptcy may be sensible people who encountered bad luck or foolish people who trod an obvious path to financial failure. We do not know. But they are not in financial trouble just because they could not wait another few months for a VCR, and then a new car, and then a winter vacation to the islands. Instead, many of them worked nights and weekends, put the kids to work after school, read trade catalogues at the dinner table, and woke up in the night in cold sweats when they could not figure out how to make the business pay. Most of the entrepreneurs are in trouble because they made what turned out to be bad business decisions, not because their consumer spending was undisciplined.

Entrepreneurs raise a very special question in bankruptcy: If we really are a capitalist country, committed to the notion that people should try to start their own businesses and nurture them into Apple Computers or Tandy Electronics,[20] just how harshly should we treat the entrepreneur in bankruptcy? The high-risk nature of entrepreneurship means, in effect, that bankruptcy policy is another part of small business policy. It seems to us that some systematic attention to the problem of small business should be placed on the agenda of bankruptcy policymakers.

Notes

1. J. Duncan, The 1981 Dun & Bradstreet Business Failure Record (New York: Dun & Bradstreet, 1983), p. 10. While the report is not entirely self-explanatory, a telephone conversation with Dun & Bradstreet personnel indicates that their reports of business failures are based almost entirely on bankruptcy filings.

2. Our sample was drawn using only two criteria: petitioners were natural persons (as opposed to legal fictions such as corporations or partnerships) and they had filed either a Chapter 7 liquidation or a Chapter 13 repayment plan. We eliminated Chapter 11 filings because these are overwhelmingly business filings, although occasionally an individual with enormous debts and complex legal problems will end up there. We judged the individuals in Chapter 11 to be sufficiently unusual that eliminating them would provide a more accurate description of typical bankrupt debtors.

3. There are some legal twists here for the property other than the home. In Chapter 7 the debtors can "redeem" their property if they have enough cash to pay its current market value rather than the outstanding loan balance. In that case, they would simply discharge the amount of the debt that exceeds the collateral value. The trouble with this provision for the Millers—as for most debtors—is that they do not have the cash to take advantage of it. They then face the option of returning the property or paying the loan in full.

4. 104 Monthly Labor Review (September 1981), Table 3, p. 61.

5. For consistency in coding, the only petitioners classified as currently self-

employed in these data are those who either listed themselves as "self-employed" on their bankruptcy forms or filed a Form 8 supplement for "Debtors Engaged in Business." A debtor who ran his own restaurant but listed his occupation as a cook rather than as self-employed was coded as a current wage earner. Such a debtor might be recoded as formerly self-employed if we had the necessary information.

We can estimate the number of wage earners who, like the Millers, were formerly self-employed. A question on the bankruptcy forms asks if the debtor has been in a partnership or a business within the six years preceding filing. This response does not perfectly define former businesspeople, because some wage earners may have been in passive partnerships as an investment. Nonetheless, our review of the files indicated that most of the "yes" answers to the partnership/business question were given by debtors who had failed in busness and who were bringing substantial business debts into bankruptcy. That impression is strongly reinforced by the debt structure of those who reported a former partnership or business. As we explain in detail later in this chapter, their debts look more like those of the self-employed debtors and unlike those of the wage earners. On this basis, we characterize them as a group as "failed entrepreneurs." Collectively, we refer to the currently self-employed and formerly self-employed simply as the self-employed or as entrepreneurs, noting the more specific designation only when we need to identify one of the subgroups.

6. By several tests, the formerly self-employed look more like the currently self-employed than they do the wage earners. The currently self-employed and the formerly self-employed report significantly higher mean total debt/income ratios and nonmortgage debt/income ratios than do the pure wage earners, although the ratios for the currently self-employed are insignificantly higher than those for the formerly self-employed.

TABLE 6.4. Total and Nonmortgage Debt/Income Ratios for Pure Wage Earners, Currently Self-Employed, and Formerly Self-Employed Debtors

	Total Debt/ Income Ratio	Total Nonmortgage Debt/Income Ratio
Pure wage earners	2.5	1.4
Currently self-employed	8.6	5.6
Formerly self-employed	6.1	4.2

Source: Consumer Bankruptcy Project.

A one-way analysis of variance showed that the unsecured debt of the currently and formerly self-employed was statistically different from that of the wage earners but not from each other. An analysis of variance of total debt, secured debt, and assets showed that all three groups were significantly different from one another, but in every case the formerly self-employed occupied a position that was closer to that of the currently self-employed than it was to that of the pure wage earners.

TABLE 6.5. Debts and Assets for Pure Wage Earners, Currently Self-Employed, and Formerly Self-Employed Debtors

	Total Debt	Unsecured Debt	Secured Debt	Assets
Pure wage earners	$26,753	$ 9,827	$16,850	$22,835
Currently self-employed	97,897	40,455	57,813	73,123

TABLE 6.5 (*Continued*)

	Total Debt	Unsecured Debt	Secured Debt	Assets
Formerly self-employed	72,745	35,522	37,223	36,517

Source: Consumer Bankruptcy Project.

The pure wage earners and the formerly self-employed are similar in family income. This makes sense, because the formerly self-employed are earning like other wage earners but carrying debts like other self-employed workers. The mean family income of pure wage earners at $15,642 was statistically indistinguishable from that of the formerly self-employed at $15,524. See the discussion at note 10, where we compare all wage earners (including the formerly self-employed) with the currently self-employed.

7. When we could not verify that a debtor was or had been self-employed recently by the forms in the file, we left that debtor classified as a "wage earner." As a consequence, all debtors with ambiguous or missing information on self-employment are lumped with the wage earners, which probably overstates that group and understates self-employment.

We also undercount self-employed individuals by eliminating debtors in Chapter 11. Individuals choose Chapter 11 largely because the size of their debts makes them ineligible for Chapter 13. Some debtors, like the Millers, give up the business completely and file Chapter 7. In Chapter 7 they face no debt limitations. But those with large debts who try to maintain the business will end up in Chapter 11. While we believe that it was sound judgment to eliminate the individual debtors in Chapter 11 to understand the "typical" debtor, we recognize that the debtors who have been eliminated are more likely to be running their own businesses. The consequence of eliminating them is once again to understate the proportion of self-employed debtors in bankruptcy.

A number of debtors in our sample went into bankruptcy some months after the failures of their employers' businesses. This chain reaction, in which one failure triggers a later bankruptcy by other businesses and employees, is beyond the scope of this work. But some court clerks considered this a "business bankruptcy" and some readers might consider this another source of undercount.

8. There is a small, growing empirical literature on farm bankruptcies. One source suggests that the current fiscal crisis began in 1981, which would explain our scarcity of farmer petitioners. J. P. Smith, The Social and Economic Correlates of Bankruptcy During the Farm Fiscal Crisis, 1970–1987, 12 Mid-American Review of Sociology 35–53 (Spring 1987). For a detailed analysis of farmers in our sample, see L. W. Potter, A. Singer, T. Sullivan, "Big Is In, Small Is Out: The Crisis of the Small Farmer in Consumer Bankruptcy," paper presented at the 1986 annual meeting of the Rural Sociological Society, Salt Lake City, Utah.

9. Professionals who petition for bankruptcy often attract media attention. See, e.g., L. Simross, "An Endangered Species," Los Angeles Times, v:1 (April 6, 1988), about a lawyer specializing in discrimination suits and the economics of law practice.

10. Table 6.6 presents income data for current wage earners and currently self-employed. Among current wage earners are some formerly self-employed persons.

11. The income figures presented here are family figures, just as we used in earlier chapters. Among the self-employed, however, the methods of computing income varied a bit within Chapter 7. In Chapter 7, the debtor declares his financial circumstances

TABLE 6.6. Distribution of Income, Current Wage Earners and Currently Self-Employed[a]

Distribution	Income	Assets	Total Debt	Secured Debt	Unsecured Debt
Wage Earners					
Mean	$15,630	$24,309	$ 31,696	$19,030	$12,590
s.d.	9,122	28,979	44,482	31,449	26,353
25th percentile	9,500	2,496	9,215	2,178	3,672
Median	14,811	11,579	18,618	8,694	6,510
75th percentile	21,000	40,700	38,983	27,018	12,225
N	1,198	1,336	1,340	1,346	1,339
Missing	148	10	6	0	7
Self-Employed					
Mean	17,743	73,124	97,897	57,813	40,455
s.d.	14,511	78,226	89,090	67,015	52,240
25th percentile	7,000	13,779	31,816	8,530	9,906
Median	15,169	54,210	64,566	34,962	24,137
75th percentile	25,000	98,118	139,752	81,360	49,914
N	19	154	156	155	156
Missing	65	2	0	1	0
Statistical Test					
t-value	−1.37	−7.68*	−9.15*	−7.12*	−6.57*

[a]Cases with extreme values on assets, total debt, or income are removed.

*Significant at $p \leq 0.05$

Source: Consumer Bankruptcy Project.

on Form 7 (for debtors not engaged in business) or on Form 8 (for debtors engaged in business). It would seem logical for all our self-employed debtors to file Form 8, but many of them instead filed Form 7 and a few cases included both a Form 7 and a Form 8. Where Form 7 was available, we estimated annual income by adding together the primary filer's income in the preceding year, the primary filer's "other income" in the preceding year (for instance, transfer payments such as unemployment or alimony), and any other income reported by the second filer in a joint petition. Form 8, however, asks no questions about profits, salaries paid to the family, or any direct income question; instead, it asks only about "other income" of the filers. As a result, we are able to report income for only a portion of our self-employed sample: 91, or 58% of the self-employed, reported a usable income figure.

12. The forms in bankruptcy are ill-suited to reporting the financial affairs of the self-employed, but the lawyers or others filling out the forms also appear to be confused. Many regard "self-employed" as a sufficient description of the means of livelihood, so that information on occupation was available for only 83 debtors and information on industry was available for only 88 debtors. The current status of the business was often difficult to determine as well. Another 26 debtors reported that their business is now defunct, but they are still self-employed, perhaps in a new incarnation of the old business. In at least a few instances, we were aware that the case preceding or following the one we drew in the sample was our debtor's bankruptcy filing for a corporation or perhaps a partner's filing in bankruptcy.

Using the data available, we repeated the tests used in Chapter Five to determine why self-employed debtors have lower incomes than the CPS self-employed. Is it their industry and occupation composition, or their low rates of earnings within those categories that accounts for the lower incomes of the debtor sample? One way to examine this question is through direct standardization. As Table 6.7 shows, applying the CPS industrial composition of the self-employed to our debtors' incomes would lower their incomes by about $1,000. That is, using our debtors' current rate of earnings in every industry but changing their industrial composition to put more of them in agriculture and construction would actually lower their incomes. By contrast, if we kept the debtors' current industries but let them earn at the rate of the CPS sample, the debtors' mean income would rise by about $3,000 ($20,856–17,595).

Turning to the same exercise with occupation, we find substantially the same results. Give our debtors the occupational profile of the self-employed nationally, and their income would drop by about $1,900. Despite the fact that this control would create more well-paid doctors and lawyers, it would also "create" more farmers and construction contractors, hence the net decline in income. On the other hand, if our debtors could somehow manage in their current occupations to earn what the national sample earned, their incomes would rise almost $4,000 ($21,441–17,516).

Both these standardizations suggest that the debtors' industrial/occupational location does not explain their lower incomes. Instead, these data imply that it is their relative rates of earnings *within each category* that account for their lower incomes.

If we decompose the earnings difference to partition the difference between indus-

TABLE 6.7. Decomposition and Standardization of Income Differences for Currently Self-Employed in Bankruptcy Sample[a] and National Sample

Bankruptcy Grand Mean:	$17,257	N = 66
National Grand Mean:	22,291	N = 593,544
Decomposition		
Difference		$ 5,034
Difference due to		
Composition		−3,757
Rates		−9,633
Interaction		8,356
Standardization by Industry		
National sample mean income		$22,291
Standardized to bankruptcy sample composition		20,856
Bankruptcy sample mean income		17,595
Standardized to national sample composition		16,416
Standardization by Occupation		
National sample mean income		$22,291
Standardized to bankruptcy sample composition		21,441
Bankruptcy sample mean income		17,516
Standardized to national sample composition		15,642

[a]Cases with extreme values on assets, total debt, or income are removed.

Source: Consumer Bankruptcy Project; March 1981 Current Population Survey.

try/occupation location and earnings rates, we find the differences presented in Table 6.7. The overall $5,000 gap in earnings is partly attributable to composition ($3,800 of the gap) but more attributable to rates ($9,600 of the gap). This overexplains the gap because of an interaction effect ($3,757 + $9,633 = $13,390). When the interaction term is added to the equation, it subtracts $8,400 and reduces the gap to the original $5,000. An interaction effect of the opposite sign is counterintuitive. What it means in this case is that in the bankrupt debtor sample, there is an offsetting effect such that some industry/occupation groups that are relatively large in the debtor sample are also relatively high in earnings. The best case of this is probably the self-employed truck drivers, who are relatively overrepresented in the debtor sample and who are also earning more than their counterparts in the CPS sample. By the same token, some low-earning industry/occupation groups, such as self-employed farmers, are underrepresented in the debtor sample but are a large part of the national sample. They too contribute to the interaction effect. The large interaction effect helps explain the equivocal effects of composition that we have seen. In the direct standardization, the CPS composition actually *reduced* the income of the debtors. In the decomposition, compositional differences contributed to the *higher* earnings of the CPS sample. How could composition do both of these things? The interaction effect shows us that composition makes a little difference, but what is more important is that the CPS has a large number of low-earning specialties absent in bankruptcy, and bankruptcy has a large number of relatively high-earning specialties that are proportionally less important in the national sample.

These results, then, confirm that the self-employed debtors as a group earn less than the national average principally because of their lower earnings within most categories. These results are analogous to those that we earlier reported for the entire sample, but with the interesting twists we have noted.

We repeated these analyses using personal work-related income rather than family income. This change reduced mean income in CPS drastically, from over $22,000 to only $14,500. In the CDS sample, income dropped from a mean $17,300 to about $14,600.

Standardization analysis showed little effect of occupation and industry. This finding shows that the self-employed in the general population apparently have a "cushion" of other income not available to the bankrupt self-employed. This cushion amounts to about $7,000 at the mean, or roughly one-third of family income, compared to only $2,000 for the bankrupt self-employed. We discuss further the significance of other family workers in Chapter Eight.

13. Because the primary usefulness of debt/income ratios is measurement of a debtor's capacity to repay, the text table is the most relevant one. For a comparison, however, we set forth here the debt/income ratios for current wage earners (including former entrepreneurs) and for the currently self-employed:

TABLE 6.8. Distribution of Debt/Income Ratios for Current Wage Earners and the Currently Self-Employed

	Debt/Income Ratio	
Distribution	Current Wage Earners	Currently Self-Employed
Mean	2.82	8.61
s.d.	8.91	22.43
25th percentile	0.67	1.28

TABLE 6.8 (*Continued*)

Distribution	Debt/Income Ratio: Current Wage Earners	Debt/Income Ratio: Currently Self-Employed
Median	1.36	2.37
75th percentile	2.48	7.66
N	1,159	82
Missing	187	74
Statistical Test		
t-value	−2.33*	

[a]Cases with extreme values on assets, total debt, or income are removed.
*$p \leq 0.05$
Source: Consumer Bankruptcy Project.

14. In our preliminary report, we reported self-employed debt as a percentage of all debt, including the "outliers," or extreme cases, and it was even greater: 34%. T. A. Sullivan, E. Warren, J. L. Westbrook, Folklore and Facts: A Preliminary Report from the Consumer Bankruptcy Project, 60 American Bankruptcy Law Journal 293, 302 (1986). To maintain comparability among the analyses in this book, we have removed the outliers.

15. As we noted in Chapter Two, most aggregate analyses have been done using Administrative Office figures that muddle consumer and business cases.

16. Reports of means, medians, standard deviations, and quartiles expose this problem somewhat. These fuller reports describe something closer to reality. We use the descriptions of central tendency, medians or means, to approximate the "average" debtor.

17. For example, debtors whose debts are primarily business obligations are exempt from the "substantial abuse" test in Chapter 7. 11 U.S.C. §707(b).

18. Congress put a seven-year sunset provision in the current Chapter 12 so that Congress will be forced to reevaluate the need for a special farmers-only bankruptcy scheme. Some in Congress seem aware of the possibility of special help for special groups, but they may rightly be worried about opening yet another Pandora's box of special-interest legislation.

19. It is also possible that many entrepreneurs would not benefit from special help. Professor Lynn LoPucki's study of business bankruptcies concludes that by the time of bankruptcy filing, most small businesses are beyond any reasonable chance of successfully recovering. L. LoPucki, A General Theory of the Dynamics of the State Remedies/Bankruptcy System, 1982 Wisconsin Law Review 311.

20. Both businesses, according to legend, were started in a home garage only a few years before they were traded on the Big Board.

7

The Homeowners

Home ownership is the usual signal that someone has arrived—both financially and socially. Our finding that homeowners are a sizable proportion of bankruptcy petitioners raises both social and financial issues. The social significance lies once again in the similarity of the bankrupt debtors to mainstream Americans. The financial significance is the commitment of an important number of debtors to long-term mortgages in the face of powerful, imminent economic instabilities.

Homeowners Are the Backbone of America—And of Bankruptcy

Home ownership has long been regarded as a mark of social, economic, and political stability. Thomas Jefferson argued that an independent yeomanry, whose independence was founded on their ownership of land, was an essential bulwark against tyranny and corruption, and the only true foundation of republican virtue. As America grew, the lure of cheap land drew settlers west. As towns grew, propertyowners became responsible for providing basic social services through property taxation, which was the primary source of local government revenue well into the twentieth century. Land ownership conferred status and satisfied dreams, even when the plot was small and the cabin rude.

Home ownership continues to be a telling indicator of status and responsibility. Everything from taxes to insurance rates is priced to favor the homeowner over profit-motivated landlords. Neighborhoods are judged by the proportion of the property that is owner-occupied, and many creditors decide to lend when they see a "yes" next to their query about home ownership. In much of America, becoming a homeowner takes on a social significance that is second only to taking a job.

The social importance of home ownership derives in part from its economic importance. The homeowner owns an asset—a nice home that might appreciate beyond the homeowner's wildest dreams, implicitly proving the homeowner to be both a sound financial manager and a social pillar of the community. Nevertheless, most homeowners face relentless mortgage payments, upkeep, and repairs that sometimes cannot be deferred. The homeowner who goes into bankruptcy is the middle-class American who has precisely what everyone else is working for, but who is in deep financial trouble nonetheless.

More than half of the bankrupt debtors—52%—are homeowners, compared with 64% of the general population. Just over 7.5% of the bankrupt homeowners own mobile homes, about the same proportion as in the general population.[1] The bankrupt debtors' homes have a median value of $35,000, which does not suggest a palace, but the mean value is $50,000, which is not too different from $56,100, the average home value for all American homeowners. This chapter explores the circumstances of the homeowners in bankruptcy, people for whom the American dream has soured.

A Homeowner's Bankruptcy

Joel Wesley Hammond, Sr., and his wife, Sally Elizabeth Hammond, filed Chapter 7 bankruptcy in Pennsylvania. They list their home, located on a corner lot of Lackawanna Township, as a two-and-a-half story brick and stucco dwelling with a one-story frame garage. They give the value of their home as $45,000. The Hammonds list many other assets, which do not add up to much. Theirs is one of those cases in which the lawyer or the debtors are compulsive, listing everything. They own $3,756 in household goods, detailed and valued down to a rolling pin ($5.00) and seven men's undershirts ($0.25 each). They also own a seven-year-old Jeep worth $2,000. Mr. and Mrs. Hammond record separately each of their pictures, claiming "1 large portrait (Jesus) $30.00, 1 medium portrait (Jesus) $20.00, (4) 11″ × 15″ portraits (Jesus) $100.00."

The Hammonds list familiar consumer debts. They owe the power company, the gas company, and the telephone company for about one to two months' service, for a total unsecured debt of $363.29. They owe property taxes to the school district, the county, and the township, for a total of $437.24. And there are Pennsylvania taxes: each of them owes an occupation tax of $81.00 apiece, and a personal tax of $15.75. Their tax debts total $630.74. The Hammonds also owe $850 on a personal loan from Reliance Consumer Discount Company. This loan is secured by a lien on their household furnishings.

The Hammonds' big debt is their home mortgage, and they have had an uneasy relationship with their mortgage company, Prince Deposit Bank. The Hammonds claim a principal loan amount due of $28,500 (evidently the amount originally borrowed), but they list the current balance on this mortgage as $31,552.10. This sum suggests they have several arrearages, incurring charges for more interest and penalties, and that missed payments have increased the total amount owed. The Hammonds have a second mortgage on their home, also from Prince Deposit. They borrowed another $3,840.34 on this second mortgage, and now it will take $4,118.88 to pay back the bank, suggesting arrearages on the second mortgage as well. The Hammonds indicate they have been sued once, a mortgage foreclosure action by Prince Deposit Bank when they were behind in their payments. Now, however, the Hammonds and Prince Deposit are evidently working things out. Mr. and Mrs. Hammond plan to keep their home and continue payments after their Chapter 7 is complete, and Prince Deposit raises no objections. The debtors and the creditor have apparently agreed that the mortgage will survive bankruptcy and the debtors will keep the house as long as they pay, all without any formal reaffirmation agreement.

The files give some indication of the Hammonds' problems. They fail to list their 1979 incomes, but there were evidently serious financial difficulties in 1980. Mr. Hammond worked only the last two months of the year, earning $2,000. He received another $5,000 in "no-fault benefits," a somewhat cryptic reference that suggests an injury or accident. Mrs. Hammond worked part-time for six months for the school district and earned $985.50. Mr. Hammond indicates he now has a job as an inventory control clerk with the school district and has been there for ten months; he earned $4,088 during the first eight months of 1981. Mrs. Hammond now lists herself as a housewife, and there is no indication she plans to work outside the home.

The Hammonds' first and second mortgages were incurred in 1979, suggesting that only one year before their troubles began they had passed fairly stringent financial screening. The Hammonds had borrowed over $7,000 from a Household Finance Consumer Discount Company during 1979, but they paid off the balance due in a single lump $4,275.58 in 1980. Perhaps this payment represents financial health in part of 1980, or perhaps the Hammonds passed on the $5,000 no-fault payment to the finance company, whose loan kept them going while they waited for the payment.

When they file bankruptcy, the Hammonds appear solvent on a balance sheet. Their combined assets total $53,339.50, while their debts add up to $38,499.62—making them one of the "richest" families we studied. Their wealth, of course, is largely the equity in their home, that is, the difference between the market value of the home and the outstanding mortgages. They have only a very modest amount of personal possessions.

It is interesting to speculate on the effect of the Chapter 7 bankruptcy discharge on the Hammonds. They had less than $400 in dischargeable, unsecured debt—less than the attorney charged for the bankruptcy case. There is no indication that they were able to discharge their $630 worth of tax debts nor that their attorney challenged Reliance Financial's $850 secured claim against their furniture.[2] Even if they had eliminated their tax debts and the finance company claim, those debts totaled less than $1,500. This file raises a troubling question: Why file for bankruptcy, why suffer social stigma and a seriously damaged credit rating, for so little apparent benefit?

The most likely answer is that the Hammonds' attorney advised a bankruptcy filing to stop Prince Deposit Bank's foreclosure action. Once the foreclosure was halted, the parties may have used the opportunity to work out a payment schedule privately. This is an especially likely possibility because the Hammonds were evidently back on schedule with their payments by the time of filing, and their "agreement" with Prince Deposit may have been simply to continue paying on schedule. In that case, there would have been no need for court intervention.

Bankruptcy might have bought the Hammonds some negotiating room with their mortgage lender, but they received little debt relief from their filing. Bankruptcy was just a procedural device that enabled them to negotiate a way to keep their home.

Basic Economic Comparisons

Homeowners and Nonowners

Homeowners and nonhomeowners in bankruptcy have distinct financial profiles. Table 7.1 shows that homeowners have higher incomes and greater assets than the nonowners in bankruptcy. The median income for homeowners is $17,000; the nonowners have a median income of $12,500. Median total assets for homeowners are $43,000, while median assets for nonowners are only a fraction as large at $3,000. The higher incomes are consistent with the screening these debtors survived in applying for home mortgages; a qualifying income is necessary for a lender to approve a mortgage. The higher assets—nearly 15 times higher for homeowners—reflect the fact that the most valuable asset most consumers will ever purchase is their home.

The bad news for homeowners comes in the debt columns, where the burden of debt offsets the high assets. The total debt burdens for homeowners are about three times those of nonowners. The secured debt burdens reflect the large home mortgages; homeowners list median secured debts of $29,500, while nonowners list median secured debts of $3,100. However, even the nonmortgage secured debt of homeowners is higher.[3] Unsecured debts between the two groups are much closer but still significantly different. Median unsecured debts for homeowners are $7,600, while nonowners' median unsecured debt is $6,600.

The debt/income ratios present the same picture. Total debts compared to incomes show the homeowners in considerably worse shape, with mean debt/income ratios of 4.7 compared with 1.8 for the nonowners. Without the home mortgage, homeowners and nonowners look remarkably alike in the relationship between their debts and their incomes. The nonmortgage debt/income ratios of the two groups are statistically indistinguishable, with nonowners

TABLE 7.1. Distribution of Income, Assets, and Debts for Bankruptcy Petitioners, by Home Ownership Status[a]

Distribution	Income	Assets	Total Debt	Secured Debt	Unsecured Debt	Nonmortgage Secured Debt
Homeowners						
Mean	$17,616	$51,210	$57,965	$40,732	$17,314	$10,041
s.d.	9,899	43,082	62,683	46,930	30,414	27,618
25th percentile	10,600	25,564	24,148	16,419	3,703	341
Median	17,000	43,050	39,238	29,477	7,632	3,341
75th percentile	23,724	64,100	64,100	48,631	16,792	7,688
N	615	715	717	716	716	716
Missing	102	2	0	1	1	1
Problem[b]	66	66	66	66	66	66
Nonowners						
Mean	$13,739	$ 5,900	$18,720	$ 5,401	$13,304	$ 5,401
s.d.	8,567	15,733	32,441	10,421	30,444	10,421
25th percentile	8,066	1,030	6,846	0	3,903	0
Median	12,500	2,975	10,865	3,107	6,640	3,107
75th percentile	18,000	6,541	17,862	6,795	12,104	6,795
N	617	716	717	719	717	719
Missing	102	3	2	0	2	0
Statistical Test						
t-value	7.35**	26.42**	14.89**	19.67**	2.48*	4.21**

[a]Cases with extreme values on assets, total debt, or income are removed.

[b]Petitioners whose claim of home ownership cannot be verified are removed from this statistical analysis.

*$p \leq 0.05$

**$p \leq 0.01$

Source: Consumer Bankruptcy Project.

owing debts equal to about 1.8 years' income and homeowners owing nonmortgage debt equal to about 2 years' income.

The Hammonds got a boost in their net worth from the equity in their home. Most homeowners follow the same pattern, showing a little better net worth picture as a group than do nonowners. But the difference for most debtors—homeowners and nonowners alike—is simply one of how far below zero they find themselves. The mean net worth of a nonowner is $−16,300, and the mean net worth for a homeowner is $−14,000, a difference that is not statistically different. Homeowners may do slightly better, but both groups are still drowning. Home equity values, like larger incomes, are largely offset by greater debt burdens. For homeowners to show large negative net worth while they own a substantial, often appreciating asset is one measure of the depths of their financial trouble.

One source of cash available only to a homeowner is a second mortgage. In Texas, debtors are permitted to encumber their homes with second or third mortgages only for home improvements. But no other state in the country is so restrictive, and in Illinois and Pennsylvania debtors are free to borrow as much as lenders wish to lend, using their homes as collateral. In Illinois and Pennsylvania, 32.6% of the homeowners in bankruptcy report at least two separate mortgages on their homes, and 6.2% report three or more. There is some reason to believe that this number understates the proportion of debtors who took out second and third mortgages.[4] Second mortgages whittle away the residual value in a home, but even with second mortgages an Illinois or Pennsylvania debtor, on average, still had a home worth $9,424 more than the combined mortgages.

The basic financial comparison shows two groups in bankruptcy: nonhomeowners with lower earnings and lower assets and homeowners with somewhat higher earnings and assets—and considerably higher debts as well. The data comparing homeowners with nonhomeowners in bankruptcy show two somewhat different groups in relatively similar states of financial collapse.

Bankrupt Homeowners and All Homeowners

Homeowners in bankruptcy carry larger mortgages than the homeowning population in general. The mean home mortgage in the general population is $27,100.[5] The median, not inflated by the few really large mortgages at the top of the range, is $21,000. For debtors in bankruptcy, however, the mean is $29,400 and the median is $24,200, both higher than for the general population.

The relative impact of these home mortgages is even greater than the direct comparison suggests. Not only do bankrupt debtors have higher mortgages, but they must pay them from lower incomes. In the general population, the average income for a person with a mortgage of $30,000 is $45,000.[6] This is a synthetic mortgage debt/income ratio of 0.67. (We call it synthetic because it is constructed from national group means, not from debtor-by-debtor analysis.) In bankruptcy the mean mortgage is $29,400, but the mean homeowner income is only $17,600. Comparing these two means yields a synthetic mortgage debt/income ratio of 1.70.

The homeowner in bankruptcy supporting a mortgage about the same size as the homeowner in the general population is making the mortgage payments from an income that is far lower than the income of the counterpart homeowner not in bankruptcy. The burden of the mortgage debt on this average homeowner–debtor is almost three times larger. This gives some idea of the extraordinary burden a home mortgage has become for many debtors in bankruptcy when they can no longer balance their incomes and debt obligations.[7]

In fact, the bankruptcy data are worse than these synthetic debt/income ratios suggest. We compare mean mortgages and mean incomes for the bankrupt debtors only to make the comparison with the nationally reported data. But when we compute mortgage income ratios for all the homeowners in bankruptcy on a debtor-by-debtor basis, the mean mortgage/income ratio jumps to 2.6. This means that for the typical homeowner in bankruptcy, mortgage debt alone is more than two and a half years' income.

In the general population, about 9.8% of all homeowners put second mortgages of any size on their homes,[8] compared with 32.6% of the bankrupt homeowners living in states permitting second mortgages. Second mortgages generally have a much shorter payback period than first mortgages, so that a second mortgage is usually a larger monthly burden than the amount outstanding initially suggests. This intensifies the squeeze on the debtor. Any mortgage—first, second, or tenth—will cause the debtor to lose the home if it is not paid in full and nearly on time. Second mortgages are short-term, higher payment obligations, which force debtors to pay an even larger share of their income to keep their homes.

These data suggest that while the bankrupt debtors' homes may be their biggest assets, often they are also a bigger burden for them to maintain. Independent of their other debt problems, bankrupt homeowners as a group face a much tighter financial squeeze just to meet their mortgage obligations so they can stay in their homes.

Signs of Debtor Determination

Debtors who want to keep their homes must pay their home mortgages—and the bankruptcy files are full of people determined to keep their homes. Attorneys and judges we interviewed talked about how fiercely the homeowners fought. Just how far homeowners will go to protect their homes is confirmed by an interesting source: the errors in mortgage reporting.

We noted in Chapter Four that errors in data reporting necessarily introduce some bias into the data. Ample evidence suggests that reporting errors almost always understate debt. We believe this understatement to be particularly acute with home mortgages.

Debtors are required to list all their debts so that the court can notify all creditors of a debtor's bankruptcy. There are no exceptions, and a debtor who fails to comply risks possible perjury charges and denial of discharge. Most debtors report their home mortgages, and their reports give us the data from which we draw the grim inferences about homeowners' financial circumstances. These files show substantial home mortgages that debtors are supporting on meager incomes—with no indication that they have missed a single payment. A number of debtors, however, fail to report their home mortgages, and a number of attorneys and judges evidently look the other way when presented with obviously incomplete files.

Ten percent of the debtors in bankruptcy who own their own homes—80 homeowners—do not report any mortgage debt. We were so astonished by this finding that we pulled each file and examined it in detail. In 61 cases these debtors make inconsistent reports: They list no home mortgage in their schedule of debts, but elsewhere in the files the debtors indicate they will be paying their mortgages "outside the Chapter 13 plan" or they are current on all their mortgage payments, so there is "no need to contact bank about the home loan." The remaining 19 give no indication of a mortgage, and there are no inconsistencies evident within the papers filed.[9]

Many of the usual reasons for failing to list a debt—forgetting about it, uncertainty about the identity of the creditor—do not apply to home mortgages. In at least 61 of the 80 cases, the inconsistent information provided shows that the debtor remembered.

So why is there no mortgage listed? Attorneys and judges explained that some debtors do not want their mortgage companies to hear about the bankruptcy. These debtors are generally current on their payments, and they do not want any trouble. Although few mortgage lenders would foreclose a mortgage held by someone now in bankruptcy if all payments were current, debtors still worry.[10] Both the attorneys and the courts are indulgent enough on the point that some debtors passed through bankruptcy with their files uncorrected.[11] And even when the homeowners correctly report their home mortgages, sometimes the mortgage company's name and address are deleted from the files or from the mailing list for the notifications to creditors. After all, if the debtor will keep paying this particular debt, why stir up trouble?

Some debtors, such as the Hammonds, are in bankruptcy to deal directly with their mortgages, holding off a foreclosure while they negotiate a settlement or making up their late payments through their bankruptcy plans. Others, however, have evidently avoided trouble with their home lenders, and they intend to continue to be model borrowers regardless of the remainder of their economic condition. "Save the house" seems to be their clearest goal in bankruptcy, even if they are otherwise crippled by their financial circumstances.

How Can Homeowners Be in So Much Trouble?

The staggering debt burdens of homeowners in bankruptcy make for tales of deep worry and enormous struggle as debtors try to keep their homes. But they also raise a puzzling question: Why are putatively successful people in so much trouble? The widespread perception of homeowners as financially stable people is backed up by a compelling piece of evidence: People who borrow money to buy houses undergo the most rigorous financial scrutiny most consumers will ever face. Most mortgage lenders are conscious of their borrowers' overall debt burdens and concerned that they not take on more than they can reasonably handle. The homeowners passed the screening.[12]

The discrepancy between once passing a rigorous credit test and ending up in bankruptcy can be explained by the hypothesis that the bankrupt homeowners are people with once-reasonable debt burdens and subsequent income interruptions. Mr. and Mrs. Hammond, if not typical in all respects, were part of a pattern that reappeared in our files. The Hammonds owned a home worth

$45,000, which they very much wanted to keep. They owed principal mortgage debts before arrearages and penalties of $28,000. This mortgage was incurred just two years before the bankruptcy filing. We do not know what their income was when they got the mortgage, but we can be fairly sure that the lender required a stable income source.

By 1980, just a year after incurring their mortgage, the Hammonds' combined earned income was $2,000. They already had a second mortgage on their home, a "personal loan" of $4,840, and a $7,283 loan from a finance company that the Hammonds repaid before they declared bankruptcy.

We know from their income reports that the Hammonds had suffered serious work interruption the year before their bankruptcy filing. They made a substantial payment on their finance company loan, but they fell into trouble with their mortgage lender. Mr. Hammond found work, although his income may still have been lower than it was the year of his mortgage approval. After he returned to work, Mrs. Hammond either quit or lost her job. Ten months after Mr. Hammond returned to work, and one month after Mrs. Hammond's employment ended, the Hammonds filed for bankruptcy, eliminated many of their other debts, and focused their energies on trying to repay their home mortgage.

Although not all files give so much detail about when mortgages have been incurred or what debts have been paid off before the bankruptcy filing, elements of the Hammonds' story are repeated frequently through the files. As we discussed in Chapter Five, a large proportion of bankrupt debtors show sharp fluctuations in their incomes, and homeowners are no exception to this finding.

From data on the incomes of homeowners filing in Chapter 7 one and two years before bankruptcy, we find a similar pattern of losing and gaining for homeowners and nonowners. More than 42% of the homeowners and 47% of the nonowners had a shift in income of at least 10% between the second and first year preceding bankruptcy.[13] About 22% of all the homeowners and 26% of the nonowners had an income change of more than 30%. Fluctuating incomes affect homeowners as much as they affect other bankrupt debtors.

Another explanation for the presence of so many homeowners in bankruptcy lies in the substantial number of multiple mortgages on their homes. The high proportion of multiple mortgages suggests that homeowners in bankruptcy may have tried to forestall financial collapse by borrowing against their homes. By using a second or third mortgage to raise cash, a homeowner can continue to feed a family and meet payments even when income is interrupted. The bankruptcy files may be, in part, the stories of debtors who planned to use debt during a rough time, but whose debts mounted too quickly until the risk of losing their homes overwhelmed them. The files do not give enough detail to be certain, and for some debtors the inference is clearly not true, but the high proportion of multiple mortgages (32.6%) in Illinois and Pennsylvania suggests some debtors fall into this pattern.

Similarly, the relatively high nonmortgage debt of homeowners may indicate efforts to finance their consumption while freeing up cash for mortgage payments. Debtors may charge other goods during hard times to make sure there will be cash for the monthly house payments and file bankruptcy once the debt puts their homes at risk. Or the homeowners may once have passed credit checks with ease, then amassed consumer debts they could not possibly repay—only to flee to bankruptcy when the combination became unmanageable. The data are sketchy, and the moral overtones not entirely clear.

Homeowners and Entrepreneurs

The complex relationship between financial stability and home ownership shows up among debtors who, according to many of our analyses, are in the worst shape in bankruptcy. Nearly three-quarters—70.8%—of the currently self-employed in bankruptcy are also homeowners.[14] There is a higher rate of home ownership among the self-employed than among wage earners in bankruptcy (50%) or home ownership in the general population (64%).

Home ownership and self-employment may go hand in hand for a variety of reasons. People who want to own their own businesses may also be people who want to own their own homes. In addition, or perhaps alternatively, the correlation may be financial. Home ownership gives a business lender an important source of collateral. In states where second mortgages are unrestricted, it is common for a bank to lend an entrepreneur the money to start a business only if the businessperson will give a second mortgage on the family home. As one banker explained to us, "It makes good sense. We may get something out of [the home] if the business fails. But even if we don't, a second mortgage gives incentive. This guy knows he can't just walk away from the business." Without a home, it may be harder for a would-be entrepreneur to get a start—hence the high correlation between home ownership and entrepreneurship.

We may see more homeowning entrepreneurs in bankruptcy because the double risks of home ownership and small business ownership put these people at disproportionate risk for financial collapse. Mortgage payments must be made regularly, even if business is slow. Homeowners cannot easily cut personal expenses by moving to a cheaper apartment. As we saw in the last chapter, entrepreneurs have taken on huge credit obligations, and these obligations often deplete their equity in their homes. With more obligations, fewer opportunities to cut costs, and multiple pledges against their homes, these debtors have fewer options if their businesses start to falter. They might survive some portion of these risks, but the combined burden may explain why so many homeowner–entrepreneurs find themselves in bankruptcy.

Comparative studies of the self-employed in and out of bankruptcy would be necessary to provide definitive answers to these questions. But the possible links between home ownership and small business failures emphasize the conclusion that the relationship between home ownership and financial collapse is not straightforward, and that home ownership does not insulate anyone from catastrophe.

Homeowners and Bankruptcy Law

In bankruptcy, as in so many other areas of the law, special provisions apply exclusively to homeowners. In the upside-down world of bankruptcy, the twist is that these special sections make life harder for the homeowner.

Home mortgages are not treated in the same way as other secured debts. Both Chapter 7 and Chapter 13 offer the debtor some help with most secured creditors, such as a car dealer or a furniture company that kept a security interest in the goods sold. A debtor who owes on a car, for example, can terminate the car lender's lien in bankruptcy by paying the full value of the car, even if it is less than the outstanding loan amount. The remaining loan balance can be discharged along with the other unsecured debts. On a $10,000 car loan, for example, secured by a car worth only $6,000, a debtor who can come up with $6,000 in cash can keep the car and discharge the balance. In Chapter 13, a debtor owing on the same car can reschedule payments, making smaller payments over a longer time, and the total payments need add up only to the value of the car ($6,000) plus interest. The remaining $4,000 in debt is discharged. Even when the car is worth more than the loan, the Chapter 13 debtor can get a break. A loan due to be paid off in a year or two can be stretched to three to five years under the Chapter 13 plan, sometimes at reduced interest rates. Although both Chapter 7 and Chapter 13 contemplate some repayment for secured creditors, the timing and amount of the repayment may vary dramatically from the original agreement.

The home mortgage lender, however, enjoys greater protection in bankruptcy than *any* other lender. The Bankruptcy Code specifically exempts home mortgages from the readjustments that can be made on all other secured loans. Homeowners who take out mortgages vow to repay that mortgage on time and in full or lose the home—even in bankruptcy.

The one exception to this rigid rule is found in Chapter 13. There, by court interpretation of some ambiguous language rather than by clear legislative prescription, the homeowner is given one break: If the owner is behind in mortgage payments, Chapter 13 will permit the debtor to forestall foreclosure by proposing a plan to pay the accumulated arrearages plus interest plus the regular monthly payments as they accrue. In the meantime, the debtor must make all regular mortgage payments on time, or the lender can foreclose.

The homes of bankrupt debtors are still not entirely safe, even if the debtors manage to keep up their mortgage payments. Even if the mortgage lender can be satisfied, the debtors face losing their homes because other creditors want them sold to satisfy the debts owed to them. Once again, bankruptcy provides very little additional protection beyond state law.

Unpaid general creditors can bring actions in state court requiring debtors to sell their homes to pay their creditors. Texas forbids this action under most circumstances, and all states restrict it.[15] Generally a debtor is entitled to a certain amount of equity in a homestead free and clear of claims of creditors other than a mortgage holder of tax liens. That amount is the homestead exemption. An unsecured creditor cannot force a home sale unless the home is worth more than the home mortgage plus the debtors' exemption amount. By law, the home mortgage always gets paid first, and the debtors keep from the remainder an amount equal to the exemption in that state.

The three states we studied had three different homestead exemptions, and bankruptcy laws incorporate the state exemption schemes. As a practical matter, the Texas debtors could keep their homes from their general creditors, regardless of the home's value or the size of the mortgage.[16] The Illinois debtors could keep only $10,000 in value from a home. If the value of an Illinois home exceeds the mortgage by more than $10,000, Illinois law requires that the home be sold to satisfy the other creditors. Because Pennsylvania debtors may use the federal exemption, a single person can keep $7,500 in home equity and a married couple can keep $15,000. Thus a home belonging to a couple in bankruptcy in Pennsylvania would be sold only if the value of the house exceeded the mortgage by more than $15,000 (e.g., if a house with a $30,000 mortgage were worth more than $45,000).[17]

Bankruptcy does provide one additional protection for homeowners. For a family that files Chapter 13 and keeps up the house payments, there will be no home foreclosure. Even if they have $50,000 in value in the homestead and live in Illinois, they can keep their home. But there is a catch. The Chapter 13 payments must be at least equal to the amount of equity that exceeds the state law exemption. In Illinois, for example, that means that a family with a $50,000 home and a $30,000 mortgage has excess equity equal to $10,000 ($50,000 value minus $30,000 mortgage minus $10,000 exemption equals $10,000 excess equity). In effect, the family can "buy" their excess equity in their home from their other creditors by paying it back over time with interest. Because the alternative is losing the home in a sheriff's sale under state law or seeing it sold in bankruptcy under Chapter 7, the Chapter 13 choice is on its face attractive for a homeowner. That fact makes the findings of the following section all the more surprising.

Homeowners and Chapter 13

There is a widespread perception that any homeowners who declare bankruptcy will be in Chapter 13. Only there, where they could pay off their arrearages to hold off their mortgage lenders and pay out their equities to hold off their general creditors, would homeowners find some relief in bankruptcy.

The data do not support this perception. The homeowners split almost evenly between Chapter 7 and Chapter 13. Because all debtors show a greater propensity for Chapter 7 (61% of the entire sample is in Chapter 7), the even split between 7 and 13 shows homeowners with a greater inclination to Chapter 13 than the overall sample—but the surprising fact is that the difference is relatively small.[18] In Chapter Thirteen, we will use multivariate statistical techniques to analyze the variables that explain debtor choices between Chapter 7 and Chapter 13 and to see how home ownership stacks up against a range of other variables. For now, it is sufficient to note that homeowners do not flock to Chapter 13 as conventional wisdom posits.

This finding has immediate relevance to questions of law and policy: If homeowning debtors are not using Chapter 13 as predicted, they may be using bankruptcy differently from the way policymakers presume.

We began this chapter with the story of Mr. and Mrs. Hammond, homeowners who had chosen Chapter 7. The files indicate that they fully intend to keep their home, although they had had so much trouble paying their mortgage that their lender had initiated a foreclosure action before the bankruptcy filing. The Hammonds discharged little unsecured debt and, as a matter of law, debtors cannot change the terms of their home mortgage loan, yet bankruptcy may still have been useful for the Hammonds. If the mortgage foreclosure were pending at the time of filing, the bankruptcy action bought the debtors time to negotiate. Once they filed, the foreclosure stopped, at least until the mortgage lender could fill out new papers and get back into court. In the meantime, the debtors, usually represented by a lawyer for the first time, could talk with the lender about their prospects for full repayment. And, as in the Hammonds' case, they can work out an agreeable plan. The critical feature of bankruptcy for some homeowners may be the automatic stay, the pause in collection activities mandated by a bankruptcy filing, not any discharge of debt or change in legal status of the home mortgage.

The Chapter 7 homeowners can offer one positive element in their discussions with the mortgage lender: They will no longer be burdened by unsecured debts. Following bankruptcy, the debtors will be free to concentrate on the home mortgage and any other secured loans they have decided to pay. For debtors who have built up substantial unsecured debt totals (as most of the bankruptcy debtors have), this is an important shift in financial circumstances. The biggest homeowner protection may be the general Chapter 7 discharge, which affects all the nonmortgage creditors. Given mortgage lender acquiescence, the limited additional help found in Chapter 13 may not be terribly useful or attractive.

We have the strong impression, supported by the files, that many mortgage lenders are perfectly willing to continue the mortgage relationship notwithstanding Chapter 7 bankruptcy, so long as they receive timely payments. This attitude makes sense, because the alternative is a foreclosure sale almost certain to cost the lender time and money. After a Chapter 7 discharge, a mortgage lender will usually have a one-debt debtor and still have the ultimate security—the right to repossess the house if payments are not made.

This scenario also suggests there may be a considerable amount of acquiescence from the nonmortgage creditors as well. The 80 debtors who showed no mortgage and therefore very substantial equities in their homes, for example, should have been closely questioned by their nonmortgage creditors, who could have demanded the debtor sell the home and pay them pro rata or, if the debtor was in Chapter 13, pay at least the present value of the home equity in Chapter 13 payments. We cannot know whether the creditors inquired informally and found out that the mortgage actually reduced the equity, or whether the trustee may have made such a determination. It is possible that the creditors simply did not bother. They may have decided that checking any debtor's file for hidden assets simply was not worth the occasional payment it would yield, and so these debtors slipped through with substantial home equity. Or they may have concluded that any pro rata distribution was too small to be worth filing papers, especially since the distribution is always split among the active and inactive creditors alike. This suggests that homeowners may be able to save more than the law allows. It also suggests that some of the Chapter 13 filings are simply the consequence of attorneys who assume that the creditors will otherwise object if a homeowner stays in Chapter 7 without selling the house, even if the assumption is wrong.

Far from being the necessary choice for all homeowner–debtors, Chapter 13 has significant disadvantages if a debtor's primary aim is to keep the home. Unless they need Chapter 13's special cure provisions because the mortgage lender is recalcitrant, homeowners are likely to find Chapter 13 more dangerous for retaining their homes. Most debtors in Chapter 13 agree to divide their incomes among the home mortgage and all their other debts. Later we discuss the enormous failure rates in Chapter 13, with debtors who have higher hopes of repayment than their incomes allow. For now, we simply note that homeowners who choose Chapter 13 repayment run a substantial risk that they will do little to save their homes that they could not have accomplished in Chapter 7.

Policy Implications

The data on homeowners show once again that the debtors in bankruptcy are not some "other," but part of mainstream America. Although home ownership in bankruptcy is lower than the national norm, more than half of all the debtors in bankruptcy own their homes when they file. The bankrupt homeowners once survived a rigorous credit check. They once had good jobs, cash for a down payment, and clean credit records—and yet they ended up in financial ruin. This high proportion suggests a certain fragility in the factors that make people economically safe.

The homeowners in bankruptcy earn less and owe more than homeowners in the general population. They struggle with nonmortgage debts that would (and did) sink debtors without homes. On top of these debts, they manage larger mortgages with much less income. Even with the equity they build up in their homes, debtors in bankruptcy have an average net worth so deep in the hole ($-13,337) that it would take the best part of a year's earnings without any expenses just to make it to "flat broke," zero net worth.

Some bankrupt homeowners have experienced dramatic shifts in their incomes, and many have used their homes as a source of cash by taking out second mortgages. A surprising number are entrepreneurs. The debtors in bankruptcy show how quickly a home—and home mortgage—can shift from being a source of financial security to a relentless economic burden.

The homeowners provide another perspective on how bankruptcy happens. Financial disaster is not always a function of living at the economic margins and drifting in and out of jobs and debts until a bad combination wipes the debtor out. Instead, it is a fair inference that for these homeowners bankruptcy represents a very real decline in fortunes.

The data show, for the first time, that homeowners are substantial users of bankruptcy. This finding raises the same issue as in the last chapter: Should there be special legal protections for this subgroup? To analyze this problem, it is important to consider both the role of state law and the adequacy of current bankruptcy law. Both are important, but the variety of state homestead exemptions suggests that legislators are far from reaching a consensus.

State homestead laws must be considered in the context of bankruptcy. These state laws governing mortgage foreclosures provide homeowners important protections that interact with the protections of bankruptcy law. Some homeowners find that bankruptcy helps them forestall a mortgage lender or a general creditor insisting on sale to satisfy an overdue debt. Others may find that the only way to stay current on their mortgages is to discharge their other debts. Just as bankruptcy law must be considered a part of the social support for the unemployed and as a small business aid for the entrepreneur, bankruptcy should be considered a part of a broader net of laws that protect homeowners from losing their homes in precipitous debt collection actions.

But the scope of protection in bankruptcy may not be adequate. There has been a widespread perception that Chapter 13 would handle whatever problems bankrupt homeowners might have. Many lawyers we interviewed were so convinced of this that they routinely advised: "All debtors should file Chapter 7 and get their discharges, except the occasional homeowner—he should be in Chapter 13." Even judges repeated the conventional wisdom, with one explaining that he was opposed to Chapter 13—"except, of course, if you had a homeowner." With lawyers and judges making such strong assumptions about where homeowner–debtors should be, it is all the more remarkable that the homeowners split evenly between Chapter 7 and Chapter 13. At the least, these data demonstrate that the bar's complacency about the present structure is misplaced.

If home ownership is a status we wish to protect, then a restructuring of the bankruptcy laws to focus on homes—in Chapter 7 and Chapter 13—may make sense. At present, neither Chapter 13 nor Chapter 7 is satisfactory. Chapter 13 is useful only for those who can make significant payments in a Chapter 13 plan. For the debtor who needs Chapter 13 to cure an arrearage on a mortgage, the price of saving the house is making payments to all other creditors, which may be more than he or she can reasonably manage. For the debtor who needs to get rid of crushing nonmortgage debt, Chapter 7 makes sense, but the debtor cannot cure any mortgage problems in Chapter 7, except with voluntary cooperation of the mortgage lender.

In current bankruptcy policy home ownership is not the protected status; mortgage lending is protected instead. When the current bankruptcy laws are reviewed in light of home ownership data, they are curiously out of step with other bankruptcy provisions. Elsewhere in bankruptcy, all creditors give up something when their debtors declare bankruptcy. Home mortgage lenders, however, give up less than their counterparts who are not relying on a home.

Given the fact that laws usually favor homeowners, with special tax breaks to homeowners and state law provisions that make it much harder to repossess a home than a car or furniture, it might be surprising to see so little special bankruptcy protection from home mortgage lenders. The rationale is that mortgage lenders require special protection or home mortgages will dry up. If home mortgage lenders had to worry about their payments being rescheduled in bankruptcy, the argument runs, they would charge more for home mortgages and make it more expensive for every homeowner to take out a loan. Of course, every creditor uses this argument in connection with every type of credit. The difference is that home mortgage lenders have made their argument more persuasively.

This argument turns ultimately on facts. Is it true that giving homeowners more help in dealing with their home mortgages in bankruptcy would make such mortgages less available or raise the interest rates for all homeowners? One way to find out would be to compare experiences (and interest rates) in states with varying mortgage lender laws. For example, it is much harder to foreclose mortgages, even after nonpayment, in some states than in others. A study could determine if those differences affected the terms of mortgages in those states. Few such studies have been done, so that the arguments about the high costs of additional consumer rights remain matters of faith on all sides.[19]

There may be a second factor involved in current bankruptcy policy prohibitions on restructuring home mortgages. If homes are so important that debtors would go to virtually any length to protect them, then Congress might deliberately decide not to provide special help. Help with a home mortgage might be too great an incentive to enter bankruptcy. This argument supports the creditors' contention discussed in the preceding paragraph. It may be that fewer homeowners go into bankruptcy now because they receive little help on their mortgages. If they had more help, the argument runs, they might file bankruptcy in greater numbers.

This argument contains a good deal of truth, and both the high proportion of homeowners already in bankruptcy and the intensity of their desire to keep their homes support this analysis. On the other hand, the argument is not without ironies, too. This argument amounts to saying "We can't make bankruptcy law too useful or lots of people will use it." This argument is the basis of a perpetual tension in bankruptcy laws: How do they provide enough help for the truly needy but not so much help that everyone will use them?

The picture of homeowners in bankruptcy is one of people struggling to keep their homes. Whether fighting their mortgage lenders or concealing the fact of their bankruptcy while they scramble to meet their mortgage payments, the debtors in bankruptcy have not given up. The data reinforce the notion that debtors do whatever they can to save their homes.

Should the homeowner's incentive be used to squeeze every last payment from a homeowning debtor or as a reason to expand bankruptcy protection for homeowners? People with different normative views will see the answers differently. What the data show is that homeowners are a very important part of the bankruptcy story.

Notes

1. In 1979, 7.0% of all owner-occupied housing units were mobile homes. U.S. Bureau of the Census, Statistical Abstract of the United States, 1981 (102 ed., Washington: U.S. Government Printing Office, 1982), Table 1372, p. 760.

2. If Reliance Financial lends the Hammonds the money to buy the furniture in which they took a security interest, the security interest is enforceable in bankruptcy. But if Reliance took a security interest on furniture the Hammonds already owned to secure a cash loan, the security interest would be nullified in bankruptcy and the loan would become unsecured. There is no notation in the file that the Hammonds' attorney tried to set aside the security interest, which may have been an oversight or may have been because the security interest was valid. Either way, with the security interest left in place in the bankruptcy, the Hammonds either forfeited their furniture or they paid this creditor in full.

3. Both differences are statistically significant, as are all the differences in Table 7.1.

4. The percentages given are of homeowners, excluding nonowners. The case base has been reduced by 23 cases in which home ownership was unclear. Mortgages are likely underreported for reasons discussed on pages 134–35. On the other hand, there may be some overreporting in our analysis because some debtors list arrearages on a mortgage separate from the mortgage itself, making arrearages look like second mortgages. We have eliminated for this analysis mortgages equal to or less than 10% of the value of the home to avoid overreporting, based on separate listings for arrearages.

5. Survey of Consumer Finances, 1983: A Second Report, Federal Reserve Bulletin (December 1984), Table 1, p. 858.

6. *Id.*, Table 2, p. 859.

7. For those who remember the one-time adage that debtors can carry home mortgages about twice as big as their annual incomes, we note that most homeowners have not just taken out a home mortgage. Instead, both the national data and the bankruptcy data bring together all debtors—those who are in the first month of mortgage repayment and those who are in the last, all averaged together. It is unlikely that the bankrupt homeowners are all in the early months of their mortgages, but it is possible that the average duration of a mortgage differs between our sample and the national sample.

Of course, size of the mortgage is less important than the size of the monthly payment. Mortgages are generally spread over 30 years. Bankruptcy, with its orientation toward total debts and total income, does not require all debtors to report their monthly mortgage payments. But we infer from the relative size of their mortgages and the relative size of the debtors' incomes that they probably make mortgage payments that consume a large portion of their incomes.

8. U.S. Bureau of the Census, 1980 Census of Housing (Residential Finance), Table 15: Income, 1-Unit Homeowner Mortgaged Properties: 1981.

9. For data analyses about mortgages and home mortgage debt, we eliminate the 61 debtors with inconsistent reports about home mortgages, adding them to the debtors who listed their mortgages as "unknown in amount." We do not eliminate the 19 debtors who list no mortgages. Although these cases may be hard to believe, they show no indication of reporting error. Even if it seems implausible, 19 debtors are indicated as outright owners of their homes, which they might be. These 19 debtors with no reported home mortgages are included along with other homeowners in the calculation of mortgage data. Once again, we acknowledge that these data may understate debt actually owed, and, in turn, overstate the financial position of the debtors.

But the interesting implication is not simply that this analysis may paint too rosy a picture of bankrupt homeowners' circumstances. What interests us about this reporting problem is the explanation offered by attorneys and judges for why we found so many debtors who claimed no home mortgages.

10. Although technically the Bankruptcy Code accelerates and causes all debt obligations to be in breach, both in practice and, in some courts, by judicial decree, the debtor who is current on a secured loan will probably not face losing a home so long as the debtor continues to make payments as originally scheduled.

11. Indeed, the incentives seem strong enough that we have serious reservations whether the 19 debtors who do not list any information about mortgage debt actually own their homes free and clear. The protocols of data collection require that we list them as such, and their mortgage-free home values are included within these calculations. Once again, however, we may be sketching a picture of debtors in bankruptcy that is somewhat rosier than the harsh reality.

12. Some debtors in bankruptcy could be homeowners through mistakes in the mortgage process—applications that were not fully checked or debtors' names that were somehow confused. Some may hold mortgage assumptions that the lender failed to check carefully because the original borrower remained liable. Nonetheless, we find it very difficult to believe that many of these 637 families got their mortgage through their lenders' carelessness.

13. There was no significant difference between the homeowners and the nonowners in the distribution of losses and gains. Of 76 homeowners who were income losers, 46% lost 30% or more, 62% lost 20% or more, and 84% lost 10% or more. Of 114 nonowners who were income losers, 54% lost 30% or more, 66% lost 20% or more, and 81% lost 10% or more.

Another 126 homeowners gained income: 37% gained 30% or more, 48% gained 20% or more, and 71% gained 10% or more. Among 205 nonowners who gained income, 38% gained 30% or more, 50% gained 20% or more, and 76% gained 10% or more.

14. Among the formerly self-employed, 53.7% were homeowners. This led us to some speculation about whether the loss of a home might have accompanied the demise of the business, but no firm data are available on this point.

15. The procedures that states devise for selling a debtors' home to satisfy unpaid debts vary widely. Texas has taken the simplest position—and the most restrictive. Only the home mortgage lender, the taxman, or a home improvement lender can force the sale of a homestead in Texas. Even the position in Texas is somewhat more complicated than we suggest, with various commentators arguing that Texas does permit judicial sale of a homestead, but only if the value exceeds the homestead allowance, which means, in effect, that the nonhomestead portion is being sold. With the generous homestead exemption in Texas, this amounts to the same thing as saying that in most cases the nonmortgage creditor cannot force the sale of the home. Other states permit

general creditors to force the sale of a home, but they require various notices, postings, other opportunities to satisfy the debt, proof of value in excess of exemptions, and so on, making the sale of a home possible, but a fairly cumbersome process for most nonmortgage creditors.

16. This conclusion overstates the situation in 1981 in a very few cases where the debtors' land value exceeded $10,000, exclusive of all improvement including the house, and the mortgage was less than the amount of the excess. Even in such cases when general creditors could, as a matter of statutory law, force a sale of the homestead, the courts were very reluctant to let such cases proceed. It is a fair summary that for virtually all the debtors in bankruptcy, general creditors could not reach the debtors' homestead in Texas.

17. By using the federal "wild card" exemption of $400, a Pennsylvania debtor would increase the homestead exemption to $7,900, or $15,800 for couples.

Pennsylvania also permits another protection for the home. The state recognizes tenancy by the entireties, which means that if one spouse incurs a debt, the spouse who does not owe the debt may block the sale of the joint homestead to satisfy this debt. There is no limit on the value that can be saved in this way, but few debtors are able to take advantage of it. If both husband and wife are liable for the debt, the homestead can be sold and tenancy by the entireties is no protection. Most creditors know this, and most require that both husband and wife sign debt applications. Only debtors who choose the Pennsylvania exemptions rather than the federal exemptions can use this option. In our sample, only 26 Pennsylvania homeowners (6.5%) selected Pennsylvania exemptions, and there is no indication in the files that they used tenancy by the entireties to protect their homes. (Of the 26 cases, 16 were in Chapter 13, where the exemptions made less difference.)

We consider the effect of tenancy by the entireties to protect homesteads again in our discussion in Chapter Eight, note 10, of married debtors filing alone or singly.

18. This does not mean that 61% of all debtors are in Chapter 7. We deliberately oversampled Chapter 13 to make more accurate statements about Chapter 13 debtors, especially in districts with very few Chapter 13's. See discussion of sample selection in Chapter Two.

19. Professor Philip Shuchman has just completed a study focusing on another aspect of home mortgage foreclosures. Parts of the country are governed by a rule called the *Durrett* rule, which permits a debtor who later files bankruptcy to set aside a real estate foreclosure sale if it fails to yield at least 70% of the market price of the real estate. Other courts have specifically ruled that they will not follow this approach, and a foreclosure sale stands in a subsequent bankruptcy regardless of the sale price. Professor Shuchman compared lending rates in states with different legal rules and found no correlation between those that offered greater consumer protection and higher borrowing rates across the board. P. Shuchman, Data on the *Durrett* Controversy, 9 Cardozo Law Review 605 (1987). Although his focus was elsewhere, Professor Shuchman's research tends to negate the idea that the cost of mortgages will rise for everyone whenever the debtors receive foreclosure protection. Congress should demand empirical evidence before granting mortgage lenders extra protection.

8

Women and Bankruptcy

For American men, economic security is a function of income and property. For American women, economic security has often depended on American men. But ever since the early years of the Republic, and long before an identifiable feminist movement began, there has been mounting pressure and erratic progress toward providing economic equity to women apart from the institution of marriage. Over the last one hundred and fifty years, married women were first permitted to own property and then to make their own contracts, including labor contracts.[1] Although the Great Depression of the 1930s saw efforts to ban employment for wives of employed men, today by law employment rights are independent of gender,[2] and women, including married women, have entered the work force in record numbers.

Bankruptcy law has never discriminated by gender or by marital status, but creditors have discriminated on both grounds until very recently. For decades, few women filed for bankruptcy on their own, because few had credit on their own. The credit picture began to change in 1970 when Congress enacted the Equal Credit Opportunity Act to provide that women would be entitled to credit in their own names.[3]

The increase in credit available to women should cause the relative proportions of women in bankruptcy to increase over time. One study of women in bankruptcy indicates they have begun filing in greater numbers.[4] Because our data were collected in one year only, we can neither verify nor dispute this conclusion. What we can do is describe the women in bankruptcy and compare them with other men and women. These data etch graphic pictures of single women struggling to make it alone, in precariously similar financial circumstances in and out of bankruptcy, and of married women filing bankruptcy when they discover that a single income no longer supports a family.

Two Women in Bankruptcy

As in other chapters, we begin with case studies from our files. Since we have already looked at several married women who filed bankruptcy with their husbands, our examples here are two women who came to the bankruptcy court alone.

Opal Marvin lives on a rural homestead in central Illinois. She filed her Chapter 7 alone. As an assembly line worker, she earns $5.10 an hour in a plant that processes livestock feed. If she had worked the "standard" 2000-hour work year in 1981, she would have earned $10,200. In 1980, the year before she filed for bankruptcy, she earned $7,000. In 1979, she earned $6,000. The data do not indicate why Ms. Marvin earns a relatively high hourly wage but had a low annual income. She may have worked earlier at a lower paying job, or she may have worked only part time. Her job may be seasonal, or she may have had occasional layoffs during the previous two years.

Ms. Marvin is listed in our data as married. The classification of her marital status comes from the notation on her home mortgage, "Note and Mortgage to FHA Joint tenant with husband, James Warren Marvin." "Joint tenant" does not refer to living together in the home, but to the legal status of the property, which was evidently purchased by both of them with both of them liable on the mortgage. According to the files, Ms. Marvin has lived in this home for at least the previous six years.

Ms. Marvin indicates that she owes $20,000 on the home mortgage and $200 secured by her car. She lists 11 unsecured creditors for a total unsecured debt of $2,721.14. Her unsecured debts alone represent 40% of her 1980 income. Even if she had been able to work a full year at $5.10 per hour, her unsecured debts would still have been more than a quarter of her gross income.

The unsecured creditors listed in Ms. Marvin's bankruptcy include Montgomery Ward, to whom she owes $1,100 for a new stove, and four medical providers to whom she owes over $300. Other creditors are four clothing stores, for a combined $1,300. We cannot tell from the file whether the clothes were work clothes for her or school clothes for her children. They could have included a ball gown, but it seems unlikely. Two creditors are mail-order establishments known for their inexpensive clothing.

Under the Illinois exemption statute, Ms. Marvin exempted $10,000 of the family homestead, her car, and her few household goods. Although the file does not disclose any reaffirmation of debt, it appears she will keep the house and the car, presumably by an informal arrangement with the lien holders.

Ms. Marvin paid her attorney $250, and she has agreed to pay another $190. She leaves bankruptcy keeping all her property and discharging about $2,700 in unsecured debt. The amount of debt discharged is small, but, as we noted earlier, it represents a large fraction of her annual income. She evidently concluded that relief from those obligations was worth the fees and possible loss of future credit.

Another single-filing debtor is Carmelita Gentry. She lives in Philadelphia, where she works at an electronics plant. She lists her occupation only as "service girl" without further elaboration. Her 1980 earnings are listed as $11,520; no amount is listed for the preceding year, although the form requests this information. No source of income other than her job is listed. She has lived at the same address in Philadelphia for at least the preceding six years.

Ms. Gentry owns little and she claims all of it as exempt. Her clothing and household goods are valued at $1,000. She owns a house whose worth she lists as $15,000, which she claims as exempt using the federal exemption.[5] There is no record of a car, savings account, pension fund, or any other assets.

Ms. Gentry's debts might also appear to be modest. The only secured debt her lawyer identifies is a $1,900 secured debt to Beneficial Finance with unspecified collateral. Another—or perhaps the same—$1,900 debt to Beneficial is listed under unsecured debts. Her total unsecured debts are $6,558.17, or about 57% of her 1980 income. She owes a bank and a savings and loan $1,800 each. She owes Wanamaker's nearly $200, and a clothier another $575. She lists debts to utility companies for $450. She lists no co-debtors on any of her obligations.

Although her debts are modest, we can assume they have been understated. There is a mortgage on the house, and the statement of creditors lists the name and address of the bank holding the mortgage. This information has been carefully lined through and the words "omit mortgage" have been typed in the space reserved for the amount of the mortgage. (It seems obvious that the attorney, reviewing the draft form, wrote an instruction to his secretary to "omit mortgage," the secretary dutifully typed in "omit mortgage," and the attorney failed to see the mistake on the final version that was filed in court.) The protocols of data collection require that Ms. Gentry appear as a homeowner who owns her house free and clear (see Chapter Seven). In fact, her postbankruptcy situation apparently includes a mortgage of unspecified amount.

The papers refer neither to Ms. Gentry's marital status nor to whether she is a parent. Indeed, her life prior to 1980 is a complete blank, save for the information that she has never before been in bankruptcy and has not moved. We do not know whether she is a displaced homemaker or widow who has just found her job as "service girl." We do know that a bank trusted her with both a mortgage and a personal loan, and she had also passed credit checks at a thrift institution and at least one major department store in the years before she filed bankruptcy.

Filing Status and Marital Status

Opal Marvin and Carmelita Gentry are examples of women who file individual cases in bankruptcy. In this chapter, we refer to these women as "single-filing women." About 43% of our sample cases, 645 debtors, were bankruptcies filed by a single debtor, male or female. Of these lone filers, 261 were single-filing women. Thus single-filing women constituted about 40% of the single filings and about 17% of all the cases in the sample.

Joint bankruptcies comprise the larger share of consumer bankruptcies. In our sample, 858 women filed with their husbands, creating a group we refer to as "joint-filing women." Some of these women were introduced in Chapter Three: Winona Todd, Martha Fredrickson, Betty Sue Havco, and Laura Mae Spice. Joint-filing women have also shown up in chapters on homeowners and the self-employed, and others will appear in later chapters on debtors with high medical debts and repeat filers. Altogether, 74% percent of our cases have a woman debtor. Our total number of petitioners is 2359, counting two petitioners for each joint petition, and the proportion of men and women is almost equal: 53% men, 47% women.

To a large extent, women filing bankruptcy alone are single or well on the way to being single. The bankruptcy forms do not ask marital status, so we must infer whether a debtor is married from other information in the files. Joint filers, because of the restrictions imposed by law, are all married couples at the time of filing.[6] Single filers may or may not be married. We searched the files of all single-filing women for any mention of a spouse, and in 88% of the cases we found none.

A variety of factors make it likely that the overwhelming majority of single filers are not people living with spouses. The 1978 Bankruptcy Code made it easier and less expensive for married couples to file bankruptcy, so that one filing fee, one set of forms, and one attorney's fee produces a discharge for both spouses. Husbands and wives are usually jointly liable for their debts, so the discharge of only one spouse would usually leave the remaining spouse to face the same collection efforts for the outstanding total debts.[7] The low cost and broad benefits of joint filing make it likely that most married couples living together would file a joint bankruptcy.[8]

Some single-filing women may be married at the time of filing, but only because the bankruptcy court is faster than the divorce court. We recall the file of Elaine Dover, who was trying to save her Chevy Blazer and support her six children. Ms. Dover filed her Chapter 13 bankruptcy petition alone, explaining that she and her husband "are not yet separated but [he] contributes less than $200 a month" to the family. Ms. Dover was married at the time of filing and is listed as such in our data, but she will likely face the future alone.[9]

Only a few circumstances would justify a single filing for a married woman. If she had incurred debts for which her husband is not liable, either debts that preceded the current marriage or debts from a small business of her own, single filing might be sensible. Those circumstances are rare, however, especially because a person starting a business is typically asked to guarantee business loans, and the lender nearly always asks for the signatures of both husband and wife.[10] Because nearly all single-filing women were advised by attorneys or legal clinics, we assume that they would have used joint petitions if they had been married. Because they filed alone, they probably were not married.[11]

In this chapter we discuss the circumstances facing women filing bankruptcy either alone or with their husbands. We also compare our debtors with the single and married women in the general population. These data provide a unique perspective on the grim economic realities facing women alone, whether they have declared bankruptcy or are living at the edge of financial collapse. The data also show the economic vulnerability of one-income families, giving a harsh economic twist to the decision of many married women to enter the workplace.

Single-Filing Women: Life at the Bottom

The economic story of women in bankruptcy is the story of women everywhere: They earn less money than men. Lower incomes for women have been documented many ways, but the bankruptcy data add to the story of the economic vulnerability of women trying to support themselves and their families.

The first column of Table 8.1 compares the incomes of families with a male worker with families headed by women.[12] Family income includes income from all sources, including all wage earners in the family, alimony and child support, and income supplements from the government.[13] The table shows the mean family income of families with a male worker is about $26,300. Comparable income for families with a male earner in bankruptcy is about $18,100, a 30% difference between male-earner families in and out of bankruptcy. This is about the same relative position we saw in Chapter Four when we compared the incomes of all families in bankruptcy with the incomes of families in the general population.

When we compare families headed by women, we find that the families

TABLE 8.1. Family Incomes and Personal Earnings, National Sample and Bankruptcy Sample, by Sex

Group	Mean Family Income[a]	Mean Personal Earnings[b]	Difference Between Mean Family Income and Mean Personal Earnings
National sample[c]			
Males	$26,329	$18,524	$7,805
Females	14,122	9,871	4,251
Bankruptcy sample			
Males[d]	18,073	15,591	2,482
Single-filing females	10,638	10,113	525

[a]Includes income from all sources.

[b]Work-related income of primary earners.

[c]Primary individuals, husband/fathers in primary family, and wives/mothers in primary families with no husband/father present.

[d]This figure is for all males, including those who file jointly. For single-filing males, family income was $15,808 and personal earnings were $15,055.

Source: Consumer Bankruptcy Project; March 1981 Current Population Survey.

headed by women in and out of bankruptcy are closer to each other, with family incomes of $14,100 in the general population compared with $10,600 for the women in bankruptcy, a 24% difference. The gap between women's families is narrower because of the unhappy fact that women outside bankruptcy make so much less than men.

The national data show that families headed by women generally receive about 54 cents for every dollar that families headed by men make, or about $12,000 less per year on average. The gender gap in income is similar in bankruptcy.[14] Mean income for bankrupt families headed by men is $18,000, compared with a mean income of $10,600 for families of single-filing women. Families headed by a woman in bankruptcy receive 59 cents for every dollar of income in a bankrupt family headed by a man, about the same fraction as women earn generally.

Table 8.1 also shows what happens when we compare only the wages of men and women primary earners, omitting all family income received from other sources. The gaps between men and women grow. Men primary earners in the general population report mean personal earnings of about $18,500, compared with $9,900 for women. Mean earnings for men in bankruptcy are about $15,600, whereas women single filers in bankruptcy earn $10,100. Comparing only their individual wages, women in bankruptcy earn 65 cents for every dollar men in bankruptcy earn, a better proportion than the 54 cents in the general population, but still depressingly far from equal incomes.[15]

These data suggest four income groups. At the highest income are men in the general population. Well below them are the men in bankruptcy. Still lower are the women in bankruptcy and the women in the general population, standing near each other and very close to the poverty line.

Single Women's Occupations and Incomes

Single-filing women in bankruptcy work in occupations and industries that are similar to those of all women heads of households. Male single filers work in somewhat less similar occupations and industries than all male heads of households, but the differences in occupation and industry are still small.[16] This reinforces our finding in Chapter Five that the debtors in bankruptcy generally work in roughly the same industries and occupations as the national labor force.

Much greater differences are found in comparing women with men. In the general labor force, female heads of households and male heads of households have an index of dissimilarity of 43 for occupations and 33 for industries. Among the single-filing bankrupt women and men, the differences are almost as large, 40 for occupations and 29 for industries.[17]

We cannot be certain of all the reasons for the striking differences in employment between male and female heads of households.[18] The women tend to be concentrated in fewer occupational specialties, and this tends to increase the dissimilarity between their job distributions and those of men. What is important to our analysis is the extent to which these occupational/industrial differences account for the parallel pattern of income differences that we find.

In Chapter Five we compared the differences in occupations and industries for bankrupt debtors with those of the general population. We found that differences in occupations and industries explained very little of the differences in incomes among the two groups. This time we repeat the decomposition analysis, but we subdivide the two groups, examining whether differences in industries and occupations explain differences in earnings between men and women.

In the general population, the segregation of men and women into distinct occupational and industrial specialties helps perpetuate income differences between men and women, but other studies have shown that it only explains a small portion of the difference in their earnings.[19] A larger part is explained by differences in wages within occupations, perhaps because women are more likely to work part-time, because women tend to have lower paying jobs within each occupational category, or because of outright wage discrimination.

The same finding holds true in the bankruptcy sample. Although there are large differences between the occupations and industries of the men and women in bankruptcy, these differences do not account for the large income gap between men and women. Only about $1,000 of the $15,000 difference is explained by the fact that women work in different occupations and industries.[20] Women work in different jobs from men, but their lower income is not attributable solely to low-paying occupations or industries. The remaining $14,000 differences in income between them is explained by differences in wages within their occupations and industries, perhaps for the same reasons that exist in the general population.

These data etch a clearer picture of women in bankruptcy. Occupational differences have little to do with the large differences in income between men and women. Gender and income are linked directly. A woman heading her own household without a man's income to balance some of the difference feels the impact more sharply.

Other Financial Data

Table 8.2 compares various occupational and financial characteristics of single-filing women, single-filing men, and joint-filing couples. A key point is a comparison of assets and debts, the good new and bad news of a balance sheet. Single-filing women have much less of both.

Mean household assets for joint filers are valued at $36,500, more than double the mean assets of single women filers at $15,300. Median assets show an even greater difference, with joint filers claiming $25,500, compared to a relatively paltry $6,400 for single women filers. Men single filers also do worse than joint filers, showing the greater accumulation of assets in a two-adult family. But they also do better than single-filing women, with mean assets

TABLE 8.2. Financial and Job Descriptors of Male and Female Single Filers and Joint Filers[a]

Characteristic	Mean	Standard Deviation	25th Percentile	Median	75th Percentile	N
Assets**						
Male	$23,245	$37,637	$ 1,400	$ 6,558	$35,560	379
Female	15,309	19,363	1,200	6,400	23,350	259
Joint	36,472	44,081	5,395	25,500	52,850	851
Income last year[b],**						
Male	13,861	9,318	8,455	12,500	18,186	320
Female[c]	8,829	6,105	4,403	9,000	12,927	224
Joint	14,720	9,230	8,940	14,830	20,000	739
Household income**						
Male	14,560	9,527	9,000	13,248	19,013	346
Female	9,745	5,790	6,000	9,600	13,125	234
Joint	18,441	9,638	11,728	17,800	24,000	701
Total debt**						
Male	37,182	57,331	8,281	17,155	40,649	373
Female	20,609	22,903	6,692	11,136	25,419	260
Joint	44,927	59,355	12,672	27,267	49,617	855
Secured debt**						
Male	19,214	35,627	878	6,364	24,300	375
Female	12,180	16,670	1,013	5,496	17,476	261
Joint	28,197	43,525	4,374	14,256	36,386	857
Unsecured debt**						
Male	17,913	40,788	3,668	6,842	15,258	372
Female	8,382	11,832	3,212	5,404	8,577	260
Joint	16,664	30,412	4,131	7,852	15,025	855
Tenure (years)						
Male	4.9	6.9	0.0	2.0	8.0	189
Female	4.4	6.1	0.0	2.0	6.5	133
Joint	14.5	6.4	0.0	2.0	7.0	480
Prestige**						
Male	37.8	12.3	32.0	37.0	47.0	308
Female[d]	40.0	11.9	32.0	38.0	48.0	212
Joint	36.6	11.7	29.0	36.0	47.0	712

[a]Cases with extreme values on assets, total debt, or income are removed.

[b]Work-related income only.

[c]Females are significantly lower; no significant differences between single-filing men and joint filers.

[d]Females are significantly higher; no significant differences between single-filing men and joint filers.

**F test is significant at $p < 0.01$ for all groups unless otherwise noted.

Source: Consumer Bankruptcy Project.

54% higher, although median assets were nearly identical. Debtors in bankruptcy are generally in economic trouble, but women filing alone face bankruptcy with considerably fewer assets than do couples in bankruptcy and with somewhat fewer assets than single-filing men.

The pattern reverses when we compare debts. Single women filers have significantly lower debts than joint filers, and a greater proportion of their debt is unsecured. Single women filers owe, on average, $20,600. Joint filers report a mean total debt more than twice as high—$45,000—with a slightly higher proportion of secured debt. Men filing alone again had debts that straddled about halfway between the lower debts of single-filing women and the higher debts of married couples.

These data show single people approaching bankruptcy with fewer debts and assets than married couples, but with single women trailing single men on all financial measures.[21]

Income and asset comparisons give some idea of the grim financial circumstances of women in bankruptcy, but women also carry lighter debt burdens. As a result, single-filing women, single-filing men, and joint-filing couples have remarkably similar debt/income ratios.

The comparisons are gathered in Table 8.3. We separately test the debt/income ratios of joint filers, single-filing women, and single-filing men to look for statistically significant differences. There are none. Nonmortgage debt/income ratios are even closer for the three groups.[22] Married couples, women alone, and men alone file bankruptcy at about the same proportion of debts to income, although the absolute amounts of such debts and income vary among the groups.

Women and Economic Dependence

These comparative financial data juxtapose two important economic facts about single women in bankruptcy: They are persistently at the lowest end of all income measures, and they file bankruptcy in the same state of relative collapse as other bankrupt debtors. Because of their sharply lower wages, sin-

TABLE 8.3. Total and Nonmortgage Debt/Income Ratios for Single-Filing Males and Females and for Joint Filers[a]

Group	Mean	s.d.	25th Percentile	Median	75th Percentile	*N* (Missing)
Total Debt/Income Ratio						
SF males	3.71	11.85	0.64	1.23	2.59	324(52)
SF females	3.48	14.35	0.74	1.37	2.70	224(37)
Joint	2.89	8.00	0.72	1.48	2.58	636(171)
Total Nonmortgage Debt/Income Ratio						
SF males	2.62	10.44	0.46	0.77	1.50	321(55)
SF females	1.67	2.92	0.51	0.83	1.44	224(37)
Joint	1.65	6.42	0.47	0.71	1.34	636(171)

[a]Cases with extreme values on assets, total debt, or income are removed.

Source: Consumer Bankruptcy Project.

gle women are more vulnerable to a small disruption—a few unanticipated medical bills, a short layoff, a handful of credit card charges run up too quickly. These data highlight the economic vulnerability of women heads of households and emphasize the continued economic dependence of women on men.

Women's financial dependence is demonstrated by comparing the personal and family earnings of women in and out of bankruptcy (see Table 8.1). Women heads of household in the general population have total family incomes 25% higher than women single filers in bankruptcy—$14,100 versus $10,600. But a comparison of just the earnings of the two groups of women from their own jobs changes the picture dramatically. The stunning fact is that women in and out of bankruptcy earn statistically indistinguishable amounts—$10,100 versus $9,900. Comparable women in the CPS sample of the population actually earned *less* than the women in our bankruptcy sample. The women in the general population have higher total incomes only because they received $4,200, or 30% of their total family incomes, from other sources. The single women who filed bankruptcy received an average of only $500 annually from all other income sources. What distinguishes women in bankruptcy from other women trying to make it alone is the supplemental income the survivors get and the bankrupts do not.[23]

When these data are combined with the earlier data on the similarities in occupations, industries, and occupational prestige of the women in and out of bankruptcy, the position of women heads of households becomes even clearer: The majority are perched near the edge of bankruptcy, worrying about even small financial disruptions. These data suggest that supplemental income, such as alimony or a child's income, may represent the difference for many women between staying out of bankruptcy and going in.

The One-Income Family

The other women in bankruptcy have filed jointly with their husbands. Joint filers in bankruptcy have higher family incomes and higher assets than do either men or women single filers, but the data also show that they have correspondingly higher debts, leaving them in a comparable state of financial trouble.

The startling fact about these married couples in financial trouble is that they are one-income families in far greater proportion than one-income families in the general population. In the national population in 1981, about 60% of all married women were employed, compared with only 45% of the wives in our bankruptcy sample.[24] In addition, 10% of the wives in our sample who were working in 1981 had not worked in 1980. Therefore, during the year before the bankruptcy filing, only about a third of the wives in bankruptcy were employed, compared with almost two-thirds of the wives in the general population. These data show that married couples in bankruptcy are considerably less likely to be two-income families than are other American families.[25]

Of the wives in bankruptcy who were employed, it appears that many worked only part-time. While the bankruptcy data do not ask whether employment is full-time or part-time, we infer that many of the working married women in bankruptcy worked only part-time because of their total wages. The mean income of employed bankrupt wives was $6,000—considerably below what a full-time minimum-wage job for 1980 would have paid. The equivalent mean income for wives in the general population was $8,557—below the $9,900 mean income for women primary earners, but 43% higher than the working wives in bankruptcy.

We compared the industries and occupations of women in the general population, women single filers in bankruptcy, and women joint-filers in bankruptcy. The industries and occupations of all the women were very similar. The small differences fail to explain the income differences among women, particularly the dramatic drop for the working wives in bankruptcy.[26] The occupational and industrial similarities among all women make it a fair inference that what separates working wives in the general population from working wives in bankruptcy is the lower proportion of bankrupt wives who work full-time.[27]

These data show the couples in bankruptcy are far more likely to be one-income families than are families in the general population, and the data suggest that even among the two-income families, fewer wives hold full-time jobs. The bankruptcy data portray the increased risk faced by lower income families that do not follow the national trend toward two incomes.

The most obvious explanation for the greater proportion of one-income families in our bankruptcy sample is that our sample contains a disproportionate number of couples who chose a traditional family life (i.e., a wife who does not work outside the home). The decision may be motivated by a belief that a mother should be home with the children. Or the one-income family may be driven by the economic reality that a person with few job skills cannot pay child care, clothing, and transportation costs and still earn any money. The grim realities are compounded if children are ill or handicapped.

Other families live on one income because they have no alternative. Some of them might have been two-income families in which the second income disappeared through disability or layoff. The income disruptions that affect the general bankruptcy sample may have affected the wives in particular, resulting in a lost job or a temporary cutback to part-time work.

The data give no reasons for there being only one or one-and-a-half incomes in most bankrupt families. Regardless of the reason, these data suggest that a second earner, especially in lower income families, may spell the difference between minimal success and economic collapse.

No group in bankruptcy presents a cheery picture, but the economic circumstances of women are the worst we have examined, and they reflect the precarious position of women not in bankruptcy. Single women and married women in bankruptcy present two different pictures of people struggling to maintain a middle-class existence. The implications for shaping bankruptcy policy are different for women in different circumstances. But both raise troubling normative questions and implicate other areas of public policy beyond bankruptcy.

The data show single-filing women at the bottom of the economic basement. They have the problems of women everywhere—earning only a fraction of what their male counterparts in the same industries and occupations earn, but trying to maintain an economically viable household.

The similarity in debt/income ratios for single-filing women and all other groups raises an interesting point: It may be that neither debtors nor creditors needed our study to tell them about the difficult economic circumstances and the special vulnerability of women. These women earned less than men, but they were also able to buy less and to borrow less. Whether the women's frugality or their creditors' wariness were the cause of low spending, it is clear from these data that the women in vulnerable economic conditions accounted for less than their share of the bankruptcy losses. Evidently their grim circumstances were clear enough to force caution on someone in the credit system.

One finding that may be of particular importance is the critical role of outside support for women. We noted in other chapters that bankruptcy policy fits within a broader framework of social support laws. Effective enforcement of child support and alimony undoubtedly affects whether some women will need bankruptcy. State and federal income supplements for families headed by single women are also likely to have a powerful effect on how many women face bankruptcy.

These data also implicate bankruptcy policy directly. Single women may often be in the position of being too broke to go bankrupt. Certainly many of the single women who did file for bankruptcy were just able to afford a filing fee and a lawyer's fee. Think of Opal Marvin, for whom a $500 legal fee was about a month's take-home pay. Of course there are male debtors in equally tight circumstances, but single women are there in great disproportion. When we discuss various provisions of the bankruptcy laws that provoke expensive litigation—or reforms that threaten to do so—one likely cost is higher lawyers' fees for bankruptcy assistance. It will be well to remember the circumstances of Opal Marvin and other single women, who might thereby be priced right out of bankruptcy, leaving them with no help.[28]

The circumstances of married women in bankruptcy also suggest hard policy choices. The married debtors belie the caricature of the married couple parking the children in day care and taking on two jobs to chase material frills. These data suggest that when only one spouse works, the consequences may not be forgoing a new car or missing out on a VCR, but may be economic collapse. Not everyone needs two salaries to survive, but our sample of economic failures is littered with Americans in the lower half of the income range who tried to get by on only one full-time salary.

This finding raises a troubling policy point: Should creditors have a right to demand that families be two-income families to repay their debts? In the context of bankruptcy, these couples are saying that they cannot handle their debts. But have they really tried? In only 45% of the joint cases does the wife have a job, and even then there is ample evidence that she is often working only part-time. Should bankruptcy relief be tied to getting these people out into the mainstream, to getting a job and paying off their debts, rather than taking bankruptcy and writing them off? Currently, the discharge is not conditioned on both spouses working. There have been a few reported cases the hinted to the contrary, but no holdings require a family to become a two-income family.

Some of these single-paycheck families have not made a voluntary choice to keep a spouse at home. Disability or layoffs or even economic rationality related to lack of salable skills may make it impossible for both spouses to work. The data do not tell. But even if we could sort out the one-earner families who had no alternative but to leave a wife at home—on someone's normative view of what is a true alternative and what is not—should the law tell the remaining couples that both must work?

The law could condition the discharge on both spouses' entering the labor force. Such a rule would require the judge to make an inquiry into the reasons the wife was not working or why she had not yet found work, an inquiry that would be both intrusive and expensive. More profoundly, the notion of requiring both spouses to work is an experiment in social engineering on which there is no normative consensus.

Facts have an ugly virtue: They make unpleasant realities hard to avoid. One dour reality in bankruptcy is the continued dependency of women on men. Even in bankruptcy, wives are far better off than women alone, although wives earn less and work less. Single women remain critically dependent on supplemental income beyond their own earnings. Despite television depictions of women doctors and lawyers and routine assertions of equal pay for equal work, women continue to earn two-thirds or less of what their male counterparts earn. For women on their own, bankrupt and nonbankrupt financial circumstances are frighteningly close.

These data explain the financial box in which women find themselves, trying to hold on to a middle-class existence in the 1980s. A woman can tie her future to a man, and the data relentlessly show she will do better. But nowadays even that will not insulate her from disaster. The days of counting on one income to support a family are rapidly diminishing for those people with middling incomes and some economic disruptions. And many women trying to make it alone—whether they were intent on an independent existence from the beginning or were displaced homemakers thrust into the working world—cannot make it without outside support.

If we enjoyed true equality between the sexes, the comparisons between married and single women, and the highlighted importance of wives working, would simply represent the natural economic superiority of the family unit. Instead, the data present the grim economic realities that, even now, face many American women.

Notes

1. For a general discussion of the development of laws relating to the status of married women's legal control over their property, see R. Chused, Late Nineteenth Century Married Women's Property Law: Reception of the Early Married Women's Property Acts by Courts and Legislatures, 29 American Journal of Legal History 1 (1985); R. Chused, Married Women's Property Law: 1800–1850, 71 Georgetown Law Journal 1359 (1983).

2. Bona fide occupational qualifications restrict a few occupations (e.g., wet nurse) to one gender, but the civil rights laws guarantee that access to jobs and pay once on the job shall be equal for men and women. Some states also restrict any discrimination based on a person's marital status, but that restriction is not a part of the federal scheme.

3. 15 U.S.C. §§ 1691–1691(f) (1982). Today creditors are still permitted to require signatures of each spouse for married couples, so long as the request is made "for the purpose of creating a valid lien, passing clear title, waiving inchoate rights to property, or assigning earnings." 15 U.S.C. § 1691(d) (1982). Before the equal credit laws were passed, as a routine matter, whether there was justification or not, many creditors refused married women credit without their husbands' signatures. By extension of prejudice more than logic, creditors often refused to lend to unmarried women as well. Although federal law restricts the creditor's right to demand both signatures, it is currently the practice of most creditors to request that both husband and wife sign credit applications even when no lien in jointly held property is created. It is our sense that most couples comply, although we have no data on the point.

4. Shuchman notes that "there appears to have been a substantial, perhaps even dramatic, increase in the number of separate female bankrupts within the past decade." P. Shuchman, The Average Bankrupt: A Description and Analysis of 753 Personal Bankruptcy Filings in Nine States, 1983 Commercial Law Journal 288, 289.

5. The maximum allowed for her homestead exemption was $7,900. But she lists the value of the home as $15,000 without giving her mortgage, so her actual exemption (homestead minus mortgage) may be considerably less than $15,000. We cannot tell from this file.

6. Joint filing is available only to married couples. 11 U.S.C. § 302.

7. When only one spouse files for bankruptcy, the creditor can continue to collect against the remaining spouse. The only exception is during a Chapter 13 plan when actions against a co-debtor are stayed. After the plan is dismissed or completed, however, the creditor can go after the co-debtor for collection of the unpaid portion of the debt.

8. Joint petitions in bankruptcy are so sensible in many cases that even couples on the verge of divorce sometimes stay together for this last legal act. For one filing fee, they can both get a fresh start and wipe out some of their earlier disasters, a use the bankruptcy judges repeatedly discussed. The debtors need not worry that a spouse will leave them with large bills, or that one spouse will file bankruptcy, thereby forcing the other spouse into a later bankruptcy. Although we correctly state that all women filing jointly are married, they may not remain so for long. For our data analysis, however, this point is more social than statistical because we use the prebankruptcy incomes and assets of the couples to analyze the financial position of married women during their marriages, even if some are about to change their marital status.

It has been a common finding that divorce is associated with bankruptcy. In summarizing a variety of studies, the Bankruptcy Laws Commission Report notes, "All studies considering this factor indicated a [divorce] rate higher than for the general population or for a control group used in the study." Report of the Commission on Bankruptcy Laws of the United States Part 1, (Washington, D.C.: U.S. Government Printing Office, 1973), p. 42. But in the Western District of Texas, where local interrogatories required the debtors to state the cause of their bankruptcy, divorce and related family problems were cited by only 3.4% of our sample.

9. Some cases, such as Opal Marvin's, are simply a puzzle. She lists Mr. Marvin as her co-debtor husband for the mortgage on her home for the past several years, but nowhere else in the file is there any indication that he has any part in her life, economic or otherwise. It could be that except for the home, Ms. Marvin and Mr. Marvin live carefully independent financial lives. Or it could be that Mr. Marvin is long gone and Ms. Marvin pays her bills alone, and she has neither the interest nor the time to get his signature for a joint bankruptcy petition. Or there may be a more complex arrangement that defies any neat classification.

10. Some commentators argue that a married person might file alone in a state that recognizes tenancy by the entireties. This legal device permits one spouse to keep the home free of all debts incurred only by the other spouse, without a limit on the value preserved. This puts a premium on treating the husband and wife separately, not joined in one bankruptcy. If both husband and wife are liable for a debt, however, the device does not save the home, and other commentators speculate that the sophistication of most creditors on this point causes the device to be worth little. In our sample, Pennsylvania recognizes tenancy by the entireties, which might cause more single filing by married people in that state. In fact, single-filing women are slightly underrepresented in Pennsylvania (28% of the single-filing women, rather than the expected 30%), whereas they are slightly overrepresented in Illinois, which has no similar legal provision (40% rather than the expected 30%).

11. Of the 261 single-filing women, 248 list an attorney representing them in bankruptcy. Most of the remainder seem to have consulted legal clinics for advice on filing.

12. For these comparisons, we use our entire common debtor sample, self-employed and wage earners alike, to parallel the United States labor force.

13. Our national figures are compiled from the March 1981 CPS data tape. The women identified in the table were either primary individuals or they were former wives or mothers now living in a family with no husband present. The men were either primary individuals or the husbands/fathers in a primary family. In 1980, the Census Bureau abandoned the practice of automatically classifying married males as household heads. We revert to the older usage and terminology for clarity in distinguishing the groups.

14. For the whole population we find that women earn 54¢ to every dollar earned by men. The commonly reported 59¢ is based on comparing only full-time, full-year workers, excluding part-time workers who are disproportionately female.

15. Both gender and the bankruptcy–income gap hurt the women in bankruptcy. The relative impact of each factor can be calculated from the first column of Table 8.1. The largest income gap is the $15,700 separating males in the national population and single-filing women in bankruptcy. A statistical decomposition shows that 78% of this gap is due to the national gender gap (males versus females in the national sample); the remaining 22% is the bankruptcy gap (the additional difference between the female heads of household in the national sample and the single-filing females in bankruptcy). For the women in bankruptcy, the "price" of being a woman is, on these averages,

about $12,244 of their lower family incomes, while the lower income associated with bankruptcy accounts for only $3,453.

16. For single-filing women compared with all female household heads, the index of dissimilarity for occupations is only 8.7 and for industries it is 11.5. The mean occupational prestige scores are statistically different at 40.0 for single-filing women and 39.1 for all women household heads, but the difference is substantially unimportant. For single-filing men compared with all male household heads, the index of dissimilarity for occupations is 13.5 and for industry it is 17.7. The overall prestige score for single-filing male bankrupt debtors was lower than that for men in the general population, 37.8 versus 41.6. As with the women, the difference is statistically significant but small.

When we examine the occupational prestige scores within each industry, there are two industries, nondurable manufacturing and finance, in which the bankrupt women had significantly higher prestige than the comparison sample of women. In retail trade, the bankrupt women had significantly lower prestige. These data indicate some occupational and industrial differences between women in bankruptcy and in the general population, but the differences are nothing like the differences when any combination of men and women are compared.

The women in bankruptcy are more likely than the general population of women workers to be service workers or administrative-managerial workers. In the national sample, women are more likely to be professional-technical and clerical workers.

17. But in the general population, women have statistically significantly *lower* occupational prestige (39.1 versus 41.6 points for men), and among the bankrupt sample, the women have significantly *higher* occupational prestige scores than men (40.8 points versus 37.8). However, these small prestige differences have little substantive significance.

18. These index numbers are much larger than those in Chapter Five because they refer to the male and female household heads, rather than to all male and female workers. Male household heads are likely to include some of the most stable and well-situated workers. Female household heads include disproportionate numbers of displaced homemakers, widows, unmarried mothers, and other women whose labor market choices are likely to be limited. Thus the index of dissimilarity is likely to be greater because the composition of the two groups differs so much.

19. See B. Reskin and H. Hartmann, eds., Women's Work, Men's Work: Sex Segregation on the Job (Washington: National Academy Press, 1986), p. 10.

20. One way to understand whether the income differences between men and women in and out of bankruptcy are a function of different occupations is by standardization, a technique we explained and used in Chapter Five. Here we standardize incomes first by giving everyone the occupational distribution of single-filing bankrupt women.

TABLE 8.4. Family and Personal Incomes Standardized by Single-Filing Women's Occupational Distribution, by Sex, CDS and CPS

Group	Standardization by Single-Filing Women's Occupational Distribution: Family Income	Personal Earnings
Men—national	$25,325	$17,652
Women—national	14,424	10,149

TABLE 8.4 (*Continued*)

	Standardization by Single-Filing Women's Occupational Distribution	
Group	Family Income	Personal Earnings
Men—bankruptcy	16,330	15,332
Women—bankruptcy	10,638	10,113 (unchanged)
Maximum income gap	14,687	7,537

Source: Consumer Bankruptcy Project; March 1981 Current Population Survey.

By comparison with Table 8.1, this shows that giving everyone the same occupational distribution as the single-filing women would have its maximum effect on the family and personal earnings of men in the national sample, but the effect would be to reduce earnings by only $1,000. For women in the national sample and for bankrupt men, the effect would be to raise slightly family and personal income, but the increase would be less than $500. The maximum income gap would shrink by only 6% for family income and by only 10% for personal earnings.

For comparison, we standardize by using the mean income for single-filing bankrupt women.

TABLE 8.5. Family and Personal Incomes Standardized by Single-Filing Women's Incomes, by Sex, CDS and CPS

	Standardization by Single-Filing Women's Mean Income Within Each Occupation	
Group	Family Income	Personal Earnings
Men—national	$11,183	$10,562
Women—national	10,288	9,778
Men—bankruptcy	10,952	10,397
Women—bankruptcy	10,638	10,113 (unchanged)
Maximum income gap	545	449

Source: Consumer Bankruptcy Project; March 1981 Current Population Survey.

If we let all of our sample members keep their own occupations but assign to them the mean earnings for each occupation that bankrupt women have, the income gap shrinks by over 95%. Everyone is worse off. In terms of family income, all men lose 58%, bankrupt men lose 31%, and all women lose 27%. Thus we conclude that it is low income within occupations, not occupational segregation, that accounts for the low income of single-filing women. What we do not know is the extent to which the low income is due to part-time or seasonal work or to periods of unemployment.

21. Single-filing women have significantly higher occupational prestige than men (Table 8.2). This finding probably reflects the prevalence of women in nominally higher status but poorly paid white-collar jobs.

22. When the home mortgage is removed, the debt/income ratio for men is significantly higher than that for women: 2.6 versus 1.7. At the median, both men and women have nonmortgage ratios of 0.8, and even at the 75th percentile men have a ratio of 1.5 versus women's 1.4. The principal difference between the sexes in the total nonmortgage debt/income ratio lies among the top quartile of men and women.

23. The supplements for women heads of household may come from a variety of sources, including alimony and child support, public assistance, interest and dividends, survivor's pension or social security benefits, or contributions from other working family members. We cannot identify with precision the sources of supplemental income in our data.

24. More than a fifth—22%—of the women filing joint petitions list their occupations as "housewife," an indication that they are not currently working outside the home, nor are they looking for outside work. Another 26.5% of the wives did not report an occupation, which might mean they were not part of the labor force. About 7% of the jointly filing women reported they were "unemployed," leaving about 45% of the wives employed.

Husbands and wives filing jointly in bankruptcy share some job-related characteristics. For example, eight of the ten self-employed wives are married to men who are also self-employed. The Pearson correlation coefficient between spouses on occupational prestige is a significant 0.23; the higher the prestige of the husband's job, the higher the prestige of the wife's job. Similarly, tenure has a significant correlation of 0.25; the longer the husband has been employed by his employer, the longer the wife has been employed by hers. On the other hand, if the husband has recently taken on a new job, it is very likely that the wife has as well. The one correlation that is negative (although not significant) is for income; the higher the husband's income, the lower the wife's income.

25. Among these bankrupt couples, when the wife is working the husband may not be. In 12% of the joint cases, the wife reported earnings but the husband did not. Thus among joint-filing couples in bankruptcy, 67% had only one earner. According to the Current Population Survey the comparable figure among husband–wife families in the national population in 1981 was 49%.

26. Mean occupational prestige scores were similar: 40 for the single filers, and 39 for the joint-filing wives. The occupational distributions of the two groups are also quite similar. About 30% of both groups are clerical workers, 20% of both groups are service workers, and about 15% are professional-technical workers. The single filers are somewhat more likely to be managerial workers or to be operatives, and the joint filers are somewhat more likely to be sales workers or private household workers. But the differences are slight: the index of dissimilarity between the two groups is 9.6.

The index of dissimilarity for industry is 11.8, only slightly higher. In both groups, a little over one-quarter of the women are employed in "professional services," such as educational and health services. Retail trade accounts for 20% of the joint filers and 15% of the single filers. The single filers are slightly more likely to be employed in manufacturing and in finance and other business services; the joint filers are somewhat more likely to be employed in transportation and in personal services.

Self-employment does not explain the income difference because not many women filers are self-employed. The single-filing women were twice as likely to be self-employed as married women; 7% of them are self-employed, versus only 3% of the joint filers. More importantly, the self-employed single filers had mean earnings of less than $7,000, and so the greater numbers of the self-employed among the single-women filers should have decreased the income gap between them and the joint filers. When both husbands and wives in the general population work full time, the wives' mean income is $13,250. U.S. Bureau of the Census, Current Population Reports, "Money Income of Households, Families, and Persons in the United States: 1981" (Washington: U.S. Government Printing Office, Series P-60, 1981), p. 137.

27. In 1984, three years after our data were collected, about 43% of wives were

part-time workers. About 33% of women who maintain families were part-time workers. U.S. Bureau of Labor Statistics, "Linking Employment Problems to Economic Status," Bulletin 2270 (September 1986), Tables B-1 and B-2, pp. 40–49.

28. Single-filing women paid significantly lower legal fees than did other petitioners, a mean fee of $405 versus $502 for everyone else ($t = -6.18$, $p = 0.00$). Single-filing women were no more likely than other filers to consult specialist attorneys or to pay their filing fees in installments. It is possible that they were more likely to use legal services but we could not tell from our data.

9

Medical Debt and Bankruptcy

Medical debt has had a particularly ambiguous and erratic impact on the making of consumer bankruptcy policy. Policymakers veer from indifference to sympathy, waiting for any convincing evidence of the relative importance of medical debts.[1] One classic bankruptcy stereotype pictures a debtor devastated by crushing medical bills who files bankruptcy as a last resort. There are such debtors. We begin our discussion of medical debts with two such cases.

Medical Routes to Financial Devastation

Fred and Janet Waller were not in comfortable financial circumstances during the years before bankruptcy, even without considering medical problems. In the year immediately preceding their filing their combined incomes totaled $13,084.75. Janet had worked three years as a presser with One-Hour Martinizing, but her income was modest. Fred started his job as clerk in a state agency in Peoria, Illinois, seven months before filing. Evidently he had been unemployed for some period before that, because his income the preceding year had been only $1,960, bringing their combined incomes that year to $7,418.

The Wallers seemed to manage on this income. They report little nonmedical debt. They owe $40.00 on their Illinois income taxes, $200 on their utilities, $30 to the bank for a safe deposit box rental, and $108 to a finance company. They do not have a car loan, a home mortgage, or any outstanding credit card charges. Their property is similarly modest. They own a 15-year-old Volkswagen and a 13-year-old Grand Prix, their clothes, and little else.

The picture of a very modest, stable financial condition is shattered by the inclusion of the Wallers' medical debt. The Wallers owe almost $20,000—

nearly 90% of their total debt—for medical bills. They owe for surgery and slings, dental care and physical therapy. They owe ambulance services, private physicians, physician groups, a medical school, a clinic, and a community hospital. Along with doctors of unspecified specialties, they list debts to radiologists, anesthesiologists, dentists, and to an obstetrician/gynecologist for "surgery." Not all the bills are from Peoria; some are from neighboring communities. There is good reason for this: the Wallers list 18 different addresses for the six years preceding their bankruptcy.

Besides their medical debts, the Wallers owe $902 for legal services rendered in 1978 by a lawyer now deceased. Also, one Mary Moran has filed a claim for "$995.95 for injuries received and damage done due to collision in which car owned by Janet Waller was involved." And here is where the clues about the medical claims begin to surface.

The Wallers are parties to a personal injury action, and one of the medical debts incurred in 1978 carries the tag "X-rays from accident." The remainder of the medical bills stretch across a period from 1978 through the 1981 filing. These may be the direct consequence of the accident, or there may be other medical problems as well. It is interesting to note that the Wallers are another example of the lag between the onset of financial trouble and the filing of bankruptcy—in this case three years.

The Wallers did not use their personal injury lawyer in their bankruptcy. Instead, they promised to pay their bankruptcy lawyer $590. No part of the fee had been paid at the time of filing, and there is no indication of the arrangements for fee payment. For their troubles, the Wallers discharged all their debts except the $40 tax payment, an amount in excess of $22,000. They had so little property that its value was well below the small Illinois exemption levels. They kept their property and began bankruptcy's fresh start. Clouding the fresh start was the possibility of further medical problems and the possible difficulty of getting future medical treatment except on a cash basis.

For Christy Brunini of Lebanon, Pennsylvania, an automobile accident in April 1979 was obviously the precipitating event for disastrous medical bills and an eventual bankruptcy. At the time of her bankruptcy, which was filed by a legal services attorney, Christy was unemployed; her only income during 1980 had been $2,064 in general assistance. She requested an installment plan for her filing fee, because she did not even have the $60 court fee to file bankruptcy.

When Ms. Brunini filed bankruptcy, her creditors were closing in. She owed $36,500 to medical providers, about 93% of her total unsecured debt of nearly $39,000. She was being sued by an ambulance company and by her landlord. There was a constable's levy on her personal property, which consisted of household furnishings valued at $1500, clothes valued at $500, and a 15-year-old Buick listed at $100. She reported $5.00 in her checking account. Ms. Brunini had moved several times—nine times in the past six years, all in neighboring small towns in Pennsylvania.

Among her creditors were an ambulance company and a hospital. Two persons injured in the accident had sued for personal injuries, and one of them was also suing to recover her insurance deductible. Under the Pennsylvania assigned claims plan, Ms. Brunini owed over $33,000 to the Insurance Company of North America.

Ms. Brunini received her discharge. She still might have to pay $22 on a disputed school district per capita tax, and she owed another $20 on her filing fees, but her other debts—nearly $39,000—were discharged. If she were at fault in the accident and liable for the injuries to the people who had sued her, those obligations were discharged as well and the injured people would have only her insurance, if any, to pay their medical bills. On the other hand, she did not have any assets worth seizing or income with which to pay them anyway, so the practical impact of bankruptcy for these creditors may not have been great.

The Importance of Medical Debt

There are at least two ways to measure the significance of a kind of debt in bankruptcy: Did it have a dramatic impact on a few bankrupt debtors, or did it have a measurable impact on a large number of debtors? The importance of medical debts depends on which definition one elects.

Christy Brunini and the Wallers are examples of bankruptcy petitioners for whom medical debt has a dramatic impact. The largest total medical debt in the sample, $129,400, was owed by an East Texas couple; the files revealed only that the debts were incurred through the illness of their child. In such cases, medical debts provide as clear an inference of the direct cause of financial catastrophe as we are ever likely to see from the bankruptcy files.

Cases that reveal crushing medical debts are as rare as they are dramatic. Only 27 debtors in our sample owed more than 85% of their unsecured debt for medical services or supplies. Only 20 debtors reported medical debts in excess of $10,000, and 9 debtors listed medical debts as their only unsecured debts. Depending on which number indicates the clearest picture of true medical catastrophe driving a debtor into bankruptcy, at most only 1% to 2% of the debtors in bankruptcy are demonstrably there because of catastrophic medical losses.

Altogether, the 1502 debtors in the CDS bankruptcy sample owed $1.4 million in medical debts, but these debts were unevenly distributed. Debtors in 717 cases reported no medical debts at all and another 7 had unspecified dollar valus for their debts. Among the 778 who reported a dollar value for medical debt, the median medical debt was $616. The mean debt was much higher, $1,755, once again reflecting the impact of a few debtors with extraordinary burdens.[2] Medical debt was about 11% of the mean total unsecured debt, but for individual debtors the proportion of unsecured debt ranged from 1% to 100%.

The first point these data illuminate is that dramatic medical losses are critical for only a tiny fraction of the bankrupt debtors. More modest medical debts are typical.

It is possible, however, that the data may understate medical debt because the sources of debt are not always apparent. The impact of disability, disease, or injury is not indicated only by a dramatic, overwhelming medical debt. Medical problems may contribute to financial troubles through ancillary effects. Illness may cause a debtor to lose his job or to lose paychecks through absenteeism. A debtor may need to move to a ground-floor apartment because of an injury, or stomach problems may require someone to buy a food processor and eat expensive foods. Parents of a sick child may travel to a distant city for treatments, staying in motels and eating in restaurants. Even direct medical charges, such as those for drugs and doctor visits, may show up as MasterCard and Visa charges rather than as classifiable medical debt.

Our data suggest that there might be another indirect impact of medical debt. Debtors with greater burdens of medical debt also have significantly more lawsuits filed against them when they file for bankruptcy.[3] Some of these lawsuits could be products of accidents that also caused the medical debts. Some may be from health care providers who are suing for repayment. In either case, the lawsuits may contribute to the debtor's decision to seek legal help and eventually to file bankruptcy.

The point once again is that reality is more complex than summary numbers can show. For a tiny fraction, medical catastrophe struck, and financial catastrophe was close behind. For another group of indeterminate size, medical debt may be an important part of a collapsing financial condition, but one that is difficult to discern. For the great majority of debtors in bankruptcy, however, medical debt is just one more unpaid bill among many.

Patterns of Distribution of Medical Debt

We looked for some pattern in medical indebtedness among the debtors to see if debtors with medical problems shared other characteristics. The possible groupings turned up few regularities. The amount of medical debt did not correlate significantly with occupational prestige, job tenure, self-employment, income in the previous year, gains or losses in income, family income, assets, secured debts, exemptions, migration, marital status, casualty losses, or attorney choice.[4] Medical debt did not vary significantly by state or by district.

It was somewhat surprising to find no correlation between medical debt and job tenure, because we had assumed that the illness or injury associated with high medical debts would imply job interruption as well. One explanation is that job tenure is so low for these debtors overall that medically caused job interruption is masked by all the layoffs and terminations unrelated to medical causes.

Debtors with medical debts were somewhat more likely to be in Chapter

7, and those in Chapter 7 owed more medical debt.[5] The mean medical debt owed by Chapter 7 filers was $2,032, significantly more than the $1,154 owed by Chapter 13 filers. About $1.1 million of the medical debt listed in our sample was scheduled in Chapter 7, with only about $0.3 million listed in Chapter 13. The few debtors with extraordinarily high debt were nearly all in Chapter 7.

Our efforts to find a pattern failed to suggest a special subgroup of debtors with medical problems. Other ways to analyze the data, however, give some insight into which debtors may be more at risk for financial collapse following medical trouble.

The Medical Debt/Income Ratio

A medical debt, much like any other debt, is overwhelming only in its proportion to income. Ms. Brunini and the Wallers had incomes that were very low, even by the standards of this sample; their debts other than their medical debts were also fairly low. For them, the medical debt/income ratio makes it clear that bankruptcy was almost inevitable. For other debtors, however, medical debts might or might not contribute significantly to their financial collapse, depending on the balance between debts and income. To explore this relationship, we constructed a medical debt/income ratio.

When we eliminate anyone who did not report any medical debt, the mean medical debt/income ratio is 0.20. This indicates that for roughly half of the debtors with some medical debts, a debtor at the mean would have to spend over two months' income to pay those debts alone. As earlier comparisons with the national population revealed, that figure indicates that the mean medical debt was enough to put a debtor family into the 5% of most indebted Americans, even if they did not owe another dime to anybody. These debtors would have had to struggle just to pay their debts to doctors and hospitals.[6]

Nonetheless, the central finding is that medical debt is not an especially important burden for most debtors. The median medical debt/income ratio for those with any medical debt is 0.04.[7] Some debtors have very great burdens of medical debt in relation to their incomes, and these cases pull up the mean. Across the sample, medical debts do not seem to play the central role in most consumer bankruptcies.

Medical debt/income ratios do not vary significantly by state or district, but they do vary by chapter. Not only do those in Chapter 7 owe more medical debt, but their medical debts are also a greater proportion of their incomes. For those in Chapter 7, the mean medical debt/income ratio is 0.25, significantly higher than the 0.09 of those in Chapter 13 ($F = 5.57$, $p = 0.02$). As we discuss later in Chapter Thirteen of this book, we have a difficult time sorting out Chapter 7 and Chapter 13 debtors on most economic criteria, but debtors with very large medical debts seem to find their way more quickly into Chapter 7.

The Special Hardship of Medical Debts for Some Groups

The medical debt/income ratio clearly shows the differential impact of medical debts on bankrupt petitioners, with single women suffering most. In Chapter Eight the data showed that women single filers had very low incomes. If we examine only the dollar value of debts owed, there is no significant difference between joint filers and single filers, men and women. But if we examine the medical debt/income ratio, then a significant difference emerges. Joint filers' mean medical debt/income ratio is 0.12, well below the sample mean, and the mean for single-filing males is 0.24, which is slightly higher than the sample mean of 0.20. But single-filing females report a mean medical debt/income ratio of 0.43, which is significantly higher than any other group ($F = 5.56$, $p = 0.00$). Thus the impact of medical debt on single-filing women is much greater, at least partly because they have lower incomes available to pay their debts.

The unemployed are also less likely to have an income to repay their medical debts.[8] Some unemployed are eligible for government support, such as Medicaid, but many still manage to be close enough to income levels above the standards required for state or federal medical assistance so that they acquire significant medical debt for which they are personally responsible. Those who are currently employed face a medical debt/income ratio of about 0.15, whereas the medical debt/income ratio for the unemployed is far higher at 1.19.

Causality for either group is ambiguous. Single women more often support children than do single men, and women face the costs of medical care for pregnancy. Sick children and pregnancy can also cause income loss. Similarly, a sick person is less likely to be able to hold down a job and a person out of work is less likely to have medical insurance. In all these cases the medical difficulty can affect both income and medical debt, driving the medical debt/income ratio beyond the repayment ability of the debtor.

These data suggest that, in addition to those who faced huge medical debts (such as the Wallers and Christy Brunini), more modest medical debts may contribute to the financial demise of some single women filers and unemployed debtors.

Lack of Medical Insurance

Whether a family is financially crippled by a medical problem is not a function of income only; it is also a function of whether the debtor is insured and can shift most of the medical bills to a third party. We explore the possibility that employed debtors with no medical benefits might be more likely to seek bankruptcy as a way to deal with their medical debt.

It is startling that the courts, which ask for detailed information on income, require no information on a debtor's total compensation package, even though fringe benefits now add as much as 25% of wages to the compensation packages of many working Americans. Because the courts do not ask about fringe benefits, we cannot know with certainty which of our petitioners were not covered by insurance. Some industries, however, are less likely to offer workers fringe benefits, and we made a rough calculation from the trends in each industry. Among the industries with fewer fringe benefits are agriculture, retail trade, and personal services.[9] In all three industries, employment is likely to be seasonal or part-time, which further reduces the likelihood of substantial fringe benefits. Moreover, employment in these fields is highly decentralized, with many small, marginal companies employing workers. Their workers are unlikely to be able to bargain collectively for fringe benefit packages. National data show that women are disproportionately found in retail trade and personal services,[10] and we speculate that single women filers might be especially likely to find themselves in such industries and without medical coverage.

This reasoning suggests that employees in industries with low fringe benefits are more likely than the norm to have high medical debt/income ratios and that women in bankruptcy are more likely to be in these industries than in others. Our hypotheses are supported. Being in an industry with low fringe benefits is significantly related to higher medical debt/income ratios,[11] and there was a significant interaction between being a woman single filer and being in one of these industries.[12] A measurable amount of variance could be explained by just two variables: filing status (e.g., joint, single male, single female) and industry (low fringe benefit, not low fringe benefit).

Table 9.1 shows the effects of these two variables in a multiple classification analysis.[13] The unadjusted deviations show how much is added or subtracted

TABLE 9.1. Multiple Classification Analysis of Medical Debt/Income Ratio by Filing Status and Likelihood of Fringe Benefits[a]

Variable and Category	*N*	Unadjusted Deviation	Eta
Filing status			
Joint	315	−0.02	
Single male	95	−0.02	
Single female	80	0.09	
			0.10
Fringe benefits			
Unlikely	72	0.14	
More likely	418	−0.02	
			0.15
Grand mean = 0.14			
Multiple R^2	0.032		
Multiple R	0.178		

[a]Cases with extreme values or assets, total debt, or income are removed; excludes cases without any medical debts or without any income.

Source: Consumer Bankruptcy Project.

from the mean medical debt/income ratio by the petitioners' characteristics. Thus being a joint filer or a single male subtracts 0.02 from the medical debt/income ratio, and being a single filing woman adds 0.09. Being in an industry with fewer fringe benefits had an even more powerful influence. It adds 0.14 to the medical debt/income ratio, which doubles the mean medical debt/income ratio. Thus the double whammy of being both female and in an industry with low fringe benefits raises the debtors' medical debt/income ratio from 0.14 to 0.37.

This analysis does not by any means explain every nuance involved in medical debts. Indeed, the multiple R squared indicates that only 3% of the variance in medical debt/income ratios can be explained by these two variables.[14] On the other hand, these data give some clue that the consequences of occupational differences show up in the relatively greater medical debts women have when they face bankruptcy.

Policy Implications

Medical debt arouses our sympathy because illness is socially defined as something that is "not the fault" of the sick or the injured. Given the morally ambiguous atmosphere of bankruptcy, illness is one cause that most policymakers would be willing to excuse. Medical debt, after all, can literally be a matter of life and death. To buy medical care—even if one cannot pay for it—is more acceptable than buying fine clothes or fancy cars for which one cannot pay.

Our central finding is that crushing medical debt is not the widespread bankruptcy phenomenon that many have supposed. To the extent that the typical debtors in bankruptcy are painted as sympathetic characters because they are struggling with insurmountable medical debts, these data show that "typical" is the wrong adjective. Only a few debtors find themselves in such extreme circumstances. Once again, a stereotype tossed back and forth in heated debates is too insubstantial to justify a policy position that affects all debtors.

A somewhat larger group of debtors supports a less dramatic, but still sympathetic picture: A number of debtors add medical debt to their already overburdened balance sheets, and, at some point, they finally tumble over into bankruptcy. About half of all debtors carry some medical debt, and many carry substantial medical debt. Although these medical debts are not the obvious cause of the debtors' bankruptcies, they are part of their financial troubles. Moreover, medical problems may manifest themselves in a number of financial consequences, including lower incomes and higher nonmedical debts. This is probably the most sympathetic group of debtors, but their numbers are difficult to pin down.

These data again illustrate the interaction between bankruptcy and other policy decisions. For example, most industrialized democracies provide medical coverage for all citizens, but the United States has been unwilling to do so. Bankruptcy once again plays a role in the larger social support system, functioning as an insurer of last resort for persons hit with medical catastrophe well beyond their means to repay. Mr. and Mrs. Waller need not struggle forever, facing one collection suit after another. They washed away nearly $20,000 in charges for medical debt through their discharge. Christy Brunini discharged nearly $39,000, and the East Texas couple with the sick child shed debts totaling over $129,000. From the point of view of the individual with enormous medical debt, bankruptcy releases the debtors from an indentured future, much as comprehensive medical insurance would have.

But the differences between medical insurance and bankruptcy should not be overlooked. Bankruptcy worked well for the Wallers and Ms. Brunini because they had very little property. For debtors in somewhat more prosperous circumstances, bankruptcy would have been a costly alternative—perhaps involving loss of a home, furniture, life savings, a retirement nest egg, and so on. Indeed, we cannot know how much the Wallers or Ms. Brunini managed to pay before the debts piled up too far and they lost all hope of repaying. The files do not tell whether they once had assets, a home or a decent car, that are now gone. We see only the debtor who has or has been reduced to little property, who has no reasonable hope of repayment, and who faces bankruptcy as the only real hope to gain economic stability. Depending on the generosity of the available exemptions, the debtor family with a medical catastrophe can make their creditors stop their collection efforts, but only after the debtors wipe out virtually all their financial assets.

Bankruptcy is a niggardly insurer of last resort in other ways. In Ms. Brunini's file it was clear that the accident had happened more than three years before her filing. She had already been sued on two debt collection actions. The file does not tell how many collection letters and phone calls she received, how hard her creditors tried to collect, and how hard she worked to stay out of bankruptcy. The Wallers filed only after Mrs. Waller's wages had been garnished, and Ms. Brunini filed only after a creditor had a judgment threatening to take away everything she owned. The personal cost of the prebankruptcy collection system should not be ignored. Obviously, if these debtors could have paid with medical insurance rather than the "insurance of last resort" of bankruptcy, the nonmonetary costs they suffered would have been much lower.

Moreover, we cannot tell how many medical providers refused service when these debtors could not show proof of insurance, especially since these medical debts were incurred over a period of two or three years. Debtors who can say "Please call my insurance company to take care of all this" are obviously in a different position from the debtors who end up in bankruptcy to deal with their financial problems. After bankruptcy, as we noted with the Wallers, the debtors may find it impossible to get medical services unless they pay in cash.

In the second half of this book, we discuss the impact of bankruptcy on the creditors. Here we pause to note that although bankruptcy may give the debtor a fresh start, it passes those bad debt losses on to the health care providers. Unlike insurance or a public medical plan, bankruptcy does not spread these costs over a large group of workers or taxpayers. Instead, particular hospitals, doctors, and ambulance services, among others, suffer the effects of these bad debts. These creditors can to some extent spread the costs among their paying patients, but the net result is that the burden of a substantial social problem is borne disproportionately.

As an insurer of last resort, the bankruptcy system works to alleviate pressing medical bills. But it does so at high cost to the debtor, and potentially to their creditors and other citizens. Bankruptcy is part of a social support system, but it is less than generous.

Finally, we note that the data on medical debt show a great randomness. With the exception of associations between medical debts and employment in certain industries, unemployment, and being female, medical debt showed no important correlations with other financial or social circumstances of the debtors. The apparent lack of pattern in medical debts is part of the overall story of bankruptcy, part of the theme that no one is exempt from financial catastrophe. Illness or injury is part of the story for most bankruptcy petitioners and the central theme for a few.

Notes

1. One study of the Northern District of New York concluded that, contrary to published reports, health care costs were a negligible proportion, less than 2%, of scheduled debts. B. A. Gold and E. A. Donahue, Health Care Costs and Personal Bankruptcy, 7 Journal of Health Politics, Policy, and Law, 734–39 (Fall 1982). This study, however, was limited to a single district, and it did not distinguish secured from unsecured debt.

By contrast, many studies identify medical debts as a significant factor in the financial difficulties of the debtor. See Commission on Bankruptcy Laws of the United States, Report (Washington: U.S. Government Printing Office, 1973), Part 1, p. 44 (review of studies of personal bankruptcy). One researcher has reported that large medical debts appear to be an important influence in the bankruptcy of single-women filers, an issue we consider later in this chapter. P. Shuchman, The Average Bankrupt: A Description and Analysis of 753 Personal Bankruptcy Filings in Nine States, 88 Commercial Law Journal 288, 289, note 7 (1983).

In one of our sample districts, the Western District of Texas, a locally required form asked debtors the reason for their bankruptcy. A little over 8% of our sample reported health problems to be the principal reason for their bankruptcy. The health problem might not be reported in medical debt, however; it might instead be reflected in shorter working hours, disability leaves, and other conditions that affect income more than debt.

2. The standard deviation was $5,721.

3. Debtors received a score of 1 for each type of action that had been filed against them: judgments, seizures, repossessions, or lawsuits. This index of legal actions correlated significantly but not strongly with medical debt ($r = 0.07$, $p = 0.01$). We compared the index of lawsuits a debtor had with the medical debt/income ratio. There was a significant difference among the debtors in their medical debt/income ratio depending on their score on this index ($F = 3.92$, $p = 0.01$). For those with one action,

the medical debt/income ratio mean was 0.19; with two actions, medical debt/income ratio rose to 0.55; with three or more it was 0.47. Debtors in the top 5% of medical debts reported twice as many pending lawsuits than others with medical debts.

4. We found that persons with higher levels of medical debts were less likely to be homeowners. Although the finding was statistically significant (that is, a similar difference would likely occur between homeowners and nonhomeowners in another sample), the magnitude of the difference was small ($r = -0.07$, $p = 0.03$). Thus the substantive importance of the finding is not great.

We also found that medical debt correlated with the number of unsecured creditors ($r = 0.12$, $p = 0.00$), but the reason for this is probably the specialization within the medical community. Each specialist bills separately and becomes a separate creditor. Thus the ambulance, hospital, anesthetist, laboratory, radiologist, surgeon, pharmacy, and many other potential creditors may be involved in just one episode. And, as expected from its part–whole relationship with unsecured debt, medical debt correlated positively with the total unsecured debt value ($r = 0.22$, $p = 0.00$).

5. The correlation between chapter and size of medical debt was statistically significant but substantively weak ($r = -0.07$, $p = 0.02$). Chapter 13 filers had a standard deviation of only $1900, but the standard deviation among Chapter 7 filers was 3 1/2 times larger at $6,800.

6. The medical debt/income ratio becomes quite high for those with the largest medical debts. Among the top 5% of the sample in terms of the dollar value of medical debts, the mean medical debt/income ratio is 1.69, or about 20 months' income. Medical debts may not be the only problems of this group, but they clearly are staggering in themselves.

7. The standard deviation was 0.88. The range was from 0.001 to 17.7. The 25th percentile was 0.01 and the 75th percentile was 0.12. There were no significant differences in medical debt/income ratios by state, district, attorney, or whether the debtor received government payments.

8. We use the term "unemployed" to describe those who are apparently unemployed from the reports in their bankruptcy files. As we indicate in Chapter Five, the term has special significance for labor statistics, and we cannot be sure that our debtors meet all the qualifications of those standards.

9. The industries least likely to be covered by pensions are personal services (10.3% of workers covered), agriculture (10.7%), entertainment and recreation (16.1%), and retail trade (19.6%). The same industries are the least likely to be covered by group health insurance: only 22.6% are covered in personal services, 24.5% in agriculture, 29.8% in entertainment and recreation, and 36.8% in retail trade. By contrast, health plans cover 82% of workers in mining and 81% in manufacturing. U.S. Bureau of the Census, Statistical Abstract of the United States, 1988 (108th ed., Washington: U.S. Government Printing Office, 1987), Table 656, p. 396. There were virtually no members of the consumer bankruptcy sample in entertainment and recreation, so we excluded that industry in the text. The three remaining industries account for over 70% of the nonsupervisory private sector employees who were exempt from minimum wage legislation in 1985: 1.0 of 1.6 million agricultural workers, 2.5 million of 15.9 million retail trade workes, and 3.8 million of 17.0 million service workers were not covered even by minimum wage. S. Levitan and I. Shapiro, Working but Poor: America's Contradiction (Baltimore: Johns Hopkins University Press, 1987), p. 54.

10. Women workers accounted for 71% of retail sales clerks and 59% of service workers in 1980. U.S. Bureau of the Census, Statistical Abstract of the United States,

1981 (102d ed., Washington: U.S. Government Printing Office, 1981), Table 675, pp. 402–4. Women are in general less likely to be covered by fringe benefits. In 1980, for example, 61% of male workers but only 45% of female workers had group health insurance. *Id.*, Table 544, p. 334.

11. $F = 10.83$, $p = .00$. This finding comes from a two-way analysis of variance, a multivariate technique used here to examine medical debt/income ratio using type of industry and filing status as independent variables.

12. $F = 4.50$, $p = 0.012$.

13. Multiple classification analysis is similar to multiple regression analysis, except that the independent variables are measured in categories (single, joint) rather than intervals (dollars). The beta coefficient is the analogue of the unstandardized regression coefficient; it shows the effect of each variable controlling for the others.

14. There is actually a triple whammy, because the single filers and those in low-benefit industries are more likely to have lawsuits filed against them. We combined our legal actions index with the other explanatory variables used in this chapter, filing status and low–fringe benefit industry. Explained variance rose to 5%, and the main effect of the legal action index on medical debt/income ratio was highly significant ($F = 6.0$, $p = 0.00$). In addition, there was a significant interaction between legal actions and being a single-filing woman ($F = 3.0$, $p = 0.00$), and the three-way interaction was significant ($F = 26.6$, $p = 0.00$).

10

Credit Card Junkies

The credit card symbolizes the turbulent consumer economics of the 1980s. Soaring real interest rates through the decade have made the credit card business enormously attractive to card issuers, while consumers have seemed singularly willing to live life on the plastic edge of financial disaster. A staggering 572.2 million credit cards—2.5 cards for every man, woman, and child in the United States—were outstanding in 1981.[1] Creditors and debtors have cooperated in creating a mountain of credit card debt.

Most observers believe that this trend has contributed to the great increase in consumer bankruptcies during the 1980s. Many debtors trace their financial trouble to excessive use of credit cards. Credit counseling services encourage debtors to cut up their credit cards as a ritual encouragement to financial recovery.

Creditors shoulder part of the blame here: Who has not received unsolicited offers of credit cards with substantial "preapproved" credit lines? The stories of excessive credit extension abound, including the pussy cat in Ohio who got a credit card in the mail, the inmates at a state prison who all got credit cards because "they had stable addresses," and the fellow in Dallas who went home from the foreclosure sale on his house to find waiting for him a new $5,000 Gold MasterCard.

Many people share an intuition that credit cards represent a peculiarly dangerous form of credit. The cards may give fraudulent debtors opportunities for chicanery that are unavailable with other forms of credit. More commonly, credit cards may tempt the marginally irresponsible debtor into truly serious irresponsibility. For some people, presenting plastic to the cashier may not seem like spending. Debtors who never dream of seeking a $5,000 bank loan might run up $5,000 in charges of $50 at a time. Each month the debtor might make the small minimum payment with a vow to start paying off the balance the next month. When the maximum credit limit is reached on one card, a new card with a new credit line may arrive in the mail—the debtor's reward for having made all those minimum payments right on time. At the end of that road may lie bankruptcy.

In addition to the seductiveness of incremental irresponsibility, credit cards may be particularly insidious because of their high interest rates, often approaching 20%. Once a debtor becomes seriously overcommitted to credit card debt, the interest charges alone can make it impossible to recover.

Because we shared the common perception that short-term debt might represent a special problem for consumers, we wanted to analyze our data to see if credit card debt were especially important in consumer bankruptcy. We begin with the stories of people with staggering credit card debts, then we turn to the numbers.

A Couple of Junkies

We searched the files for debtors with very large credit card debts relative both to their other debts and to their incomes. We were not looking for the typical debtor who uses a credit card, but rather for one who might illustrate serious credit card abuse. After we read a number of files, our nominees for the award for sleaziest use of a credit card (consumer division) were Hubert and AnneMarie Voelker.

The Voelkers filed Chapter 7 bankruptcy in South Texas. They claimed to own very few assets, valuing their personal goods at only $3,000. They did not own a home, and they have one car. The Voelkers had about $1,700 in secured debts, most of it apparently for the purchase of some furniture and other household goods. There is no record that they reaffirmed any of this secured debt once in bankruptcy. They may have arranged informally with their secured creditors to keep paying on these bills or they may have surrendered the collateral to their creditors.

The Voelkers had about $15,000 in unsecured debt. About 80% of it, almost $12,000, was owed on credit cards. Other than that, they had medical debts, about $2,200, and a small bank loan. Except for the medical debt, Hubert and AnneMarie present a picture of overconsuming debtors looking for a discharge on a pile of unsecured debt.

Although we cannot know all their circumstances, their file tells no obvious tale of woe. Hubert had a job as a furnace operator that paid him $20,000 per year, and he had been in that same job for seven years. AnneMarie was a housewife, apparently not employed outside the home. The file contains no evidence of an income interruption—no layoff, job change, or the like. These seem to be people who got the credit cards, ran up charges without buying anything of lasting value, and evidently hopped right into bankruptcy.

As bad as this sounds, it gets worse. The Voelkers filed for bankruptcy in 1981 precisely six years and two weeks after their last Chapter 7 bankruptcy. As we discuss in the next chapter, true repeaters are rare birds in our sample. The Voelkers waited just the legally mandated six years between bankruptcies, with only 14 days' cushion (just in case they had counted wrong?). Perhaps they circled in red on their calendar the final day of the sixth year since they last stiffed their creditors, while Hubert and AnneMarie charged to the tune of almost $15,000 on a $20,000-a-year income. They may have waited for the big day when they were once again eligible for bankruptcy the way most of us wait for Christmas.

These facts suggest to us that the Voelkers were eager to tap the "enrichment" of bankruptcy "as often as the law allows," as one study put it. As far as we can tell, the Voelkers succeeded. No creditor objected to discharge, and Hubert and AnneMarie went forth free of the shackles of debt once more, perhaps with a new bankruptcy-eligible day marked on their 1987 calendar. On the evidence of the file, these are the classic abusers of consumer credit.

Before we close this story, we pause to play devil's advocate. The Voelkers' file, complete as it is, could not stand for the proposition of unmitigated abuse without much more individualized inquiry. The same facts would fit a rather different story. Spinning a tale from the medical debts listed in the file, it is possible to envision Hubert as holding down a middling job whose primary benefit is health insurance. AnneMarie may have been at home because of chronic debilitating medical problems. If AnneMarie's hypothetical troubles were longstanding, the Voelkers' earlier bankruptcy could have been the solution to crushing medical burdens. They could have been overwhelmed by medical debt when Hubert finally landed a job with decent health insurance. Within a year after he started on the job, the Voelkers might have seen that they could never make a dent in their old medical bills, so they declared bankruptcy.

Things never got that bad again, now that they had insurance with Hubert's employer, but over the next six years they gradually charged a little more than they could pay off each month. While the health insurance covered 80% of the outpatient bills and all the hospitalization, the Voelkers struggled on a $20,000 income to pay their 20% share of doctor bills and drug bills and to buy all the other nonprescription medical supplies and small luxuries that make life more comfortable for AnneMarie. The widespread acceptance of bank cards means that most of these charges show up in their bankruptcy files as credit card debts rather than medical debts. The charges added up along with the interest compounding at 19½%. Within six years they owed $15,000 on a $20,000 income, and bankruptcy looked like the only solution again. They waited until they were eligible, and they filed.

The point of the second story is one we make with pedantic frequency. The reality about these debtors is impossible to know from the records, where the nuances and shadings that make us laugh or cry are not always fully revealed. The sad story we tell here is one that takes an imagination—quite a leap from $2,200 in medical bills into a long tale of woe. But the point is a fair one: The tale of woe and the treatise on greed could be supported by exactly the same file.

The way that two stories could emerge from one file reminds us that the normative elements—the part that makes us call debtors "junkies" or "victims"—is not rigorously quantifiable. Instead, normative judgments can emerge only on close, individual questioning. Having said that, we wish a creditor had objected to the Voelkers' discharge and the judge had called them in and explored all this, because we strongly suspect these folks were seriously abusing the consumer credit system. On the other hand, any creditor who lent them all that money may well have been too lax to object to their discharges.

The necessity for individual inquiry should not be taken to mean that a statistical approach is useless. We have no doubt that from among the cases that look like the Voelkers, a good number would be found to represent abuse of the credit system and of the bankruptcy system. For social science and policy purposes, we can safely assume that a fair portion of such cases represent abuse and draw such conclusions as we think appropriate. The second Voelker story merely emphasizes that from a judicial perspective numbers can only isolate possible abusers; individual inquiry is required to separate the unfortunate from the unscrupulous.

A second debtor in our files has a more typical story, but one with its own ambiguities. Anthony Allegro filed Chapter 7 bankruptcy in the Eastern District of Pennsylvania in July 1981. He had no secured debts. He listed over $10,000 of unsecured debts, of which about $7,000 had been rung up on four Visas and three MasterCards from seven different banks. His credit card debt alone represented more than 80% of his 1980 income, which was about $8,500. If we stop with these cold numbers, Anthony looks like a runner-up in the abuse award sweepstakes, and his creditors look like dummies for giving him so much credit.

Allegro's file, slim as it is, adds more depth to his story. His historical income was probably closer to the income he reported for 1979, almost $16,000. Each of the seven banks that had issued cards to him might reasonably have granted a credit limit of $1,000 against a $16,000 income. We cannot tell from the files when the credit cards were used, but much of the debt may have been incurred when Anthony had the larger income. He may have charged the rest during 1980, after he apparently lost his job as a salesman, but when he may have expected to be reemployed shortly. By July 1981, when he filed for bankruptcy, he still had not found another job. It is plausible that Anthony was carrying too much consumer debt even before he lost his job and that the credit card issuers had granted rather more credit to him than they should have. Both debtor and creditors may have been too sanguine in assuming that incomes only go up—and that they never go away. Yet both may have been guilty in Anthony's case merely of working close to the edge rather than borrowing or lending irresponsibly.

Besides losing his job, Anthony was in the middle of a divorce. Perhaps because of his separation, he listed only about $1,000 in property, consisting of a one-third share of a burial plot co-owned jointly with his mother and brother as well as miscellaneous household goods. He had already borrowed the total value of his life insurance as well. The separation suggests another possible explanation for the credit card charges: His soon-to-be-former wife may have incurred the charges, and Anthony may have been ordered to pay them as part of his divorce settlement.

Anthony's bankruptcy presents a picture of someone who had incurred too much credit card debt relative to his income, perhaps in part because of the financial strains of divorce. With continued employment, he might have climbed back from his debts, but a year of unemployment triggered his bankruptcy. Of course, it is possible to reverse his story, as with the Voelkers. On examination in court, we might find that he charged wildly just before bankruptcy, raising questions about his motives. But without a creditor's objection and a subsequent inquiry in open court, we cannot tell.

We can be sure of one thing the Voelkers and Anthony Allegro had in common: Their creditors had approved credit card charges that ultimately rivaled their yearly incomes.

Measuring Credit Card Debt

Our data base includes two categories that cover most of the debt conventionally associated with credit cards. "All-purpose cards" includes travel and entertainment cards, such as Diner's Club and American Express, and bank cards, such as MasterCard and Visa. The second category, "store cards," embraces virtually all unsecured credit extended by a seller of goods and services for its own products. This category includes department stores that issue their own cards and local merchants who sell on credit without using a plastic card. It does not include the specialized categories of debt, such as gasoline companies, medical debt or utilities, set forth separately in Table 14.1, but it does include some general debts not usually put on a credit card. Debts to plumbers or lawyers or funeral homes show up as store card charges because they are debts for goods and services, even though a plastic card may not have been used. This sort of general open-account debt is like credit card debt in that it is short-term, unsecured credit. It is sometimes unlike credit card debt when creditors expect it to be paid promptly and in full (no small monthly payments), or when they do not charge the high interest rates associated with credit cards. Our work in the files gives us the sense that the great bulk of the "store" debt owed by wage earners in our sample is similar to credit card debt; it consists of charges to Marshall Field's and Sears, rather than general open-account debt. Because we did not separately code the various types of charges, however, we cannot state with certainty the relative proportion of store credit card debt versus general open-account debt, and we necessarily inflate somewhat our reports of consumers using store credit cards by including general-account debt.

We eliminate the self-employed and the formerly self-employed from the analysis in this chapter. Because much of the store debt of the self-employed is actually business debt, owed to contractors and suppliers, including them in this analysis would wildly distort our reports of credit card debt. By removing the presently and formerly self-employed, we limit our reports of store cards primarily to consumer debt, although some entrepreneurial debt undoubtedly remains and tends to inflate the amount of debt in this category (see the discussion in Chapter Six).[2]

The General Picture

Nearly nine out of ten wage earners—88%—had at least some outstanding credit card debt when they filed bankruptcy. Wage earners in our sample carried a total of $3.9 million of credit card debt, a mean debt of $3,700 for each debtor. Credit card debt is certainly one common denominator for debtors in bankruptcy.[3]

The number of debtors carrying credit card debt and the total amount of debt listed is not surprising, given the ubiquity of open-account credit. These data affect the financial health of the debtor even more than the initial figures might suggest. Credit card debt is short-term debt, often requiring payment in 30 to 90 days, and it carries very high rates of interest, often 20% or more. If the first pressure, short-term repayment, is relaxed by credit card issuers, the solace is balanced by the second pressure as interest mounts.

Table 10.1 describes credit card debt for the wage earners in our sample. Half the debtors have combined credit card debts in excess of $2,100, and a quarter have debts over $4,200. Fewer debtors had all-purpose cards than store cards, but most of them had some kind of plastic card. The store cards repre-

TABLE 10.1. Distribution of Credit Card Debt (never self-employed debtors)[a]

Distribution	Total Credit Card Debt	All-Purpose Credit Card Debt	Store Credit Card Debt
Mean	$ 3,741	$ 2,010	$ 2,933
s.d.	7,606	1,847	$ 7,364
25th percentile	922	865	732
Median	2,097	1,523	1,524
75th percentile	4,178	2,528	3,064
Total $	3,939,774	930,769	3,009,005
N	1,053	463	1,026
Unspecified amount	6		
Missing	149	739	176
Proportion of debtors with total credit card debt/income ratios:[b]			
	At least 0.200	38.3%	
	At least 0.250	30.8%	
	At least 0.500	12.8%	

[a]Cases with extreme values for assets, income, or debt have been excluded. Currently or formerly self-employed debtors are excluded.

[b]As a percentage of debtors with computable credit card debt/income ratio (N = 934).

Source: Consumer Bankruptcy Project.

sent a higher mean debt burden ($2,900) than the all-purpose cards ($2,000), but the difference is not statistically significant. Store card debt and general-purpose card debt are identical at the medians, suggesting that debtors use their Sears and Visa cards about the same way.

The debt/income ratios for credit card debt at the bottom of Table 10.1 show how much of each debtor's income had been committed to a credit card debt before the bankruptcy filing. Almost one-third of the wage earners owe credit card debt equal to or greater than three months' gross income, a debt/income ratio of 0.25. Given the fact that credit cards offer generally the most short-term, high-interest consumer debt available, these ratios are remarkable, even in our debt-burdened sample. That ratio means that debtors making $20,000 per year would owe $5,000 to Montgomery Ward, Visa, and the rest, with the interest meter running at around $1,000 per year while they worked on it.

Even more striking are the numbers further out at the margins. Nearly 13% of the debtors in this sample owe more than half a year's income in short-term credit card debt. That is $10,000 or more from a $20,000 annual income. The interest payments are about $2,000 per year, or 10% of their total incomes just to stay even on this one type of debt! Although these figures are doubtless inflated by a few hidden entrepreneurs and their business debts, they reveal serious signs of credit malfunction. Imagine owing more than half your yearly income to J.C. Penney and MasterCard and see how long the shudder lasts. The only ones who might shudder longer are the credit managers at Penney's and your bank.

Defining Junkies

The term "credit card junkies" has become popular in recent years to describe people who abuse credit, who do not or cannot use credit responsibly. In this section we examine the data to uncover the potential abusers frequently expected to populate the bankruptcy files.

Although the aggregate data on credit card use reveal some breathtaking numbers, they are far too blunt an instrument to indicate how many debtors could be classified as junkies, so we try to create more refined tests; however, we are mindful that we can make neither the clinical diagnoses nor the moral judgments implied in much of the discussion about credit card junkies. As the two stories with the Voelkers' file show, without a specialized, fact-finding inquiry, we cannot be sure of abuse even in a case that seems dramatic on its face. As a consequence, the tests we use to refine the data analysis are tests only to narrow the range of suspects—people who, on more individualized inquiry, might be credit card junkies.

There is no generally accepted criterion for identifying a credit card junkie. To look for debtors who might be junkies or abusers, we use a process of elimination. As we did in Table 10.1, we again eliminate the 300 debtors who are or were self-employed, taking out their large commercial debts. We then have 1202 wage earners, of whom 143 (12%) owe no credit card debt of any description. This pares the base of suspected credit abusers to 1059.

For the remaining wage earners with some credit card debt, there are several ways to identify abusers. One method is to identify those with disproportionate credit card debt relative to their income. This definition is attractive because it relates the individual's debt to the income available for repayment, but it is insensitive to the actual dollar amounts and it ignores the fact that these debtors may have truly stunning debts of other kinds as well. As we saw in Table 10.1, about 13% of the debtors owe one-half or more of their annual income in credit card debt. This group we call the "high debt/income group." They account for about 34% of the credit card debt in the sample.

A second definition of the junkie examines debt composition. We define the "short-term debt junkie" as the person with at least $100 in credit card debt whose credit card debt represents at least 75% of total unsecured debt.[4] For this person, the credit card debt was probably a major influence on the decision to petition for bankruptcy. This group also accounts for 153 persons, or about 13% of the wage earners in the sample, and they account for nearly one-quarter (24.7%) of the credit card debt in the sample.[5]

A third definition of the junkie is the person who causes the creditors the greatest loss. We identified the 15% of the debtors who reported the largest credit card debts as the "heavy users." By definition, this group consisted of 159 debtors (15% of the wage earners), and together they accounted for over half (52.9%) of the credit card debt.[6]

There was substantial overlap among our three differently defined groups, and 23 debtors were "junkies" by all three definitions. These are people whose characteristics we can analyze in further detail.

Table 10.2 summarizes the characteristics of the potential junkies compared with the other wage earners. In general, the first two definitions of junkies yield more similar results than does the definition of the heavy users. According to the first two definitions, the junkies look similar to nonjunkies in many respects, but they have lower incomes and higher debts. Even though the entire sample is characterized by low earnings, debtors with high credit card debt relative to their income or relative to their other debt have much lower incomes. The two groups do not differ from other wage earners in their assets, secured debt, occupational prestige, or migration histories. But they have significantly higher unsecured debt and they are significantly less likely to be filing jointly.

There are also some differences between the junkies who are defined by the debt/income ratio and those defined by the proportion of their unsecured debt due to credit cards. Compared with other wage earners, the junkies defined by the debt/income ratio (first number column) have significantly lower job tenure, are significantly more likely to be in Chapter 7, and if in Chapter 7, are significantly more likely to report a recent income drop of 10% or more.[7] Thus it is possible that their high debt/income ratios reflect a shrinking denominator (reduced income) and not just an expanding numerator (debt).

A third approach to identifying the potential abusers is examining the top

TABLE 10.2. Characteristics of Credit Card "Junkies," by Three Definitions (never self-employed debtors with some credit card debt)[a]

Variable	High Debt/ Income Group[b]	All Others	Short-Term Debt Junkies[c]	All Others	Heavy Users[d]	All Others
Family income (mean)	$ 9,669***	$17,505	$13,825***	$16,601	$19,954***	$15,558
Assets (mean)	$24,430	$23,148	$24,316	$22,630	$36,207***	$20,524
Unsecured debt (mean)	$23,180***	$ 7,984	$ 7,236***	$11,198	$26,765***	$ 7,748
Secured debt (mean)	$23,238	$16,808	$16,896	$17,292	$28,307***	$15,272
Occupational prestige (mean)	39.1	37.0	37.8	36.9	42.5***	36.1
Job tenure (mean)	2.6***	5.0	4.2	4.7	5.2	4.5
Proportion in Chapter 13	0.25**	0.44	0.36	0.37	0.28*	0.39
Intrastate mover (%)	0.34	0.35	0.37	0.36	0.28*	0.38
Interstate mover (%)	0.13	0.10	0.08	0.12	0.16	0.11
Joint filers (%)	0.42**	0.57	0.48*	0.58	0.63	0.56
Proportion who are income gainers with 10% or more gain[e]	0.31	0.37	0.27	0.30	0.31	0.29
Proportion who are income losers with 10% or greater loss[e]	0.39**	0.19	0.22	0.18	0.22	0.18

[a]Cases with extreme values on assets, income, and total debt excluded. Currently and formerly self-employed debtors excluded.

[b]Credit card debt/income ratio equals or exceeds 0.50.

[c]Credit card debt equals or exceeds $100 and constitutes 75% or more of unsecured debt.

[d]The 15% of all debtors with the highest credit card debts.

[e]Computed for Chapter 7 only.

*$p \leq 0.05$

**$p \leq 0.01$

***$p \leq 0.001$

Source: Consumer Bankruptcy Project.

15% in total credit card debts ("Heavy Users" column). This is an absolute dollar definition; we do not look here at their debt/income ratios or at the composition of their debts. Compared with the other wage earners, they appear to be both better and worse off. They are significantly better off in terms of income, assets, and occupational prestige. It might be that their higher incomes and assets made creditors less concerned about their mounting credit card debts. At any rate, the heavy users are significantly worse off in terms of both secured and unsecured debt. They are no more likely than other debtors to file jointly, to have gained or lost income, or to have moved interstate, but they are more likely to be intrastate movers and to have filed in Chapter 7.

We were unsuccessful in our efforts to predict credit and debt using indicators such as income, prestige, job tenure, chapter, and joint filing for our various "junkie" groups. For example, although we know from Table 10.2 that job tenure varies among these groups, it was not a significant predictor of credit card debt. While we can identify small numbers of debtors who are heavily burdened with debt, we conclude that in many respects they resemble the other debtors.

Even if researchers cannot identify credit card abusers using general indicators, surely the credit records should signal creditors of potential abuse. Anthony Allegro's file causes a shudder—how could anyone run up charges in excess of 80% of a year's income?—but Allegro was given seven credit cards and a line of credit that permitted him to charge 80% of a year's income in high-interest, short-term debt.

We ask the question even more pointedly for the Voelkers. How did Hubert and AnneMarie get all that nonmortgage credit, almost a year's income, after they had already been through bankruptcy? The record of bankruptcy remains in credit reporting agencies' files for ten years. Every creditor on their list, secured and unsecured, knew or should have known that they were high-risk debtors. To lend so much to any $20,000-a-year couple would be very imprudent, but to pile that amount of debt on a ship that has sunk before seems absolutely mad.

Why were the debtors charging so much and why were their creditors smiling in approval? One answer is based on the data we discussed earlier relating to sharp fluctuations in income. If it is madness for both debtor and creditor to let charges exceed half a year's income, perhaps in some cases it happens because both debtor and creditor were basing credit on an income very different from the income the debtor earned in the year before bankruptcy.

Many bankrupt debtors have suffered income interruptions. As we noted in Chapter Five, just under half the Chapter 7 debtors had a substantial swing in income during the two-year period before bankruptcy, and low job tenure for debtors in bankruptcy contributed to their low incomes. Because income interruption is a part of the economic story for so many of the debtors in bankruptcy, it is one possible explanation for the terrible mismatch between debts and incomes for the credit card junkies.

Although we earlier found that both short-term debt junkies and heavy users had about the same job tenure and income interruptions as the remainder of the debtor group, the debtors with the worst credit card/income ratios (including the Voelkers and Mr. Allegro) were more often debtors with low job tenure or income swings than are the remainder of the debtors in bankruptcy.

Nonetheless, income interruption is not a complete explanation for the amazing amounts of credit card debt incurred by the debtors with the worst ratios of credit card debt to income. Nearly 60% of those for whom we can measure income changes did not experience an income change of 20% or more. This subgroup of cases likely contains some credit card abusers. It also necessarily includes creditors who accepted charges that even at the time of the charge were obviously well beyond the debtor's capacity to repay.

Policy Implications

Credit card debt is a substantial portion of what typical, wage-earning consumers carry into bankruptcy, but its impact is different from what we had anticipated. The stereotypical debtors with a special weakness for credit card debts are represented, but their number is small. Out of 1202 cases, we could find only 23 debtors (less than 2%) who met all three criteria indicating abuse: high credit card debt/income ratio, high proportion of unsecured debt in credit cards, and in the top 15% of the absolute amount of credit card debt carried into bankruptcy. Other potential abusers do not meet these criteria, although they might on some normative scales be abusers in every sense of the word. On the other hand, even among the 23 debtors, including the Voelkers and Tony Allegro, there might be debtors whose tales would make us pause before we branded them abusers.

Even when we use a broader classification of abuse, looking at debtors who meet only one or two of the tests, the data in the files introduce ambiguities. A large fraction of the debtors with staggering debt/income ratios had serious income interruptions during the years before bankruptcy, suggesting that a downturn in income rather than an upswing in discretionary spending accounted for their financial circumstances. But an almost equal number of debtors with high debt/income ratios had stable incomes; they had amassed huge credit card debts on the basis of incomes far too low to repay them.

The data on credit card debt/income ratios signal serious problems besetting the credit industry. Our data almost certainly include cases of debtors who have been irresponsible, even fraudulent, in their use of cards. But creditors have dispensed the cards recklessly, even if the exact numbers are maddeningly elusive. The presence of even a few junkies raises questions about whether penalties should attach to those who abuse the credit system. And if the answer is yes, they also raise the question of whether it is the debtor or the creditor who should bear the penalty.

Is mere irresponsible use of a credit card enough to deny protection to a debtor, even if the credit limits were never exceeded and no misrepresentation was made about how many cards the debtor had? And if there is a penalty, such as nondischarge of the credit card debt, what is the moral implication of rewarding the creditor who was also irresponsible in granting the credit?

The problem of matching irresponsibilities is not one limited to credit card issuers, nor is it one we can fully explore in this chapter. Instead, we raise the problem here and we return to this theme later in the book when we discuss the role of the creditors in greater detail.

Credit card debt is an important part of consumer credit and therefore it is not surprising that it represents a substantial part of the debt we found in bankruptcy. For a very small subset of consumer bankrupts it seems to be the "devil card" of which consumer credit counselors speak. In that subset can be found irresponsible borrowing and irresponsible lending. If Congress should decide to try to police abuses of the consumer credit system through bankruptcy, rather than directly, then this subset of debtors and creditors would be the ones to examine. For most debtors, however, credit card debt is just one problem among many, neither the stuff of tragic stories nor a good reason to make important changes in the bankruptcy laws.

Notes

1. This number was supplied by the people who put together the Nilson Report, a credit card newsletter used by numerous industry analysts. The figure includes bank cards, travel and entertainment cards, and most retail cards. It does not include certain private label cards used in limited areas, such as a card issued by a local pharmacy or local gift shop.

2. The six cases with the greatest credit card debt ($131,000–$292,000) were all currently or formerly self-employed and are among those excluded from analysis in this chapter.

3. Texas debtors had nearly twice as much average credit card debt than those in Illinois or Pennsylvania. A number of Texas debtors with very high store debt account for the statistical difference. It seems likely that some hidden entrepreneurs in Texas skew the figures because Texans are no different in their use of general-purpose cards, a subcategory that is subject to little distortion from business debts. Furthermore, the finding is counterintuitive because Texas is by far the most debtor-favoring of the three states we studied. If debt collection laws are in fact important to the availability of unsecured credit, we would expect Texas debtors to get less, rather than more, of the general unsecured credit reflected in this table.

4. Twenty-three debtors were excluded because they had less than $100 in credit card debt. We also excluded 6 more debtors who had credit card debt, but in unspecified amounts, bringing our sample for these calculations to 1030. The test we devised may be too broad because a debtor could have relatively small unsecured debts but have a real problem with car loans, a home mortgage, or other secured debts. A debtor with only $100 in unsecured debts, but all of it on a Visa card, would show up as a potential junkie by this definition, even though this debtor's real problem might be that a car was about to be repossessed or a home foreclosed. We searched again, limiting potential junkies to those debtors for whom at least 75% of all their nonmortgage debts were

on credit cards. This reduced the potential junkies to only 39, about 3% of the wage earners. The discussion in the text is based on the larger number of debtors with credit card debt at least 75% of all unsecured debt.

5. The credit card junkies, defined as all those with at least $100 credit card debt and whose unsecured credit was at least 75% credit card debt, represented only 7% of the total unsecured debt and 11% of the total nonmortgage debt in the sample, amounts not even proportionate to their number.

6. The heavy users, 15% of the sample, accounted for 35.3% of all credit card debt, almost 40% of total unsecured debt, and 31.1% of total nonmortgage debt. Furthermore, these debtors have a special affinity for credit card debt. The credit card debt for these heavy users of cards is 51% of their total unsecured debt, on average, as compared to 34% for the rest of the wage earners. Thus it is fair to characterize the heavy users of credit cards as people who run up higher debts than most wage earners and who are more dependent on credit cards as a form of credit.

7. They are also significantly more likely to report an income loss of 20% or more. Among the high debt/income ratio debtors, 34 had lost 10% or more of their income, and most of this group—30—had lost 20% or more. This is significantly different from the other groups. The debtors in Chapter 13 may be experiencing the same income interruptions, but, as we discussed in Chapter Five, only Chapter 7 debtors give the relevant information for calculating income over two years. Chapter 13 debtors give information only for the current year of filing.

11

The Repeaters

We observed several times that debates about bankruptcy are permeated by a deep-seated suspicion that bankruptcy petitioners are not the needy of America, but instead are clever manipulators who have found a way to beat the system. No factual question comes closer to addressing that concern than the one posed in this chapter: Are debtors going into bankruptcy over and over, slyly running up debts and then taking to the bankruptcy courts when their creditors ask for repayment?

This question has terrific emotional punch—and practical implications for changing the bankruptcy system. If many bankrupt debtors are repeaters, then it is reasonable to infer that what separates them from other working people—including other people in financial trouble—is that they have learned to work an angle. Their activities may not be illegal, but they certainly are distasteful to most of us. If many bankrupt debtors are repeaters, then there is a good argument for much tougher restrictions on repeat bankruptcies, which would significantly reduce the number of bankruptcies.

The argument is not new. Less than five years after the 1898 bankruptcy law had been adopted, it was on the verge of repeal because of pressure from creditors. One of their most bitter complaints was that debtors (usually from the Big Cities) were filing bankruptcy over and over. Rather than repeal the bankruptcy law, Congress adopted the rule that no debtor could receive a bankruptcy discharge more often than once every six years. Currently, a debtor can get a Chapter 7 discharge only once in six years, although Chapter 13 can be used more often if the debtor completes a payment plan.[1]

Today's vital concern about bankruptcy repeaters is sustained by credit industry allegations that bankruptcy has become so attractive that debtors will "enrich" themselves "as often as the law would allow."[2] Other commentators, economists who study bankruptcy, in particular, see the economic rationality of repeatedly declaring bankruptcy. The bankruptcy repeater should be the ultimate rational actor; he has no moral scruples against taking maximum advantage of the legal devices available to discharge lawful debt.

How Many Repeaters?

The bankruptcy forms require debtors to disclose whether they have ever declared bankruptcy before. In the discussion that follows, if either a husband or wife in a joint filing has filed a bankruptcy petition, we treat them collectively as repeaters. In our sample of 1502 petitions, 120 debtors had filed a bankruptcy petition at some time in the past, about 8% of the debtors in bankruptcy.[3]

Because the numbers were relatively small, we examined each file separately to see what we could learn about people who declare bankruptcy more than once. For this purpose, we define a "true repeater" as someone who files bankruptcy and discharges all accumulated debt, only to follow that fresh start by running up more debts and getting yet another bankruptcy discharge. If debtors choose Chapter 13 either the first time or the second time and pay their debts in full, for example, they cannot properly be called repeaters, because they paid their debts at least once rather than obtaining successive discharges. By the same token, if they file bankruptcy twice, but one or both cases were dismissed (for example, a Chapter 13 payment plan failed and the case was dismissed), then they have not received two discharges and are not true repeaters.

Ultimately, we cannot determine the precise number of true repeaters even by looking at the files, because the files are incomplete. Debtors do not always explain whether previous filings were in Chapter 7 or Chapter 13 and whether they resulted in any discharge, a partial discharge, or no discharge.[4] Nor is it always clear that the current bankruptcy will result in a discharge. We can identify only the debtors who are "potential" repeaters, those who filed prior bankruptcies and who *may* have been discharged previously. Our figures represent the maximum possible number of true repeaters.

Who Are the Repeaters?

No-Repeat Discharges

The first story that emerges from the files is that a number of repeat filings can be explained by debtors whose circumstances caused them to file twice in their attempt to get one discharge. The group includes the debtors who had filed bankruptcy within the year or two preceding the filing we studied. They had not filed bankruptcy, recovered, run up debts, and filed again. Instead, these debtors made successive attempts to craft a bankruptcy solution to a single set of economic troubles. There were 23 debtors who made two filings to accomplish one bankruptcy.

The circumstances that would cause a debtor to file two bankruptcies within the same year are illustrated by Martha and James Perkins. They filed a Chapter 13 in September 1980 that was dismissed in November 1980 because they were unable to make their payments. They gave up on the idea of partial repayment and filed a Chapter 7 in January 1981. Thus they are listed as repeaters, although, in fact, their first filing had no effect on their debts. They simply took two tries to find a solution to their financial problems.

The 23 stories have several variations. Many are failed Chapter 13's, with subsequent Chapter 7 filings. Some are failed Chapter 13's followed by new attempts at a Chapter 13. There is even a Chapter 7 that was voluntarily dismissed when, according to the notation in the file, "the debtors changed their minds"—followed by another Chapter 7 when they evidently changed them back again.

Why these debtors have two filings rather than the more typical conversion of a case from one chapter to another or modification of their first Chapter 13 plans depends on some legal technicalities. In some cases, if their attorneys had been quicker (or, to be fair, if the debtor had warned them earlier about what was happening), the case could have been converted to another chapter and would have shown up in the files only as a conversion or modification. In other cases, the debtors actually waited a period of time between bankruptcies, perhaps making their second try at a Chapter 13 after one spouse got a new job. Some debtors may have been involved in a scam, using Chapter 13 refilings as a device to get the benefit of the automatic stay and to stave off creditor collection a little longer without any hope of ever paying a Chapter 13 plan or getting a discharge. Regardless of motive, the short periods between filings combined with the serious financial condition of the debtors reveal continuous financial disaster that the debtors were unable to resolve in one run at the bankruptcy courts.

A second group of debtors who filed two bankruptcies in quick succession includes those who are not receiving a second discharge. These are debtors who filed for Chapter 7 bankruptcy between two and six years after their first filing, long enough to rebut the presumption that this was effectively a double filing to solve a single problem, but a short enough time to bar them by law from a discharge in Chapter 7.[5] There were five debtors in Chapter 7 within six years of their earlier filings, which means either they had not received a discharge earlier or they would be dismissed from this bankruptcy without a discharge.

A third group of debtors who filed twice will not receive two discharges. These are 32 debtors who made their second filing in Chapter 13 and were dismissed without a discharge. They are also necessarily out of the category of true repeaters.

Finally, some debtors made it clear that they were not looking for a second discharge. These debtors were in Chapter 13 the second time around, trying to pay 100% of their debts. Among these Chapter 13 debtors, 14 had promised to pay 100% of their debt and were not yet in trouble on their payment plans. Whether they succeeded and paid or failed and were dismissed, they were not on the path to two discharges.[6] One other debtor had paid in full all creditors in her previous Chapter 13 case. Another noted that his earlier Chapter 13 had been dismissed without a discharge. Neither of these debtors would be seeking a second discharge.

When we exclude the double-filers, the Chapter 7 nonrepeaters, the Chapter 13 dropouts, and the 100% payers in Chapter 13, the number of debtors potentially receiving two discharges drops to 56 debtors, about 3.7% of the sample.[7] We focus on these 56 potential repeaters to understand better the circumstances of their repeat trips to the bankruptcy courthouse and to see how their presence should affect bankruptcy policy.

High-Risk Businesses

One group that stands out among the potential repeaters are those who are or have been self-employed. Among the 56 potential repeaters, 11 are currently self-employed and 6 formerly self-employed.

The files of the self-employed reflect many of the ambiguities of the other files, especially the incomplete information about earlier filings. Some of these debtors may not be repeaters, because they did not discharge debt in their previous bankruptcies.

Even the 17 self-employed debtors who are repeaters do not fit the stereotype of debtors who repeatedly run up debts by overspending and bail out when their creditors press. Instead, the entrepreneurs are people who tried a very risky venture and got into trouble. As we indicated in Chapter Six, they probably poured all their money and all their time into the businesses, amassing substantial business debts for which they were personally liable. The impossibility of ever paying off their staggering business debts makes these bankruptcies comprehensible, if not excusable.

Among these 17 debtors are Leslie and Rose Malachuk, doing business as The Music Outlet. They filed in Chapter 7, listing $29,394.43 in income taxes and employer's unemployment compensation, $109,833.60 in debts secured by inventory, their home, and various household goods, and $102,265 in unsecured debt. Their unsecured debts ranged from $18.93 to a book club to $7,914.23 to J. D'Addario & Co. for "goods sold." Their income from 1968 through the present has come from Mr. Malachuk's income as "an independent sales rep and sole proprietor wholesale distributor of musical equipment and accessories."

The Malachuks knew the risks of running a small business in the music field. They explain in their files that they had "filed individual [bankruptcy] petition and corporate petition for Holiday Music House" in 1968—about the time they switched to the current version of the business. Many of their creditors knew the risk as well, since most were music suppliers and banks making commercial loans, working with many similar small businesses, and, in some cases, evidently lending to the Malachuks over a long period of time. Generally their lenders were professionals who were fully aware of the risks and who decided nonetheless that there was enough promise of profits to support such lending.

The Malachuks leave their Chapter 7 with few personal assets and, notwithstanding their bankruptcy discharge, agreeing to pay some of their debts—perhaps those due creditors with whom they hope to do business in the future. Whether they will try again in the music business, only to amass nearly a quarter of a million dollars in debt and show up once again in bankruptcy in another dozen years, is beyond our knowledge. But the Malachuks and other self-employed debtors who use bankruptcy to deal with their overwhelming business debts are not the repeaters portrayed in the horror stories of bankruptcy abuse. Instead these are people who illustrate that bankruptcy is a part of the support system for small businesses, especially for those who may pick up and try again after a failure.

Wage Earners

If we separate the entrepreneurs from all potential repeaters, we are left with a group of 39 wage earners—just under 2.6% of the sample. Among these 39 debtors are 6 who are in Chapter 13 attempting a partial repayment—and seeking some discharge. The remaining 33 debtors are in Chapter 7 for a full discharge. This group includes the debtors most likely to use bankruptcy more than once to escape debt payment in the ways portrayed in the bankruptcy debates.

We examine these 39 potential repeaters to see if they differed from the rest of the population. Our findings are all negative: no significant differences in debt/income ratios, no significant differences in employment status, no significant differences in white-collar versus blue-collar status, and no significant differences in occupational prestige. In short, the wage-earning repeaters look a great deal like the rest of the sample.

How many of the 39 wage earners are true repeaters remains a puzzle. Missing information on their first filing makes it problematic to assume an earlier discharge. For the six now in Chapter 13, a subsequent discharge may also be tenuous. We have only a maximum estimate of potential repeaters, not a certain class of people with two discharges.

The Potential Repeaters

These data show that among those debtors who traveled to the bankruptcy courts before, fewer than half are even potential repeaters, trying to discharge debt more than once. Less than 2.6% of the debtors are wage earners who are eligible for two discharges, and, because some of them are in Chapter 13, less than 2.2% are going for a straight Chapter 7 discharge the second time around.

The relatively low proportion of repeaters is somewhat surprising when the data from the preceding chapters are considered. Generally, the debtors in bankruptcy have very low earnings relative both to the population at large and to others in their industries. They have frequent income interruptions and extraordinary debt burdens. They have fewer working spouses and slightly larger families. They have higher mortgages relative to their incomes. Some have huge medical debts. Bankruptcy can rid these people of their previous debt burdens, but it does not give them a raise or more job security. It does not reduce the expenses of raising children or make the car run without costly repairs. The point, of course, is that what put the bankrupt debtors in precarious financial positions did not go away simply because they filed for bankruptcy. Their precarious incomes and uncertain expenses remain. Nonetheless, the overwhelming message from these data are that relatively few debtors come through the system twice.

Finding a low proportion of possible repeat players raises speculation about the debtor—creditor system. Perhaps the events that have a significant hand in pressing people toward bankruptcy, such as job interruptions throughout all industries and occupations, are a more recent phenomenon, so that typical debtors are facing these crises for the first time in the 1980s. The proportion of debtors caught twice in the web of financial catastrophe may be low in our sample, but it may be climbing as more middle-class Americans face layoffs and cutbacks. If so, repeat filings may increase over time as more debtors face repeated financial reversals.

Another interpretation of these data is that debtors who have survived bankruptcy are different from those who have not. Despite their low incomes or job interruptions, they may be unlikely to pass through bankruptcy twice. The debtor who has gone through bankruptcy may never garner enough credit to need bankruptcy again. Whether self-discipline or creditor vigilance is the reason, only a small portion of these debtors may find themselves with enough high debt and low income to file for bankruptcy twice in their lives.

On the other hand, debtors once through bankruptcy may find credit again. Both the Malachuks and the Voelkers (discussed in Chapter Ten) had previous bankruptcies in their credit files, but they managed to run up extraordinary debts. If former bankrupts can garner substantial debt, as these files indicate, and if their financial circumstances remain shaky, once-bankrupt debtors may have found other ways to cope with subsequent financial problems. Perhaps these debtors move a lot to avoid paying their debts, or maybe they develop hard shells about creditor collection activities, or maybe they save more money during good times. A study focused on the instant in time when the filing occurs tells little about the long-term effects of the bankruptcy. But the low rate of potential repeaters—especially in the face of the economic model predicting that these debtors have found economic nirvana—suggests that debtors will not flock to bankruptcy "as often as the law allows." Perhaps bankruptcy is not as attractive as many commentators have assumed.

Policy Implications

The findings about repeaters are among the most significant negative findings from the Consumer Bankruptcy Study. The image of clever debtors who declare bankruptcy when their six-year waiting period has ended and their debts have peaked is a vision from policymakers' nightmares more than it is a reality in the bankruptcy system.

These data raise a recurring bankruptcy policy question: How much should bankruptcy law be driven by problems that rarely occur? General restrictions and disincentives to filing bankruptcy—as opposed to direct limits on the frequency of filing—affect all debtors. In our sample, that involves making life tougher for 1502 filers to reach 39 who *might* have misbehaved.[8] We question whether a broad-sweep approach, toughening bankruptcy laws generally and testing all debtors who come into bankruptcy, makes any sense. As it is, the current six-year limit on debtors' discharging debt in bankruptcy seems to work well.

Yet what is "rare" is in the eye of the beholder, and some may find a potential 2.6% rate of repeaters troubling. Moreover, even a small proportion of repeaters may represent a serious problem because they undermine public confidence in the system. Every time the popular press finds another debtor who has gone into bankruptcy once again or a flimflam man working the area who has already declared bankruptcy three times, reasonable, bill-paying citizens are roused. Few such stories explain that this debtor is the unusual case, and that the story is newsworthy precisely because it is as rare as it is outrageous. It may be tempting to spend resources and to impose costs on all debtors to dissuade a few repeaters, simply to promote the image of fairness within the system.

If this problem of perception is important, we believe it would be better to attack the problem directly by requiring a bankruptcy judge to interrogate each repeater about the justification for a second bankruptcy. A second discharge could be denied where the justification seems inadequate. Of course, such procedures would create a new set of problems. Standards for "second bankruptcy abuse" would have to be developed. The standard might involve a troubling breadth of judicial discretion and might vary from judge to judge and court to court. It is also legitimate to ask whether it makes good sense to expend limited court resources on so narrow a problem. But at least this solution focuses on the specific concern and addresses it directly.

Another question lurks in these data: What role have the creditors played in multiple bankruptcies? Although this is the section about debtors, we must pause to ask how the debtors in our sample—including the Voelkers from the last chapter—got so much credit after having already filed bankruptcy once. Prior bankruptcies are listed in credit reports for ten years. But these debtors amassed debt/income ratios that are statistically indistinguishable from the rest of the debtors who had no track record of bankruptcy. The repeaters got the same large amounts of credit relative to their incomes, with no apparent differences in how it was structured (e.g., secured versus unsecured). In Part II we explore further the operation of a credit system that permits such results.

We conclude this chapter with a recurring theme. The image of the debtor in bankruptcy as someone very different from the rest of us is unsupported. This time we tested the notion that debtors differ from middle-class Americans only in their willingness to use the bankruptcy laws without hesitation. The data show that relatively few debtors are eager to enjoy the benefits of bankruptcy more than once.

Notes

1. The rule stated in the text is roughly correct but oversimplified. Without exhausting the details, a debtor cannot get a second Chapter 7 discharge within six years of prior Chapter 7 or a Chapter 7 discharge within six years of a Chapter 13 bankruptcy unless the prior Chapter 13 had paid the creditors in full. 11 U.S.C. §727(a)(9), (10). A prior Chapter 13 on rare occasions is treated like a full payout if the debtor paid at least 70% and the court finds the payments were the debtor's best effort. On the other hand, a debtor may get a new Chapter 13 discharge regardless of prior bankruptcies. 11 U.S.C. §1328.

2. This is the phrase used to summarize the Purdue Study suggestion that bankruptcy is such a good deal that debtors will take it whenever they can to enhance their economic position. Purdue University, Credit Research Center, Krannert Graduate School of Management, Consumer Bankruptcy Study (1982), Vol. II, p. 133.

3. This number is drawn from the common debtor sample. As we do throughout the book, we exclude outliers here. (See Chapter Two.) Among the 27 outliers were 2 repeaters.

4. The bankruptcy forms ask the following questions: What cases under the Bankruptcy Act or Title 11, United States Code have previously been brought by or against you? (State the location of the bankruptcy court, the nature and number of each case, the date when it was filed, and whether a discharge was granted or refused, the case was dismissed, or a compostiion, arrangement, or plan was confirmed.)

While this would seem to give adequate information concerning discharge, the question was often incompletely answered. And in the case of a previous Chapter 13, knowing that a plan had been confirmed still does not tell the subsequent researcher whether the plan resulted in a full payment or a partial payment and some discharge. Nor do we have any information about secured debt, reaffirmations, and voluntary repayments from previous filings.

5. See explanation in note 1.

6. When a debtor promises 100% and succeeds in completing his plan, obviously there is no debt discharged. When the debtor promises and fails, the debtor may be dismissed, and there will still be no discharge. In the flexibility of the Bankruptcy Code, however, the debtor may promise 100% and, if he gets into trouble, persuade a court to modify the plan to a lesser payment or convert the plan to Chapter 7. The latter events could result in the discharge of debt in what is classified at the time the data are gathered as a 100% plan that is still pending.

7. These figures are of the same magnitude as those found in the Brookings Study, although they are not directly comparable. D. Stanley and M. Girth, Bankruptcy: Problem, Process, Reform (Washington: Brookings Institution, 1971), p. 59.

8. This omits the 17 self-employed debtors on the notion that their bankruptcies evidence a different kind of problem, which is not part of the current debate about consumer abuse.

12

Can These Debtors Pay?

The generous willingness of Americans to help those in trouble is balanced by a demand that only the truly needy be helped. Ultimately, the central question most people pose about bankruptcy is whether those who file could have repaid their debts if bankruptcy had not been available. Is the process one of humane discharge or sanctioned abuse?

No single question has a more profound and direct influence on bankruptcy policy. If it is the needy who use bankruptcy, the bankruptcy system can focus on efficiency and fairness. The present system has a number of provisions directed at abuse and there will always be concern with abuse, but it would be a peripheral issue in a system perceived to serve the truly deserving. On the other hand, if the system is shot through with slick manipulation, bankruptcy should be structured around protections to weed out abusers even at greater cost to everyone, including the needy.

As we noted earlier, in 1984 Congress passed amendments to the Bankruptcy Code that imposed substantial new restrictions on consumer bankruptcy. These amendments were adopted in response to a perceived problem of abuse. On a theoretical level, economists viewed bankruptcy as a very attractive alternative for the rational debtor and therefore theorized that many debtors would be eager to benefit from it.[1] This theoretical proposition seemed to be confirmed by an empirical study done by Purdue University, which claimed that many Chapter 7 debtors could pay a "substantial" part of their debts.[2]

Our data show that consumers in bankruptcy look very much like the rest of America in their work, but very different in their financial circumstances. The data for the debtors show that, on average, they are at the extreme end of the financial spectrum—earning less and owing more than most Americans, so that their overall financial condition makes them worse off than most of the population. But being at the bottom of the credit heap does not necessarily mean these debtors could not pay. If a substantial portion of debtors could repay, then bankruptcy policy must account for them. On the other hand, if the abusers are rare, the system may have braced for an onslaught that is not coming.

The Moral Definition of "Can Pay"

"How many debtors can pay?" is in part a normative question: the answer depends on moral and social value judgments. Some advocates mask this point in discussions of bankruptcy, speaking as if the ability to pay were an objective fact like height or weight. A debtor's ability to pay is a function of the level of sacrifice demanded. All of us might prefer to skip paying our monthly bills in favor of having a party or buying a new car, but we would hardly claim that this preference made us unable to pay. On the other hand, nearly all of us would agree that an elderly widow with few assets, living on her social security, "can't pay" the massive debts left by the failure of her late husband's business (a case in our files). Where to draw the line—how much sacrifice to require of people in debt—is a key question in bankruptcy.

The normative questions are inextricably interwoven with the analysis of the data, making a discussion of the data without the normative element of the question "Can these debtors pay?" so abstract as to border on useless. Our own normative analysis is necessarily intertwined with our presentation of the data. But we try to label clearly each part of the discussion and to present the data in a way that will help readers make personal normative judgments that may vary from our own.

The Costs of Finding Abusers and Policing Repayment

Our search for abuse using statistical methods has taught us the limitations of the data reported in the bankruptcy files. Abuse in a particular case cannot be determined from the cold numbers alone. There are undoubtedly abuses that we do not see in the files (for example, a stunning new job that starts next week, a debtor a heartbeat away from a fabulous inheritance). Conversely, apparent abuses might disappear if we had more information. The latter point was illustrated by an incident in a congressional hearing about bankruptcy in which a credit industry spokesman inveighed at length against bankruptcy abusers. When Chairman Peter Rodino asked for the names of a few abusers, the industry spokesman hemmed and hawed, but after a few days came up with five "typical" abusers. Subsequent inquiry by the General Accounting

Office, including personal interviews with the debtors, revealed that one of the debtors had multiple sclerosis, another had been in a serious car accident, and a third had lost his job and moved into a tiny mobile home shared with his in-laws to save on expenses.[3]

Although these "abusers" also mentioned less sympathetic reasons for their credit troubles (one flatly admitted not managing money well), the incident illustrates again that identifying abuse requires individualized inquiry. In the real world this means a judge must call in the alleged abusers and question them carefully about their particular circumstances.

Another reason that identifying abuse may require information outside the files is that our normative judgments about abuse may not depend solely on the difficulty of repayment. We might want to impose different levels of sacrifice on different debtors. For example, we might like to know why the debtor got into financial trouble. A debtor struck by layoff or suffering crushing medical bills elicits forgiveness with little demand for further sacrifice. But the petitioner whose smooth charm apparently captured the life savings of an elderly widow (whose pitiful letter we found in an Illinois court file) is someone we would like to hold below the poverty level for years. We might want therefore to evaluate these debtors' capacities to repay in somewhat different ways.

Because of the need for particularized inquiry, identifying abusers is costly. A member of Congress would ask how many new judges and how much court time it would take to identify those who "could pay" under whatever standard is adopted. One part of the answer to that question depends on whether statistical methods could substantially narrow the search. Thus the ultimate question for us is whether abuse is both widespread and subject to systematic detection. If it is, then resources could be well spent to find it.

Testing Ability to Repay

Debtors might repay by selling their assets and giving the cash to their creditors, or they might repay by committing a portion of their future income to repayment. We examine both possibilities to see if our debtors in Chapter 7, those who said in effect they could not or would not pay, would have had a reasonable likelihood of repaying their debts. Because all reform proposals to date stress that debtors who could repay should file in Chapter 13, we also examine the Chapter 13 debtors. We test first to determine how many of them seem able to pay and then to see if they are in fact repaying, as policy debates assume.

As before, we consider only the pure wage earners in this chapter, because the self-employed and formerly self-employed are so distinctly different from wage earners in a number of key respects. In particular, entrepreneurs are much less able to pay than are wage earners, so their exclusion reduces the sample to those debtors who have the best possibility of repayment.[4]

Paying from Assets

People traditionally thought of wealth as a function of ownership of property of various kinds, from real estate to corporate stock. The balance sheet, assets versus liabilities, was the heart of financial analysis. In this century that view has greatly changed, especially in the credit industry. The modern loan officer is more likely to focus on disposable income—income after taxes, living expenses, and payments on existing debt—than on assets versus liabilities.

Nonetheless, many areas of the law, including bankruptcy, still reflect an asset-based rather than an income-based view of credit. We begin by looking at the capacity of the debtors in our sample to pay their debts by selling their assets before we move on to repayment from future income.

As we have seen, more than half our debtors were homeowners. The family home is a very distinct asset, in cash value and in social policy, so we separate asset sales into two categories: the home and everything else, including other real estate. We look at the nonhome assets first.

Nonhome Assets

Characteristically, property has two very different values. Its value to the debtor is its replacement value, but its value to a creditor is its market value. The debtors' clothes provide the textbook example. A shirt that has been worn only twice is worth $30 to the debtor, who would have to spend that to replace it. But it would be worth only a couple of dollars at a garage sale, if it were sold to pay debts.

In part because of these differing perspectives on value, it is impossible for us to be sure of the accuracy of the debtors' reports of the value of their possessions or whether the errors are more likely to be plus or minus. Some debtors may report the market value of assets (the garage sale value); others give the replacement value (often the cost). No doubt debtors have an incentive to report low values to stay within dollar limits on exemptions. Yet a debtor comfortably within those limits may find it easier to list replacement value, the cost originally paid.

More importantly, for assets of any real value, debtors face perjury charges and loss of their right to a discharge if they misstate an asset's value. The active market for real estate and the publication of price books for used cars make the values of the big assets the easiest for the court and creditors to check. Estimates for small items—winter clothes or a seven-year-old dinette set—are likely to vary the most and to reflect something other than what they would bring in a liquidation, but these estimates also affect the total asset picture the least. Because nothing short of a massive survey with an army of appraisers will ever tell us what the debtors' assets are really worth, the debtors' reports, made under oath, are likely to remain the best evidence we have.

To determine recoveries for creditors from sale of assets by Chapter 7 debtors, we have to allow for paying off liens on the assets, for the costs of the sales, and for legal exemptions. Many debtors in our sample had substantial assets, but these assets were burdened with substantial liens held by secured creditors. A necessary first step is to subtract the amount of those secured liens from the value of the assets to determine how much salable value the Chapter 7 debtor would have to repay to unsecured creditors. If, for example, a debtor owns a car worth $1,000 but still owes $2,000 on it, the value of that asset to any creditor except the car lender is zero. The car lender will get $1,000 from sale of the car and will be in line with everyone else for the remaining $1,000 owed on the car loan. On the other hand, if the car is worth $3,000, the sale of the car would pay the car lender in full and leave $1,000 (minus the costs of sale) for the unsecured creditors. In our sample, this first adjustment, paying off secured debt, would leave 40% of the Chapter 7 debtors with nothing for their unsecured creditors, even before we adjust for sales costs and exemptions.[5]

We must then consider selling expenses. Sales costs, including commissions, advertising, etc., would be deducted before anything is distributed to the creditors. Trustees' fees, set by statute at 7% on the first $1,000 in value and 6% on the next $1,000, would also be deducted before any distribution. We assume total selling costs and trustees' fees would be 10% of the amount raised at the sale, a low estimate.

Next we must make some allowance for legal exemptions. Every state provides some exemptions, so that creditors cannot take literally everything that a debtor owns. If some states did not, the federal bankruptcy laws would no doubt be amended to provide some minimum exemptions, because a fresh start with absolutely no property—no clothes, no kitchen utensils, no car, no tools, no furniture—would be no fresh start at all. (You cannot go to most job interviews wearing the proverbial barrel.) Thus we must make some allowance for exemptions to produce a realistic yield for creditors.

To determine whether the sale of debtors' assets would produce much for their unsecured creditors, we computed the proportion of debt that a debtor family could repay if they sold all their assets, paid 10% in trustee and sales costs, and kept a minimum exemption. We used an arbitrary exemption figure of $5,000, a figure considerably lower than either the federal exemptions or the exemptions in many states.[6] The results are seen in Table 12.1.

Over 87% of the debtors could pay nothing at all; only 86 could pay anything. Most of those who could manage some repayment could pay relatively little.[7] A total of 10 debtors could pay in full and only 17 more could pay as much as 50 cents on the dollar. That is, 2% of the wage-earning debtors could have paid all their unsecured debts by selling off their nonhome assets[8] and less than 4% could have paid even half. A separate calculation shows that the mean amount of unsecured debt Chapter 7 debtors could pay if they sold everything above a $5,000 exemption would be 5 cents on the dollar. Selling nonhome assets is not a potential source of meaningful repayment for creditors.[9]

TABLE 12.1. Proportion and Dollar Value of Debt Repayment to Unsecured Creditors from Sale of Assets, Chapter 7 Wage Earners[a]

	Nonhome Assets[b]	Home Equity[c]
Proportions of Debt Repaid		
Number	721	260[d]
Number who can repay anything	86	25
Number who can repay 50–99%	17	5
Number who can repay 100%	10	10
Dollar Values of Repayment, for Debtors Who Can Repay Anything		
Mean	$4,815	$13,535
s.d.	5,034	13,900
25th percentile	1,293	5,375
Median	2,541	8,140
75th percentile	7,288	18,070
N	86	25

[a]Cases with extreme values on assets, total debt, or income excluded.

[b]Assumes that all assets are sold, secured creditors have been paid, 10% trustee and sales costs have been paid, and a minimum exemption of $5000 has been kept by the debtor.

[c]Assumes that home sale will yield 70% of market value, the mortgage lender is paid in full, and that homestead exemption is $10,000.

[d]Homeowners. Excludes cases of doubtful homeownership.

Source: Consumer Bankruptcy Project.

Selling Homes

Over half those in the bankruptcy sample own their homes. If unsecured creditors could insist that the debtors sell their homes and distribute what remains after the mortgage is paid off, how much would they get?

To see what home foreclosures would really yield for the unsecured creditors of our Chapter 7 debtors, we must determine a realistic sales price and net expenses that would have to be paid. First it is necessary to adjust for the difference between market value and liquidation value. Debtors are instructed by the bankruptcy forms to report the market value of their homes, which is the price the debtors would get with a broker and time to wait for a good offer. But the trustee at a court-ordered sale would get far less. One standard that the bankruptcy courts often use—although with absolutely no empirical basis—is that real estate should bring 70% of its market value when sold on the courthouse steps rather than through the regular real estate market.[10] To reflect the lower prices brought in foreclosure sales, we use the same rule of thumb the courts do and reduce the value of the home by 30%.

We also must subtract a homestead exemption, and we use a conservative $10,000. This exemption figure is the one permitted in Illinois, and it is typical of the minimum exemptions available around the country. It is less than that allowed a married couple under the federal exemption available in Pennsylvania and Texas and less than the state exemption in Texas.

Although the costs probably are still understated, these adjustments provide some idea of what home sales would yield for unsecured creditors.[11] The results are reported in Table 12.1. Over 90% of the Chapter 7 homeowner debtors could pay nothing.[12] The 25 debtors who could pay something cover a wide range of repayment, from nearly nothing to 10 debtors who could pay 100%. The average amount realized for unsecured creditors from the sale of these 25 homes would be $13,500. The median would be $8,140. Once again, we find debtors who could repay their unsecured debts from assets, but they are a tiny fraction of the wage-earning debtors in Chapter 7.[13]

Selling All Assets

Now that we have identified the effects of selling nonhome assets and of selling the family home, we can combine the two to see what payments could be obtained by forcing debtors to sell *all* their assets, subject to the same assumptions and exemptions. That calculation showed that 20 of our Chapter 7 debtors, 3% of the total, could pay all their unsecured debts by selling all assets. Twenty-two more could pay as much as half their outstanding unsecured debt. If any of our very conservative estimates of costs are mistaken in the case of a particular debtor, the number of debtors who can repay drops off even further. We conclude that selling debtors' assets—even down to minimal exemption levels—is unlikely to yield more than trivial repayments for most creditors.

Paying from Future Income

If we move away from assets and focus instead on income to see whether the debtors in bankruptcy could repay, we bring our analysis more closely into line with the credit industry's lending practices. This section considers whether bankrupt debtors might be able to repay their debts from their incomes.

Debt/Income Ratios for Chapter 7 Debtors

Because we cannot cross-examine each debtor family about income and expenses, we must use a statistical approach to estimate the debtors' capacity to repay.[14] As before, we do our first analysis using the ratio of debt to income. Across a large sample of debtors, that ratio quantifies the capacity of the average debtor to pay some or all debts and provides a way to identify questionable cases. In Chapter Four we noted that income tends to be overstated and debt understated, thus painting too rosy a picture of the debtors' circumstances. The debt/income ratios for Chapter 7 pure wage earners are given in Table 12.2.

The overall picture for these Chapter 7 debtors is grim. At the mean, a family would have to pay every dollar of its income for two and a half years to repay its debts. At the median, a family would have to pay every cent of income for over a year and three months to pay off all debts.

As before, we take a second look after segregating the generally long-term mortgage debt from the nonmortgage debt, which is almost all short-term consumer debt. These results are also reported in Table 12.2. For this computation, we leave homeowners in the sample, but we remove their mortgage debts.[15] Obviously in real life the homeowners cannot ignore their mortgages, so the nonmortgage ratio itself may be misleading for them. Neither the total debt/income ratio nor the nonmortgage debt/income ratio is an ideal way to look at homeowners' financial circumstances, but the two together give a better picture.

Because mortgage debts are so large, removing them substantially reduces debt/income ratios. What surprised us was that the ratios remained as high as they did. At the mean, a Chapter 7 debtor has nonmortgage debts equal to more than one year and five months' worth of income. Again, the mean is stretched by some debtors with very great debt burdens. Yet at the median, debtors owe more than eight months of the family's annual gross income in short-term debts. Even the debtor at the 25th percentile, the least burdened group, owes five months' income in nonmortgage debt.

The question we are addressing is the sacrifice that would be required to pay off debts. Because the ratios and the percentiles start to get numbing at some point, it might be helpful to use specific amounts. The average family in the wage-earner sample made about $15,600 per year. If that family had the median burden of nonmortgage debt, it would owe about $10,900. That is the amount the family would have to repay after paying the mortgage on a house or the rent on an apartment, as well as necessary living expenses for food, medical care, gasoline, insurance, and the like. At a more affluent level, a person with an income of $30,000 and the same proportion of debt as the median bankrupt debtor would have short-term, nonmortgage debt of $21,000. If that

TABLE 12.2. Total Debt/Income Ratio and Total Nonmortgage Debt/Income Ratio for Chapter 7 Pure Wage Earners[a]

Distribution	Total Debt/Income Ratio	Total Nonmortgage Debt/Income Ratio
Mean	2.5	1.4
s.d.	8.8	5.4
25th percentile	0.7	0.4
Median	1.3	0.7
75th percentile	2.3	1.2
N	1,047	1,045
Missing	155	157

[a]Cases with extreme values on assets, total debt, or income excluded.

Source: Consumer Bankruptcy Project.

person were even more affluent, with an income of $50,000, the median short-term debt would be $35,000.

The Effect of Interest

Even if family members were willing to sacrifice by dedicating huge portions of their income to debt repayment, they might still need the protection of the bankruptcy laws. In fact, the analysis to this point understates the burden of debt placed on these debtors by the continuing avalanche of consumer interest charges. In 1981, consumer interest rates reached heights previously unimaginable. Indeed, the fact that many of these rates remained very high, even after inflation was brought under control, became a source of considerable controversy. In deciding whether to file for bankruptcy debtors have to consider not only the debts they already have, but the interest charges that continue to mount outside bankruptcy.

We thought this practical aspect of the problem was sufficiently important that we should try to get a rough idea of the additional debt burden represented by continuing, short-term interest building up on the pile of debt each debtor owed. We omitted home mortgage interest from this calculation because it is long-term debt for which bankruptcy will offer little help, although we are not unmindful that the homeowner–debtors must pay it in addition to the debt burdens we list here. For the outstanding short-term debt, we assumed interest would be paid on the short-term debt at a conservative 15% interest rate. (The going rate for car loans in 1981 was 16% and for revolving credit was 18–21%.)[16] We assumed no interest on obligations such as medical debt, back rent, and taxes (the last because tax interest rates vary so much). We then calculated the annual short-term interest each debtor family would have to pay.

On these assumptions, we found that the average annual interest charges were equal to 16% of the debtor's annual gross income. The median was lower, at just under 9%. The average debtor family in our sample of wage earners would have to dedicate almost two months of their gross income just to stay even on the amount of debt previously described. Even if debtors could set aside two full paychecks a year to service their nonmortgage interest, they still would not reduce any of their outstanding debt principal.

This interest burden is a key piece of the consumer bankruptcy puzzle for two reasons. It helps in understanding the true debt burden on consumers who file for bankruptcy. It also aids in explaining why some debtors decide bankruptcy is the best alternative for them. Bankruptcy stops the running of interest on all unsecured consumer debt and much nonmortgage secured debt.[17] (It can stop a lot of interest for businesses also, which is said to be one reason Texaco filed for bankruptcy when the interest charges on Pennzoil's $9.2 billion judgment were running more than a million dollars a day.) Bankruptcy stops interest running on unsecured debt, and the debtors have to cope with interest on secured debt only if they want to keep the collateral. Even in a Chapter 13 100% payment plan, debtors can pay something less than they owe outside bankruptcy by escaping the relentless burden of interest charges.

Bankruptcy is not just an alternative that debtors consider when they ask whether they could repay the debts they owe today. It is an alternative most debtors need simply to stop sliding deeper into the debt hole. It seems to us that the debt/income ratios we have seen, combined with enormous ongoing interest charges, mean that it is unlikely that many debtors would be found able to pay their debts outside bankruptcy under any standard of sacrifice that would command majority support.

Hypothetical Chapter 13 Plans for Chapter 7 Debtors

Even if debtors need bankruptcy to stop interest accumulations, some of those in Chapter 7 might be able to repay the principal owed. To test this hypothesis we constructed for each of our Chapter 7 debtors a hypothetical payment plan in Chapter 13, to see how many of them could have paid had they tried. If the debtor could pay according to this plan, then we speculated that here we had someone who might have abused the bankruptcy system by filing Chapter 7.

OUR ASSUMPTIONS

First we decided how long the hypothetical plan would run. We settled on a three-year payment period, in part because the Bankruptcy Code presumes this to be the period of a Chapter 13 payout plan. For debtors like these, with extremely volatile incomes, we believed it stretched the limits of plausibility to project that they would have the same or greater incomes for more than three consecutive years. Indeed, hypothesizing stable income for three years—in the teeth of the evidence we have about their incomes for the preceding two years—was probably an act of reckless optimism. For those who believe that the debtors' employment and income roller coaster rides are not over yet, what follows is little more than an academic exercise that bears little relation to reality. For those who think debtors will consistently earn more after bankruptcy, we have understated ability to repay. We make the assumption about three-year incomes not because we believe in its accuracy, but because we need some assumption to proceed and we have no reasonable basis to vary the report the debtors have given.

For most calculations we use 100% repayment as the only meaningful standard. We gave extended consideration to testing for 75% or 50% payment of debt but finally abandoned the idea for two reasons. One was the difficulty of calculating how payments from income would be applied to debt. The second was that below full payment it becomes impossible to make meaningful comparisons with the payments already made in a Chapter 7, so one cannot be sure a Chapter 13 actually returned more to creditors.

Once a statistical analysis deviates from full payment, the difference between secured and unsecured debt makes it impossible to determine how much has to be paid to retire a given amount of debt. A majority of the debtors owe more than half their debt on a secured basis. If these debtors are going to pay anything on their debts, many of them are surely going to try to pay off the loan secured by the car or the furniture or perhaps the tools the debtor needs to work. Yet other debtors may decide that the car they bought was a mistake, they can get along with a clunker, and they will let the car go rather than try to pay off the loan.

These variations make payment levels very hard to calculate. Debtors who try to keep collateral and pay against secured debt will have to pay interest in Chapter 13. If they pay $1,000 a year toward their plans, $150 of that amount may be interest on secured debt rather than a payment against unsecured debt. Thus if we calculate that a particular family can pay 60% of their total debts, but they would in fact have devoted those payments to secured debt, the actual result might be payment of less than half the debt plus additional interest to the secured creditors. On the other hand, if that debtor surrendered the collateral, it would be sold and much of the secured debt would be paid from the sale, with income left to pay against unsecured debt.

Any attempt to calculate debt repayment below 100% also presents an intractable problem of comparison with what is already going on in Chapter 7. We know that debtors already make considerable repayment in Chapter 7. As we discuss subsequently, about a fifth of the Chapter 7 debtors reaffirm some debts, so they are legally obligated to pay them after bankruptcy. Those who reaffirm are disproportionately those who have better debt/income ratios and thus appear better able to pay. Therefore it is probable that a number of Chapter 7 debtors we could identify as able to pay part of their debts are already doing so by reaffirmations. There is also substantial anecdotal evidence that a number of debtors are repaying some debt without an official reaffirmation, especially where the debt is secured. In effect, both debtor and creditor proceed without formality, and as long as the monthly payments are made the debtor keeps the collateral. This sort of implicit reaffirmation seems especially common with home mortgages, where a number of Chapter 7 debtors appear to keep their homes with no sign of a formal reaffirmation of the mortgage debt. We recall Carmelita Gentry in Chapter Eight; her mortgage had been carefully crossed off her list of debts, but she was probably still paying it to live in the house.

In Chapter 7 the debtors are making exactly the same decisions about their secured debt that they make in the hypothetical Chapter 13: Keep the car? Try to pay off the washer? If the debtors want to keep the item subject to a security interest, they will have to pay the value of the collateral.[18] In other words, if the debtors are struggling to keep property, which almost all the debtors are, the Chapter 13 purporting to pay half the outstanding debt may yield exactly what the Chapter 7 yields—partial discharge of unsecured and secured debt with debtors paying the debts on collateral they want to keep and giving up other collateral and discharging those debts.[19]

Chapter 7 debtors are not always nonpayers, both because they must cope with their secured debt and because they reaffirm some unsecured debt. The inability to calculate payment percentages accurately because of the impact of interest on the secured debt the debtor chooses to pay compounds the problem, making the comparison between putatively not paying in Chapter 7 and partially paying in Chapter 13 useless. For these reasons, we decided that the only meaningful approach was to limit our analysis to hypothetical three-year 100% payment plans.

CALCULATING THE PAYMENT PLAN

To find which debtors could repay their nonmortgage debt in full in three years, we calculated each family's capacity to pay by figuring how much money it would take to meet a Chapter 13 plan that repaid debts in full and subtracting that amount from the debtors' family income. The remainder would be the amount the debtor would be expected to live on, an amount we could evaluate according to normative conclusions about the appropriate degree of sacrifice. The number of necessary conditions and calculations defies readability, so we offer a brief summary in the text and greater explanatory detail in the notes for those who want to follow the details.

For each debtor we calculated what would be required in a Chapter 13 repayment plan. We calculated each debtor's income, less federal income taxes, although we could not make appropriate deductions for union dues, state taxes, insurance payments, or retirement contributions that might actually reduce the take-home pay.[20] We then deducted payments to the home mortgagee,[21] payments to the secured creditors,[22] and a statutory fee to the Chapter 13 trustee.[23] Finally, we deducted a household budget for each debtor. When the required Chapter 13 payments and the budget were subtracted from the after-tax income, the remainder was applied against the unsecured debt under the hypothetical Chapter 13.

The hardest issue we addressed was the budget question: how much the debtor needs to live, to have an incentive to continue getting up for a job, to feed the kids and have lunch money, to pay a doctor bill, and so on. Rather than calculate our own untested budgets, we used budgets published by the Bureau of Labor Statistics.[24] The Bureau published three budgets each year, low, moderate, and high.[25] In broad terms, they represented the expenses incurred by an average American urban household of four (husband, wife, two children) in the bottom third, the middle third, and the upper third of the population by income. The budgets are not merely a gross report, however, because they build up expenses item-by-item, and they apply a minimally acceptable standard rather than the average costs Americans incur. For example, the housing costs in the low budget are calculated only for minimum housing, with adequate heat (no air conditioning), running water, and so forth. The low budget is not a poverty budget, because the assumptions that go into calculation of the federal poverty budget are based on very different criteria, and a poverty budget provides too little detail for a meaningful comparison with the bankruptcy data.[26]

The low budget assumes that families rent, and the other two assume the families own their homes. The pretax low budget for 1981 was $15,323, the moderate was $25,407, and the high was $38,060.[27] All in all, these budgets represent the government's best estimate of the personal expenses of each third of Americans by income.

We adjusted the Bureau of Labor Statistics budgets to reflect the actual mortgage obligations of the bankrupt debtors[28] and a closer estimate of their tax liabilities.[29] To reflect the various normative views policymakers might take, we calculated the hypothetical Chapter 13's three times for each debtor, once for each budget.

Table 12.3 shows the results of our first calculation. There were 721 wage-earner households in the Chapter 7 sample who gave enough data to make this calculation. The first number column of the table reveals that 75—about 10%—of these households could have paid all their debts in three years while living on the Labor Department's low budget. Only 15 of these households, about 2%, would have had the moderate budget after full payment, and 4 households could have paid and still enjoyed the high-budget existence—not affluent, but not brutal either. The three categories cumulate; that is, the 4 families are also included among the 15 and the 15 are also included among the 75.

These figures reflect only absolute budget levels. The 75 families who "can pay" on the low budget include families with incomes double the low budget, so that the calculations to this point require those families to live on half, or less than half, of their incomes.[30] Should the law require a family earning $35,000 a year to live on $15,000? Policymakers have to decide if it is fair, socially desirable, and economically sensible to have this family living so dra-

TABLE 12.3. Number of Chapter 7 Wage Earners at Estimated Living Levels, Given Hypothetical Chapter 13 Plans[a]

Variable	All Chapter 7 Pure Wage Earners[b]	Non-Homeowners	Homeowners
After paying taxes and creditors, number of creditors whose remaining income is at			
BLS low budget[c]	75	47	28
BLS intermediate budget[d]	15	3	12
BLS high budget[e]	4	1	3
Of 75 who would be at low budget level, number remaining if income floors were set at			
80% of take-home pay	23	19	4
70% of take-home pay	50	36	14
60% of take-home pay	65	44	21

[a]Cases with extreme values on assets, total debt, or income excluded. Chapter 13 plan is three years and assumes constant income, 100% repayment to unsecured creditors, continued mortgage payments, and trustee fees. See text for details.

[b]N = 721. Excludes cases for which home ownership could not be determined.

[c]$15,323.

[d]$25,407.

[e]$38,060.

Source: Consumer Bankruptcy Project.

matically below their income for three years. It may also be difficult to maintain these income levels on an involuntary basis. Will a debtor work overtime, will a spouse keep a part-time job, when only the creditors profit?

Beyond perceptions of fairness, these figures conceal some serious anomalies. The Bureau budget data are based on spending patterns for people at the income levels studied. Yet working members of the higher income family may have higher expenses for their jobs. They may need to wear suits and dresses rather than employer-provided uniforms or jeans accounted for in the low budgets; they may need more for lunches and transportation. These differences matter when every penny is accounted for. Our calculations necessarily squeeze these expenses out.

To respond to concerns about disproportion, we reanalyzed the data to exclude the debtors for whom the difference between what they earned and the budget on which they would be required to live would be the greatest. We ran the figures leaving debtors with 80% of their take-home pay with which to pay their mortgage and budget expenses. Thus a family would not be included in "can pay" under this test unless it would have at least 80% of take-home pay left for expenses after debt service. Of the 75 families in the table, 23—about 3% of the Chapter 7 total—qualified under this test.

A 70% floor yielded 50 debtors—7% of Chapter 7 debtors—who could meet a low budget. A 60% floor produced 65 debtors, about 9%. Thus 9% of our wage-earner Chapter 7 debtors on a posttax basis could pay all their debts in three years while living on the Bureau of Labor Statistics low budget and dedicating up to 40% of their incomes to debt repayment.

CONCLUSIONS: PAYING IN HYPOTHETICAL CHAPTER 13's

These data reveal some extreme findings. The overwhelming majority of Chapter 7 debtors—90% by any measure—could not pay their debts in Chapter 13 and maintain even the barest standard of living. But we might want to examine even these few debtors more closely. The debtors who could pay all if they gave up 40% of their income are merely suspects. Some have already lost their jobs or they may be saddled with continuing medical or other expenses; for them the projected income and the low budget are unkind jokes. Still others may be discharging debt they might be able to repay, but, like the "abusers" reported to Congress and interviewed by the GAO, they might tell tales of hardship that would make debt forgiveness more justified than the cold numbers suggest.

The ultimate question for policymakers is whether the abusers are worth finding. Some would not hesitate to say that if 3%, or 7%, or 9% of these deadbeats are able to pay, we should track them down. We count ourselves among those who are not convinced. A complex statistical analysis yields about 3–9% of the debtors who are suspects for further, more extensive investigation. By law, these debtors are already paying some substantial portion of their secured debt, either by continuing their payments or by relinquishing the collateral for liquidation. A new bankruptcy regime that invested more time to find and to investigate the potential can-pay debtors would prompt only a small amount of new repayment. This is the classic case in which a policymaker asks if the game is worth the candle.

Already Trying to Pay—Chapter 13 Debtors

In the bankruptcy debates, the Chapter 13 debtors are frequently idealized as the family in financial trouble struggling to regain financial responsibility and to pay their debts. Virtually all debate has been premised on this view of Chapter 13 and the corollary proposition that if more Chapter 7 debtors would simply file Chapter 13 instead, abuse would be a thing of the past.

The Purdue University Study argued for putting more debtors in Chapter 13, but this study considered Chapter 7 debtors only. Evidently the researchers thought it was axiomatic that the Chapter 13 debtors must be paying. After all, no one can force a debtor to declare Chapter 13, so those who attempt to repay are the volunteers, declaring themselves in effect to be "can-pay" debtors. Given the terrible financial circumstances of most bankrupt debtors, we were skeptical about whether Chapter 13 debtors in fact enjoyed such successes.

We conducted two analyses. First we analyzed the Chapter 13 debtors hypothetically, as we had the Chapter 7 debtors, to see how many of them could pay 100% within the constraints of the assumptions previously discussed. Then we examined how many had actually succeeded in paying whatever percentage they had in fact promised to pay in their plans.

Chapter 13 Debtors and Hypothetical Chapter 13's

For our hypothetical test, we use exactly the same criteria we used to find "can-pay" Chapter 7 debtors, including the proposition that the debtor is making a 100% repayment. In fact, many Chapter 13 debtors propose to pay only a small percentage of their debts, and many Chapter 13 debtors fail to pay whatever percentage they promised—both factors overlooked in the idealization of the Chapter 13 debtor. To determine, however, whether the Chapter 13 debtor is in fact paying anything more than the Chapter 7 debtor who settles up with his secured creditors and perhaps even reaffirms an unsecured debt or two, the only meaningful comparison comes from putting the Chapter 13 debtor through a full, hypothetical repayment plan.

Table 12.4 shows how many Chapter 13 debtors could pay all their debts and still have enough left to live at the Bureau of Labor Statistics low-budget level. About 18%—79 current Chapter 13 debtors—can pay all their debts and maintain at least a low budget. Less than 5%—21 debtors—could maintain a moderate budget, and 2 debtors could maintain a high budget. These proportions are higher than among Chapter 7 debtors, but they are not much higher.

As with the Chapter 7 debtors, we reanalyzed the "can-pay" debtors to see how many could pay and still have 60–80% of their take-home pay. These

TABLE 12.4. Number of Chapter 13 Wage Earners at Estimated Living Levels, Given Hypothetical Chapter 13 Plans[a]

Variable	All Chapter 13 Pure Wage Earners[b]	Non-Homeowners	Homeowners
After paying taxes and creditors, number of creditors whose remaining income is at			
BLS low budget[c]	79	27	52
BLS moderate budget[d]	21	1	20
BLS higher budget[e]	2	0	2
Of 79 who would be at low budget level, number remaining if income floors were set at			
80% of take-home pay	26	13	13
70% of take-home pay	51	27	24
60% of take-home pay	68	27	41

Cases with extreme values on assets, total debt, or income excluded. Chapter 13 plan is three years and assumes constant income, 100% repayment to unsecured creditors, continued mortgage payments, and trustee fees. See text for details.

[b]N = 433. Excludes cases for which home ownership could not be determined.

[c]$15,323.

[d]$25,407.

[e]$38,060.

Source: Consumer Bankruptcy Project.

results are also shown in Table 12.4. With an 80% floor, 26 of the Chapter 13 debtors could have paid, at 70%, 51, and at 60%, 68 Chapter 13 debtors could have paid. These figures represent 6%, 12%, and 16% respectively of the Chapter 13 debtors. They are improved over the comparable figures in Chapter 7, where 3%, 7%, and 9% of the debtors respectively could have paid, but they are not as dramatically improved as policy debates have assumed.

How can it be that we find so few Chapter 13 debtors able to pay 100%, when these debtors have declared themselves "can-pay" debtors? There are two reasons. One is that many of these debtors are undertaking to pay much less than 100% and therefore may not be paying more than many Chapter 7 debtors actually pay. The second reason is that most of these Chapter 13 cases are failing.

ACTUAL OUTCOMES IN CHAPTER 13

There is a fundamental problem in studying the success rate of Chapter 13 cases. One would have to wait at least five years after the date of filing to be sure all the cases were closed and success or failure was duly noted in the files. By then, however, the files on the cases that failed soon after filing would have been archived and, in some cases, destroyed.

For many of the cases in the Bankruptcy Project, we cannot report final results. Our inspection of the files in each district was a snapshot taken at the time of our visit to that district. In districts we visited early in the study, our snapshot was taken near the beginning of the Chapter 13 plans we reviewed. In other districts, we were looking at plans in their second or third years.

OUR DATA

The results we found are set forth in Figure 12.1, which we present in the form of a flow chart, showing the percentage of wage-earning Chapter 13 debtors who fell into each of our categories of possible results at the time we reviewed the files. There are two yes-or-no points in the flow chart for each case: the plan proposed was confirmed or was not confirmed; and, postconfirmation, there were or were not signs of "bad news," such as a motion to dismiss for nonpayment. There are four result categories: still paying, failed, troubled, and missing. When we looked at the files, those in the first category, "still paying," were still making their Chapter 13 payments or in some cases had even completed their payments. Those in the second category, "failed," are a combination of "switched to Chapter 7" and "dismissed," both results being an abandonment of payment under their plans. Some cases failed before confirmation and others after. The "troubled" category consists of cases in which the case had not yet been dismissed or converted but (1) no plan had been confirmed at the date of our inspection or (2), postconfirmation, there was some sign of serious trouble with the case, such as a motion to dismiss or convert. The cases listed as "missing" are those where it was impossible to tell what had happened to the case.

Because we looked at these cases before the full payment period had elapsed in most instances, the failure rate is necessarily understated. Cases that had failed by the time we looked had definitely failed, but some of the cases that were still paying at the time of our inspection may have failed later. The cases in the still-pending and bad news categories might have succeeded or failed, but our interviews with judges and attorneys suggested that most of them probably failed. A case still pending many months or even years after filing is a sure sign of trouble and is generally doomed.[31] The "bad news" cases could have been revived if the debtors were able to resume payment, but the judges and practitioners tell us that most often such cases fail.

Indeed, many of the cases had undoubtedly failed by the time we looked at the files in the sense that the debtor had quit paying and would not resume payments. But the court system moves slowly, and the paperwork after the fact moves even more slowly, especially in busy courthouses. These troubled categories probably included a high proportion of cases that had already failed but were still awaiting proper clerical burial.

Overall, 32% of the cases for which we had usable data had already failed by the time we looked at the files. Another 31% of the cases were troubled, leaving about 32% still paying at the time of our sample. About 4% of the cases were missing. For a rough comparison, if we assume that as many trou-

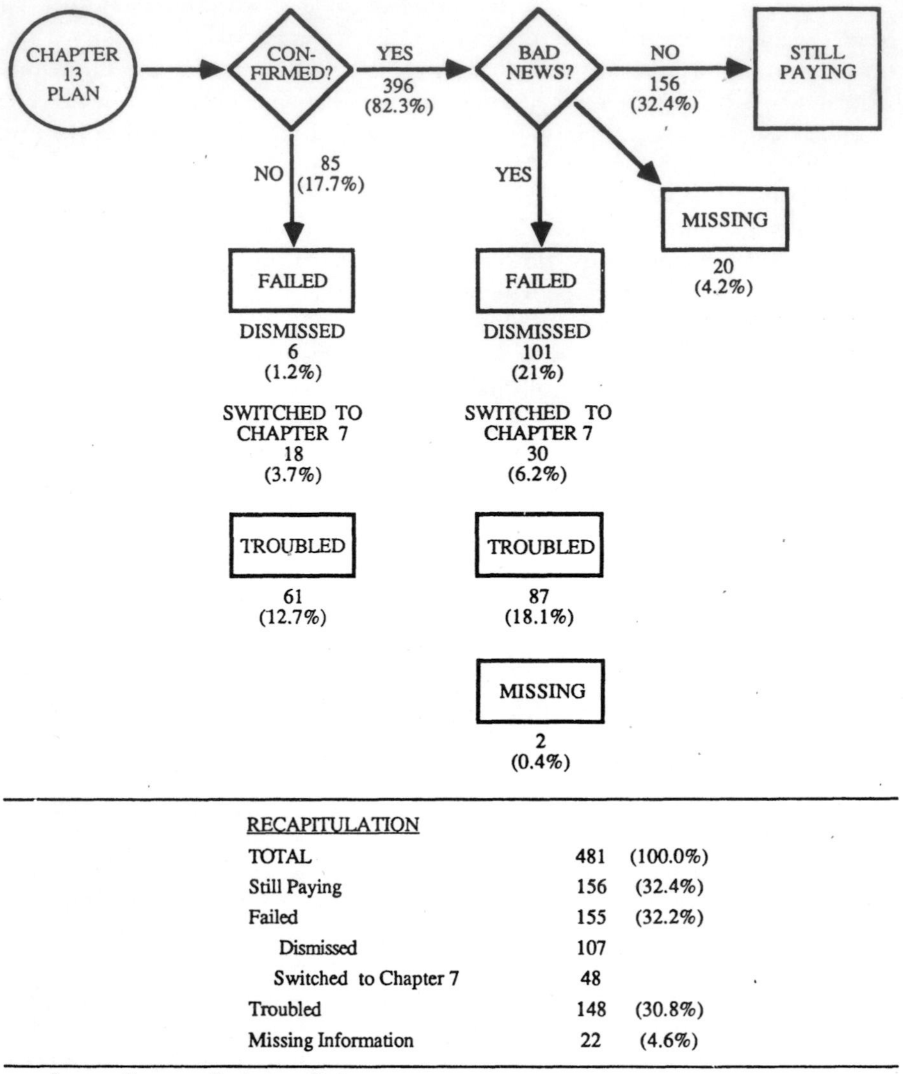

RECAPITULATION

TOTAL	481	(100.0%)
Still Paying	156	(32.4%)
Failed	155	(32.2%)
Dismissed	107	
Switched to Chapter 7	48	
Troubled	148	(30.8%)
Missing Information	22	(4.6%)

Source: Consumer Bankruptcy Project

FIGURE 12.1. Outcomes for Chapter 13 Cases (N = 481, pure wage earners). Source: Consumer Bankruptcy Project.

bled cases revived as still paying cases later failed, then about one-third of the Chapter 13 cases made it through the payment process to the end; two-thirds of them failed.[32]

THE RICE DATA

The low success rate in Chapter 13 is confirmed by another source, Claude Rice, who runs a data processing service for Chapter 13 trustees, handling their mailings and routine collections for a fee. Mr. Rice closed 20,235 cases for Chapter 13 trustees during 1980–81, and he testified before Congress that 29.6% of the cases closed that year had paid to completion.[33] The Rice data are not exactly comparable to the Bankruptcy Project, primarily because Mr. Rice receives cases only after a trustee decides they are worth sending to him to set up a collection file. Most trustees would not send Mr. Rice cases not yet confirmed, a point where about 18% of our debtors stumbled. Some trustees might wait for early payments before sending the file on to Mr. Rice, so that some portion of the early dismissals after confirmation would also be omitted from Mr. Rice's files. Finally, those who use Mr. Rice's service may be differently motivated to monitor their Chapter 13's, choosing a sophisticated and regular billing service to keep track of the debtors and prevent them from falling behind. This means that Mr. Rice may well have a higher success rate on Chapter 13's than a sample of all filings would show. Yet his data are consistent with ours. If anything, his data may suggest that our success rate is overstated.

POSSIBLE EXPLANATIONS FOR THE CHAPTER 13 FAILURES

Even within these limitations on the data, the Chapter 13 failure rate is extraordinarily high. Several factors may contribute to that outcome, but the overriding fact may be the simplest one. Almost none of the debtors in either chapter can pay, except at the price of enormous sacrifice and on the very shaky premise that they will not again suffer the income interruptions and high expenses so many of them have suffered in the past. These data indicate that those who choose Chapter 13 are doing so not because of some careful calculation of their ability to pay, but for other reasons—and the financial realities they face often spell failure.

Indeed, one could reasonably ask, given the preceding data, how can nearly a third succeed at their plans? The preceding section showed that only 18% could live on a government low budget and pay their creditors in full. Only 6% could pay and make a low budget without giving up more than 20% of their income. Does a possible one-third success rate indicate some hidden source of wealth?

The answer to the puzzle lies in what the debtors in Chapter 13 actually promise to pay. On average, our debtors promised to pay only about half of their debt, and still two-thirds of them failed. The debtors Claude Rice saw, after each case played out, had paid even less (44.1% payment) and failed even more (29.6% success rate).[34]

The Prize Debtor

Having tried every statistical way to shake loose the can-pay debtors, we finally used an anecdotal approach. We asked the computer to locate the debtor who most likely could have repaid his or her creditors but who took Chapter 7 bankruptcy and discharged the debt instead.

Our candidate for the debtor who can pay the most is a boat captain who filed Chapter 7 in Houston. The numbers are stunning: He owed $2,300 on a six-year-old Toyota and $10,925.34 in unsecured debts. He had worked at his present job for three years, and he made $54,000 in each of the two years preceding his filing. We know nothing about him except the information in the file, but on the face of it he looks like a guy who could pay.

The reason for his filing is elusive, but there is one hint: His only other brush with courts was in the California divorce court. The captain and his wife divorced the same year as his bankruptcy filing. Evidently they had been separated for some time before the divorce (he has lived in Texas for three years and the divorce was in California). Most of the debts he lists are with California stores, and his wife evidently has the car he owes money on. Possibly this debtor filed to avoid paying joint debts with his ex-wife, although no allegation of that sort is in the files.

This ruse obviously is not what Congress had in mind when it drafted a bankruptcy statute to relieve the hopelessly overburdened consumer debtor. But the story does not end here. The ambiguities in the system have a funny way of reasserting themselves.

The captain paid his bankruptcy attorney in cash before the filing. The attorney prepared the schedules and filed, but when it came time for the 341 hearing to answer the creditors' questions, the debtor was nowhere to be found. The meeting was rescheduled, but still no debtor. The trustee then moved on two separate occasions to dismiss the complaint, but no action had been taken when we saw the captain's file. We were sufficiently curious to recheck this file six years later, and we found that the Houston court was so backlogged that there still had been no court action on either motion. This debtor is in a state of legal limbo: technically in a pending bankruptcy, but very unlikely to see a final discharge.

The files do not tell whether this debtor was killed in a barroom brawl, was enjoying the southerly breezes off the coast of Madagascar, or was drinking a beer in his apartment in Shuster, Texas, and muttering, "To hell with all of them." Evidently he never reappeared, and no creditor cared enough to go after him.

Another irony in this case is that the debtor could have accomplished much the same result outside of bankruptcy without spending $500 on an attorney. He owed each creditor relatively small amounts. The $2,300 car loan was the biggest debt, but we think the debtor would not have minded if the repo man had visited his ex-wife in California. The other creditors would have had to track him down in Texas (or wherever he had sailed by then) or just given up. If this debtor is gone, it is not bankruptcy that caused the creditors' losses.

The bottom line is that the debtor chose to skip, and it was probably not worth it for the creditors to hunt him down for relatively small sums.

This debtor is undoubtedly not a shining example of how the bankruptcy system helps the unfortunate. But he is not quite the clear case of bankruptcy abuse we hoped to find. No bankruptcy judge ever gave him a discharge, and he could elude his debtors without bankruptcy help. The captain is a likely can-pay debtor, but the problem he presents is only incidentally a bankruptcy problem.

Policy Implications

To most people, abuse of the bankruptcy system means use of bankruptcy by those who could pay if they were willing to give up those assets that they had bought and now want to keep without paying. In the more sophisticated debates that have taken place in Congress, the assumed source of repayment is the debtor's future income, which would be ample to pay creditors if the debtor had a truly moral view of the obligation to keep promises. Because these concerns are powerful, we devoted this chapter to a careful analysis of our debtors' capacity to repay from asset sales or from future income. We found very little capacity to repay in either way, although some will feel that the little we found justifies expending considerable resources to ferret out "can-pay" debtors and make them pay. We have sympathy with this point. But we also have great reservations.

We see bankruptcy as a social safety net. The data from Chapters Four, Five, Six, and Seven show that those who use bankruptcy are not the underclass, the homeless, or the chronically unemployed. Not surprisingly, those in the worst economic circumstances are unlikely to gather sufficient credit to find themselves in bankruptcy. Instead, the debtors in bankruptcy are those who own homes, who work alongside other Americans, who participate in a middle-class lifestyle.

The first source of repayment is forced sale of almost all of a debtor's assets, with very low exemptions. What bankruptcy promises to entrepreneurs who start a new business or homeowners or wage earners is that debt will not push them back to a less-than-middle-class existence. The homestead exemption is designed to permit people to keep their homes and not be forced to start all over again. The personal property exemptions are there to keep debtors from the wrenching loss of wedding bands and winter coats to yield no more than a few dollars for their creditors. The discharge and protection from seizure and garnishment assures wage earners that they will not spend their lives in indentured servitude, even if they make a serious credit mistake. The discharge and the property exemptions are middle-class protections, reflecting the middle-class nature of bankruptcy itself.

The human pain and social dislocation associated with the sale of a person's possessions or the loss of a home escape statistical measurement. The data show that the return to creditors would be very modest, in our view too modest to balance the adverse social effects. For the middle class, struggling to hang on, it seems to us that the fresh start should include a reasonable equity in a home and a modicum of consumer goods.

The second source of repayment is future income. In the same year that our data were collected, bankruptcy experts testified before Congress:

> There was a broad consensus that bankruptcy had become an extremely serious financial problem which was having a definite impact on members of the consumer credit industry. . . . Persons seemed to be using bankruptcy who did not need it—the new bankrupts had substantial income and assets, and often, had not even been delinquent prior to filing their petitions. . . . There was a sense that bankruptcy had gotten out of hand, and was threatening the very fabric of an entire industry. . . . Consumers have considerable ability to pay debts out of future income.[35]

The Purdue Study went one step further, claiming in Congress—and widely quoted in the popular press—that Chapter 7 debtors discharged "$1.1 billion dollars in debt they could have repaid."[36]

The point of our complicated financial scrutiny has been to test the level of abuse, to see whether the system requires tightening. We scrutinized the Chapter 7 debtors, forcing them into repayment plans that kept them on the government's "low budget" regardless of what they really earned.

After an exhaustive (and exhausting) search for a sizable group of can-pay debtors, we find so few likely prospects for repayment that we conclude the effort to keep can-pay debtors out of bankruptcy or force them into Chapter 13 is a wasteful misdirection of energy. Out of 1202 wage earner debtors, only a handful could pay their debts by making payments from future income. The self-employed debtors, with their much higher debt/income ratios, were in worse shape with even lower repayment prospects. Of course, our conclusion is laden with normative assumptions. A policymaker who would demand great sacrifice would put more debtors in the can-pay category than we would. Nonetheless, these data should be useful and interesting to that policymaker. These data give some idea of the general range of repayment capacity. One observer might say 3% of the Chapter 7 debtors could repay; another might say 9%. What these data show is that it is not true that 70% of the debtors abuse the system. Or 40%. Or even 20%.

We conclude that bankruptcy laws should not be shaped around the can-pay question. When Congress responded to allegations of widespread abuse in 1984, it wrote a law to correct a problem that did not exist. The "solution" was costly to debtors who later used the system even though the changes would have little appreciable affect on actual abuse.

To conclude that abuse is not a widespread problem that should drive bankruptcy policymaking leaves open another question: How should a system respond to occasional abuse?

The circumstances of most debtors should be the crucial fact in shaping a sensible bankruptcy policy. But the way a few debtors come out will also have an important influence on that policy. We recognize that the individual who may have cheated the system is important, if for no other reason than as a symbol for all debtors, creditors, policymakers, and members of the general public who lack confidence in the system.

One possible response is simply to decide that occasional abuse is the cost of a large system that generally works. In bankruptcy, potential abusers are so few and far between that no easily identifiable criteria flag them and no program of vigilant scrutiny is likely to yield more than a handful of suspects. Moreover, scrutiny is expensive. Even before the 1984 amendments, creditors had many opportunities to object to abusive behavior, but our review of files suggests that few creditors bothered, presumably based on their own cost/benefit analyses. Similarly, we could decide that dedicating public resources to the careful review of files is simply not cost effective.

A modified response to the problem of occasional abuse is to restructure the system to permit it to nab the occasional abuser, but to spend no resources to look for that abuser. In effect, if abuse comes to the court's attention through the newspapers or some other source, a particular debtor could be stopped cold, with a system that otherwise runs as before.

The 1984 amendments included one feature of the latter variety. In addition to reducing exemptions for all debtors and several other system-wide features, the amendments included a "substantial abuse" test that permits the bankruptcy judge to examine a debtor's circumstances to see if the debtor's decision to file Chapter 7 is a substantial abuse of the bankruptcy system. If the court finds abuse, the debtor faces the choice of filing in Chapter 13 or staying out of bankruptcy altogether. It is likely that the scheme identifies some abusers, but no announced standards for the search exist and judges are supposed to make the investigation on their own without any prompting from the creditors.

The failure to use announced standards permits the court to pursue any "abuse" it finds, but it also has the potential to create a random system of justice. One leading case interpreting the new provision stated that there should be no finding of abuse unless the debtors could pay substantially all their debts in Chapter 13,[37] while another decision seems to bar from Chapter 7 everyone who could pay anything whatever to creditors under Chapter 13.[38] The views and energy of the bankruptcy judge are obviously critical to the task of finding, labeling, and tossing out the abusers, and in some districts uninterested judges make the new provision little more than window dressing. The chances of being labeled an "abuser" are low anywhere,[39] and they may be too haphazard to affect the debtor who tries to take advantage of the system or the perception of fairness it was supposed to promote.

On balance, we think that the mitigation of a relatively small level of clear abuse is not worth idiosyncratic, luck-of-the-draw justice. We have enough confidence in the operation of the consumer bankruptcy system to tolerate the occasional story of the local paper about a debtor who kept a mink coat, knowing that the debtor is rare and the details might reveal a very different picture.

The other major conclusion of this chapter is that Chapter 13 has not turned out to be what was promised. For years participants in bankruptcy policy debates have talked about Chapter 13 as if it were a panacea, as if getting a debtor into Chapter 13 were virtually the same thing as getting all or most debts paid. Congress struggled in the 1978 Code to make Chapter 13 attractive, so debtors would file there and repay.[40] The Purdue Study concluded that $1.1 billion would be repaid, if only those Chapter 7 debtors would take Chapter 13—their enthusiasm unencumbered by facts from a single Chapter 13 file.

Our data show the contrary. Debtors in Chapter 13 fail at extraordinary rates, with fewer than a third still making payments an average of two years after confirmation. On average, those who are paying have proposed plans that promise to pay only about half their debts. This is not surprising, considering how little they have. And some might say that a debtor who repays something is better than a debtor who does not. But with plans paying considerably less than 100%, it is not possible to know whether Chapter 13's pay creditors more than Chapter 7's. The possible range of economic outcomes in consumer bankruptcy is more than a simple Chapter 7–Chapter 13 dichotomy. Instead, there is a continuum of payment levels, with a prototype Chapter 7 at one end, paying nothing and discharging everything, and a prototype Chapter 13 at the other, paying all creditors 100%. In fact, most debtors lie in some hazy field in between, with an important overlap. A Chapter 13 family may be doing for their creditors as little—and possibly considerably less—than many Chapter 7 debtors.

The implications of these findings for establishing policy are far reaching. In 1981 choosing Chapter 13 was an entirely voluntary act, with no legal bar to a Chapter 7 nor any creditor leverage to force a Chapter 13, which makes the failure rate in Chapter 13 all the more noteworthy. High failure rate among volunteers raises serious questions about the efficacy of proposals to force debtors into Chapter 13. If success eludes most debtors who evaluate their own finances and their own desire to pay their debts, and choose to try to pay, how much payment can we expect from those who are coerced into payment plans? We conclude that continued efforts to force more debtors into Chapter 13 may drive up Chapter 13 filing rates but will not necessarily add up to creditor repayment.

Occasionally we hear of districts that announce they have managed high repayments in Chapter 13. We cannot draw any conclusion until we see the data, but we wonder how that could be. If the debtors in other districts are like the ones we saw, there must be some special circumstance that permits high-payment plans. It could be that some trustees can squeeze out high payments by pressing the debtors to live below minimum budgets, to liquidate assets, or to find other ways to produce income—which would make us uneasy about the notion of a court trustee turned debt collector. Another possibility is that these debtors enjoy bonanza 13's, where many creditors fail to file and the debtor's 100% plan really pays far less than all the outstanding debt. It could also be that attorneys and trustees in those districts pick only the best debtor families for Chapter 13's or that in those districts some people are attracted into Chapter 13 who would not have filed bankruptcy at all in another district, including people who might have gone to nonbankruptcy debt counseling services if they were available. Until we know more, we seriously doubt that a cross section of Chapter 13 debtors contains very many people who can pay much debt.

The larger question is whether we have done debtors any service by promoting Chapter 13. Debtors have filed Chapter 13 in record numbers since the adoption of the 1978 Code. Would Chapter 13 be so attractive if the debtors knew that two-thirds of them would either be in Chapter 7 or out from under bankruptcy protection altogether in a short time? How would they feel about paying an attorney's bill of several hundred dollars and a $60 filing fee if they knew that 20% of them would be tossed out of court before they could even propose a confirmable plan?

Many of our friends in the bankruptcy field and many of the good people we interviewed for this study would be shocked to hear us question Chapter 13's value. Chapter 13 is popular among policymakers and academics alike, but these data cause us to ask whether it makes much sense for most debtors in bankruptcy. Until Chapter 13's are routinely filed by a group of debtors better able to repay their debts—people who currently stay out of bankruptcy—we see relatively little return to creditors and little benefit to most debtors.

It is not ridiculous to suggest that it might be better not to have Chapter 13 at all. One could argue that its benefits are outweighed by the harm done to people who waste money and mental anguish on impossible payment plans. But we are not ready to go that far. Chapter 13 is an important option for people who feel a strong desire to try to pay but who need the protection of the bankruptcy laws to give them time to do so. It is probably true that most debtors who could pay in Chapter 13 could do so just as well in a good credit counseling program. Yet is is also true that such programs do not exist in many communities and therefore Chapter 13 may be the best available solution for some debtors in those communities. Finally, Chapter 13 offers unique assistance for a small number of debtors who can pay but who need help with a recalcitrant secured creditor, such as a home mortgage holder.[41]

All in all, we think it would be better if the volume were turned down on Chapter 13 promotion. Judges could encourage lawyers and trustees who are selective about putting debtors in Chapter 13 and discourage those who routinely file 13's that obviously have little chance of success. As part of that process, local court orders could establish debt/income ratios above which filing a Chapter 13 requires a written justification from the lawyer and a special court hearing. (For those who are still concerned about the tiny minority of can-pay Chapter 7's, the converse could be required for a Chapter 7 that was below a certain ratio.) Local rules could forbid lawyers to advertise Chapter 13 under headlines that say "Avoid Bankruptcy." Above all, praise and self-congratulation should be reserved for judges, lawyers, and trustees who have a high proportion of successful 13's (without the use of high-pressure collection tactics), rather than simply for a high proportion of Chapter 13 filings.

In the last chapter of this book, after looking at bankruptcy from the perspective of creditors, we discuss more about bankruptcy policy. Here it is sufficient to lay to rest a fantasy, the phantom legions of debtors who could pay if only they would. Putting that fantasy to one side would permit the bankruptcy debates to return to their true foundation: a fair balance between debtor and creditor.

Notes

1. Many economists talk about the "attractiveness" of bankruptcy and how its "attractiveness" would cause many debtors to use it. E.g., M. White, Personal Bankruptcy Under the 1978 Bankruptcy Code: An Economic Analysis, 63 Indiana Law Journal 1, 3 (1987–88).

2. Purdue University, Credit Research Center, Krannert Graduate School of Management, Consumer Bankruptcy Study (1982), Vol. I, pp. 88–91. For a detailed critique which concludes that the study is "unreliable and misleading, and . . . does not offer a sound basis for any contemporary discussion of bankruptcy policy," see T. A. Sullivan, E. Warren, and J. L. Westbrook, Limiting Access to Bankruptcy Discharge: An Analysis of the Creditors' Data, 1983 Wisconsin Law Review 1091, 1093 (1983). Also see our discussion of this study in Chapter Two, p. 17.

3. U.S. General Accounting Office, Report to the Chairman, Committee on the Judiciary, House of Representatives, "A Profile of Selected Personal Bankruptcy Cases" (1982). Two of the five debtors refused to talk with the GAO, so their stories are not reported.

4. Chapter Six documents that the formerly self-employed look much more like the currently self-employed than they do like wage earners in terms of debt. For the purposes of this chapter, we compared capacity to pay from assets and from future income of the self-employed, the formerly self-employed, and the pure wage earners.

For the first, we tested a "debt/asset" ratio, debts divided by assets, and found that pure wage earners differed significantly from the formerly self-employed ($F = 3.45$, $p = 0.03$). The mean total debt/asset ratios were 38.1 for the Chapter 7 pure wage earners, 321.2 for the currently self-employed, and 955.4 for the formerly self-employed. Asset values of 0 were recoded as one dollar for this calculation. Nonmortgage debt/asset ratios were also significantly different: 37.7 for pure wage earners, 320.3 for the currently self-employed, and 954.7 for the formerly self-employed.

As to ability to pay from future income, the formerly self-employed and the self-employed look very different from the pure wage earners on both total debt/income ratios and nonmortgage debt/income ratios and the difference is significant at $p < 0.05$. The mean total debt/income ratios for the self-employed and formerly self-employed are 8.6 and 6.1, respectively, compared to 2.5 for the pure wage earners. The mean nonmortgage ratios for the three groups are 5.6, 4.2, and 1.4. The differences between the ratios of the self-employed and the formerly self-employed are not statistically significant at $p < 0.05$. Nonetheless, to be doubly sure, we recalculated the debt/income figures in this chapter for pure wage earners and the formerly self-employed combined. The results showed consistent reductions in the percentage who appeared able to pay.

5. For technical reasons, we did not subtract debt from assets on an asset-by-asset basis. Instead we subtracted aggregate nonhome secured debt from nonhome assets. The result should be approximately the same for the purpose of seeing how much

unsecured debt could be paid by forcing the sale of those assets. The result is to understate assets, because the unsecured part of a secured debt may be subtracted from an unencumbered asset. In the example in the text, a $2,000 loan on a car worth only $1,000, our calculation might subtract that remaining unsecured $1,000 from the value of a second car that was fully paid off. If the second car was worth $1,500, we would understate its value by $1,000. However, when we are comparing assets to unsecured debt, the result is rough justice. The reason is that the $1,000 of unsecured debt on the first car would be added to the total unsecured debt, an addition our calculation does not do. Thus the $1,000 understatement of asset value is roughly balanced by the $1,000 understatement of unsecured debt. In any case, the undersecurity is approximately one-quarter of the nonhome secured debt, because nonhome collateral in our sample was worth around 76% of secured debt. See Chapter Seventeen for a more detailed analysis of this point.

6. Because state exemption laws vary so much, we cannot develop a clear idea of where the debtors would have been under various exemption schemes. We cannot compute the full effect of exemptions even under the laws of our three sample states, because the law limits what a debtor can keep both by dollar amount and by description of the item. (Debtors in Texas, for example, can keep horses and rifles, but not cash.) This defeats any statistical attempt to analyze what these debtors could keep. As an approximation, we calculated a middle-of-the-road $5,000 exemption for nonhome property, with no category limitations. Because this exemption is so small, it probably overstates a possible repayment from liquidation sales.

7. For the small group who could pay anything, the mean repayment would be 33% and the median payment would be 20%.

8. For this computation we have not added the undersecured portion of secured debts to the total unsecured debt, the converse of the problem in note 4. The effect here is to overstate the percentages of unsecured debt that we report as payable. The debtors actually had more unsecured debt and thus could pay a smaller percentage from a home sale than the figures to follow indicate. For the homes themselves, however, we deducted the aggregate mortgage amounts from one or more mortgages on each house from the stated value of the house, so the equities are as reported by the debtors.

9. Even the Chapter 13 debtors, those promising to repay some of their debts over the next three to five years, could not pay much if they sold off their nonhome assets instead of trying to pay. They could do better than the Chapter 7 debtors, but only 19 of them could pay 100% of their unsecured debts and only 12 more could pay as much as 50%.

10. The 70% figure comes from a leading case, *Durrett v. Washington National Insurance Co.*, 621 F.2d 201 (5th Cir. 1980), in which a court ruled that any home foreclosure sale that failed to yield at least 70% of the fair market value of the home might be subject to later attack in bankruptcy. There has been a huge outcry from the mortgage lending industry, arguing that foreclosure sales rarely meet the 70% test and the *Durrett* opinion would impose great hardships and costs on the mortgage lending industry. The issue in the debate with regard to the 70% figure itself centers on the contention that it is an unreasonably high percentage of fair market value to hope for in the context of a forced sale. For additional discussion and data about the consequences of the *Durrett* decision, see P. Shuchman, Data on the *Durrett* controversy, 9 Cardozo Law Review 605 (1987).

11. Figuring gross recoveries at fair market value, with no sales costs and no exemptions, 186 debtor families could pay something by selling their homes. Within this

group, the median recovery would be $8,000 and the mean $11,700. We thought it right to report these figures, but it must be emphasized that they have nothing to do with the reality of assets sales.

12. Texas creditors would benefit the most. Texans account for 23 of the Chapter 7 homeowners who could repay *any* unsecured debts by selling their homes.

13. Once again, the Chapter 13 debtors do better, but not much better. Less than 10%—34 of them—could pay all their unsecured debts by selling their homes, ignoring nonmortgage secured debts.

14. Since 1984, Chapter 7 debtors have been required to estimate their living expenses, something not available in the 1981 files. The primary purpose of the requirement was to enable judges to determine whether Chapter 7 debtors who could pay were abusing the bankruptcy process.

However, we have a serious question about the reliability of the reported information. The debtors obviously have an interest in overstating their expenses so that it will not appear that they are able to pay. On the other hand, it is by no means clear that the errors would all be in the direction of overstatement. Judges, lawyers, and credit counselors are virtually unanimous in saying that most debtors in financial trouble consistently underestimate their expenses. Indeed, it is likely that some of them developed such deep financial trouble precisely because they underestimated living expenses in the past, failed to budget for contingencies, and so forth. The problem of underestimating expenses has been repeatedly explained to us as the major cause of the frequent failure of Chapter 13 plans. The debtors trying to pay in Chapter 13 are often ridiculously optimistic about the amount they can live on. We are reminded of Elaine Dover in Chapter Four, who believed that she could meet all the incidental expenses of six children, including three teenagers, on five dollars a week. It seems just as likely that the estimates of expenditures now being made by Chapter 7 debtors are often too low.

We use an objective measure of the debtors' capacity to pay, with no attempt to estimate individualized expenses. We believe this yields a better statistical conclusion, even though it would obviously be necessary to look at expenses to determine how much a debtor should be forced to pay from income in individual cases. Some debtors might be able to do better than standardized expenses, and some might do worse. As we show in Chapter Four, people who file bankruptcy have larger families than Americans generally, and it seems reasonable to assume that they have concomitantly greater expenses.

15. We removed all mortgages, not just home mortgages, so there are a few other real estate mortgages ignored as well, such as mortgages on rental property and on homes occupied by ex-spouses.

16. Federal Reserve Board Bulletin (December 1983), p. A41.

17. Bankruptcy does not stop interest from accumulating on oversecured loans, particularly on home mortgages. Bankruptcy does permit debtors to restructure secured loans, except for real estate mortgages, which must be paid according to their original terms. See discussion in Chapter Seven.

18. There are many legal complications paying now or over time, depending on whether the loan is in default and how much has to be paid, which we ignore for now because they have little bearing on the basic point.

19. Indeed, the ability to pay only the allowed secured claim in Chapter 13 may mean that the debtor in Chapter 13 who keeps all the property promised under a security agreement pays less than a debtor in Chapter 7 who does not have the cash for

a redemption and must pay the full loan value to keep property encumbered by a security agreement.

20. Based on average effective tax rates for 1981, a family earning $35,000 a year would pay $7,400 in taxes (income and FICA). Income tax rate from IRS, Statistics of Income Bulletin (Spring 1984), Table 4, p. 93. We used average figures that do not apply in every case. We deducted the resulting tax payments from each debtor family's income so that the income remaining is posttax take-home pay, ignoring other deductions such as union dues and insurance.

The tax effects are difficult to figure on an average basis, because deductions depend on so many variables, including household size. This problem was more acute under prior law, because in 1981 more deductions were available to the average family and the tax rates were higher and varied more. Thus a set of figures applying an average tax rate might be misleading in one case, but figures without any tax deduction would be more distorted.

21. Mortgage payments were based on the outstanding principal, assuming a 10% interest rate. We almost certainly underestimated the payments, because most debtors had larger initial balances, and repayment amounts are figured on the initial balance, not the balance after some years of payment. We also assumed two months of arrearages that would have to be made up over the three-year payment plan. We cannot determine from our data the actual average arrearages, so we made a conservative estimate based on our impressions from reviewing the files. Once again, we believe we understated arrearages. The mortgage calculation at this point is only principal and interest, not insurance and tax escrow payments. We account for these expenses later. See note 28.

22. We calculated nonmortgage secured debt assuming a 15% interest rate. Based on aggregate calculations, we found that nonmortgage collateral for the pure wage-earner sample was generally worth about 73% of the outstanding loan value, so we calculated an interest payment based on that amount. See Chapter Seventeen for data on undersecurity.

23. The fees for such trustees varied from district to district, with a statutory maximum of 10% of the debtors' monthly payments. We assumed a conservative 6%.

24. These budgets were referenced by Congress for considering proper levels of sacrifice for bankrupt debtors. S. Rep. No. 98-65, 98th Cong., 1st Sess. (1983), at 22.

25. See U.S. Bureau of Labor Statistics Bulletins, Urban Family Budgets and Comparative Indexes for Selected Urban Areas, annual (supplements to Bulletin 1570-5). Ironically, 1981 was the last year such budgets were calculated. The federal government cited cost as the reason for dropping the budgets. This means, of course, that unless other data emerge, these calculations cannot be made for years after 1981.

26. The poverty level is based on the government's determination of the proportion of a poor family's budget that was spent on food in 1955, which was 33%. The poverty level was originally the cost of a minimally nutritious diet, as purchased by expert dieticians and accounting for no food preferences or allergies, multiplied by three and adjusted for the number of adult males (who get the full allowance), adult females (who get a partial allowance), and children (who get a smaller partial allowance). U.S. Bureau of the Census, Current Population Reports, "Money Income and Poverty Status of Families and Persons in the United States: 1981 (Advance Data from the March 1982 Current Population Survey)" (Washington: U.S. Government Printing Office, Series P-60, No. 134, 1982), pp. 1–5. While the poverty level figure purports to include things like taxes and shelter, the gross nature of the calculation makes it impossible for

us to do the kinds of calculations necessary to produce an accurate "can-pay" figure. For example, there is no shelter component that would reflect the nonmortgage housing costs of a homeowning debtor family. Furthermore, the poverty budget ignores the value of food stamps, subsidized housing, and other subsidies available to the poor that would not be available to our debtors because their incomes before debt service would be well over poverty. The true poverty level figure for them would be $2,000–$3,000 higher, which would have been much closer to the Labor Department 1981 low budget. Finally, the poverty level has not been fundamentally recalculated for over 20 years; it has only been readjusted for inflation. Given all these imponderables, we were unable to devise a fair and comparable analysis based on poverty-level figures.

27. These figures are for urban, four-person families, Autumn 1981. U.S. Bureau of the Census, Statistical Abstract of the United States, 1982–83 (103d ed., Washington: U.S. Government Printing Office, 1983), Table 763, p. 465.

28. We already had taken out home mortgage payments for homeowners, whereas the budgets included shelter costs. We adjusted the budgets by removing the allowance for mortgages in the moderate and high budgets, leaving in the allowances for home maintenance, insurance, and so forth, which we had not included in the mortgage calculation. In the low budget we had the problem that the Bureau of Labor Statistics assumed that all low-budget people would be renters. If we eliminated the shelter component, we would leave homeowners with no allowance for their shelter expenses beyond the mortgage payments to cover the insurance, property taxes, and maintenance. We therefore left the shelter component in, assuming it would roughly balance the cost of maintaining a home for the homeowners in the sample.

29. We adjusted the Bureau budgets to eliminate the allowance for federal taxes because we calculated taxes based on income on a debtor-by-debtor basis for greater accuracy.

30. The average pretax income of the 75 Chapter 7 debtors who can pay all and live on the low budget is $27,500, far above the average income in the sample. A debtor family with that income living on the Labor Department low budget would have 56% of its income available for living expenses, with the remainder dedicated to debt repayment.

31. Failure to confirm a plan within a few months after proposal indicates a serious problem. Sometimes this indicates that creditors objected to the plan; perhaps the debtor is not paying enough to meet the good faith test or perhaps a creditor believes the law entitles him to more. The judge may permit the filing to pend to see if the parties can work something out. After a few months, if nothing happens, it usually means the debtor cannot develop a plan to meet all the statutory requirements. Alternatively, a confirmation may typically be delayed if the trustee or the judge notices that the debtor has wholly unrealistic plans for repayments, such as payment plans that exceed the debtor's income. When the debtor comes up with a story about how his income will rise or he is moving in with his family to save on expenses, before the 1984 amendments courts often indulged the debtor several months in "pending" to see if the debtor had a chance. The judges tell us that few debtors made it from pending to confirmed. Since 1984, payments must begin within 30 days of filing, which should leave fewer pending cases.

32. The clear failures are those debtors who converted to Chapter 7 without confirmation (18 debtors, 3.7%), those debtors dismissed without confirmation (6 debtors, 1.2%), those debtors who converted to Chapter 7 after confirmation (30 debtors, 6.2%), and those debtors dismissed after confirmation (101 debtors, 21%). "Troubled"

cases on the flow chart are those debtors who still had no confirmed Chapter 13 plan and those debtors with bad news about their payment histories in their files.

The flow chart shows points of failure in the progress of a Chapter 13 case. For example, almost 20% of the cases still had not confirmed plans at the time of our visits, while 61% of the confirmed cases for which we had data were already in trouble ("bad news"). At the preconfirmation stage, most of the failures converted to Chapter 7 liquidation cases. After confirmation, more than two-thirds of the failures were dismissed from bankruptcy entirely. The debtors thus dismissed may have filed a new Chaper 13 to try again, may have filed a Chapter 7, or may have decided to try to deal with their debts outside bankruptcy.

33. Hearing before the Subcommittee on Courts, Committee on the Judiciary, U.S. Senate, 97th Cong. 1st Sess., October 20, 1981 (testimony of Claude Rice), pp. 36, 52 (hereafter "Hearings"). Mr. Rice's data are for cases filed earlier than his testimony, including some filed recently and already failed and some filed three to five years earlier and paying to completion during 1980–81.

The Rice data also contain a tantalizing piece of information. Mr. Rice reports that the success rate of cases closed from 1960 to 1980 was 41.4%. *Id.*, p. 53. These data are aggregated and thus the trends are impossible to discern, but they suggest that perhaps as the number of Chapter 13 filings have risen, the proportion that succeed has declined. This is an area requiring further study before any conclusions can be reached.

34. "Hearings," p. 52.

35. "Hearings," April 3 and 6, pp. 58, 51.

36. Purdue University Study, pp. 88–91.

37. In re Edwards, 50 Bankr. 933 (Bankr. S.D.N.Y. 1985).

38. In re Walton, 69 Bankr. 150 (E.D. Mo. 1986).

39. American Bankruptcy Institute, Perception and Reality: American Bankruptcy Institute Survey on Selected Provisions of the 1984 Amendments to the Bankruptcy Code (Washington: ABI, 1987), pp. 69–70. The other major element of the 1984 consumer amendments, the "disposable income" test, is also unlikely to have affected the can-pay levels that we found. The inquiry into expenses required by that test was largely going on earlier under the good-faith standard, which in any case continues to be applied in many courts in addition to the new disposable income test.

40. Professor Vukowich discusses congressional attempts to make Chapter 13 more attractive than Chapter 7 through broader discharges, unlimited exemptions, and plans that are easier to pay, although he is critical of the devices used. W. Vukowich, Reforming the Bankruptcy Reform Act of 1978: An Alternative Approach, 71 Georgetown Law Journal 1129, 1135–38 (1983).

41. Chapter 13 also serves various quasi-legitimate functions—for example, delaying foreclosures and permitting payment of attorneys' fees over time—but those functions would be better served by specific statutory provisions providing some relief to debtors in these respects while constraining possible abuses.

13

Laws, Models, and Real People

We think of The Law as a governing instrument: A law is passed and people obey. But often the law has been used to influence more than to govern. Perhaps coincident with the rise of economics as a discipline central to government planning and political debate, Congress and state legislatures have increasingly designed laws to influence conduct by incentives and disincentives, usually economic ones, rather than by direct command or prohibition. No one is required to develop raw land or to refurbish a historic building, but we attempt to influence people to do so by zoning laws, tax codes, utility regulations, and a host of other laws structured around various incentives and disincentives.

Carrots and Sticks

The line between encouragement and coercion in the law is indistinct, but the difference is real. If the law required jailing people who do not pay their debts, only an economist would describe that penalty as a disincentive. The rest of us would say the conduct is prohibited, the prohibition enforceable by imprisonment. On the other hand, if the law forbade extending credit to a bankrupt for ten years after bankruptcy, we would probably think of that as a disincentive to bankruptcy, as well as a prophylactic measure. The movement in debtor–creditor law has been toward adopting incentives to encourage favored behavior while discouraging less desirable activity.

Typically, the incentive approach to social control relies on the premises of economics, including a picture of "economic man" as the rational maximizer who calculates costs and benefits. Economic man acts in socially useful ways as a response to economic incentives and disincentives. Change the incentive structure and the behavior will change. Sometimes these economic carrots and sticks are developed from observed behavior. Too often, they are abstract models created by armchair theorists, along the lines "Suppose we're on a desert island and you have a nickel and I have a banana. . . ." The theorists conclude with a stunning restructuring of law to encourage all those rational maximizers to conform to the desired behavior.

Until recently, the ultimate example of incentive-laden laws was the Tax Code, in which literally thousands of provisions were intended to encourage some activities and discourage others, quite apart from their revenue-raising function. Ironically, while the tax reform statutes have explicitly abandoned attempts to "fine tune" economic conduct, the carrot-and-stick approach to bankruptcy has flourished.

Our data offer an opportunity to evaluate the economic incentive approach to bankruptcy where it is based on simple armchair models. What these data show may also provide insights into the strengths and limitations of using simple, abstract economic models as the basis for other consumer statutes.

Economic Models and Bankruptcy Laws

When the first permanent bankruptcy law was enacted in 1898, congressional debate centered on the plight of oppressed debtors, usually farmers and small businessmen, caught in the latest economic recession.[1] The only bankruptcy proceeding available to individual debtors was Chapter VII liquidation (called Chapter "7," after Congress switched to arabic numerals in the 1978 Bankruptcy Code). Because the law was perceived as too debtor-oriented, it faced quick repeal, until amendments were hammered out in 1903 that better balanced the collection interests of the creditors with the relief needed by debtors.[2] The Great Depression prompted a flurry of new amendments. In 1938 Congress added Chapter XIII, a provision specifically designed to stay creditor actions while a wage earner repaid his debts.[3]

The author of the new Chapter XIII alternative explained its need:

> There are thousands of wage earners all over this land who desire to pay their honest debts but who cannot. For the first time we have the machinery set up in this bill whereby a court order is issued to stay all creditors' actions against a wage earner. A hearing is had, he sits at a table with his creditors and the judge, and they decide how much he and his family need to live on during the pendency of the settlement, and then in the most friendly way they arrive at how much he can pay into the treasury for the benefit of his creditors, to be distributed week by week. That has been done under a voluntary system that has grown up in Birmingham, Ala., . . . where in some 2,000 cases it has worked out and the creditors have gotten dollar for dollar of what was due. In practically all of these cases bankruptcy has been avoided.[4]

The 1938 amendments left Chapter VII largely unchanged and available for all the debtors it had served: people in need of debt discharge. The new Chapter XIII was proposed as a voluntary system designed to attract the debtors who would not use Chapter VII, but who nonetheless needed protection to have time to repay their creditors in an orderly fashion.

In the 1960s and 1970s, while Congress was gearing up to reconsider the bankruptcy laws, a different approach to bankruptcy issues gradually infiltrated the debates. Some bankruptcy experts began to evaluate proposed changes in the bankruptcy laws based on the "incentives" these laws created either for debtors to stay out of bankruptcy or for debtors to choose Chapter XIII repayments rather than Chapter VII discharges.[5] This development was roughly coincident with the discovery of bankruptcy by economists. In a major symposium on bankruptcy reform, William Meckling, then dean of the Graduate School of Management of the University of Rochester, delivered his paper, "Financial Markets, Default, and Bankruptcy: The Role of the State." He delineated the economic view of consumer bankruptcy.

> Changes in bankruptcy law which lower the costs or raise the benefits to debtors of one of these three options [Chapter VII, Chapter XIII or informal settlements] will without question increase both the number of debtors who elect that option and the total number of debtors who elect one of the three in preference to repayment.[6]

Much of the ensuing debate centered on property exemptions—the amount of property debtors could keep in Chapter VII.[7] High exemption levels "encouraged" relatively well-off debtors to choose Chapter VII to discharge all their debt while protecting all their property, while low exemptions "encouraged" relatively worse-off debtors to avoid bankruptcy altogether or to attempt some debt repayment through Chapter XIII. The bald assertion that manipulating the laws would produce predictable effects in debtor behavior both in the decision to take bankruptcy and the choice between chapters was evidently so obvious as to require no empirical substantiation. Not even a note mentioned that an as-yet unproven empirical assumption formed the premise of the economists' call for substantial adjustments in the bankruptcy laws.[8]

Congress was also hit directly with the shifting debate. Testimony before congressional subcommittees considering bankruptcy reform used the incentive terminology of economic models to debate the merits of various proposals. Commentators discussed the possibility that a federally imposed minimum on debtor protections "would substantially increase the number of bankruptcy cases filed by consumer debtors," but that state variations in exemption levels would cause debtors to "shop" for favorable property exemptions.[9]

With increasing frequency the guiding policy question shifted from the adequacy (or excessiveness) of debtor protection to a question of whether the protections created the correct "incentives" for debtors in financial trouble.[10]

The new economic focus was only half-realized by the time the 1978 Bankruptcy Code was adopted and its impact was not often explicitly stated, but the structure of the new Code reflected the shifting approach. The new Chapter 13 gave consumer debtors much greater power to deal with their secured creditors and a much broader discharge, including the remarkable power to discharge liability for fraud and other intentional torts.[11] Chapter 13 was now much more attractive for debtors who wished to preserve nonexempt property or property subject to a security interest, as well as debtors facing a discharge objection if they filed in Chapter 7. Many commentators had difficulty justifying such protections on grounds of fairness to creditors or a reasoned decision about why certain debtors should be protected in certain circumstances. Instead, these provisions came increasingly to be seen as incentives to encourage the use of Chapter 13 by those debtors who could pay and as economic sorting devices to separate the can-pay debtors into Chapter 13 from their can't-pay counterparts who would take Chapter 7.[12]

On one level, the new Chapter 13 provisions were a stunning success. The number and proportion of Chapter 13 cases rose dramatically and became a national phenomenon.[13] Oddly enough, this tremendous increase in pay-out cases was largely ignored by creditors, whose organizations focused instead on the also dramatic rise in the overall number of consumer bankruptcies. The industry began a concerted effort to prove that the new Code had caused the dramatic rise in bankruptcies. The consumer credit industry lobbied Congress, provided witnesses for key congressional hearings, funded the Purdue Study purporting to document consumer bankruptcy abuse, and paid an advertising firm to spread the word on the study.[14] Newspaper editorials poured forth to argue that the generous new laws encouraged people to take bankruptcy even though they could pay their debts. At the same time, academics, many with motives quite different from those of the industry, churned out a flurry of bankruptcy-incentive articles. Attention was directed toward limiting access to Chapter 7, ensuring larger payments in Chapter 13, and sharply reducing the attractiveness of Chapter 7 by reducing the federal exemption levels.

The credit industry was also active in the state legislatures, where it argued that the availability of the relatively generous federal exemptions had made bankruptcy too easy for shiftless consumers. It urged the states to "opt out" by exercising the option granted by the Bankruptcy Code to bar use of the federal exemptions by the citizens of an opt-out state. Within four years, 34 states opted out. The rationale for opt-out was clear:

> Perhaps more important, the argument that larger federal bankruptcy exemptions will induce the filing of voluntary bankruptcy petitions has probably influenced the opt-out decisions of the thirty-two states which have thus far opted-out.[15]

Congress soon fell into line. Accepting the argument that generous exemptions in the 1978 Code were "causing" too many Chapter 7 bankruptcies, in 1984 Congress restricted the debtors' federal exemptions still available in the 14 states that had not opted out. It made other changes responsive to the credit industry's concerns, including a new restriction on access to Chapter 7 and a more demanding payout requirement for Chapter 13.[16]

The shift in the bankruptcy debate was more than semantic. Where concerns once had focused on what a family needed to get back on its feet, or on whether high exemptions offended the community sense of justice, the central issues now became finding the "right" exemption level to promote low bankruptcy filing rates and, for those in bankruptcy, encouraging debtors to choose Chapter 13 over Chapter 7.

By the early 1980s the economic model had reached such a level of acceptance that its efficacy was simply assumed. In 1983, for example, a prominent bankruptcy law professor explained: "To overcome the major criticisms of the new Bankruptcy Act, one simple and relatively minor change is needed. The exemption policy should be modified by reducing bankruptcy exemptions."[17] The author explained that reducing exemptions would cause the number of bankruptcy filings to decline by making bankruptcy more costly, and debtors with nonexempt assets "would have a stronger incentive to file in Chapter 13," thus causing the proportion of debtors in bankruptcy to file Chapter 13 to rise.[18]

Although dozens of different proposals about exemptions and other statutory adjustments littered the debates, the premises of the model were by now so widely accepted as to require no documentation. Some protested vigorously, but Dean Meckling's assertion that the economic model of bankruptcy would "without question" produce the desired results carried the day. In not much more than a handful of years it had become so clear that debtors in financial trouble would respond in predictable ways to statutory incentives that the only interesting question was exactly how to fine-tune those incentives.

Testing the Model

With the data from the Consumer Bankruptcy Project we examine the effectiveness of the economic incentive approach that has been popular with policymakers and academic commentators alike. Although Dean Meckling described the workings of incentives in formal economic terms, the model is so simplistic that it may seem strange to describe it as a model at all. Yet it represents a specific set of predictions about how debtors will behave both in filing for bankruptcy and in selecting a chapter in which to file. These predictions have powerfully influenced both the course of the bankruptcy policy debates and subsequent changes in the bankruptcy laws. In that sense, it has been widely accepted as a model and therein is found its political power.

The premises of the model, as they are found in the debates and in academic analyses of bankruptcy, are these: (1) that bankruptcy is a very attractive method of improving one's economic position, so attractive that debtors who are able to pay their debts must be prevented from using it by powerful disincentives; (2) that disincentives to use bankruptcy and incentives to choose Chapter 13 payouts will strongly influence debtors to pay their debts outside of bankruptcy or in Chapter 13; and (3) that property exemptions are the key incentive/disincentive in influencing debtor behavior, so that establishing just the right level of exemptions will cause can-pay debtors to avoid bankruptcy or to pay in Chapter 13. Underlying all three premises is the central proposition of economics as applied to bankruptcy: that debtors are rational maximizers whose behavior can be predicted and controlled (or strongly influenced) by economic incentives.

We test the premises of the simple economic model of bankruptcy in three ways. First, we examine the sorting effect of the elaborate statutory incentives built into Chapter 13 in the 1978 Code. When the Code was enacted, the bankruptcy debates were in transition, with the new economic incentive approach to Chapter 13 vying with the more traditional focus on helping the willing debtors to pay. Descriptions of the new Chapter 13 were couched in terms of incentives, but those incentives were not often linked explicitly to the notion of encouraging debtors to pay according to a carrot-and-stick model. Nonetheless, the new Chapter 13 was loaded with incentives that should have attracted can-pay debtors. These incentives included much broader power to keep property subject to liens, notably by provisions permitting the debtor to keep the property by paying only its value, not its full cost, and other provisions that permitted homeowners to keep their homes while paying arrearages on their mortgages over three years. They also included the new, very broad discharge. If the general premises of the model are correct, these incentives should have guided more can-pay debtors into Chapter 13 while leaving can't-pay debtors in Chapter 7. We begin by testing that hypothesis against our data. We compare debtors in the two chapters according to their ability to pay as measured by the ratio between their debts and their incomes.

Second, we test the more specific prediction of the model, the idea that property exemptions will directly influence can-pay debtors to avoid bankruptcy or to choose Chapter 13. We test each prediction, to see if exemption levels influence the decision to file bankruptcy and then to see if they influence choice of chapter among those who ultimately file. If the predictions of the model are correct, we should find that high exemptions have tempted many debtors into bankruptcy who have greater capacities to pay, while low exemptions should operate as a gate-keeper that will keep from bankruptcy all but those least able to pay. Similarly, the data should show that high exemptions encourage debtors to take the easy way out in Chapter 7, even if they are relatively able to pay, while low exemptions should force all but the most impoverished into Chapter 13.

Finally, we test all the economic variables together to see how much predictive power they have in explaining debtors' choice of chapter in bankruptcy. We do that by including all the principal economic variables in a multiple regression equation to predict choice of chapter. In this way we explore the possibility that some economic model, even if not the one proposed, might be powerful in explaining debtor behavior and thus permitting manipulation of that behavior by economic incentives. If the economic variables are not very powerful in explaining the debtors' choices, then the basic premises of the current economic analyses of bankruptcy are called into serious question.

We also explore factors absent from the economic model, including social-demographic variables and the effects of local legal cultures, to determine their effect on debtor decision making. The data indicate that the economic model has surprisingly little predictive power, while social-demographic factors have far greater explanatory power. When we combine all three types of variables, we are nonetheless unable to explain even half the variance. These data suggest to us that the relatively simplistic economic models used in bankruptcy policymaking do not work, a conclusion that we believe has relevance in other areas where a simple new model promises to revolutionize policymaking.

Correlations with Choice of Chapter

The first step in examining the effect of economic incentives is to correlate the raw economic indicators of debtors' financial circumstances with the debtors' choice of chapter. The fundamental premise of the economic incentive approach is that bankruptcy is an economic exercise and debtors are economic creatures. Because Chapter 7 and Chapter 13 provide different economic incentives depending on a debtor's financial circumstances, the model predicts that debtors choosing Chapter 7 should differ measurably from those choosing Chapter 13.

The analysis begins with a correlation matrix whose entries are coefficients, one for each pair of variables.[19] A correlation coefficient shows if two variables are related and whether the direction of the relationship is positive or negative. A homey example that makes direction easy to understand is that, among newborns, longer babies tend to be heavier babies and shorter babies tend to be lighter babies; thus weight and length of newborns are positively correlated. On the other hand, a negative correlation is illustrated by a fixed supply of formula in the pantry and an infant's weight. As the supply of formula goes down, the weight goes up, so the two are negatively correlated. In our case, a positive correlation between a variable and chapter choice indicates that debtors with more of the variable (e.g., income) are more likely to be in Chapter 13. A negative correlation (say, with unsecured debt) indicates that the more the debtor has of that variable, the less likely the debtor will be in Chapter 13. The reverse also holds. A negative correlation with Chapter 13 necessarily means a positive correlation with Chapter 7.[20]

In addition to determining direction, a correlation coefficient also shows the strength of the relationship. A very high correlation, one with an absolute value of 0.8 or larger, would suggest that the two things not only are correlated, but they might measure the same thing. For example, shoe size and foot size would correlate highly because they measure the same thing. At the other end of the spectrum are statistically significant correlations that are so weak they have little practical significance. With a sample as large as ours, statistical significance is so easily found that we use ± 0.2 as a rough benchmark for minimal substantive importance.

We explore five economic variables for each debtor: assets, exemptions, family income, unsecured debt, and secured debt. The debt/income ratio is not included directly, but its components—unsecured debt, secured debt, and family income—are. The correlation coefficients are reported in Table 13.1.

The simple economic model of bankruptcy predicts that assets and family income would be positively correlated with choice of Chapter 13. Those who have more property to protect and those who have more income with which to pay should file Chapter 13, saving their assets and paying over time. The correlation coefficient shows this to be the case, although the relationship is weak. The correlation between assets and Chapter 13 is a minimally important 0.25; between income and Chapter 13 it is a substantively unimportant 0.12. The anticipated correlation is evident, but it fails to demonstrate much power.

An economic approach might also assume that unsecured debt would be negatively associated with Chapter 13, indicating that debtors with higher debts are more likely to find themselves in Chapter 7 discharging that debt than in Chapter 13 trying to repay it. This prediction is true, although the absolute value of the correlation ($r = -0.12$) is so low that it also has little substantive value.

Plausible predictions could be made that secured debt would be positively or negatively correlated with Chapter 13. Debtors might choose Chapter 13 to give them the opportunity to pay their secured debt over time while keeping their property. On the other hand, debtors too tied up with secured debt might have nothing left to make plan payments and might simply reaffirm their secured debt in Chapter 7. As it turns out, the correlation is positive (more secured debt means more likely to select Chapter 13), but the relationship again is so weak ($r = 0.08$) that it tells little.

Finally, the debtors' exemption claims are an important economic variable that should bear a relation to the debtors' choice of chapter. The greater the amount of property that can be exempted, the more attractive Chapter 7 should be. A more generous exemption should be a disincentive to repayment. To the contrary, our data show a positive correlation between exemption claims and choice of Chapter 13 ($r = 0.12$), but, once again, the correlation is too weak to have any substantive impact. We explore that relationship more fully just ahead.

TABLE 13.1. Pearson Correlation Coefficients of Choice of Chapter with Variables in the Analysis

Economic Variables		Social–Demographic Variables		Local Legal Variables	
Family income[a]	0.12	Married	0.07	Metro district	0.13
Assets	0.25	Intrastate move	−0.49	Texas practice (1 = Texas)	0.10
Exemptions	0.12	Interstate move	−0.21	Attorney specialist	0.27
Unsecured debt	−0.12	Self-employed	0.03		
		Homeowner	0.24		
Secured debt	0.08	Prestige	0.06		
N	1,080				

[a]All sources reported. Debtors filing Form 8 in Chapter 7 (for debtors engaged in business) were not required to indicate the amount of income or profit from their business.

Source: Consumer Bankruptcy Project.

The correlation matrix shows some correlations in the direction predicted by the economic model and others in conflict with it. The key finding, however, is that the correlations are too weak to provide substantial support to the economic model.

Sorting by Ability to Pay—The Chapter 13 Incentives

The simple economic model promises a way to sort debtors who can pay from those who cannot, encouraging the can-pays to select Chapter 13 repayment while the can't-pays take a speedy discharge in Chapter 7. In Chapter Four we used debt/income ratios as a rough measure of whether debtors are likely to be able to repay their debts. The comparison of Chapter 7 with Chapter 13 petitioners by ability to repay is reported in Table 13.2.

The critical finding is at the bottom of Table 13.2, where the tests of significance show no statistical difference between the two groups. A glance at the numbers makes this finding somewhat counterintuitive. The mean debt/income ratio for a Chapter 7 debtor is 3.56, indicating that these debtors owe debts equivalent to over three and a half year's income, while the mean debt of the Chapter 13 debtor is only 2.75, less than three years' income. But a

TABLE 13.2. Distribution of Total Debt/Income Ratio, by Chapter[a]

Distribution	Total Debt/Income Ratio
Chapter 7	
Mean	3.56
s.d.	11.89
25th percentile	0.71
Median	1.42
75th percentile	2.58
N	686
Zero income	29
Missing	202
Chapter 13	
Mean	2.75
s.d.	8.32
25th percentile	0.67
Median	1.40
75th percentile	2.67
N	555
Zero income	18
Missing	12
Statistical Test	
t-value	1.40[b]

[a]Cases with extreme values on assets, total debt, or income excluded.

[b]Not significant at $p \leq 0.05$.

Source: Consumer Bankruptcy Project.

closer examination shows why the statistical tests show the two groups are indistinguishable. The first, second, and third quartiles of debt for the two groups are separated by less than a tenth of a percentage point. The means are distorted, once again, by a few debtors with debt/income ratios of truly astronomical proportions. The great majority of debtors, according to the statistical analysis, have about the same debt/income ratio whether they are in Chapter 7 or Chapter 13.

In earlier chapters, we recalculated debt/income ratios excluding home mortgage debt to get another picture of the debtors' ability to repay. As before, we leave the homeowners in the sample but exclude their home mortgage debts. The results of this reanalysis are reported in Table 13.3. The critical number at the bottom this time shows a statistically significant difference. The nonmortgage debt/income ratios of Chapter 7 debtors are significantly higher than the nonmortgage debt/income ratios of Chapter 13 debtors.

The difference is statistically significant, but it is not necessarily substantively significant in demonstrating the efficacy of the economic model. One problem is that nonmortgage debt/income ratios leave homeowners in the sample while omitting their most important debt—the home mortgage. Be-

TABLE 13.3. Distribution of Total Nonmortgage Debt/Income Ratio, by Chapter[a]

Distribution	Total Nonmortgage Debt/Income Ratio
Chapter 7	
Mean	2.33
s.d.	7.55
25th percentile	0.58
Median	0.88
75th percentile	1.70
N	685
Zero income	29
Missing	203
Chapter 13	
Mean	1.38
s.d.	6.86
25th percentile	0.35
Median	0.61
75th percentile	1.00
N	553
Zero income	18
Missing	14
Statistical Test	
t-value	2.31*

[a]Cases with extreme values on assets, total debt, or income excluded.

$*p \leq 0.05$.

Source: Consumer Bankruptcy Project.

cause there is a larger portion of homeowners in Chapter 13, exclusion of their biggest obligation may make them look more able to pay than they really are.

More importantly, the difference between the debtor groups is statistically significant, but it is still small. Even with the artificial exclusion of mortgages, most Chapter 7 and Chapter 13 debtors appear unable to pay. In Table 13.3 the first quartile of the Chapter 7 debtors about matches the median of the Chapter 13 debtors, a substantial overlap in ability to pay. Furthermore, the median ability to pay in Chapter 13 is only modestly higher than the median in Chapter 7. The statistical difference seems to come from a number of the most swamped Chapter 7 cases, which pull up the mean debt/income ratio, even though the bulk of each group of debtors looks remarkably alike.

These findings are not inconsistent with the Purdue Study conclusion. The 1982 study financed by the credit industry argued that many Chapter 7 debtors were able to pay. If that were true, the presence of can-pay debtors in Chapter 7 would tend to make the distribution of debt/income ratios similar between chapters, the result we have found. On the other hand, our data suggest the complementary conclusion: Many people in Chapter 13 cannot succeed in paying. Whether can-pay debtors in Chapter 7 or can't-pay debtors in Chapter 13 are the cause, it seems clear that the economic incentives built into the 1978 Code fail to sort debtors by their capacity to repay.

The overall picture of debtors in the two chapters is one of economic randomness. Among debtors who look very much alike, some are attempting three- to five-year payouts while others in the same financial circumstances take their discharge in bankruptcy within a few weeks of filing. The absence of a significant difference between the groups suggests that congressional economic incentives have not succeeded in dividing debtors by ability to pay.

Using Exemptions to Encourage Repayment

Many of the state "opt-out" decisions had been made by 1981, the year in which our sample cases were filed. Illinois had opted out, leaving its citizens with relatively meager state exemptions to protect assets in bankruptcy. Pennsylvania and Texas had not opted out. Pennsylvanians, facing extremely limited state exemptions, almost always chose the federal exemptions. Texans often found their state exemptions more generous that the federal ones. As a result, these three states in 1981 presented a natural experiment, a laboratory in which to study the effects of exemption levels on the choices made by debtors.

Illinois had low exemptions, Texas had high, and Pennsylvania was in the middle, so the effects predicted by the exemption–incentive model should have been directly reflected in the patterns of bankruptcy filings in those three states. According to the economic model, when exemptions are low, only the most desperate debtors will file bankruptcy, but when exemption levels are high, debtors who could repay fairly easily will opt for bankruptcy rather than the discipline of repayment. A Texas debtor who could pay should more readily say "Heck, I can keep everything in a Chapter 7 bankruptcy, why should I go on short rations to pay?" An Illinois debtor equally able to pay should be convinced to avoid bankruptcy because the alternative is the loss of many assets.

If the economic model were correct, the exemption differences should produce a different composition of debtors in each state, with Texas debtors in the best shape, Illinois debtors in the worst shape, and Pennsylvania debtors somewhere between. To test this model, we return to the nearest proxy for relative ability to repay—the debt/income ratio. The results of this test are reported in Table 13.4. Once again, the key finding is at the bottom. There is no statistically significant difference among the debt/income ratios for debtors in Texas, Pennsylvania, and Illinois. The debt/income ratios between debtors in one of the highest exemption states and one of the lowest exemption states are effectively the same.

This finding was somewhat surprising because, as we have noted, a data base the size we are using makes statistically significant differences, if they exist, relatively easy to detect—even when they are small enough to indicate little substantive difference. Here the debtors showed no significant difference in their relative ability to repay whether they were in high-, low-, or middle-exemption states.

We considered the possibility that home ownership and large home mortgages might be masking other differences among debtors in their relative ability to repay. We reanalyzed the debt/income ratios by state, this time omitting all home mortgages, as we did in earlier analyses. The results were the same. No significant difference in the nonmortgage debt/income ratios emerged

TABLE 13.4. Distribution of Total Debt/Income Ratio, by State[a]

	State		
Distribution	Texas	Illinois	Pennsylvania
Mean	3.05	3.49	3.10
s.d.	11.37	12.55	5.24
25th percentile	0.67	0.67	0.82
Median	1.28	1.36	1.64
75th percentile	2.42	2.50	2.84
N	498	391	352
Zero income	23	10	14
Missing	112	44	58
Statistical Tests			
F ratio	0.228[b]		
Significant differences in state means	None		

[a]Cases with extreme values on assets, total debt, or income excluded.

[b]Scheffe ranges test used for multiple comparison of means. *F* ratio of 0.288 is not significant at $p \leq 0.05$. This test was repeated with six other ranges tests with no change in results.

Source: Consumer Bankruptcy Project.

among debtors in the three states, despite greatly differing levels of assets that could be kept in each.

These data dispute the central premise that debtors will respond to economic incentives according to a simple economic model. The data also suggest that the effects promised when the legislatures and Congress amended exemption laws have not come to pass.

Chapter Choice and Exemption Levels Working Together

The influence of the economic incentive approach on bankruptcy policymaking was not limited to the claim that exemptions would influence some debtors not to file bankruptcy. The model also promised that exemptions would influence whether debtors in bankruptcy attempted Chapter 13 repayment or simply shrugged off their debts in Chapter 7.

According to the economic model, debtors in a high-exemption state would rarely choose Chapter 13 because they did not need it to protect all their property. Thus the debtors in Chapter 7 in a high-exemption state such as Texas should cover a broad economic range, from those debtors in the most trouble to those relatively more able to repay. On the other hand, the debtors declaring bankruptcy in a low-exemption state such as Illinois should choose Chapter 7 only if they had no possible hope of repayment because the available exemptions protected so little. The Illinois Chapter 7 debtors should be a narrower band of debtors in desperate financial condition, whereas the Chapter 13 debtors should cover a wider range as more debtors struggle to avoid the harsh consequences of Chapter 7 and its low exemptions. Once again, Pennsylvania debtors should be somewhere between.

To test this hypothesis, we compared the debt/income ratios for debtors in Chapter 7 and Chapter 13 in Texas with the same data for debtors in Illinois and Pennsylvania.[21] Once again, exemptions did not have the predicted impact on debtor behavior. We found no significant difference in the comparison of debt/income ratios between Chapter 7 and Chapter 13 debtors among the states. Chapter 7 debtors in Texas and Chapter 7 debtors in Illinois have about the same repayment prospects even though Texas debtors can keep more than ten times as much property as Illinois debtors.[22]

These direct tests of the economic model demonstrate that the model—the central intellectual construct for exemption laws in 33 states and in the federal Bankruptcy Code—does not accurately predict debtor behavior.

Why Does the Economic Model Fail?

It is inconceivable that economic factors do not influence debtor behavior. After all, bankruptcy is about money (or lack of it), so economic incentives must have something to do with debtor decisions to enter bankruptcy.

In every chapter of this book we have found debtors in bankruptcy to be financially distinct from the general population. Bankrupt debtors earn a third less than the general population, and a quarter of the debtors are below the poverty level. Bankrupt debtors' assets are about one-third the size of the assets of most American families. Their unsecured debts are four times larger than most Americans' debt burdens. More than 90% of the bankrupt debtors have consumer debt/income ratios dramatically greater than 95% of the general population. The typical bankrupt debtor owes debts greater than three years' income. These numbers show a clear economic sorting so obvious it is easy to overlook: People in financial trouble are the people entering bankruptcy. Those not in bankruptcy are, on average, much better off financially. At the grossest level, economic sorting works impressively; it simply does not work according to a simplistic economic model.

The proponents of the economic model used in debating bankruptcy policy assumed this basic sorting would *not* work, that rich and poor alike would use bankruptcy, making more powerful economic restrictions necessary. According to a purely economic view, bankruptcy without severe limitations is so attractive that debtors should "enrich" themselves by discharging their debts even if they could pay. Carrots and sticks were essential to correct this perceived problem, and the property exemptions were a gatekeeper provision to keep out the rich and let in the poor. In fact, most debtors avoid bankruptcy until they reach an economic crisis, suggesting that bankruptcy seems more attractive to economists than to debtors.

The data show that property exemptions do not have the desired effect, but they also show that those in economic calamity make very similar decisions regardless of exemptions. The debtors file when they are in about the same relative circumstances, regardless of the different degree of legal restrictions facing them in Texas or Illinois. It appears that their financial travail swamps the effects of incentives.

Debtor Decision Making

Debtors may fail to follow the economic model of the bankruptcy debates because the circumstances of their decisions inhibit the economic rationality predicated by the model. Here we turn from the quantitative data to our extensive interviews with judges, trustees, and lawyers to enrich our understanding of the circumstances attendant when debtors make the most critical bankruptcy decisions.

The economic model presumes that a decision to file bankruptcy is made by a rational maximizer coolly calculating the gain from bankruptcy against the loss of nonexempt assets based on an informed understanding of the bankruptcy laws. Our own experiences and the reports of those intimately involved in the bankruptcy process tell us that the reality is very different.

It is difficult to envision the debtors in our sample—the Williamses in Chapter Seven, who struggled so hard to save their home, or Ms. Dover from

Chapter Three, who supported six children on her part-time salary and who had just lost her Chevy Blazer to the repo man—sitting at the kitchen table valuing assets and calculating state exemptions, like an investor considering a takeover bid. If someone had told them they were deciding whether to "enrich" themselves in bankruptcy, they probably would have smiled for the first time in weeks.

Debtors on the verge of a bankruptcy filing are under enormous pressure from their creditors. They are often filled with anxiety and self-loathing. There may be terrific tension in their homes, and they know very little about bankruptcy, beyond what a friend told them and the lawyer's ad they saw in the TV section of the Sunday paper. Most of those intimately associated with the bankruptcy process—the judges and the lawyers—explain that the debtors' emotions and their lack of information do not leave them in a position to "calculate" much of anything, except that the next paycheck will not stretch around even the most pressing payment demands.

Debtors decide between Chapter 7 and Chapter 13 in a lawyer's office based largely on that lawyer's advice. We surmise that they are unlikely to receive advice not to file for bankruptcy.[23] Bankruptcy is an efficient way to deal with creditors, one that often takes less lawyer time than telephone negotiations—an off-the-rack solution that is easier than a custom-made response to each problem. Even if the debtors are motivated to file in Chapter 13 specifically to avoid loss of assets, their desire to save assets may blind them to the fact that they have little capacity to make the necessary payments. The filing of a doomed Chapter 13 in some irrationally optimistic hope that "everything will come out all right" may be more typical than a thoughtful cost/benefit calculation.

We have no doubt that there are some debtors camped out on the cost curve, waiting to abuse the bankruptcy system the moment it is profitable to do so. We talked about some of them in the last two chapters. But they are few and far between in our sample, far too few to have any great impact on the bankruptcy system—much less the consumer credit system as a whole.

Social–Demographic Variables

The economic model is global in that it purports to explain choice of chapter anywhere, any time, by looking only at economic variables. Its narrow focus excludes other characteristics that may impinge on debtor decision making, and this may contribute to its weak explanatory power. Social and demographic factors may have a more powerful influence on debtors' decisions to file Chapter 7 or Chapter 13 than any statutory incentives thus far designed. Our data base gave us only a limited number of demographic and social variables to examine, and not necessarily the most important ones. The five social–demographic variables we explored were marital status, migration history, home ownership, business ownership, and job prestige.

MARITAL STATUS AND MIGRATION HISTORY

As our first test of the hypothesis that social and demographic variables might have a significant impact on debtor choices, we examine bankrupt debtors' marital status as indicated by joint filing or by references in the file to a spouse.[24] About 64% of our sample were married at the time of filing.

Once again, a correlation coefficient gives an initial idea of the relationship between demographic variables and whether the debtor is in Chapter 13 or Chapter 7. We expected marital status to be positively correlated with Chapter 13 choice, simply because a married couple may feel that they are better able to complete a plan than a single adult might. As expected, the correlation was positive but too weak to support any inference ($r = 0.07$).[25] Among joint filing couples, we note that those in Chapter 13 are significantly more likely than those in Chapter 7 to have a working spouse.

We also examine each debtor's migration history. The bankruptcy files require debtors to report all previous addresses within the past six years, primarily so that creditors can be certain they have the right Bea Smith or David Anderson in mind.[26] The last move of about one-third of the sample had been an intrastate move, and the last move of one-tenth had been an interstate move. The mean number of moves was 2.2.

A debtor's migration history may be a clue to the debtor's ability to cope with debt. Most moves in the United States are believed to be economically motivated: some are moves to search for work and some are job-related transfers.[27] Others may be moves to stay one step ahead of the creditors. Many routine credit applications inquire about the applicant's residential history. Despite the fact that this a country with very high geographic mobility, residential stability is often seen as a correlate of financial stability.

Migration is an old concern of creditors; historically, there was a close association between moving and escaping debt. Indeed, moving to escape one's debts was one frequently cited motive for the passage of the 1898 Bankruptcy Act. States' laws also reflect their views of migration history. Texas, for example, has a populist tradition with strong debtor-protection laws that have been traced to settlement by debtors moving from other states to escape their creditors. In parts of the South, a sheriff trying to enforce a debt judgment often merely scribbled the initials "G.T.T." on the file to indicate that the debtor had Gone To Texas, implying that further collection efforts were probably useless. Today, instant communication and national links between credit bureaus give creditors more information about debtors who move, but staying put and paying are still linked in many creditors' minds.

We examined the data to see if the perceived link between staying put and paying (this time in Chapter 13) or moving and escaping payment (through Chapter 7) made sense in the bankruptcy context. We examined whether there had been an interstate move reported during the previous six years and whether a move had been made within the state where the debtor filed. We expected both interstate and intrastate migration variables to be negatively correlated with the choice of Chapter 13, and this was the case. Intrastate migration shows a strong negative correlation with choosing Chapter 13 ($r = -0.49$); interstate migration shows a weaker but still significant negative correlation ($r = -0.21$). In other words, moving a lot is characteristic of Chapter 7 debtors.

STABILITY AND STATUS VARIABLES

In addition to the demographic variables about marital status and migration, we also examine three other social variables that give some indication of the debtor's social position in the community: home ownership, ownership of a business, and job prestige. Just as frequent moves signal instability, home ownership indicates stability. The homeowner is believed to have a "stake" in the local community. Similarly, the self-employed person is believed to have a "stake" in the local business community and, all other things being equal, to be someone who will try to stay and work things out. Occupational prestige also gives some indication of a person's social standing. There have been suggestions in the scholarly literature, and certainly in the lawyers' advertisements that we have examined, that higher status persons are more likely to see Chapter 13 as an "honorable" route in bankruptcy. If debtors who are more stable, who have homes and businesses and higher status jobs, are more likely to attempt repayment even when they are in financial trouble, we would expect to see these attitudes mirrored by debtor choices in bankruptcy. This would create a positive correlation between each of these variables and Chapter 13.

All three variables indicating a debtor's stability within a community are positively related to Chapter 13, but none of them is correlated very strongly. Self-employment is only very weakly related ($r = 0.03$). Occupational prestige is higher in Chapter 13 (38.5 points) compared with Chapter 7 (36.9 points, $p = 0.01$), but the correlation is virtually imperceptible ($r = 0.06$).[28] Home ownership shows a stronger correlation with choice of Chapter 13 ($r = 0.24$). Overall, the correlations show a weak but generally predictable relationship between social and demographic factors and whether a debtor files for Chapter 7 or Chapter 13.

Another Possible Influence: Local Legal Cultures

In addition to the influence of economic and social–demographic factors, we believe that debtors' bankruptcy decisions may be importantly influenced by the local legal culture they encounter when they seek legal help. We believe that the "uniform" system of bankruptcy laws is in fact very different in different courts, so that debtors in one area and those in another encounter distinct legal systems.

The clue that there were significant influences at the local level came initially from the reports published by the Administrative Office of the Courts indicating how many debtors file bankruptcy and what proportion of those debtors file in Chapter 13. Despite the difficulties with these data,[29] it is clear that there are huge differences in the proportions of Chapter 7's and Chapter

13's filed in different districts. From the very start of our study, we suspected that these district variations must contain an important element of the explanation for debtors' choice of chapters.

The large district-to-district variations in the relative proportions of Chapter 7 and Chapter 13 filings found all over the country were evident in the states we studied. Among the ten districts we sampled, the rate of Chapter 13 filings varied from a high of 49.6% in the Western District of Texas to a low of 2.8% in the Middle District of Pennsylvania.[30] In other words, a debtor in financial trouble in San Antonio was 17 times more likely to file Chapter 13 than was a debtor in Harrisburg.

Furthermore, the districts varied greatly within each of our three states, as they do in many others throughout the nation. The differences in Chapter 13 filing rates within each state were enormous, in Texas from 16.7% (Eastern District–Tyler) to 49.4% (Western District–San Antonio), in Illinois from 10.3% (Central District–Springfield) to 39.1% (Northern District–Chicago), and in Pennsylvania from 2.8% (Middle District–Harrisburg) to 41.3% (Eastern District–Philadelphia).

If statutory incentives influenced the Chapter 7 versus Chapter 13 decision, there should have been little variation within states; the variation should have been between states. The wide variation in Chapter 13 filing rates within a state suggests two competing hypotheses: (1) the debtors in each district within a state differ in critical ways that cause them to prefer Chapter 13 or Chapter 7 or (2) the actual bankruptcy process in each district must differ in ways that make Chapter 7 or Chapter 13 relatively more attractive.

The first possibility has a commonsense appeal, and, if true, would help resuscitate the economic model. If, for example, debtors in the Southern District of Illinois are consistently poorer than debtors in the Northern District of Illinois, differences by district would be a function of differences among debtors. Without additional quantitative information about the debtors, it has been impossible to tell whether the district variation was a function of characteristics special to the debtors or were a function of the local legal systems themselves.

The Bankruptcy Study data indicate that there are no important economic differences among the debtors in these districts that would explain the dramatically different district filing rates. No substantial variations in debts or debt/income ratios separate the debtors in high-filing, middle-filing, or low-filing districts. Nor are there consistent variations in social–demographic characteristics that separate the debtors of one district from the debtors of another.[31]

If, as the data indicate, the debtors do not differ by district, then we are left with the alternative hypothesis: The debtors are the same, but the local legal cultures they encounter affect their choices of Chapter 7 and Chapter 13. The data suggest that something in the locale explains a great deal of the difference among Chapter 13 filing rates from east Texas to west Texas, upstate Illinois to downstate Illinois, Harrisburg to Pittsburgh.

To believe that there are distinctive local legal cultures is one thing; to quantify them for use in a statistical analysis is quite another. Although many variations in local culture may be important, the obvious place to look for local variations in a legal proceeding is at the courthouse.[32] The attitudes of different judges toward Chapter 13 was one variable we could not reliably quantify because of variations in the procedures used to assign cases to judges. We would also have liked to examine the attorneys, questioning both their views about Chapter 13 and the routines they used in interviewing clients and advising them about bankruptcy options, but restrictions imposed by limited time and money curtailed this inquiry. Ultimately, we were left with our less systematic interviews and our own observations of the local systems.

During the course of the study, we observed very different local operations and we learned about twists in local practices that made Chapter 13's more onerous or more attractive than they were elsewhere. Sometimes the variations were overt, such as court rules that effectively permitted the debtors to pay their attorneys over time in a Chapter 13, whereas Chapter 7 debtors would need the entire fee up front. In other districts, there were no obvious procedures that favored Chapter 13 or Chapter 7, but the attitudes of the lawyers and judges in the community were clearly inclined to one chapter or the other. In one district, attorneys who were not bringing in a share of the Chapter 13's were not "team players" and were not accorded high respect.

Local variations were sometimes grounded on differences in the communities involved. For example, based on some semiconscious assumption that God-fearing farmers would try to pay, we had expected to find more Chapter 13's in rural districts—but the numbers would not bear us out. When we asked one rural bankruptcy lawyer about the small number of Chapter 13's in his district, he replied, "If the debtor can pay, he doesn't need bankruptcy, because we can work it out with the creditors and avoid the pain and credit damage of bankruptcy; if he can't pay, he needs to be in Chapter 7 and start all over again." In effect, the lawyer was saying that the creditor community in the rural area in question would work with debtors informally if they could pay; the only people who needed bankruptcy were those who needed Chapter 7.

The judges are an obvious source of important district variations. During our interviews, we met some judges who are real trend-setters in their districts—dynamic, forceful people who see their roles as administering a just and workable bankruptcy system. When they genuinely believe, for example, that Chapter 13 balances the best interests of both debtor and creditor, they are not inclined to hide that view behind some notion of judicial neutrality. Instead, they swing into action, lecturing attorneys about how to handle Chapter 13's more efficiently, creating streamlined administrative procedures, and, in some cases, making life in court uncomfortable for attorneys who bring in Chapter 7's day after day without "encouraging" some of their clients to attempt a Chapter 13.

Judges have many informal devices available to make known the strength of their views. By encouraging the staff, the smooth processing of one kind of file can be assured. If all cases of one kind are scheduled to be heard before another, attorneys can count on less delay if they file in the preferred chapter. One judge bluntly explained how he had such a high proportion of Chapter 13's in his district:

> Well, I watch the lawyers that come in. One comes in with a Chapter 7, that's OK. Even two or three. But it gets to be about four or so, and I ask counsel, nicely now, "Did you inform your client about the Chapter 13 alternative?" Sometimes I'll spend a minute or two talking about how Chapter 13 might have worked out pretty well. Lawyer doesn't look too great in front of his client like that. Then, if he comes back another time or two still in Chapter 7, I ask the lawyer to swear in the client. Then I start asking the client questions. "Your lawyer explain the Chapter 13 alternative? . . ." I usually conclude there hasn't been full explanation, so the client isn't making an informed decision. I recommend that the attorney go back, talk with the client and come back again later. All the while, the clock is running. It doesn't take too long before the attorney will at least try some Chapter 13's.

Judges who are unwilling to affect debtors' decisions directly can nonetheless influence attorneys, who, in turn, influence clients. Once the word is out that a judge prefers one chapter over another, any bankruptcy attorney knows that cooperating with the judge's preference is likely to be a good practice over the long run. After all, this is the same judge who will approve the attorney's fees, agree to drive into court from home on the weekend to hear an emergency matter, and grant an extension just because the attorney is having scheduling problems. Whether the attorney or the judge is aware of it, the chances that an attorney could escape the influence of a judge with strong views about Chapter 7 or Chapter 13 are exceedingly slim.

Even judges who maintain stalwart neutrality in the face of the competing views about the advisability of Chapter 7 and Chapter 13 may have significant influences on the local legal system. We interviewed one judge who repeatedly asserted he was completely indifferent to whether debtors filed Chapter 7 or Chapter 13. He explained that Chapter 13 could work, and he proudly pointed to a high success rate among the Chapter 13's in his district. The judge explained that it took a very special debtor to make a Chapter 13 work, and he approved a Chapter 13 plan only after scheduling time to swear in the debtor, and to go over the elements of the proposed plan line by line. He indicated that he was willing to spend "about an hour on each Chapter 13, just to make sure they were right." Considering that the judge's Chapter 7's were completed in a matter of minutes, the attorneys wouldn't have to work very hard to figure out that in fixed-fee cases (as virtually all consumer bankruptcy cases are), it would be much more cost-effective to encourage most clients to enter Chapter 7. Not surprisingly, this district with a scrupulously neutral judge had one of the lowest Chapter 13 rates in the country.

In other districts, judicial attitudes may be less important. Some judges had no discernibly strong feelings about Chapter 13 or any practices we observed that would obviously influence attorney advice. Moreover, in districts with several judges and random assignment of cases, the importance of the views of any one judge would necessarily be diluted. In one district we met a judge who was clearly hostile to Chapter 13's, but he was paired with a Chapter 13 supporter—and case assignment was random. (We often speculated on what it must be like to practice in such a district. With each case filed, finding out which judge was assigned to your case must feel a little like picking up a Community Chest card in a Monopoly game—something was going to happen, good or bad.)

In searching for other clues about local legal practices that might affect debtors, we speculated that the attorneys might have formed views that would influence their interactions with their clients even when they were not responding to the influence of the local judge. Years of teaching at seminars for bankruptcy attorneys had convinced us that many attorneys had definite opinions about the advisability of Chapter 7 and Chapter 13 generally. As one could predict with a roomful of attorneys, they held strong views both ways, with one attorney adamantly arguing that Chapter 13 made no sense for most debtors while another shouted that Chapter 13 was the best invention since the saltshaker. If attorneys could influence their clients to declare Chapter 7 or Chapter 13 in response to the incentives a bankruptcy judge built into the local legal system, it would be an even easier matter for an attorney with strong feelings to influence most clients to file the preferred chapter.

Even attorneys who took no strong position on either Chapter 7's or Chapter 13's might nonetheless wish to influence their clients' decisions. Among those who file bankruptcies are the occasional general practitioner who, between writing wills and closing real estate deals, handles a consumer bankruptcy or two. Chapter 13 is generally more complex for an attorney, with more forms to fill out and more calculations to make. Moreover, the complexity of a three- to five-year payout plan offers many more opportunities to make a serious error in proposing and confirming a Chapter 13 plan, something an attorney unsure of the forms might like to avoid. In some bankruptcy courts, there is also the risk that Chapter 13 might involve later court appearances without an additional fee. The attorneys interviewed indicated that a general practitioner doing an occasional bankruptcy would have more difficulty with Chapter 13. Even some bankruptcy specialists find Chapter 13's intimidating. As one bankruptcy clerk put it, "John does a lot of bankruptcy, but he can't even spell Chapter 13. He'd rather give up the fee than take one of those on." These attorneys were, in effect, Chapter 7 attorneys.

The fee structures in Chapter 13 and Chapter 7 might influence some attorneys. Chapter 13's usually pay more—for more work. On average, a lawyer in our sample received \$535 for filing a Chapter 13, significantly more than the \$459 charged for a Chapter 7 (p = 0.00). Different attorneys, based on different cost/benefit calculations, see one or the other as more profitable. Some attorneys standardize their office practices, training legal assistants to prepare most of the forms and schedules required in the files. An office set up to handle Chapter 7's efficiently may have both more cost and greater errors in handling a Chapter 13. Although some attorneys set up procedures for both, some attorneys believe they have found the key to smooth operations in only one. Finally, every attorney faces the problem of debtors who need bankruptcy but who don't have the money for the filing fee. Some decide that repayment as part of a Chapter 13 plan balances the debtor's need for bankruptcy relief with the attorney's need for some assurance of repayment. Such an attorney would see any debtor without the requisite fee as needing a Chapter 13, regardless of whatever else was going on in the case. Other attorneys might analyze the problem differently, suggesting the debtor ask for a family loan or pay for the bankruptcy fees rather than making this month's rent payment. An attorney may emphasize any of a wide variety of incentives and opportunities to influence the debtors' choices, and the complexity of the subject matter makes it possible to justify almost any path chosen.

It is a fairly easy matter for attorneys to have a dramatic impact on debtors' choices in bankruptcy. Bankruptcy laws are technical and difficult (as the reader will undoubtedly believe by now), and it is the attorney's job to present the legal summaries on which the debtor will make a decision.[33] There are so many advantages and disadvantages to either chapter that it is a simple matter of emphasis to make one sound much more appealing. And, if the attorney genuinely believes one is better, the client is getting just what he paid for: the expert opinion of a knowledgeable attorney.

We have no scale to measure which attorneys thought Chapter 13 was a creative solution to debt problems and which attorneys thought recommending Chapter 13 was only slightly short of selling their clients into bondage. But the data do offer an indirect glimpse at whether attorneys might have an important influence on their clients.

Consumer bankruptcy is handled by a relatively small bar, and our sample of bankrupt debtors turned up many attorneys who handled several cases. We speculated that attorneys who handled four or more bankruptcies from our sample were doing a relatively high volume of bankruptcy cases and were more likely to be bankruptcy specialists. Notwithstanding our observation that there are some Chapter 7 specialists, we reasoned that a bankruptcy specialist would be more familiar than a general practitioner with the complexities of Chapter 13.

Nearly 32% of all the debtors in our sample (both Chapter 7's and Chapter 13's) consulted attorneys who were specialists. The correlation matrix indicates a positive correlation between seeing a specialist and ending up in Chapter 13 ($r = 0.27$).[34] This suggests that attorneys may exert a powerful influence over choice of chapter.

We are not unmindful that our selection process was rough and ready, and that specialization can only be inferred from the frequency of filings. And we realize there might be alternative explanations for the finding, if, for example, debtors who wanted Chapter 13's were steered to a Chapter 13 specialist. We also recognize that specialists may merely be reflecting the influence of a judge. Nonetheless, other statistical tests give us confidence that the variable has some validity.[35] It is also consistent with a recent qualitative study of consumer bankruptcy that suggests how bankruptcy attorneys may shape client choices.[36] We also note that if we had been better able to segregate and identify the views of the attorneys, we could have explored attorney influence more directly and we might have documented even greater influence. For now, we conclude that attorneys influence debtor decisions in choice of chapter.

We tried another indirect measure of the influence of attorneys. We speculated that the practice of bankruptcy law might be different in large cities and small towns. Because the practice of law is usually more diverse and the bar is larger in large urban areas, we speculated that more experimentation and competition could lead to greater use of Chapter 13. We also speculated that the influence of a judge would be weaker in metropolitan areas, where several judges hear bankruptcy cases.

The correlation between Chapter 13 and metropolitan areas was positive (0.13), but it was too weak to support any conclusions. The hypothesis is not disproven, but, at least at the most basic comparative level, it is not strongly supported either.[37]

We also speculated that legal practice might simply differ among states. We created a third measure, state, which we coded 1 if the debtor resided in Texas. Texas laws are generally more favorable for debtors, which might suggest a legal practice that would generally influence debtors into Chapter 7. The correlation coefficient, although weak, indicated that Texans were more likely to choose Chapter 13 ($r = 0.10$).[38] Thus there is a weak state effect but not in the predicted direction.

The Combined Strength of Factors Influencing Debtor Decisions

Alone, no single variable is terribly powerful, but there is the possibility that variables work together to explain more about debtors' bankruptcy choices. A multiple regression analysis permits us to explore the additive effects of the economic, social, and legal factors we have already examined using correlation coefficients. This analysis, which Table 13.5 summarizes, shows that 36% of the variance between debtors filing Chapter 7 and debtors filing Chapter 13 can be explained by the six demographic variables we identify in the sample; the five economic factors combined could predict 12% of the variance in the same regression analysis, and the three local legal culture variables predict 8% of the variance. The regression equation that combines all the factors indicates that together they explain about 44% of the variance—more than any one set alone explains, albeit considerably less than a complete explanation of how debtors in bankruptcy decide between chapters.

The relative predictive value of each set of variables depends on whether we obtained the best data to show the strength of each model. The economic data are the most complete in the bankruptcy files. More financial information is available than any other kind, and the available data directly measure the variables used in the economic model. Any strong relationship between financial position and choice of chapter should show up in these data.

The predictive power of the six demographic and social variables is all the more surprising because the kind and number of social variables we can examine are necessarily limited to those available in the bankruptcy files. It may well be that age, education, religious affiliation, or some other social or demographic characteristic for which we have no data is far more important.[39]

Similarly, the limitations in these data do not permit as much statistical analysis as anecdotal inquiry into the local legal culture model, which may have far more powerful influences than our numbers suggest.

The variables we describe as social–demographic obviously are related to

TABLE 13.5. Three Multiple Regression Models for Predicting Choice of Chapter in Bankruptcy (Standardized Regression Coefficients)[a]

Characteristic	Economic Variables	Social Demographic Variables	Local Legal Culture Variables	Combined Variables
Assets ($)	0.46***			0.29***
Family income ($)	0.09**			0.07**
Unsecured debt ($)	−0.19***			−0.13***
Secured debt ($)	−0.21***			−0.13**
Exemptions ($)	−0.06			−0.13***
Marital status (1 = yes)		0.02		0.01
Self-employed (1 = yes)		−0.08**		−0.07**
Homeowner (1 = yes)		0.09**		0.05
Occupational prestige (NORC scores)		0.05*		0.04
Intrastate migration (1 = yes)		−0.56***		−0.50***
Interstate migration (1 = yes)		−0.34***		−0.32***
Texas practice (1 = yes)			0.03	0.04
Urban district (1 = yes)			0.09**	0.05*
Specialist attorney (1 = yes)			0.25***	0.17***
Constant	0.28***	0.51***	0.26***	0.40***
F	35.6***	117.9***	43.6***	61.6***
Adj R^2	0.12	0.36	0.08	0.44

[a]Cases with extreme values on assets, total debt, or income excluded.

*$p \leq 0.05$

**$p \leq 0.01$

***$p \leq 0.001$

Source: Consumer Bankruptcy Project.

economic factors. It might appear that we are, in effect, testing different elements of a debtor's economic status by testing economic variables directly and by testing them again indirectly. Home ownership is closely related to amount of debt and amount of assets, and occupational prestige is closely related to income levels. The multiple regression coefficient, however, shows the effect of each debtor variable while controlling for the effect of all other variables. In the final column of Table 13.5 we can see the effects of all of the variables even when the financial variables have been controlled. Thus we can focus on the implications of marital status, migration, home ownership, self-employment, and occupational prestige separately from the closely related economic issues of assets, income, and debts. Because of these limitations in the data, we do not offer some all-encompassing theory of who uses Chapter 13. We can, however, infer that factors personal to the debtors, their social and demographic characteristics, affect whether they will attempt a Chapter 13 repayment or take a Chapter 7 discharge. In a very basic sense, these demographic/cultural variables relate to the original foundations of bankruptcy policy, especially to Chapter 13. If an attempt to repay is based primarily on these characteristics, then the most important function of Chapter 13 may be simply to make available a repayment option for those willing to struggle to pay, not as an alternative to which some can-pay debtors can be driven. And it may be more important to inform debtors about the Chapter 13 alternative, and to give them technical help in succeeding, than it is to tinker with economic incentives that may have little to do with their choices.

These data suggest two conclusions: (1) the simple economic model can be laid to rest as a powerful predictor of debtor behavior and (2) the relative importance of noneconomic factors is unknown, except that some social–demographic factors have an obvious influence whereas others must be more fully developed. Different studies of the bankruptcy process, such as qualitative assessments of judges and attorneys and special inquiries into debtors' demographic characteristics, may suggest additional variable to be explored to provide a better basis for other models of debtor behavior.

The Trouble with Simple Models

We note from the correlation matrix that several variables within each model not only correlate with choice of chapter, but they also correlate with each other. Not surprisingly, a high correlation occurs between home ownership and assets ($r = 0.56$) and between home ownership and secured debt ($r = 0.44$).[40] Multiple regression analysis permits us to hold each variable constant while others are measured, so that the effects of home ownership as a predictor of filing Chapter 13 are separated from the effects of high secured debt. But the combination of three models to explain debtor behavior suggests that the relationship among the variables grouped within the models is even more complex than a simple multiple regression equation will reveal.

The complexity of the interaction can be shown by another analysis that identifies how some of the factors influence one another and how they directly or indirectly influence the debtor's choice of chapter. The technique is path analysis, a procedure designed to decompose the findings of a multiple regression analysis, showing which variables used in the regression had what kinds of influence on other factors and on the final decision.

We offer one approach to such an analysis in Table 13.6 and Figure 13.1, which are explained in detail in the appendix to this chapter. We begin with seven regression equations. The variables are nested, that is, all the variables used in the first equation appear in all subsequent equations; all variables used in the second equation appear in all subsequent equations, and so on. Substantively, this permits the social–demographic variables to explain everything they can explain about assets and family income; then assets and income are added to the social–demographic variables to explain levels of unsecured and secured debt,[41] and so on. Eventually this permits us to isolate the effects of each variable on other variables and to determine how each tends to increase or decrease the likelihood that the debtor will choose Chapter 13 over Chapter 7.

This path analysis is one possible picture of the relationships among important variables in the chapter decision. The path analysis we have constructed shows that both social–demographic variables and local legal system variables have a direct and previously unexpected effect on the choice of chapter. The path analysis also shows social–demographic variables affecting economic variables, emphasizing even more the importance of noneconomic variables in the bankruptcy decision-making process.[42]

As this picture indicates, path analysis reinforces the view that any simple model of consumer choice is necessarily oversimplified. For the reader interested in more detail, the appendix to this chapter explains the path analysis and more about the findings based on this analytic approach. But the point of the picture that is critical to our story is that path analysis confirms that interrelationships among various factors influencing debtors' choices of chapter are extraordinarily complex. This test suggests that great caution is necessary in creating a model of consumer debtor behavior.

Policy Implications

Our data go to the heart of the economic incentive model as it influenced consumer bankruptcy policy, starting with the 1978 Code. The critical role of exemption levels in shaping debtor behavior was widely assumed. Some questioned whether the approach was valid or whether it should dominate all consideration of consumer bankruptcy policy, and some argued against using it as the guiding force in determining policy. But the simple economic incentive model seemed so intrinsically rational, so sensible, that it carried the day. And in 1984, when Congress amended the Bankruptcy Code, the model was treated as completely valid when Congress reduced exemption levels for the express purpose of reversing the rise in bankruptcy filings and promoting greater Chapter 13 repayments.

The reason the economic incentive approach was so successful in the legislatures could be debated at length by political scientists and intellectual historians. The strength of the "law and economics" movement generally, and its apparently clear application to the consumer bankruptcy field, may be a part of the explanation. But one part of its strength that cannot be ignored is its simple, intuitive appeal.

This appealing economic model supported changes in laws that have affected millions of people. Now several years of field research have produced the data to show that the model was completely wrong. Intellectual development in an area such as this cannot go forward without models, but these data show that models can be Trojan horses—they sometimes contain nasty surprises. It will now be easy to say that the model was too unsophisticated and to build more elaborate models, which will better fit the known data. This alternation between data and modeling is precisely what is needed, and we look forward to these efforts. But why is it that no economist pointed out the model's lack of sophistication before Congress and 34 state legislatures passed laws changing the lives of millions of people?

Legislative bodies must sometimes go forward with only rudimentary information. They cannot always await better data. Our concern is the responsibility of model builders and data collectors to those who use their speculations and information. Criticism of a model that is mere academic speculation in the professional journals is a matter of scholarly interests and priorities. Criticism of a model that is being used to pass laws is a public duty. That duty rests on theoreticians and empiricists alike, but the former can point out analytical difficulties faster than the latter can gather data. The results discussed in this chapter should emphasize the need for regularly collected data in the bankruptcy area. They should also act as a cautionary tale about enacting laws with little more than formal logic to support them.

Appendix. Path Analysis of Chapter Choice

Figure 13.1 presents a path analysis of the debtors' choice of chapter. This path analysis decomposes the relationships presented in the regression analyses in Table 13.6 to demonstrate the internal structure of the data.

Two key findings from Table 13.5 show that all of the variables together explain 44% of the variance in chapter choice, and the block of social–demographic variables together explains 36% of the variance. Studies by other researchers have also shown the general predictive power of social–demographic variables in predicting financial variables. For example, occupational prestige,

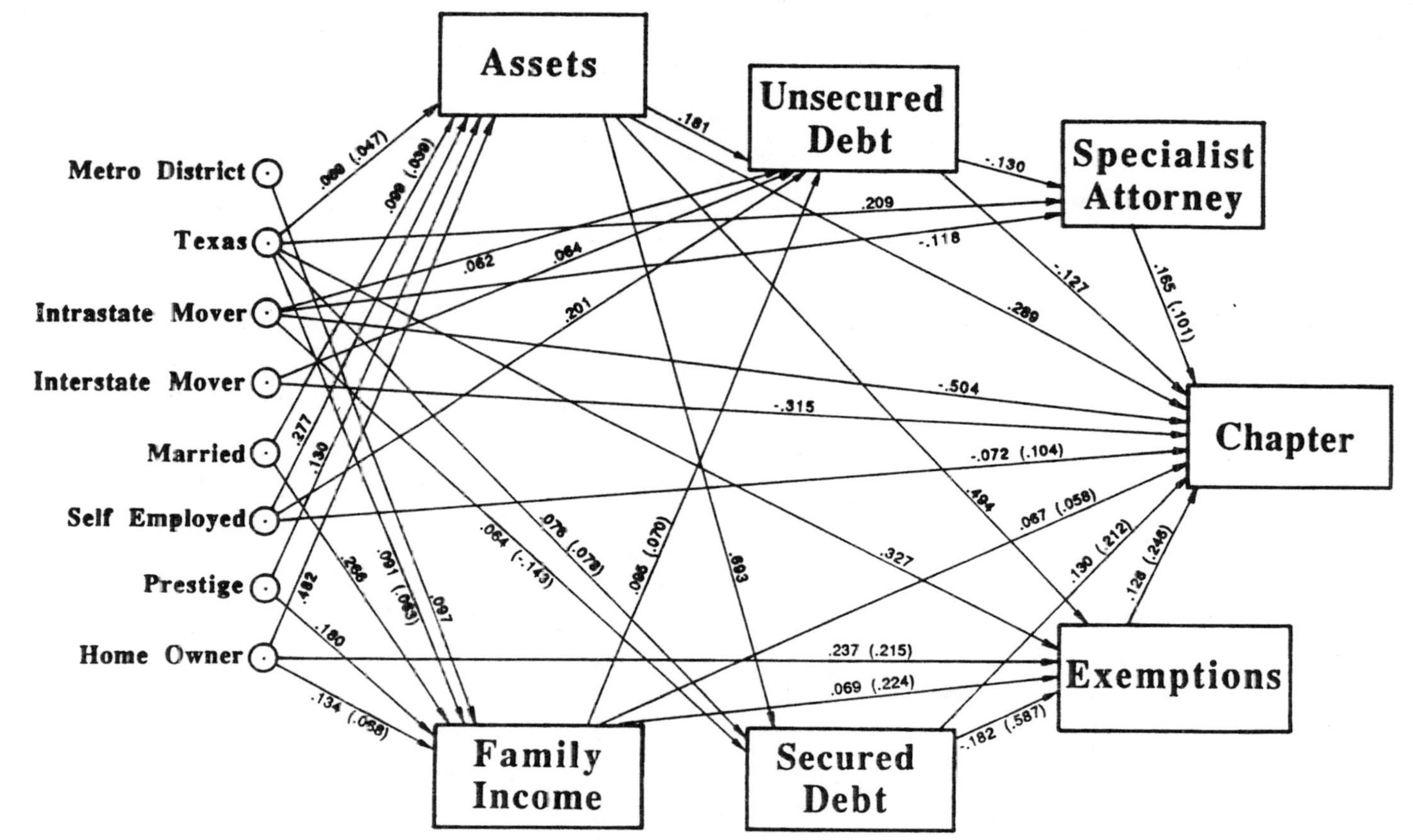

FIGURE 13.1. Path Analysis of Chapter Choice

TABLE 13.6. Direct Effects of Variables in Path Analysis[a]

Characteristic	Assets	Family Income	Unsecured Debt	Secured Debt	Attorney Specialist	Exemptions	Chapter[b]
Urban district (yes = 1)	0.034	0.097**	−0.008	−0.037	0.078*	0.018	0.053*
State (Texas = 1)	0.069**	0.091**	0.035	−0.076**	0.209**	0.327**	0.044
Intrastate move	−0.035	0.040	0.062*	0.064**	−0.118**	0.046*	−0.504**
Interstate move	−0.040	−0.013	0.064*	0.038	−0.050	−0.018	−0.315**
Married (1 = yes)	0.099**	0.266**	0.012	−0.006	−0.031	0.031	0.012
Currently self-employed (1 = yes)	0.277**	0.002	0.210**	0.049*	−0.009	0.009	−0.072**
Prestige	0.130**	0.180**	0.072**	0.044*	−0.030	0.009	0.035
Homeowner (1 = yes)	0.482**	0.134**	−0.060	0.057*	0.029	0.237**	0.046
Assets	—	—	0.181**	0.693**	−0.004	0.494**	0.289**
Family income	—	—	0.095**	0.031	0.073*	0.069**	0.067**
Unsecured debt	—	—	—	—	−0.103**	0.078**	−0.127**
Secured debt	—	—	—	—	−0.093*	−0.182**	−0.130**
Attorney specialist	—	—	—	—	—	—	0.165**
Exemptions	—	—	—	—	—	—	−0.128**
Constant	−18,129**	3,815**	−4,195	−5,016	0.3002**	−9,164**	0.3977**
N	1,235	1,080	1,080	1,080	1,080	1,080	1,080
Adj R^2	0.44	0.15	0.12	0.55	0.09	0.50	0.44
F	120.02**	25.07**	16.00**	131.74**	9.64**	91.61**	61.63**

[a]Cases with extreme values on assets, total debt, or income excluded.

[b]Chapter 13 = 1.

*$p \leq 0.05$

**$p \leq 0.01$

Source: Consumer Bankruptcy Project.

marital status, and urban residence are known to be associated with higher incomes. These earlier findings suggest to us that the social–demographic variables might be effective not only in predicting choice of chapter, but also in predicting financial variables.

Path analysis hypothesizes that a group of background ("exogenous") variables can be used to predict the subsequent ("endogenous") variables in the analysis. The exogenous variables, on the left side of the figure, are used to predict the financial variables; then the exogenous variables and the financial variables are used together to predict consulting a specialist attorney and claimed exemption value; then the specialist attorney and exemption value are added to predict choice of chapter. Another way to say this is that each variable to the right of the exogenous variables is used successively as a dependent variable and then as an independent variable. These successive regression equations can be found in Table 13.6.

The meaning of the path analysis takes shape with a series of questions: Is there a path indicated between two variables of interest? If so, what is its direction? And what is its magnitude?[43] There are potential paths available between any two variables in the analysis; in practice, there are many fewer paths, because only those variables that are significant in prediction have a path between them. The path arrowhead points toward the dependent variable and away from the independent variable. A path with significant prediction is called a "direct" relationship. For example, the migration history variables directly affect chapter choice. Occupational prestige does not directly influence chapter choice, but it does directly influence assets and income and in this way comes to have an effect on chapter choice greater than variations in assets and incomes alone will show.

The coefficients may be either positive or negative in their impact on the succeeding variable. Path coefficients are also called direct effects; indirect effects, shown in parentheses when they are large, are the difference between the correlation and the path coefficient.

The magnitude of the path coefficients indicates a relative weight in the prediction of the next variable. But path coefficients do not lend themselves to an easily interpretable metric; a path of 0.3 is not necessarily three times stronger than one of 0.1.

Ideally, the choice of exogenous variables is guided by theory; in our case, it is also guided by what was available in the bankruptcy files. The best exogenous variables cannot be changed by subsequent variables; examples are age, race, ethnicity, and religious upbringing, variables that are unambiguously prior to the debtor's subsequent activity. These were not available to us. We use as our exogenous variables the social–demographic variables and the two indicators of residence. We then decompose the economic variables to show the predictive value of the exogenous variables plus household income and assets on the values of secured and unsecured debt. The exogenous variables and the four economic variables are then used to predict two things that happen on the way to bankruptcy: (1) consulting a specialist or nonspecialist

TABLE 13.7. Mean, Standard Deviations, and Correlation Matrix of Variables in Analysis

		Mean	S.D.	Cases
Pairwise Deletion of Missing Data				
A	State (Texas = 1)	0.421	0.494	1,502
B	Urban (yes = 1)	0.419	0.494	1,502
C	Intrastate move	0.333	0.471	1,502
D	Interstate move	0.106	0.308	1,502
E	Married (yes = 1)	0.638	0.481	1,502
F	Self-employed	0.104	0.305	1,502
G	Prestige	37.525	11.903	1,238
H	Homeowner	0.520	0.500	1,502
I	Assets ($)	29,354.70	40,033.71	1,490
J	Family income ($)	15,779.44	9,609.06	1,289
K	Unsecured debt ($)	15,498.10	31,267.95	1,495
L	Secured debt ($)	23,034.440	38,565.62	1,501
M	Attorney specialist	0.322	0.467	1,502
N	Exemptions ($)	14,498.37	22,664.29	1,469
O	Chapter (13 = 1)	0.389	0.488	1,502

Minimum pairwise N of cases = 1,080

Correlation Matrix

	A	B	C	D	E	F	G	H	I	J	K	L	M	N	O
A	1.0														
B	0.20	1.0													
C	−0.13	−0.06	1.0												
D	0.13	0.00	−0.24	1.0											
E	0.09	−0.09	−0.09	0.03	1.0										
F	0.04	−0.03	−0.14	−0.05	0.08	1.0									
G	0.16	0.09	−0.09	0.08	−0.08	0.10	1.0								
H	−0.02	0.04	−0.17	−0.13	0.25	0.10	0.02	1.0							
I	0.11	0.06	−0.18	−0.11	0.24	0.37	0.17	0.56	1.0						
J	0.15	0.11	−0.04	−0.01	0.28	0.06	0.18	0.20	0.29	1.0					
K	0.09	0.01	−0.02	0.04	0.08	0.27	0.14	0.07	0.25	0.16	1.0				
L	0.00	0.00	−0.08	−0.07	0.18	0.31	0.16	0.44	0.73	0.24	0.22	1.0			
M	0.23	0.14	−0.13	0.00	−0.01	−0.04	0.00	0.01	−0.02	0.07	0.10	0.09	1.0		
N	0.39	0.13	−0.12	−0.07	0.22	0.21	0.14	0.45	0.58	0.20	0.22	0.32	0.02	1.0	
O	0.10	0.13	−0.49	−0.21	0.07	0.03	0.06	0.24	0.25	0.12	−0.12	0.08	0.27	0.12	1.0

attorney and (2) claiming a value for exempt property. Choosing a chapter is the end point of this analysis.

The path analysis shows that the relationship among these variables is complex. Looking at the currently self-employed is a good example. Self-employment is directly associated with choosing Chapter 7. Moreover, self-employment directly affects unsecured debt, and high unsecured debt is directly associated with choosing Chapter 7. Debtors with high unsecured debt also tend to consult nonspecialist attorneys, which is associated with entering Chapter 7. The path analysis then shows three types of association between self-employment and Chapter 7. First, controlling for all other exogenous variables, the self-employed are more likely to choose Chapter 7. Second and third paths of influence come about through their higher unsecured debt and their choice of nonspecialist attorneys. This type of analysis can provide guidance for new studies and for testing new hypotheses.

One example of new insights that could be tested further is the role of assets. High assets are directly associated with Chapter 13 and with high secured debt, high unsecured debt, and high exemptions. But high secured and unsecured debt levels and high exemptions are indirectly associated with Chapter 7. Thus the indirect paths have the opposite effect of the direct paths. By the same token, household income is directly associated with Chapter 13 and with high unsecured debts, yet high unsecured debts are in turn associated with Chapter 7. One reason the economic variables by themselves explain so little of the variance may be the complexity of the relationship among them.

The complex relationship between residence in the state of Texas and choice of chapter is another example of the insight from the path analysis. The simple economic model posits that residence in Texas has a strong, direct, negative influence on chapter; it does not. In fact, being in Texas is weakly correlated with entering Chapter 13, counter to the prediction of the economic model. State of residence is not a significant direct predictor of choice of chapter, but state does operate through a number of other variables. One way that this happens is through the tendency of Texas debtors, controlling for everything else, to consult specialist attorneys, who in turn are associated with more Chapter 13 filings. This could not be predicted by the simple economic model, and it is probably a function of local legal culture.

Controlling for everything else, living in Texas is also a significant predictor of having higher assets, higher household income, and lower secured debts. As we have seen, high assets are associated, via various paths, with contradictory chapter outcomes, as is household income. Lower secured debts should raise the proportions of Texans choosing Chapter 13. On the other hand, however, Texans report somewhat more exempt property, which had the effect of directing them toward Chapter 7. These complex relationships deserve further study and research, but they indicate that financial variables alone are not sufficient to predict choice of chapter. Indeed, the financial variables appear best understood within the context of other variables that themselves help predict the financial variables.

TABLE 13.8. Indirect Effects of Variables in Path Analysis[a,b]

Characteristic	Assets	Income	Unsecured	Secured	Specialist	Exemptions	Chapter
Urban district	NA	—	NA	NA	NA	NA	NA
Texas practice	0.041	0.063	NA	0.078	—	—	NA
Intrastate move	NA	NA	NA	−0.143	—	NA	—
Interstate move	NA	NA	NA	NA	NA	NA	—
Married (1 = yes)	0.139	—	NA	NA	NA	NA	NA
Currently self-employed (1 = yes)	—	NA	—	NA	NA	NA	0.104
Prestige	—	—	NA	NA	NA	NA	NA
Homeowner (1 = yes)	—	0.068	NA	NA	NA	0.215	NA
Assets	X	X	—	—	NA	—	—
Family income	X	X	0.070	NA	NA	0.224	0.058
Unsecured debt	X	X	X	X	—	0.147	—
Secured debt	X	X	X	X	—	0.507	0.212
Attorney specialist	X	X	X	X	X	X	0.101
Exemptions	X	X	X	X	X	X	0.246

Key: NA = direct effect not significant at $p \leqslant .01$; X = not in equation.

[a]Cases with extreme values on assets, total debt, or income excluded.

[b]Listed if absolute value of indirect effect is at least one-half the absolute value of the direct effects.

Source: Consumer Bankruptcy Project.

Notes

1. House Judiciary Committee Rep., H. R. Doc. No. 1698, 57th Cong., 1st Sess. (1902), at 406–07 (reprinted in Eastmann Bankruptcy 412 [1903]).

2. 32 Stat. 7970 (1903). Stricter provisions on discharge were adopted, and a series of other debtor-creditor compromises were put into place. *Id.*, p. 407, Collier on Bankruptcy (7th ed., 1909), p. xi.

3. Act of June 22, 1938, ch. 575, §1, 52 Stat, 893–905 (codified at 11 U.S.C. §3601–676).

4. 81 Cong. Rec. H. 8647 (daily ed. Aug. 10, 1937) (statements of Rep. Chandler).

5. As with all intellectual movements, the origins are complex. The premise that debtor behavior followed the predictable cause-and-effect relationship of the economic model surfaced most prominently in legal circles in a seminal exemption-reform article by the eminent bankruptcy scholar Frank Kennedy long before the economists formalized the model. F. Kennedy, Limitations of Exemptions in Bankruptcy, 45 Iowa Law Review 445, 447–448 (1960). Evidently Professor Kennedy later concluded that the model was not so clear in predicting debtor behavior. He did not use it extensively in his later work, and as head of the Bankruptcy Commission, in his testimony advocating a single, minimum federal exemption standard, he minimized the expected impact of economic incentives on debtors' actual behavior. Bankruptcy Act Revision: Hearings on H.R. 31 and H.R. 32 before the Subcommittee on Civil and Constitutional Rights of the Committee on the Judiciary, 94th Cong., 1st & 2d Sess. (1975–76) at 170.

Other commentators carried the idea. See, e.g., Note, Bankruptcy Exemptions: A Full Circle Back to the Act of 1800?, 53 Cornell Law Review 663, 673–74 (1968) (discussing the use of low exemptions to encourage greater use of Chapter 13, ultimately rejecting the proposal on grounds other than trouble with the economic analysis); Comment, Bankruptcy Exemptions: Critique and Suggestions, 68 Yale Law Journal 1459, 1509 (1959) (arguing for lower property exemptions to force more debtors into Chapter 13).

6. W. H. Meckling, Financial Markets, Default, and Bankruptcy: The Role of the State, 41 Law and Contemporary Problems 13, 27 (Autumn 1977). Dean Meckling explained that the purpose of his paper was to use principles widely accepted by economists as "an analytical framework within which to clarify issues, identify more precisely the role which bankruptcy plays, and assess the social consequences of alternative legal structures for bankruptcy." *Id.*, p. 13.

7. Other economists focused on other aspects of consumer bankruptcy laws, including the expectations about consumers' borrowing behavior and the response of credit markets. E.g., J. F. Weston, Some Economic Fundamentals for an Analysis of Bankruptcy, 41 Law and Contemporary Problems 47 (1977). Although the Weston analysis notes the absence of empirical evidence, it also adopts without questions a simplistic cause-and-effect description of consumer debtor behavior and consumer credit markets.

8. The lack of empirical verification was forcefully pointed out by Professor P. Shuchman, among others, but there was little discernible effect on the increasing reliance of the economic model as the basis for policy discussion. See, e.g., P. Shuchman, Theory and Reality in Bankruptcy: The Spherical Chicken, 41 Law and Contemporary Problems 66 (1977) (a spirited attack on Meckling's economic analysis challenging the unproven assertions of the model); J. H. Moore, Foreword, 41 Law and Contemporary Problems 1, 4 (1977) (discussing an earlier conference of economists and law professors

in which Dean Meckling had participated and which raised the questions about empirical assertions). Although Meckling acknowledges that a previous version of his paper published in Law and Contemporary Problems and cited earlier was presented at the earlier conference, he made no efforts in his revised paper to respond to the questions raised about the unproven empirical assertions.

Professor Vern Countryman is another scholar who has long lamented the absence of useful data in the bankruptcy area and who has been wary of economic models with no data to back them up. See, e.g., V. Countryman, For a New Exemption Policy in Bankruptcy, 14 Rutgers Law Review 678, 678 (1960) (discussing the lack of empirical data).

9. Hearings before the Subcommittee on Civil and Constitutional Rights of the House Committee on the Judiciary, 94th Cong., 2d Sess., Pt. 3 (1976) at 360, 369 (statement of Alvin O. Wiese, Jr., Chairman of the Subcommittee on Bankruptcy of the Law Forum of the National Consumer Finance Association, and Robert B. Norris and Vernon L. Evans, General Counsel and Associate General Counsel, National Consumer Finance Association).

10. For a summary of the general economic arguments, see J. H. Moore, Foreward [to a symposium on the economies of bankruptcy reform], 41 Law and Contemporary Problems 1, 4–5 (1977). See also W. Vukowich, Reforming the Bankruptcy Reform Act of 1978: An Alternative Approach, 71 Georgetown Law Journal 1129, 1153 (1983) (hereafter cited as Vukowich).

11. The Bankruptcy Code also set up legal incentives to enter Chapter 13. Debtors in certain circumstances are barred from Chapter 7, and a broader discharge is available to debtors in Chapter 13. 11 U.S.C. §§523, 707, 727, 1328. Our interviews with judges and attorneys had suggested that the legal incentives to use Chapter 13 (or to avoid Chapter 7) were rarely used.

Some reasons for avoiding Chapter 7 or for entering Chapter 13 could not be tested because the files contained no relevant information. For example, we could not tell if the debtor or attorney feared that a debt might be claimed as a fraud by embezzlement and not eligible for discharge in Chapter 7 but dischargeable in Chapter 13. We were, however, able to examine other reasons.

In Chapter Eleven we explored whether debtors might enter Chapter 13 because they had received a Chapter 7 discharge within the previous six years. We found only a few debtors fit this classification.

The broader discharge in Chapter 13 might be more attractive to people with educational loans or with intentional tort debts, neither of which can be discharged in Chapter 7 but both of which can be discharged in Chapter 13. Contrary to expectations, petitioners in Chapter 7 and Chapter 13 were equally likely to report educational loans ($t = -1.56$). Furthermore, Chapter 7 debtors were significantly more likely to report tort debt ($t = 3.33$, $p = 0.00$) of any kind, including both intentional tort debt (e.g., assault), which can be discharged only in Chapter 13, and ordinary tort debt (e.g., car accidents), which can be discharged in either chapter. We separately coded data on intentional torts, when the files gave enough information from which we could draw this inference reliably. Seven debtors with pending intentional tort suits were in Chapter 7, and 27 of 32 cases reporting other or undetermined tort cases pending were in Chapter 7. The Chapter 13 forms collect much less information on pending lawsuits than Chapter 7 forms do. Nevertheless, these data suggest that neither educational loans nor tort debts lead people to file Chapter 13.

The circumstances vary, but many debts involving fraud are not dischargeable in Chapter 7. We could not detect any cases of fraud, nor did we find any creditor objections to a debtor's discharge based on an allegation of fraud. Having lost or destroyed financial records or having transferred property within the preceding year could be an indication of fraud. The data show that debtors who had lost or destroyed records were significantly more likely to be in Chapter 7 ($t = 3.82$, $p = 0.00$). Those who had transferred property were equally likely to be in Chapter 7 or Chapter 13 ($t = -0.55$). Again, these indicators did not have the expected association with Chapter 13.

Chapter 13 can offer a nonspouse co-debtor protection that is not available in Chapter 7. Here we found a split in the expected direction. Chapter 13 petitioners were significantly more likely than Chapter 7 petitioners to have a nonspouse co-debtor ($t = -3.09$, $p = 0.000$). Relatively few cases were involved, however: 66 cases in Chapter 7 and 71 cases in Chapter 13.

Finally, we examined the choice of chapter for debtors who had any one of these conditions and found that Chapter 7 and Chapter 13 debtors were equally likely to have at least one such condition ($t = -0.42$).

There are also statutory bars to entering Chapter 13. For example, a debtor may not enter Chapter 13 with more than $100,000 in unsecured debts or more than $350,000 in secured debts. Yet our sample included nine Chapter 13 petitioners with unsecured debt in excess of $100,000 and two with secured debt in excess of $350,000. Seven of the former and one of the latter remained in the common debtor sample after we removed the outliers. We did not find any question raised in the debtors' files concerning their Chapter 13 filing with such large debts.

We concluded that the effort to guide debtors into Chapter 7 or Chapter 13 because of various legal disabilities is not demonstrably effective. We recognize, however, that many of the legal disabilities contemplated in the Code could not be tested directly using bankruptcy file data.

12. See M. Kaplan, Chapter 13 of The Bankruptcy Reform Act of 1978: An Attractive Alternative, 28 DePaul Law Review 1045, 1058 (1979); Bankruptcy Commission Report, 174. The omnipresence of debtors in bankruptcy who could pay was among the empirical assumptions in the debate.

13. Chapter 13 filings jumped from about 15% of all consumer filings in 1978 to nearly 30% by the year following our study. Calculation from the Judicial Conference of the United States, Director of the Administrative Office of the United States Courts Ann. Rep. (1982), Table F3B, p. 402. Whether the stated goals were met, however, is a very different question. There is a tendency to confuse the filing of a Chapter 13 with the goal of paying back creditors. Our data show that increased Chapter 13 filings by no means guarantee that result.

14. The consumer credit industry "simultaneously commissioned a study of bankrupt debtors, hired a prestigious Madison Avenue advertising firm to publicize the results of the study, and lobbied for federal legislation to remedy the problems that it was certain the study would reveal." E. Warren, Reducing Bankruptcy Protection for Consumers: A Response, 72 Georgetown Law Journal 1133, 1133–34, n.4 (1984). Testimony before Congress hammered home the economic incentive analysis. See, e.g., statement of Claude Rice, Alvin Wiese, Jr., and Jonathan M. Landers, Hearings before the Subcommittee on Courts of the Senate Committee on the Judiciary, 97th Cong., 1st Sess., 63–64 (1981); statement of Eldon Hoekstra, *id.*, p. 181; statement of Andrew F. Brimmer, *id.* at 21–23.

15. W. J. Woodward and R. S. Woodward, Exemptions as an Incentive to Voluntary Bankruptcy: An Empirical Study, 88 Commercial Law Journal 309, 311 (1983). See also W. Woodward, Exemptions, Opting Out, and Bankruptcy Reform, 43 Ohio State Law Journal 335, 345 (1982).

16. 11 U.S.C. §§522(d), 707(b), 1325(b)(Supp. IV 1986).
17. Vukovich, p. 1152.
18. *Id.*
19. The complete correlation matrix, which appears in the chapter appendix, used pairwise deletion of missing values.
20. The dichotomous dependent variable, choice of chapter, is not too skewed for ordinary least squares regression; the split is about 60–40 in our sample. We considered this an acceptable departure from homoscedasticity. To check our assumption, these equations were rerun using logistic regression (results not shown) with no resulting change in the substantive conclusions.
21. A two-way analysis of variance in the total debt/income ratio showed state and chapter both to be statistically insignificant.

TABLE 13.9. Analysis of Variance of Total Debt/Income Ratio by State and Chapter

Effects of Variables	*F* Ratio
Main effects	0.69
State	0.13
Chapter	1.63
Interaction effect of state and chapter	1.30

Source: Consumer Bankruptcy Project.

22. A two-way analysis of variance in nonmortgage debt/income ratio showed a significant effect for chapter.

TABLE 13.10. Analysis of Variance of Nonmortgage Debt/Income Ratio by State and Chapter

Effects of Variables	*F* Ratio
Main effects	2.81*
State	1.59
Chapter	6.38*
Interaction effect of state and chapter	0.15

*$p \leq 0.05$
Source: Consumer Bankruptcy Project.

Even here, there is no sorting by state for high or low exemption levels. Once the mortgage is removed, there is some tendency for people with higher debt/income ratios to be in Chapter 7. As we noted, however, this is a purely hypothetical exercise because the mortgage still has to be repaid. The analysis reaffirms that exemption levels do not have the predicted effect.

23. See G. Neustadter, When Lawyer and Client Meet: Observations of Interviewing and Counseling Behavior in the Consumer Bankruptcy Law Office, 35 Buffalo Law Review 177, 239–40 (1986) ("Economic constraints may explain the absence from the law offices observed of institutional mechanisms for consideration or implementation of potential non-bankruptcy solutions to financial difficulty"). This ground-breaking qualitative study of attorney impact on the consumer bankruptcy

process is the sort of work that is critical to understanding more completely the bankruptcy system.

24. The variable is dichotomized as married or nonmarried, with no indications of a spouse coded as "nonmarried." This may understate the number of married petitioners because some "single filers" may have been married but failed to mention a spouse, although we have anecdotal evidence that some of the married may already be separated and in the process of divorce (see Chapter Eight).

As an alternative, we used joint filing and the sex of single filers as predictors (also see Chapter Eight), but these two variables explained no more than the marital status variable alone. We did not use family size as a variable because the only data available indicate that family sizes of Chapter 7 and Chapter 13 petitioners are similar (see Chapter Four, note 13).

25. The correlation matrix appears in Table 13.7 in the chapter appendix.

26. Form 8 in Chapter 7 does not ask for migration history, and some of the Chapter 13 forms now in use ask only for differences between current mailing address and residence. We coded all information provided. Almost certainly the volume of migration is underestimated.

27. Sometimes the move precedes the job change. Among workers over the age of 16 who had been employed both in January 1986 and in January 1987, some 0.7% reported that they had changed occupations during the 12-month period because of a change in residence. (Nearly 10% had changed occupations for any reason.) U.S. Bureau of Labor Statistics, "Most Occupational Changes Are Voluntary," release of October 22, 1987, Tables 1 and 2, p. 3.

28. See Table 13.7, chapter appendix.

29. See Chapter Two and the appendix at the end of the book, "Data and Methods," for details.

30. See the appendix, "Data and Methods."

31. There is no significant difference among the districts in total debt ($F = 1.67$), secured debt ($F = 0.61$), or total debt/income ratio ($F = 1.33$). There is a significant difference in income ($F = 7.40$), assets ($F = 3.98$), and unsecured debt ($F = 3.55$) that is associated with the Northern District of Texas (Dallas, Fort Worth) and the Southern District of Texas (Houston). Because the debt/income ratios show no difference, we can assume that the higher income persons in these Texas districts are also carrying larger debts.

There are also significant differences between some pairs of districts in background social–demographic variables, but there is no clear pattern to suggest that one district is consistently different from the others. For example, the Eastern District of Pennsylvania (Philadelphia) has significantly more homeowners than the Central and Northern Districts of Illinois. (This result is from the Scheffe ranges test; using the more liberal Least Significant Differences ranges test, the Eastern District of Pennsylvania has more homeowners than any other district. About 68% of the Eastern District of Pennsylvania petitioners were homeowners, compared with the lowest proportion, 40%, in the Northern District of Illinois.) Petitioners in the Northern District of Illinois (Chicago) were significantly less likely than petitioners in other districts to be currently married: 43% versus 75% in the Eastern District of Texas (Tyler and Beaumont).

No two districts differed significantly in the proportion of self-employed petitioners using the Scheffe procedure, but the more liberal Least Significant Difference procedure showed the Central and Northern districts of Illinois to be significantly lower in self-employment than the Western and Middle districts of Pennsylvania and the Eastern and Southern districts. The range was from 5% self-employed in the Northern District of Illinois to 65% in the Middle District of Pennsylvania.

The Southern District of Texas had significantly higher occupational prestige than eight other districts using the Least Significant Difference procedure (two districts using the Scheffe procedure). Mean prestige scores ranged from 34 in the Central District of Illinois to 41.6 in the Southern District of Texas.

32. Ideally, we would like to have included the district information within our multivariate analysis, but it was difficult to code and use. Data about districts are discontinuous. A person is in District 1 or 2 or 3, etc., but there is no hierarchical ranking of districts, unlike the case of a person's debt, which may be $10,000 or $10,001, so one is always more than another. Furthermore, in four districts we had oversampled Chapter 13's, so that predicting choice of chapter using dummy variables for district residence would be erroneous. As a result, we are unable to offer a regression equation using district as a direct predictor of chapter choice. What we have done, however, is to test for the possible effects of groups of districts. The group of oversampled districts did not show a biasing effect, but the group of districts with very large metropolitan areas did have a significant predictive effect and is included in the regression equation.

33. In the 1984 bankruptcy amendments, Congress tried to force the attorneys to involve the debtors in decisions about choice of chapter. The amendments require attorneys to submit an affidavit with each filing stating that the debtor had been fully informed about both Chapter 7 and Chapter 13. The credit industry lobbied hard for the provision. (Not surprisingly, their complaint was not about Chapter 13 lawyers who put everyone into Chapter 13 without explanation, but only about Chapter 7 lawyers whose clients never heard about Chapter 13.) The efficacy of the new provisions is problematic. The principal effect of these provisions seems to have been to provide a source of jokes among the cognoscenti, as the attorney demands that a confused debtor sign an incomprehensible form stating that the lawyer has explained all the legal alternatives. These provisions required both the attorney and the court clerk to certify that each debtor had been advised of the Chapter 7 versus Chapter 13 alternatives. 11 U.S.C. §342(b).

34. See Table 13.7, chapter appendix.

35. For example, the variable is not collinear with other variables in the analysis, even with those that are the strongest predictors of Chapter 13. See Table 13.7, chapter appendix.

36. See Neustadter, When Lawyer and Client Meet, pp. 248–50.

37. There may be other legal variables that influence choice of chapter, but we have been unable to identify them (see note 4 above). Stanley and Girth found that repossessions, garnishments, and similar legal actions were precipitating factors in the decision to file bankruptcy. D. Stanley and M. Girth, Bankruptcy: Problem, Process, and Reform (Washington: Brookings Institution, 1971). We could not test their finding because we did not have a comparable sample of nonbankrupt persons with pending collection actions. But we did test whether having had a repossession or a property seizure was a predictor of the decision to enter Chapter 7 versus Chapter 13. We could find no significant association with choice of chapter, and so these variables are not reported in the subsequent analysis.

38. This test is distinct from the earlier test of the effect of exemption laws on debtor decisions, testing whether Texas debtors differed from Illinois and Pennsylvania debtors. The economic model predicts a high correlation between living in Texas and choosing Chapter 7, but the data show the opposite result.

39. Individual personality traits or a family's cultural heritage may also play a role. We had been told, for example, that Mexican-Americans in Texas were more likely to file in Chapter 13 because they perceived it as more honorable. We recoded the surnames of the petitioners in Texas, using the U.S. Census Bureau's list of Spanish surnames, and studied the association of Spanish surname with chapter choice. We could find no robust association. This test could not be repeated in Illinois and Pennsylvania, where there are large numbers of ethnic groups whose surnames are similar to Spanish surnames (for example, Italians). There may well be other racial or ethnic patterns that we cannot discern. At least one bankruptcy judge told us of seeing increasing numbers of immigrant entrepreneurs in bankruptcy. Our negative finding should not discourage other researchers from pursuing this line of inquiry.

A study of the attitudes of people in bankruptcy might suggest other lines of inquiry that would yield far better explanations of why some debtors end up in Chapter 7 while others go into Chapter 13. Several judges and attorneys suggested that the intensity of religious conviction might be correlated with choice of Chapter 13, although one went on to note that the biblical jubilee (Deut. 15: 1–18) is more analogous to Chapter 7. Without additional data, we look where there is light.

40. See Table 13.7, chapter appendix.

41. There is no uniquely correct sequence of variables for a path analysis. This sequence is designed to approximate what a creditor might ask a debtor before extending credit. As we note in subsequent chapters, however (see especially Chapter Sixteen), some creditors have little choice and no information before the debt is incurred.

42. One way in which the economic model is too simple is that some economic variables are themselves varying with the characteristics of the debtors.

43. Path coefficients are standardized regression coefficients, and they are different from the correlations. Correlations show associations without controlling for the influence of any other variables. The path coefficients show the relationship between the two variables once all the preceding variables in the analysis have been controlled. The addition of statistical controls explains why the path coefficient may differ in sign from the correlation coefficient.

II

THE CREDITORS

14

The Other Players

In the tragedy that is consumer bankruptcy, the creditors have played the role of chorus: faceless victims keening in the background behind the debtors in the spotlight. Nearly every study of the causes or effects of bankruptcy has placed the debtor center stage: Was the bankruptcy the debtor's fault? Could the debtor have paid more? The other players in the debtor–creditor relationship have been largely invisible.

One reason for the silence about creditors is that they have been implicitly viewed as monolithic in interest and as the passive victims of events beyond their control. Just as we have analyzed the composition of the debtors, we collected and analyzed data to see who made up the faceless crowd of creditors. We discovered that the monolithic image of creditors is far wide of its mark. Creditors differ greatly in many respects. Some creditors suffer repeatedly in bankruptcy, whereas others dodge the bullet. Some are passive victims of unavoidable circumstance, whereas others are knowledgeable, repeat players in the credit game, including the end game of bankruptcy.

The data permit us to see who absorbs bankruptcy losses. It is possible to tell which creditors lent frequently to poverty-level debtors, which creditors asked for security, how much the creditors' security was worth by bankruptcy time, how many creditors tried to enforce their rights through the legal process before bankruptcy, how often creditors got reaffirmations of their debts, and so on. With data, it is also possible to make projections. By evaluating the data on a case-by-case basis, it is possible to determine which creditors would be paid more if bankrupt debtors came up with some cash and which creditors are never likely to see meaningful repayment under any statutory scheme.

Chapters Fourteen to Seventeen bring the chorus out to the footlights. We explore differences among creditors and examine how these differences might shape bankruptcy policy. Data about the creditors help fill in the picture of how consumer credit operates. Bankruptcy, as the pathology of the consumer credit system, gives some insight into the weaknesses of the larger system.

Creditor Groups

The diversity of creditors listed in bankruptcy is a sharp reminder of how many ways a debtor–creditor relationship can develop. Our sample includes the expected credit card issuers and banks. In addition, there are other professional lenders in various incarnations. There are private mortgage companies and savings and loans, both engaged almost exclusively in lending to consumers for home mortgages at the time this sample was drawn. There are gasoline companies and stores, extending credit for the purchase of their goods and services. There are finance companies and credit unions, making a variety of loans from car loans to debt consolidation loans. And there are car finance companies, such as GMAC and Chrysler Credit, which finance the purchase of cars from their affiliated dealerships.

Others besides the typical professional lenders found themselves listed as creditors in someone's bankruptcy. There is a scattering of brothers-in-law and co-workers, individuals who made loans that went sour. There are debts owed to doctors, utility companies, and landlords. Educational loans and unpaid taxes are listed. There are also children and former spouses who are owed money, usually because alimony and support orders have not been met. Victims of civil wrongs—car accidents, malpractice, assaults—got judgments against debtors who ended up in bankruptcy. And there are the "others"—a potpourri of creditors who do not fit any of the earlier classifications, such as customers who left deposits with self-employed debtors.[1] In short, creditors represent the spectrum of people and companies who might have engaged in some credit relationship.

These creditor groups are listed in Table 14.1, along with the amount of money owed to each group and an indication of whether it is owed on a secured or unsecured basis. As a first dip into the creditors' data, the table simply shows who was listed in bankruptcy. In the subsequent chapters, we analyze the positions of these various creditor groups in greater detail to understand more about their losses and how they came to be listed in bankruptcy. In particular, we focus on how a creditor might be listed in bankruptcy but receive partial or even full payments, so that listings and losses are not identical.

The next three chapters examine three different creditor groups that encompass nearly all the creditors listed in our sample. Chapter Fifteen focuses on the creditors making commercial loans to small businesses. When a small business goes belly up with the owner–manager personally liable for overwhelming debts, the creditors find themselves listed in individual as well as business or corporate bankruptcies. The second group of creditors, examined in Chapter Sixteen, are the reluctant creditors—everyone from the car accident victim who never planned for a credit relationship with the guy who ran the stop sign, to landlords who try to collect the rent a month in advance, but who could not get the nonpaying tenant out quickly enough to avoid having a claim for back rent. Because of the difficulty these creditors may have in limiting their risks in a credit relationship, they raise particularly thorny problems in bankruptcy policy. Finally, in Chapter Seventeen we discuss the con-

TABLE 14.1. Amounts of Debt Owed to Creditors, by Secured and Unsecured Status, for Total Sample, Pure Wage Earners and Ever Self-Employed[a]

Creditor	Total[b]	Secured[c]	Unsecured[c]
All Petitioners			
Stores	$ 8,322,629	—	$ 8,322,629
Credit cards	1,210,371	—	1,210,371
Gas credit	570,181	—	570,181
Banks	13,924,733	$ 9,928,097	3,996,636
Credit unions	1,508,351	843,680	664,671
Finance co.–car	1,898,153	1,898,153	—
Finance co.–general	5,829,534	3,814,813	2,014,721
Private mortgage	5,737,597	5,737,597	—
Savings and loan	6,401,438	6,401,438	—
Medical	1,365,373	—	1,365,373
Utility	366,407	—	366,407
Government (nontax)	190,816	—	190,816
Tort debt	488,348	—	488,348
Back rent	289,780	—	289,780
Taxes	1,306,927	—	1,306,927
Family debt	76,800	—	76,800
Education loans	244,616	—	244,616
Private lenders	2,035,685	—	2,035,685
Other secured	4,153,615	4,153,615	—
No information[d]	123,170	123,170	—
Residual[e]	1,699,824	1,699,824	—
Total	$57,744,348	$34,600,387	$23,143,961
Pure Wage Earners			
Stores	$ 3,009,005	—	$ 3,009,005
Credit cards	930,769	—	930,769
Gas credit	467,531	—	467,531
Banks	6,346,056	$ 4,507,805	1,838,251
Credit unions	1,147,785	617,233	583,552
Finance co.–car	1,503,686	1,503,686	—
Finance co.–general	3,847,421	2,411,214	1,436,207
Private mortgage	4,830,328	4,830,328	—
Savings and loan	3,944,041	3,944,041	—
Medical	1,092,054	—	1,092,054
Utility	223,584	—	223,584
Government (nontax)	158,770	—	158,770
Tort debt	482,847	—	482,847
Back rent	69,508	—	69,508
Taxes	343,203	—	343,203
Family debt	63,474	—	63,474
Education loans	217,455	—	217,455
Private lenders	869,381	—	869,381
Other secured	1,741,431	1,741,431	—
No information[d]	89,670	89,670	—
Residual[e]	619,054	619,054	—
Total	$31,997,053	$20,264,462	$11,732,591

TABLE 14.1 (*Continued*)

Creditor	Total[b]	Secured[c]	Unsecured[c]
Ever Self-Employed			
Stores	$ 5,313,624	—	$ 5,313,624
Credit cards	279,602	—	279,602
Gas credit	102,650	—	102,650
Banks	7,578,677	$ 5,420,292	2,158,385
Credit unions	360,566	226,447	134,119
Finance co.–car	394,467	394,467	—
Finance co.–general	1,982,113	1,403,599	578,514
Private mortgage	907,269	907,269	—
Savings and loan	2,457,397	2,457,397	—
Medical	273,319	—	273,319
Utility	142,823	—	142,823
Government (nontax)	32,046	—	32,046
Tort debt	5,501	—	5,501
Back rent	220,272	—	220,272
Taxes	963,724	—	963,724
Family debt	13,326	—	13,326
Education loans	27,161	—	27,161
Private lenders	1,166,304	—	1,166,304
Other secured	2,412,184	2,412,184	—
No information[d]	33,500	33,500	—
Residual[e]	1,080,770	1,080,770	—
Total	$25,747,295	$14,335,925	$11,411,370

[a]Cases with extreme values on assets, total debt, or income excluded.

[b]This is the total debt scheduled in the petition. This total does not reflect any efforts at repayment and is not corrected for cases that were dismissed.

[c]As listed on the petition.

[d]Secured debt where creditor is listed but not classifiable.

[e]Unallocatable secured debt.

Source: Consumer Bankruptcy Project.

sumer credit industry, creditors who are lending to everyone and are listed in everyone's bankruptcy. We describe the industry's potential bankruptcy losses and how they might be reduced. We also discuss some clues these data give about how the consumer credit system operates generally.

A Little More Law and a Few More Numbers

Once again we digress for a brief discussion of the legal details of the bankruptcy system, this time as they affect the creditors. And once again, we offer the same caveats: bankruptcy specialist readers can skip this section; we have simplified some of the details; and this is not a do-it-yourself guide for creditors. We try here to summarize the provisions of the Bankruptcy Code that have the most powerful impact on a creditor's ultimate position.

The central concept for the treatment of creditors in American bankruptcy law—indeed in bankruptcy laws all over the world—is equality. Once the trustee in bankruptcy has sold all the debtor's property in excess of exemptions or has collected the debtor's Chapter 13 payments, all creditors should be paid on a pro rata basis, with every creditor receiving an equal proportion of its outstanding debt (the proverbial ten cents on the dollar). But that principle has been subject to many exceptions. There are three main devices by which some creditors do better than others in bankruptcy: liens, objections to discharge, and priority payments.

Liens

When a creditor asks a debtor not only to promise to repay, but to pledge some item of collateral that the creditor can seize to satisfy the loan if the debtor cannot pay, the creditor has taken a lien. Liens are often referred to as mortgages (with real property) or security interests (with personal property). Home mortgages and car loans are among the most typical liens, and people frequently buy home appliances or furniture with the agreement that if the debtor quits paying, the seller can come back for the goods. Bankruptcy law fully protects these security interests.[2] With court approval, secured creditors can repossess and sell the collateral to pay the debt owed to them. Oftentimes, the mere threat of repossession is enough to persuade the debtor to pay voluntarily, notwithstanding bankruptcy. In Chapter 7 or in Chapter 13, the debtor faces the same choice: pay off the lien or surrender the collateral.[3]

A security interest in effect sets aside certain property for a specific creditor. The property is usually referred to as collateral. If a debtor owns a home, for example, with a $38,000 mortgage that is sold at auction for $40,000, the secured creditor takes the entire $38,000 before anyone else gets anything from the sale of the home. Neither the debtor nor the other creditors can reach anything other than the $2,000 left over after the sale. The unsecured creditors may get other protections, but the security interest has first priority on the collateral.

Security interests sharply reduce a creditor's risk of nonpayment in or out of bankruptcy. One reason we distinguish secured from unsecured in Table 14.1 is to give a preliminary idea of the differential exposure to nonpayment, an idea developed further in Chapter Seventeen. Security interests are almost always obtained by written agreement at the time of the credit sale or loan and therefore primarily benefit the most sophisticated professional creditors, who are able to evaluate in advance the need for credit protection.[4]

Objection to Discharge

Some creditors' claims survive bankruptcy without being discharged; these creditors are able to continue any collection actions following the bankruptcy that they might have pursued before bankruptcy. A creditor can avoid discharge in one of two ways: (1) the debtor forfeits discharge completely and no debt is discharged or (2) the creditor enjoys a special status that insulates its debt from the discharge of all the other debts. Debtors lose their discharge altogether if they engage in certain nefarious conduct, such as failing to produce records to explain their losses, lying to the bankruptcy court, or secreting assets.[5] There is a long list of debtor misdeeds that may make a debt nondischargeable. They include lying to the creditor to obtain the loan, intentionally injuring someone, or causing an accident while drunk.[6] Moreover, educational loans are not dischargeable in Chapter 7.[7]

A restriction on discharge will help the creditor only if the debtor is in Chapter 7. Nearly all debts can be discharged in Chapter 13. Only alimony and child support and unpaid taxes will survive in both Chapter 7 and Chapter 13.[8] All other debts are discharged in Chapter 13—even liability for intentionally injuring someone else.

To claim a discharge exception, the creditor usually must request a specific court order declaring the debt nondischargeable. For example, if a creditor was defrauded by a debtor, the creditor must file papers in court requesting that the debt be declared nondischargeable. If the creditor fails to do so, the debt is discharged. If the creditor is an ex-spouse or a child who is owed support, the debt is automatically nondischargeable and the court will rarely require any further evidence from the ex-spouse or the child.[9] In all other cases, if the debtor disputes the creditors' request, a trial is held to resolve the dispute. The system generally requires active participation by the creditor to take advantage of special creditor protections.

Even these brief summaries show that any creditor except an ex-spouse or a child needs a working knowledge of the bankruptcy process to gain much from the nondischargeability provisions of the Bankruptcy Code. Moreover, Chapter 13 has a broader discharge than Chapter 7. If the debtor files in Chapter 13, the special creditor provisions will mean nothing for any creditor except an ex-spouse, a child, or the taxing authority. Finally, nondischargeability does not guarantee that the debtor will have any assets the creditor can reach. It guarantees only that the creditor can keep trying, notwithstanding the bankruptcy.

Priority Payment

A third special protection that the Bankruptcy Code gives selected creditors is a demand for the first payments from whatever the debtor is able to pay to unsecured creditors. These creditors receive priority payment, permitting them to collect all their debts from the bankrupt debtor before the other unsecured creditors receive anything.

In consumer bankruptcy, the crucial priority claimant is the taxing authority.[10] The same taxes that are not dischargeable are also given a priority in payment.[11] This has a powerful impact on the remaining creditors. If a debtor had $10,000 in debt and $1,000 to pay his creditors in bankruptcy, each creditor would ordinarily get 10% of its claim. But if one creditor is a taxing authority owed $1,000, the taxing authority takes all the money, and the other creditors get nothing.

In Chapter 13, the priority claimants also receive special treatment. They must be paid in full, unlike the nonpriority, unsecured creditors who may receive only a small proportion of their claims over the life of a payment plan. Thus the taxing authorities listed in Chapter 13 also get 100% payments. In a Chapter 7, if there are no assets to be distributed, priority payment is of no use. But if there are assets, favored creditors will be paid while others may be left empty-handed.

Reaffirmation

In addition to the advantages imposed by law, creditors listed in bankruptcy can ask for another boost from their debtors: reaffirmation of a debt. A debtor reaffirms by signing a paper agreeing to pay the debt notwithstanding bankruptcy.

Before the 1978 Code, so many creditors received reaffirmations that debtors lost much of the benefit of the discharge and fresh start. In the new Code, Congress required the Bankruptcy Court to approve all reaffirmations before they became binding, in effect to make certain the debtor was well advised to agree to repayment. Creditors complained bitterly about being denied access to an inexpensive means of avoiding the effects of a discharge. In response Congress provided in the 1984 amendments that reaffirmations would be effective if the debtor's attorney, rather than the bankruptcy judge, ascertained that it was in the debtor's best interest.

The special attraction of reaffirmation agreements is that any creditor can get one—if the debtor agrees. If the creditor asks and the debtor agrees, the creditor will not face discharge of its debt.

In practice, reaffirmations go to sophisticated creditors with the means to contact the debtor before the final discharge.[12] As with nondischargeability, reaffirmation does not mean the debtor will have the money to repay—only that the creditor can continue to seek repayment after the bankruptcy.

Policy Implications

Bankruptcy begins with a straightforward principle: All creditors are to be treated alike. A series of exceptions have been grafted onto the general principle. In bankruptcy, the effect of these preferences is mixed. Some creditors receive special assistance; others receive help if they know enough to ask for it. Creditors knowledgeable enough to ask for security interests when the loan is extended and aggressive enough to ask for reaffirmations when the debtor declares bankruptcy improve their positions. One creditor's improvement is always at the cost of the other creditors or of the debtor.

Although exceptions to the general principle of "equality of creditors" have long existed, the law has been erratic and rather unprincipled in selecting the beneficiaries of special treatment and in fashioning the nature of that special treatment. In part this history may reflect Congress's lack of hard information about the actual involvement of different types of creditors in consumer bankruptcy and about the effects of reforms on particular creditors. The data that follow represent a start in providing policymakers with the information needed to make intelligent decisions.

Our basic theme remains the same: Bankruptcy reform requires hard information about the players. Without it, policymaking is little more than reading tea leaves, responding to political pressures, and acting out unexamined prejudices. We do not pretend that the data in this section tell all. But they reshape some of the questions to be asked. They also give some insight into the workings of the consumer credit system that a focus on debtors alone will never yield.

Notes

1. Included within the classification of "other" secured and unsecured creditors are those for whom too little information is given to determine the creditor group to which they should be assigned. The largest single group in the category "other" consists of stores that have sold on credit, and taken a security in the goods sold. We did not separately identify any priority creditors except taxing authorities, but some of the self-employed listed employees as priority creditors who were owed wages.

2. One exception arises with some regularity in consumer cases. Security interests taken by a creditor on household goods that the debtor already owned can be set aside in bankruptcy. The typical example occurs when a debtor borrows cash from a bank or finance company and the lender insists on a security interest on all the debtor's furniture and other household goods. These security interests can generally be negated in bankruptcy. Attorneys were often confused on this point, however. Some listed such debts as "secured" and others as "unsecured."

3. The value of the security interest may be downgraded if the collateral is worth less than the outstanding loan, so the debtor must pay only the value of the collateral rather than the higher loan balance in order to own the collateral free and clear. The Chapter 13 debtor has a chance to pay over time, while the Chapter 7 debtor may face more restrictions in making installment payments if the creditor is uncooperative.

4. Reluctant creditors, especially taxing authorities, can get involuntary liens imposed by law by going to court once the debtor is in default. We found few of them. We discuss creditor collection efforts in Chapter Seventeen.

5. 11 U.S.C. §727. The exceptions to discharge are more elaborate and detailed, but the text conveys the general idea.

6. 11 U.S.C. §523. Again, the exceptions are more elaborate, and this time more diverse. Alimony and child support obligations are not discharged. Most tax debts cannot be discharged. Fines and penalties imposed for illegal activities and unscheduled debts are also not discharged.

7. 11 U.S.C. §523(a)(8).

8. 11 U.S.C. §§523 (a)(5), 1328(a)(2). To change the obligations of parents or spouses, the party in trouble must go back to family court for a reduction in the obligations. Tax debts, in effect, also are nondischargeable in Chapter 13, because debtors must promise to pay them in full or the Chapter 13 plan cannot be confirmed. 11 U.S.C. §1322(a)(2).

9. Even here, there is a complication. Sometimes a debtor's obligation is not clearly identifiable as support, for example, when a husband agrees to make a cash payment as part of the divorce settlement. The payment could be a property settlement or a support arrangement, depending on the parties' circumstances. In such a case, the creditor-spouse may have to go to court and argue the case explaining why the obligation should be deemed support and not discharged.

10. There are other priority creditors, such as employees, grain farmers, fishermen, and people who gave the debtor a deposit (for example, a tenant whose landlord goes into bankruptcy has priority for return of a security deposit). However, all these priorities are limited in amount and seldom come up in wage-earner cases.

11. In Chapter 7, this arrangement is actually helpful to debtors, because it means that any available assets will be used first to pay the nondischargeable tax debts the debtor would still have to pay if they were not paid in bankruptcy.

12. Most creditors who get reaffirmations ask for them when the debtor shows up for the section 341 hearing. Often the activity out in the halls is much more lively (and will determine more of the debtor's ultimate financial position) than what goes on in the hearing. Here the creditors' attorneys who ask may get their reaffirmations.

15

Commercial Lending

In Part I of this book, we frequently segregated the wage-earner debtors from their self-employed counterparts to give a more accurate description of debtors in bankruptcy. Similarly, in Part II we must separate commercial lending from consumer lending to develop an accurate picture of the creditors. All the loans covered in our data base were made to individual human beings, not corporations or limited liability partnerships. Our data nevertheless show that a substantial amount of lending to individuals is commercial lending, which differs in some important respects from consumer lending. These findings highlight the diversity within the creditor community and give an insight into some creditor lending decisions.

This chapter necessarily overlaps our analysis of bankrupt entrepreneurs in Chapter Six. Here, however, the focus is not on the entrepreneurs who ventured their fortunes on small businesses that failed, but on the creditors who traveled with them, lending and sometimes losing large sums of money.

Commercial Credit and Consumer Credit

Individuals who are in business for themselves incur both business and consumer debt. Because some creditors extend both consumer and commercial credit, we cannot separate the entrepreneurs' debt into its commercial and consumer components. However, the figures enable us to draw inferences about which creditors have extended commercial credit to the entrepreneurs and which have limited themselves to consumer credit.

Table 15.1 shows mean debts by category for the present and former entrepreneurs and for the pure wage earners in our sample. The categories are self-explanatory, except for the miscellaneous "other secured," which includes a hodgepodge of secured debt, most of it owed to retailers and wholesalers.[1] "Other reluctant debt" refers to unsecured creditors such as tort claimants and medical providers who might not have extended credit voluntarily. Reluctant debt is discussed in more detail in Chapter Sixteen.

The mean debt for entrepreneurs is over $82,100, more than three times larger than that for wage earners, which is $26,200. Entrepreneurs had significantly higher mean debt in all but five categories. The asterisks in the last column indicate when difference between the debts for entrepreneurs and wage earners is statistically significant.

Table 15.1 shows the average impact for each debtor. The data have been rearranged in Table 15.2 to show how the creditors' losses are distributed. Table 15.2 shows the total debt scheduled in each category and the proportion of debt scheduled by entrepreneurs and wage earners. Because entrepreneurs are 20% of the bankruptcy sample, any percentage in column 2 that is larger than 20% represents a disproportionate amount of credit extended to entrepreneurs by that category of creditor. The last entry in column 2 shows that more than 40% of the total credit from these categories was extended to entrepreneurs.

The creditors can be divided roughly into three categories: (1) those who are heavy commercial lenders; (2) those who do some commercial lending; and (3) those who do virtually no commercial lending. Listed first in Tables 15.1 and 15.2 are four types of creditors that made extensive commercial loans: stores, banks, finance companies, and savings associations. Entrepreneurs listed more than half of all the debt owed to banks and over 60% of the debt owed to stores, including wholesale suppliers. While finance companies and savings associations were less heavily involved in commercial lending, a disproportionate one-third of their credit was given to the entrepreneurs.

At the opposite end of the spectrum, three types of industry creditors apparently extended virtually no credit on a commercial basis. Gasoline companies, all-purpose credit card issuers, and automobile finance companies all gave credit to entrepreneurs proportionate to their numbers in the sample. The mean amounts lent by these creditors to each debtor were also about the same for wage earners and entrepreneurs. These two facts combine to suggest that these creditors extended little or no specifically commercial credit to the debtors in our sample. One could imagine that gasoline companies, for example, might give much more credit to a small business with several cars or trucks requiring large amounts of fuel—but they did not. They apparently treated self-employed individuals like all other consumers, with similar credit limits for all their customers.

Between the two extremes were other creditor types that apparently did some commercial lending, but not very much. Credit unions lent significantly larger mean amounts to entrepreneurs than to consumers, strongly suggesting some commercial lending, but their overall percentage of entrepreneurial credit was roughly proportional to the number of entrepreneurial cases. Their low level of commercial activity is reflected in the number of borrowers in-

TABLE 15.1. Mean Amounts of Debt Owed for Ever Self-Employed and Pure Wage-Earner Debtors by Type of Lender and Secured Status (*N* in parentheses)[a]

Type of Lender	Secured	Unsecured	Total[b]
Ever Self-Employed			
Stores	NA	$19,535 (272)	$19,535** (272)
Banks	$30,623 (177)	14,294 (151)	32,388** (234)
Finance companies–general	15,596 (90)	5,728 (101)	12,871** (154)
Savings and loans	37,233 (66)	NA	37,233** (66)
Gasoline companies	NA	1,252 (82)	1,252 (82)
All-purpose credit cards	NA	2,237 (125)	2,237 (125)
Finance companies–car	5,479 (72)	NA	5,479 (72)
Credit unions	11,918 (19)	5,365 (25)	9,745* (37)
Private mortgage companies	33,603 (27)	NA	33,603 (27)
Other secured	21,537 (112)	NA	21,537** (112)
Individual lenders	NA	11,003 (106)	11,003* (106)
Utilities	NA	1,190 (120)	1,190** (120)
Taxes	NA	7,192 (134)	7,192** (134)
Other "reluctant" debt[c]	NA	3,382 (169)	3,382 (169)
Total	49,705 (266)	38,683 (295)	82,110** (300)
Pure Wage Earners			
Stores	NA	$ 2,934 (1,026)	$ 2,933** (1,026)
Banks	$10,557 (427)	4,022 (457)	8,863** (716)
Finance companies–general	5,621 (429)	2,438 (589)	4,768** (807)
Savings and loans	$24,650 (160)	NA	$24,650** (160)
Gasoline companies	NA	1,664 (281)	1,664 (281)
All-purpose credit cards	NA	2,010 (463)	2,010 (463)
Finance companies–car	5,080 (296)	NA	5,080 (296)
Credit unions	4,143 (149)	2,358 (225)	3,499* (328)

TABLE 15.1 (*Continued*)

Type of Lender	Secured	Unsecured	Total[b]
Private mortgage companies	22,467 (215)	NA	22,467 (215)
Other secured	4,547 (383)	NA	4,547** (383)
Individual lenders	NA	4,996 (174)	4,996* (174)
Utilities	NA	572 (391)	572** (391)
Taxes	NA	1,407 (244)	1,407** (244)
Other "reluctant" debt[c]	NA	2,969 (702)	2,969 (702)
Total	19,042 (1,027)	9,960 (1,178)	26,183** (1,195)

[a]Cases with extreme values on assets, total debt, or income excluded.

[b]*T*-tests refer to differences in means between wage earners and self-employed.

[c]Reluctant debt is discussed in detail in Chapter Sixteen.

*$p \leq 0.05$

**$p \leq 0.01$

Source: Consumer Bankruptcy Project.

volved. Credit unions lent to only 37 entrepreneurs, whereas banks lent money to 234 of the 300 entrepreneurs.

Differences in the Lending Decision

The different lending patterns for these creditors reflect different approaches to credit extension. Consumer lending is generally made for consumption, and it is granted on the assumption that repayment will be made from unrelated income. Consumer lending involves relatively smaller amounts in each extension of credit and relatively greater numbers of debtors. A creditor lending to 10,000 people to purchase goods or services for consumption uses a few fairly simple tests to predict likelihood of repayment. The creditor cannot be sure which debtors will pay and which will not, but over several thousand loans the creditor can predict with some accuracy the proportion of debtors who will default, and, among that proportion, how many will eventually pay and how many debts will have to be written off. The risk can be mathematically modeled, much as insurance company actuaries model the probabilities of death or disability.

Commercial credit differs from consumer credit in its basic premise. Com-

TABLE 15.2. Proportion of Debt Owed by Self-Employed and Wage-Earner Debtors by Type of Lender and Secured Status (dollar totals in parentheses)[a]

Type of Lender	Total		Ever Self-Employed[b]			Wage Earners[b]		
			Total	Secured	Unsecured	Total	Secured	Unsecured
Stores	100.0%	($8,322,629)	63.8%	—	63.8%	36.2%	—	36.2%
Banks	100.0	(13,925,093)	54.4	38.9%	15.5	45.6	32.4%	13.2
Finance companies–general	100.0	(5,829,534)	34.0	24.1	9.9	66.0	41.4	24.6
Savings and loans	100.0	(6,401,438)	38.4	38.4	—	61.6	61.6	—
Gasoline companies	100.0	(570,181)	18.0	—	18.0	82.0	—	82.0
All-purpose credit cards	100.0	(1,210,371)	23.1	—	23.1	76.9	—	76.9
Finance companies–car	100.0	(1,898,153)	20.8	20.8	—	79.2	79.2	—
Credit unions	100.0	(1,508,351)	23.9	15.0	8.9	76.1	40.9	35.2
Private mortgage companies	100.0	(5,737,601)	15.8	15.8	—	84.2	84.2	—
Other secured	100.0	(4,153,255)	58.1	58.1	—	41.9	41.9	—
Individual lenders	100.0	(2,035,685)	57.3	—	57.3	42.7	—	42.7
Taxes	100.0	(1,306,927)	73.7	—	73.7	26.3	—	26.3
Utilities	100.0	(366,407)	39.0	—	39.0	61.0	—	61.0
Other "reluctant" debt[d]	100.0	(2,655,733)	21.5	—	21.5	78.5	—	78.5
Total	100.0	(55,921,358)	44.0	23.6	20.4	56.0	35.0	21.0

[a]Cases with extreme values on assets, total debts, or income excluded.

[b]Current and formerly self-employed. This group is 20% of the sample (N = 300).

[c]Current wage earners with no indication of self-employment. This group is 80% of the sample (N = 1195).

[d]Reluctant debt is discussed in detail in Chapter Sixteen.

Source: Consumer Bankruptcy Project.

mercial loans are granted to assist the production of income, and their repayment depends on the success of the business.

Commercial lenders do not fall into sizable entrepreneurial loans. They make cautious decisions about the condition of the small business, its prospects for success, and the lender's exposure if the company fails. The term "exposure" means exposure to risk of loss. It is used in two ways—to refer to the total amount lent and to that portion of the loan that is going to be difficult or impossible to collect—so that the total exposure on a $50,000 loan secured by $40,000 in collateral is $50,000, while the exposure to likely write-off is $10,000.

Before granting credit, a bank or wholesaler will usually have several meetings with the applicant debtor. At these meetings, the lender assesses the debtor's personal reliability. They discuss anything that may affect the business's success, including marketing strategies, balance sheets, the general health of the industry, prospects for expansion, and the talent of key employees. Commercial lenders take the time to make individualized lending decisions, and they are usually in a position to demand as much information as they want.[2]

For banks and other commercial lenders, small businesses are worth the trouble, because they represent several possible sources of profit for the bank. In some cases, the interest rate on a business loan may exceed the legal limits the lender can charge consumers. If the small business succeeds, the bank not only can expect to see its current loan repaid, but it can look forward to years of substantial banking activity with the business. A bank that lends to an entrepreneur expects to have the business's checking account, to process the business's payroll, and to meet the business's needs for letters of credit and other special business services. Employees are often attracted to the bank to cash their paychecks, and the possibility of arrangements for checking accounts, car loans, home equity loans, and other consumer lending often follow growing business accounts. Most of all, as the bank comes to know the business customer and to see its growing strength, the bank anticipates many more years of profitable loan activity. One way for a bank to grow is to cultivate business customers that grow and that keep their business with the bank.

Trade creditors, who are wholesalers and other suppliers, may not be able to spend as much time on investigation, but they often do equivalent checking, relying on their information about the industry in which they do business. Trade creditors learn about reputation in the community, and they often insist on cash in advance until a business relationship has been established. This minimizes their exposure until they have more confidence in the business.

Trade creditors make lending decisions to further their sales. For most suppliers, small businesses are important customers, and most businesses will use the suppliers that extend credit. Making good guesses about the credit worthiness and likely success of a small business may be the key to a wholesaler's success. Those who are too optimistic get burned when businesses collapse, and those who are too conservative lose sales to more aggressive competitors.

High Risk in Commercial Lending

The care with which commercial loans are made reflects the greater amount of money that is usually at stake in these loans and the greater risk they will not be repaid if a business folds. The heightened risk in entrepreneurial loans is illustrated by data collected by Dun & Bradstreet. In 1981, of each 10,000 listed businesses throughout the country, 61 failed—the highest rate in 20 years.[3] When the businesses were grouped by the amount of money owed, failures among very large (liability over $1 million) and very small (liability under $5,000) companies were a small proportion of the total; businesses with liabilities between these figures accounted for 94% of the failures. Newer businesses accounted for a larger proportion of the losses than older businesses.

The risk of failure is compounded by the relatively higher exposure per debtor for commercial loans. The data in Table 15.1 show what one would expect: larger mean loans to entrepreneurs than to wage earners. Banks, for example, lend on average three times more to each entrepreneur than to a wage-earner debtor. If an entrepreneur collapses, commercial lenders are likely to suffer greater losses than consumer lenders suffer when a wage earner fails.

Collateral and Reducing the Risk

To cope with the higher risk of failure and the larger loan values, lenders might insist on more security for their commercial loans. Conventionally, people think of small business credit, especially loans, as being secured by equipment, inventory, or accounts receivable. The figures in our sample paint a different picture.

The lenders who make both commercial and consumer loans lend on a secured basis in about the same proportion for both kinds of loans. For example, about 71% of bank loans to consumers are secured, about the same proportion as their loans to entrepreneurs. Finance companies make a larger percentage of their entrepreneurs' loans secured, but the difference is relatively small (63% secured for consumers, 70% secured for entrepreneurs). Lenders who make both secured and unsecured loans do not seem to require considerably more security for their higher risk entrepreneurial loans.[4]

These figures reflect only the nominally secured status of consumer and commercial loans. When loans are made on a secured basis, the degree of security depends on the value of the collateral. The entrepreneurial loans in our sample are much more undersecured than are loans to wage earners. A loan for $10,000 secured by a car worth only $1,000 is technically secured, but the $9,000 undersecurity represents very real risk that the creditor will never recover in full.[5] Table 15.3 shows the exposure of secured loans to entrepreneurs and wage earners. Entrepreneurial loans have almost twice the undersecurity of consumer loans. Of the total amount of commercial loans listed as secured, one-fifth is, in fact, unsecured because the collateral is worth that much less than the loans. The comparable undersecurity among the wage earners is about half as great at 11%.

Banks are by far the most undersecured lenders to entrepreneurs in our sample, and they are much more undersecured in their commercial lending than they are in their consumer lending to our pure wage earners. Over 30% of the dollar amounts lent by banks to entrepreneurs on a purportedly secured basis are in fact unsecured. By contrast, only 16% of the money owed to banks by wage earners on nominally secured loans is actually unsecured. Once again, loans to entrepreneurs were about twice as unsecured as loans to wage earners.

When this greater "false security" is taken into account, commercial secured lending suffers even more by comparison with consumer lending. Adjusting for the amounts that appear secured but are actually unsecured, half of the commercial lending is really unsecured (52%), compared with 43% unsecured lending on the consumer side.

This sort of information has not been previously reported and, remarkable as it seems, comparable data for commercial and consumer lending to the general population are not available.

Policy Implications

Although we can make only a limited foray into commercial lending in a book devoted to consumer credit, this brief look at lending to entrepreneurs reveals two points that should interest policymakers. The first is that there is a great need for more information about commercial credit for small business.

Small businesses are an enormously important part of the American economy, and as this study has shown, an important part of bankruptcy losses. Yet there are remarkably few data, in or out of bankruptcy, about lending to individual entrepreneurs. Furthermore, our data strongly suggest that one of the most commonplace assumptions about small-business lending—that it is almost entirely secured—is wrong. Commercial debt in our sample is actually less secured than consumer debt and therefore more likely to be discharged and written off. If this crucial piece of conventional wisdom is off the mark, it is likely that a good deal more of what we think we know about entrepreneurial finance is equally wrong. It follows that many programs designed to foster small business may be seriously flawed because they rest on false premises. Policymakers should demand more hard information about small businesses and, until they get it, should listen to new proposals with skepticism.

The larger point, applicable to both commercial and consumer credit, is somewhat simplistic, but easy to overlook: Reducing losses is desirable only if the loss reduction exceeds the foregone profits from making fewer loans. The loans to the entrepreneurs in our sample were high risk and seriously undersecured, but apparently small-business loans are so profitable that they are worth the increased risk. The lenders who took the heaviest commercial

TABLE 15.3. Mean and Total Values of Secured Claims and Unsecurity, Ever Self-Employed and Wage-Earners, by Type of Lender[a,b]

	Mean Claim Values					
	All Claims		Secured Claims		Exposed Claims[c]	
Type of Lender	Mean	N	Mean	N	Mean	N
Ever Self-Employed						
Bank	$16,751	235	$12,515	214	$10,399	121
Savings and loan	30,654	68	30,761	66	13,574	4
Credit union	5,506	20	4,819	20	1,250	11
Finance co.–car	4,724	67	3,613	64	1,777	48
Finance co.–general	11,463	98	10,536	89	4,319	43
Private mortgage	28,213	29	24,605	27	51,282	3
Other	2,234	122	10,648	116	4,855	53
Unknown	11,167	3	10,867	3	900	1
Total	15,444	642	13,198	599	7,075	284
Wage Earners						
Bank	$ 7,764	465	$ 6,795	445	$ 2,766	212
Savings and loan	21,210	156	21,269	153	3,205	17
Credit union	3,646	141	2,961	140	1,310	76
Finance co.–car	4,745	275	3,460	269	2,241	167
Finance co.–general	4,763	420	4,260	367	1,720	254
Private mortgage	20,591	220	20,297	217	6,618	19
Other	3,287	433	3,004	400	931	238
Unknown	5,588	11	5,128	11	1,012	5
Total	7,899	2,121	7,417	2,002	1,927	988

[a]Cases with extreme values on assets, total debt, or income excluded.

[b]Figures based on all debts where both the claim and market value of the collateral are specified.

[c]"Exposed" claims are the portion of a nominally secured claim that exceeds the value of the collateral.

[d]As a percentage of the total claim value in each category.

Source: Consumer Bankruptcy Project.

losses in our sample may be the smartest lenders in the group—high risk for high profit.

The most knowledgeable lenders—those who take time to meet their debtors, gather reams of information, and carefully evaluate the likelihood of repayment—nonetheless engage in higher risk lending with lower protection than do the less informed, high-volume consumer lenders. These data warn that more information does not necessarily eliminate loan losses, nor does sophistication of the lender, ability to demand security, or individualized lending evaluations. Loan losses are part of a much larger balance of risk and return in which all lenders engage.

Policymakers confronted with tales of creditor woe need to distinguish the cautious creditor from the highroller, and the creditor unavoidably trapped in a bad debt relationship from the creditor who took high risk for high profit.

TABLE 15.3 (*Continued*)

	Claim Values—Total Dollars				
	All Claims	Secured Claims		Exposed Claims[c]	
Type of Lender	Total $	Total $	%[d]	Total $	%[d]
Ever Self-Employed					
Bank	$ 3,936,391	$ 2,678,117	68.0	$1,258,274	32.0%
Savings and loan	2,084,501	2,030,204	97.4	54,297	2.6
Credit union	110,119	96,374	87.5	13,745	12.5
Finance co.–car	316,500	231,219	73.1	85,281	26.9
Finance co.–general	1,123,396	937,691	83.5	185,705	16.5
Private mortgage	818,171	664,326	81.2	153,846	18.8
Other	1,492,531	1,235,198	82.8	257,333	17.2
Unknown	33,500	32,600	97.3	900	2.7
Total	9,915,109	7,905,729	79.7	2,009,380	20.3
Wage Earners					
Bank	$ 3,610,335	$ 3,023,955	83.8	$ 586,380	16.2%
Savings and loan	3,308,775	3,254,295	98.4	54,480	1.6
Credit union	514,138	414,605	80.6	98,533	19.4
Finance co.–car	1,304,998	930,769	71.3	374,229	28.7
Finance co.–general	2,000,357	1,563,395	78.2	436,962	21.8
Private mortgage	4,530,082	4,404,346	97.2	125,736	2.8
Other	1,423,360	1,201,794	84.4	221,566	15.6
Unknown	61,470	56,408	91.8	5,062	8.2
Total	16,753,515	14,849,567	88.8	1,903,948	11.4

These data bring another dimension to the bankruptcy rhetoric. They suggest that identifying bankruptcy loss is only part of the story. Without some idea of the creditors' risk-taking decisions, the impact of bankruptcy filings on creditors and the need for more creditor-protective bankruptcy laws remain unknown.

Notes

1. We do not have a detailed breakdown of this category, but a review of a sample of files suggests that as much as half of this debt is owed to "stores," retailers and wholesalers of goods (other than car dealers) who took security interests. The next largest category is secured tax liens. There are no other clearly defined categories representing substantial amounts of debt.

2. We recognize that there are counterexamples to our description of actuarially based consumer lending and individualized commercial lending. There are stories of consumer lenders who checked every detail of a debtor's loan application, including the debtor's last visit to the dentist. We also hear some hair-raising stories about go-go banks and other lenders who were willing to lend millions to a couple of guys with a drill bit and an old pickup. But consumer lenders can generally turn healthy profits by

lending on a few simple, objective indicators, actuarialized across thousands of debtors. On the other hand, a bank that is casual about inquiries precedent to commercial lending will soon find that the FDIC is its principal shareholder.

3. J. Duncan, The 1981 Dun & Bradstreet Business Failure Record 3 (New York: Dun & Bradstreet, 1983). The distribution of failures by liability size of the firm was:

Under $5,000	0.7%
$ 5,000–25,000	11.1
$ 25,000–100,000	37.2
$100,000–1,000,000	45.6
Over $1,000,000	5.4
Total	100.0

Businesses with fewer than five years in place accounted for 49.1% of the failures, and businesses with six to ten years experience accounted for another 30.7%.

4. Although we do not have a precise figure for "stores," we can be sure that they do not have high levels of security for either consumers or entrepreneurs. Secured debts to "stores," retailers and wholesalers, are contained within our category "other secured." Based upon direct examination of a sample of the cases, we estimate that about half of that category represents secured store debt. But even if *all* the "other secured" debt were owed to stores, only about one-third of the store debt of either entrepreneurs or consumers would be secured.

5. In the later chapter on credit industry lending to consumers, we discuss security and undersecurity in greater detail. The data here support an anecdotal point we made back in Chapter Seven. One key function of security in a business loan is to create an "incentive" for the debtor to succeed. We quoted a commercial lending officer explaining that his bank always took a security interest in the debtor's home to ensure the debtor would not walk away from the business. A high undersecurity rate suggests that some commercial loans may be secured more for their "incentive" value than for their repayment worth.

16

Reluctant Creditors

Creditors in consumer bankruptcy have been analyzed so seldom that we were initially unsure how to sort them for comparison. Yet when all consumer debts are listed together, as they are in Table 14.1, one major distinction becomes apparent: There are industry creditors who are in the credit extension business, and there is everyone else. Except for the individual lenders, who are a special and ambiguous case and who hold only a small part of the total bankruptcy debt,[1] nonindustry creditors have one thing in common: They are not in the credit business and they do not seek credit relationships. For that reason, we call them collectively the reluctant creditors.

Reluctant creditors include completely involuntary creditors (for example, the victims of automobile accidents, who never sought any relationship with the debtor), as well as creditors who are sometimes forced by circumstance or government regulation to extend credit (doctors and utilities, for example, who try to operate on a cash basis). Reluctant creditors generally do not expect to make a profit from extending credit, yet they may find it difficult or impossible to avoid the risk of nonpayment.

This distinction between voluntary and reluctant creditors has not been a feature of previous discussions about consumer bankruptcy. Nor does the law acknowledge it in any systematic fashion. In bankruptcy, as in state collection law, creditors are divided along formal legal lines: secured, priority, and unsecured. Sporadic policy discussions of special treatment for certain creditors focus almost exclusively on the sympathetic circumstances of a particular creditor, for example, the victim of a drunk driver or the hapless employee who handled dangerous chemicals for years only to find out they gave him cancer.[2] A general distinction between those who sought a credit relationship and those who did not has never been the basis for proposed changes in the collection scheme.

Although the reluctant–voluntary distinction has not been an overt part of debtor–creditor policy discussions, it has had an important influence on the shape of bankruptcy laws. We made the point early in our discussion of consumer debtors that an image of the consumer debtor—a working-class guy down on his luck or a well-to-do sharpie willing to play every angle—will shape the direction of bankruptcy laws in critical ways. Similarly, a view of the creditor—a faceless corporation with more money than sense or a victim of the debtor's reckless driving—has a potentially powerful impact on how bankruptcy laws develop. Looking at reluctant creditors and industry creditors in consumer lending is the corollary to looking at the occupations and incomes of the debtors, filling in the other side of the equation in understanding who is affected by the bankruptcy laws.

In this chapter we focus on those lenders who do not deliberately seek credit relationships. The reluctant creditors represent about 23% of the unsecured debt in our sample and about 8% of the total debt. We describe the wide-ranging circumstances of the reluctant creditors and discuss how changes in bankruptcy policy might affect them.

Different Creditors Meet at the Courthouse

We examine eight types of creditors in our "reluctant" category: (1) tort victims, such as people injured by the debtor in an automobile accident; (2) ex-spouses and children with unpaid support orders; (3) government agencies other than taxing authorities or educational lending agencies; (4) educational lending agencies; (5) health care providers; (6) tax authorities; (7) landlords; and (8) utilities. Some of these creditors are more sympathetic than others, but none is in the business of making a profit by extending credit and all are forced from time to time to accept credit risks that a commercial creditor might refuse.[3]

The total debt owed to each reluctant creditor is listed in Table 16.1. Because these debts rarely involve any negotiation about the credit relationship at the time they are incurred, they almost never involve voluntary security interests. In our sample, all the debt listed for these creditors is unsecured.[4]

Tort Victims

Some creditors in bankruptcy are not merely reluctant; they are completely involuntary creditors. The most obvious is the tort victim, typically someone who has suffered a personal injury at the hands of the now-bankrupt debtor. The injured party probably never knew the debtor before that awful moment at the intersection. Some personal injury claims, such as medical malpractice, begin with a voluntary relationship, but even then few people would think to demand the doctor's balance sheet before the surgery. If the other driver or the doctor goes into bankruptcy following the injury, the victim will face a risk of nonpayment or reduced payment without ever having agreed to undertake any credit risk.

TABLE 16.1. Distribution of Reluctant Debt and Total Reluctant Debt Owed to Creditors (wage earners only)[a]

Creditor	Mean (s.d.)	25th Percentile	Median	75th Percentile	Total Amount Owed	Amount Owed as % of Total	N (missing)
Torts	$15,089 (25,666)	1,850	4,050	16,613	482,847	18.2%	32 (1,170)
Family	4,232 (9,164)	500	1,100	3,000	63,474	2.4	15 (1,187)
State	3,608 (9,391)	345	769	2,000	158,770	6.0	44 (1,158)
Educational loans	2,788 (3,248)	908	1,613	3,433	217,445	8.2	78 (1,124)
Medical	1,728 (5,955)	233	606	1,501	1,092,054	41.2	632 (570)
Taxes	1,407 (3,383)	193	457	1,299	343,203	12.9	244 (958)
Rent	979 (1,689)	250	521	1,096	69,508	2.6	71 (1,131)
Utilities	572 (663)	198	375	666	223,584	8.4	391 (811)
Total	3,044 (8,419)	420	1,126	2,696	2,650,895	100.0	871 (331)

[a]Cases with extreme values on assets, total debt, or income excluded.

Source: Consumer Bankruptcy Project.

The gravity of the situation facing tort victims is made clearer by the amount of money they have at stake in bankruptcy cases. As Table 16.1 illustrates, tort victims are owed the highest per-debtor amount listed among reluctant creditors. The mean tort debt is $15,100, about five times higher than the mean reluctant debt. The number of tort creditors is small—only 33 creditors in the whole sample—but together they are owed more than 18% of all the reluctant debt listed in bankruptcy.

Family Creditors

Another bankruptcy creditor who did not deliberately initiate a debtor–creditor relationship is the recipient of a support obligation imposed by law on a parent or a former spouse. No doubt some brides and grooms make well-considered financial evaluations before going to the altar, but prenuptial planning for postdivorce bankruptcy is rather more than can be expected of most of us. It is even more rare for a parent and child to think of their relationship as debtor and creditor. Even when a couple is in the midst of divorce and financial considerations seem to dominate every discussion, few participants in the drama fully appreciate that a debtor–creditor relationship is being created by a property settlement, an alimony award, or a child support order. The law imposes support obligations on a relationship that was not founded on a debtor–creditor basis.

The amount of family debt (alimony and child support) listed in our sample is suspiciously low. Only 16 of 1202 wage earners list any outstanding support obligations. The amount per debtor is substantial, $4,200, but it represents only 2% of the total reluctant debt.

The pervasive presence of divorce and separation in our files makes it difficult to believe that such a small proportion of the debtors owe any family debt. We suspect that the numbers are markedly understated because these debts cannot, by law, be discharged. With no discharge in sight, many lawyers may see little reason to list these obligations—although the bankruptcy forms clearly require them.

Health Care Providers

There are many opinions about whether doctors and hospitals should insist on payment in advance of service, and everyone has a horror story about a family member bleeding while an officious hospital clerk insists that forms be filled out in triplicate before any assistance is rendered. But even health care providers who are not so aggressive would like to avoid a credit relationship with anyone except a government agency or an insurance company. Laws requiring emergency and indigent care, ethical considerations, and simple compassion often result in credit exposure based on the pressing need for medical attention rather than on a considered view of the creditworthiness of the patient. Although we recognize their differing policies and circumstances, medical care providers listed in bankruptcy nonetheless seem to fall within the general category of reluctant creditors.

Many more debtors go into bankruptcy owing medical debt than any other kind of reluctant debt. More than half of the wage-earner debtors—55%—owed some medical debts. Total medical debt is the largest reluctant debt in our sample, 41% of the total reluctant debt.

As we noted in Chapter Nine, most medical debts in our sample are relatively small. Table 16.1 shows that half the debtors with medical debt owe $600 or less to all their health care providers combined. We also observed that medical debts, more than any other kind, are likely to be spread among several different health care providers, with different medical specialists, hospitals, clinics, pharmacies, therapists, supply houses, ambulance services, and laboratories sharing the burden represented by the medical debt. Many health care providers become reluctant creditors in bankruptcy, but the loss for each provider is not large.

Taxing Authorities

The inclusion of taxing authorities, another large category of reluctant creditors, makes the point that public sympathy is not the unifying theme of the reluctant creditor group. But taxing authorities also have had credit risks forced on them. Every taxing authority would love to have all taxes paid when due and few would regard penalties and interest as revenue sources. Of course, the tax collector is one of the most legally favored of creditors, with both a payment priority and nondischargeable status. This means that tax creditors may have to engage in credit relationships, but the structure of the current law is such that among the reluctant creditors they bear the least risk of never seeing repayment.

Taxes represent about 13% of reluctant debt, only about a third as much as medical debt, and the amounts are small in most cases. The median amount of tax debt owed was less than $500, and only 20% of the wage earners owed any tax debt at all.

Other Reluctant Creditors

The remainder of the reluctant creditors are a mixed bag. Utilities qualify as reluctant because government regulations require universal service, limit the size of mandatory deposits, and restrict or delay service cutoffs. At least some landlords qualify as reluctant creditors because delays and restrictions on eviction in many localities, even after security deposits have been exhausted, will force them to extend credit they prefer to avoid. Not all nontax state agencies would qualify, but many would because they are owed repayments for advances they never intended to make—overpayment of welfare benefits is the classic example. Educational loans fit with other reluctant creditors because the guaranteeing agency does not seek a profit and cannot apply conventional credit selection criteria to the loans, making them more like reluctant creditors than typical for-profit industry lenders. All these creditors together are owed about 25% of the reluctant debt in our sample.

Payoff for Reluctant Creditors from Increased Payments

We are more sympathetic with some groups of reluctant creditors than with others, but all of them are in a special position to argue that bankrupt debtors should be forced to pay up. Each can say, to one degree or another, that it extends credit reluctantly, that it does not make a profit on credit extension, and that it cannot freely choose its credit risks. For example, a hospital whose debt for emergency care is discharged can insist that its position is very different from that of a finance company that looked over the debtor's credit record and decided to make a loan. A public hospital can also point out to a policymaker that the cost of its discharge will be borne by others, in the form of increased insurance premiums or higher taxes, whereas a finance company loss may simply be applied to a bad debt earnings reserve set up to cover a predicted risk of default, cutting profits if losses run too high.

Since reluctant creditors are in a somewhat different position from industry creditors, it is worthwhile to determine the extent to which they would benefit from greater payments by bankrupt debtors. A rough estimate can be made directly from Table 16.1. Reluctant debt as a whole represents 23% of the unsecured debt in our sample and 8% of the total debt. Taxes already receive a special priority, putting them in a special category. Excluding taxes, the proportion of reluctant debt is 15% of the unsecured debt in our sample and 6% of the total debt.

Under present laws, however, nontax reluctant creditors would not automatically get 15% of any money paid by debtors in bankruptcy—or even 6% of the debtors' payments. One reason is that debt is not necessarily spread evenly among all the creditors, and debtors with nontax reluctant debt may have greater or lesser likelihood of repayment than those who owe money to industry or tax creditors only.

A second reason that nontax reluctant creditors will not necessarily collect a proportionate share of the debtors' repayments is the consequence of the presence of secured debt and of the current priority rules explained in Chapter Fourteen. As we discussed in Chapter Twelve, debtors' first payments are usually made to keep property subject to liens, so that unsecured creditors—which include all the reluctant creditors—are paid only after the secured creditors. Any money left after the secured creditors are paid would then go to pay any outstanding taxes. Only the part left over after secured debt and taxes would be available for the nontax reluctant creditors, and they would have to share pro rata with all other unsecured creditors.

To get a rough idea how much the reluctant creditors would profit from pushing the debtors for greater repayment, we computed a hypothetical payment for each debtor currently in Chapter 7. We assumed that each debtor family, regardless of their actual circumstances, could devote 20% of their take-home income to debt repayment. For this rough calculation, we left out budget constraints and other complications that we included in Chapter Twelve. As those data show, this necessarily overstates how much debtors could repay. We divided the putative payment according to the current practice, paying secured debt first, then taxes, then unsecured debt.[5] Under these assumptions, 187 debtors could repay some reluctant debt, but the total amount repaid would be only $95,000, or about 3.6% of the outstanding reluctant debt.

This approach is necessarily more generous to the secured creditors than the unsecured, which reflects financial reality. We can vary this assumption of better treatment for the secureds, however, and determine the effect on the reluctant creditors. Although it would involve a serious realignment of creditor rights, we could propose that all debtors in bankruptcy be forced to give back collateral subject to a security interest. If that were the law, a debtor owing on a car or buying a refrigerator on time would have to return the item, regardless of its current value or the likelihood that the creditor could sell it, and treat all the remaining debts alike. Even on that theory, the return for the reluctant creditors would be slim. Under these assumptions, 552 debtors could repay $194,000, or about 7.3% of all reluctant debt.[6]

These calculations are very rough. They omit trustee fees and diminished values in liquidation sales. They don't consider whether all the debtors could actually survive if 20% of their after-tax income were seized for creditor repayment. But they do give a rough idea of the possible benefits for reluctant creditors from a major effort to press debtors for repayment: Very little of the resulting payment would trickle down to the reluctant creditors.

Policy Implications

Reluctant creditors vary from the completely involuntary, like accident victims, to the merely reluctant, like the doctor who does not always insist on cash before the patient walks out the door. They all stand in contrast to industry creditors, however, because they are not in the credit business for a profit and they are often forced to take credit risks, rather than choosing to do so. Reluctant creditors bear a substantial portion of the total unsecured debt listed in bankruptcy—about 25%—but they are a smaller portion of the total debt—less than 8%. The corollary of these data, of course, is that industry creditors are a very large portion of all the debt listed in bankruptcy.

The mere fact of reporting the position of reluctant creditors for the first time creates a new perspective. For years people have talked vaguely about medical losses or tort debt in bankruptcy, with no clear idea of what was at stake. These data provide some basis for understanding the magnitude of such potential losses, both absolutely and relatively.

In particular, it is helpful to understand how the benefits of greater debtor repayment would be distributed between reluctant and industry creditors and within each group. The data make it clear that the combination of collateral control by secured creditors and the priority for taxes leaves little for repayment of any nontax unsecured debt. The data also show that among the nontax unsecured creditors the bulk of any repayment efforts go overwhelmingly to the credit industry.

Chapter Twelve reported how much of their debts debtors could pay. This chapter reveals who would get any repayment that could be won from debtors. These data describe the circumstances of reluctant creditors until the development of some entirely new bankruptcy regime: The debtors have little realistic likelihood of repaying any of their debts, but even if they could be forced to pay more, the chances of obtaining much increased return for reluctant creditors other than taxing authorities are minimal.

Notes

1. The individual creditors range from investors in a small business to the mother-in-law who lent the debtors survival money. By limiting ourselves here to pure wage earners, we have largely eliminated investors and other lenders seeking a profit, so the individual lenders in Table 16.1 represent primarily personal loans and credits. This category is so varied and diffuse that we cannot analyze these creditors in a useful way, so we confine ourselves to reporting their debt position in the table and leave it at that.

2. Interestingly, the former gets special treatment under the bankruptcy laws, whereas the latter lines up with all the other creditors for a pro rata distribution.

3. The principal exception is the educational loan agency. These agencies, which guarantee student loans, are in the business of extending credit, but, in common with other reluctant creditors, they are forced to accept credit risks that other creditors would not. Because they are in the business of accepting substandard credit risks, some of the arguments that might be made for special treatment for reluctant creditors would not extend to these agencies. For example, other creditors of all sorts could plausibly argue that the default risks on educational loans should be borne by the Treasury as a social cost, rather than imposed on the debtor's other creditors by way of special treatment for such loans.

On the whole, these lenders fit into the reluctant category, because the guaranteeing agency does not seek a profit and cannot apply conventional credit selection criteria to the loans, but in many ways education loans are *sui generis*.

4. Taxing authorities sometimes had involuntary liens placed on debtors' property as part of the move to collect delinquent taxes. These tax obligations, now legally secured by the debtors' property, are combined with other debts in the "other secured" line in Table 14.1.

5. The procedure we used for this calculation was to take 20% of the after-tax gross income of the Chapter 7 debtors, apply it to repayment of nonmortgage secured debt, apply any remainder to payment of outstanding taxes, and divide the remainder pro rata among the unsecured creditors. For homeowner debtors, the calculation was adjusted to take the home mortgage payment out of the gross income before the 20% figure was calculated. All calculations excluded 66 cases of uncertain home ownership for which we could not verify mortgage payments. A total of $440,970 could be repaid,

of which $346,203, or 78.5% of the pool, would go to industry creditors. The remaining $94,767 (21.5%) would go to reluctant creditors.

6. The procedure used is similar to the one described in the previous note except that we make no deductions for paying secured debts. Instead, we calculated that 20% of the secured debt would be treated as unsecured debt. (The 20% is an intermediate approximation. As we discussed in Chapter Twelve, note 22, the actual aggregate undersecurity of nonmortgage loans was 27%; the mean lender's exposure to pure wage earners, shown in Table 15.3, was 11%.) This 20% was then added to the pool of nonpriority unsecured debt. A total of $1,301,319 from this pool could be repaid, of which $1,106,885, or 85.1%, would go to industry creditors. The remaining $194,434 (14.9%) would go to reluctant creditors.

17

The Consumer Credit Industry

The companies that make up the consumer credit industry are the central players in the consumer bankruptcy drama. These voluntary lenders who lend to wage-earning consumers dominate the 11-o'clock news, the national statistics on consumer debt, and the congressional hearings about consumer bankruptcy policy. The consumer credit industry is made up of the lenders who are everywhere—and lending to everyone. Banks, finance companies, savings associations, credit unions, credit card companies, stores, gasoline companies, and private mortgage companies are among the lenders who are doing business on a huge scale with American consumers.

In 1981, consumers owed the industry about $389 billion, a number that has steadily increased since then.[1] This behemoth is generally regarded as central to economic growth and prosperity. Despite its importance, the consumer credit system is rarely scrutinized. Studies of the system tend to be sporadic and unreadable, more confusing than enlightening. Even the specialists seem puzzled. American economists, for example, tell us one month that we save too little compared with the Japanese and Germans, and warn us the next month that declining consumer spending threatens recession. Consumer credit serves as a fulcrum in this balancing act, with the credit practices that produce the indebtedness largely hidden from view. In any event, massive consumer debt represents a great engine of economic activity about which we know very little.

The central question we address in this chapter is the extent to which the credit industry could reduce bankruptcy losses. We consider how the decisions made by various types of creditors could be improved with better information and different lending practices. In the process we examine the loss exposures of different types of creditors. We are able to estimate for the first time the actual exposure of the industry as opposed to its scheduled bankruptcy debts.

TABLE 17.1. Distribution of Pure Wage Earner Debt[a]

Debt Type	Total Debt	Percentage of Total Debt
Credit industry	$27,768,057	86.7
Secured	19,555,742	(61.1)
Unsecured	8,212,315	(25.6)
Reluctant	2,650,895	8.3
Individual lenders	869,381	2.7
Residual[b]	708,727	2.2
Total	31,997,057	100.0

[a]Cases with extreme values on assets, total debt, or income excluded.
[b]Unallocatable secured and unsecured debt for which the creditor could not be determined.
Source: Consumer Bankruptcy Project.

Finally, we discuss the tension between reducing the bankruptcy losses and maximizing the profits of mass credit and the implications of all this for the consumer credit system.

The Credit Industry—Biggest Loser in the Bankruptcy Game

Most people assume the industry's decisions to extend credit to people are elaborate and thorough, from the initial credit application through the credit checks and sophisticated on-line computer updates of credit reporting agencies. One might imagine that all this credit verification apparatus would insulate the industry from large bankruptcy losses. Only the occasional clever debtor or the lucky beneficiary of a bizarre computer blip might slip through the consumer credit industry's checks and balances and thus tumble into bankruptcy owing a substantial amount to this well-run machine. Table 17.1 suggests that this is not the case. The consumer credit industry is the biggest loser in consumer bankruptcy.

Table 17.1 includes all wage-earner debt, secured and unsecured, owed to industry, individual, and reluctant creditors.[2] Once the business debt has been eliminated by removing currently and formerly self-employed debtors, the role of the consumer credit industry in consumer bankruptcies comes into sharper focus.

In Chapter Sixteen we examined the reluctant creditors, creditors who tried to avoid credit relationships but whose debtors pulled them into bankruptcy nonetheless. Reluctant creditors are only a small fraction of the creditors' bankruptcy story, about 8% of the debt listed. The consumer credit industry, by contrast, accounts for nearly 87% of the debt listed in bankruptcy.

It would be useful to examine data on total credit extended by various lenders to compare their shares of lending with their shares of bankruptcy losses. Unfortunately, we could find neither reliable nor comparable figures for nonindustry creditors such as taxing authorities, tort victims, and the rest. Thus we cannot say if the industry is exposed to bankruptcy losses out of proportion to its overall extension of credit.

But detailed comparisons we cannot make should not obscure the comparison we can make. Our data show that the most bankruptcy losses are not borne by the inexperienced lenders or by reluctant creditors. Measured in absolute dollars, consumer bankruptcy losses are lost by professionals, those who actively sought consumer lending for profit. Any changes in bankruptcy policy must necessarily affect the professional lenders most directly. By the same reasoning, if creditor planning could affect bankruptcy losses, the creditors now bearing the bulk of the bankruptcy losses are precisely the repeat players who could best make those adjustments.

Cutting Losses

Debts to lenders in the consumer credit industry in our bankruptcy sample totaled $27,768,100. Since our study covered only 1202 wage earners from only 10 of the 94 judicial districts in the United States, it does not take much imagination to infer that there are impressive amounts of debt listed in consumer bankruptcies. We saw in Chapter Fifteen that much of the secured component of this total—perhaps 90%—is likely to be repaid, but that still leaves over $10 million of unsecured debt. If we have some idea how this exposure to loss might be reduced, we should better understand the structure of the consumer credit system and its relationship to the bankruptcy component of that system.

How can bankruptcy losses be reduced? The data show that the most obvious answer to this question is wrong. For more than a decade, the assumed answer to cutting bankruptcy losses was some variant of "Make the bankrupt debtors pay more." Following that theme, Congress has worked diligently to develop incentives to attract debtors to repayment schemes. Credit industry lobbyists have agitated for statutory reform to require greater repayment, and countless popular articles have lamented the ease with which debtors shed their lawful debts.

Until we had a detailed study of the economic circumstances facing the debtors who filed bankruptcy, we could not assess whether the debtors could, in fact, pay more. The Purdue Study made some guesses, but both the methods and the political biases of that study left it far shy of a realistic assessment of what debtors could pay. Without data, "making the debtors pay more" seems to be a rational, straightforward way to cut creditors' bankruptcy losses.

The data developed in Chapter Twelve show why this answer fails: The debtors cannot pay more. Their incomes are too low to sustain minimal budgets and debt repayment, and even the proceeds from selling their assets are too meager to repay significant debt. At the edges a few debtors, perhaps 5%, might be able to pay their debts. Some debtors could repay some portion of their debts, but many of them are already doing so either in Chapter 7 or in

Chapter 13. At best, even with a high expenditure of court resources and tax-subsidized debt collection, we could reduce bankruptcy losses only slightly by pushing the debtors harder for repayment.

Some of our data suggest that the credit industry is not much more successful in collecting debts through legal action even outside of bankruptcy. The bankruptcy forms require debtors to list lawsuits filed against them and property seized from them before bankruptcy. We compiled the responses to these questions from our sample of wage-earner debtors. Creditors had brought remarkably few formal debt collection actions against these debtors prior to bankruptcy. Although most of these debtors were probably in default on most of their debt by the time of bankruptcy, not a single lawsuit had been filed against two-thirds of them. Less than 10% had suffered a property seizure or garnishment. Of more than 15,000 claims in our wage-earner sample, only 616 creditors (about 4%) had filed suit prior to bankruptcy.

Many factors influence a creditor in deciding whether to bring legal action against a debtor: The action may be nullified by bankruptcy, or the creditor may collect more money at lower cost by informal means, such as repeated phone calls and dunning letters. On the other hand, a large literature suggests that most debt collection actions are not contested by debtors and an uncontested action is not terribly expensive to prosecute, especially for a large company that can routinize procedures to cover many debtors. It is reasonable to infer that creditors realize how small their chances of payment through legal coercion are, resulting in a strikingly low level of formal legal action prior to bankruptcy. Doubtless creditors would prefer to retain this option, but the real economic benefit of formal collection action in many cases may be relatively low, even if a debtor does not file bankruptcy.

Through any scheme that is politically possible, we cannot extract more than slight repayment from consumer debtors. In effect, the bankruptcy data show that we could do as we pleased with the debtors—demand their assets, encumber their incomes, push them out of bankruptcy altogether—but we are unlikely to see much greater repayment from them than they already produced. And the creditors' own nonbankruptcy behaviors tends to confirm that conclusion. The old adage about not getting blood from a turnip applies with some force to squeezing debtors for greater repayment.

Reducing Risky Loans

There are, in effect, two opportunities to reduce bankruptcy losses—at the default stage by extracting greater repayment from debtors and at the credit-granting stage by avoiding the debtors who will take bankruptcy. The data show that the first approach is likely to be unprofitable, leaving us with the second approach for closer examination.

All professional creditors attempt to minimize their risks before lending to the extent consistent with maximizing their profits. The bankruptcy data in

Table 17.1 give some idea of how different creditors have fared in this process and which creditors have the greatest stake in doing better.

The industry creditors with the greatest bankruptcy exposure are the banks. They had lent almost one out of every four dollars owed to industry creditors in our sample. Savings associations and private mortgage companies were next, although their loans were heavily secured. Stores and finance companies had lower total amounts but carried a very large part of the unsecured debt and therefore were more highly exposed. Among them, they accounted for another quarter of the total consumer debt in the sample.

To our surprise, MasterCards, Visas, and all-purpose credit cards—everyone's credit bugaboo—accounted for only 3% of the total debt. Credit unions were also relatively minor players, with only 4% of the overall debt. At the very bottom were the gasoline companies, which totaled less than 2% of the debt listed.

It is regrettable that there are no comparable statistics for overall lending, so that we could see if particular types of creditors have been disproportionately successful or unsuccessful in avoiding debtors bound for bankruptcy. Thus, for example, it may be that banks are most listed in consumer bankruptcy only because they lend the most to consumers. Nonetheless, these data tell us which creditors would most benefit from a reduction in bankruptcy losses.

Using Security to Avoid Risks

Demanding a security interest in property is a creditor's clearest way to make a loan while limiting the bankruptcy risk. Because security interests are recognized and given favored treatment in bankruptcy, the creditor who has fully secured its loan is protected two ways: (1) the threat of repossession of the collateral gives the debtor a powerful incentive to repay this debt even if others must remain unpaid and (2) if the debtor cannot pay, the creditor can pay itself from the proceeds of seizing and selling the property. When the value of the collateral exceeds the value of the loan (a fully secured loan) the creditor faces almost no risk of nonpayment, whether the debtor files bankruptcy or not.

Some creditors use the device of security interests to reduce their bankruptcy exposure to virtually zero. Table 17.2 shows how different creditors have required security interests as part of their loan-making arrangement.[3] Savings and loans, private mortgage companies, and car finance companies made virtually all their loans on a secured basis, sharply reducing their bankruptcy exposure. Other creditors, such as stores and credit card issuers, made exclusively unsecured loans, while still others, such as banks and credit unions, made some of both.

The impact of security interests on reducing bankruptcy losses is made even clearer in Table 17.3. For this table, we make calculations on a debt-by-debt basis. We compare the value of the collateral[4] at the time of bankruptcy with the outstanding loan balance to determine the effectiveness of the credi-

TABLE 17.2. Total, Secured, and Unsecured Debt Owed to the Consumer Credit Industry by Pure Wage Earners[a]

Creditors	Total[b]	Percentage	Secured[c]	Percentage	Unsecured[c]	Percentage
Total	$27,768,057	100.0%	$19,555,742	100.0%	$8,212,315	100.0%
Stores	3,009,005	10.8	NA	NA	3,009,005	36.6
Credit cards	930,769	3.4	NA	NA	930,769	11.3
Gas credit	467,531	1.7	NA	NA	467,531	5.7
Banks	6,346,416	22.9	$ 4,508,165	23.1	1,838,251	22.4
Credit unions	1,147,785	4.1	617,233	3.2	530,552	6.5
Finance co.–car	1,503,686	5.4	1,503,686	7.7	NA	NA
Finance co.–general	3,847,421	13.9	2,411,214	12.3	1,436,207	17.5
Private mortgage co.	4,830,332	17.4	4,830,332	24.7	NA	NA
Savings and loan	3,944,041	14.2	3,944,041	20.2	NA	NA
Other	1,741,071	6.3	1,741,071	8.9	NA	NA

[a]Cases with extreme values on assets, total debt, or income excluded.

[b]This is the total debt scheduled in the petition. This total does not reflect any efforts at repayment and is not corrected for cases that were dismissed.

[c]As listed on the petition.

Source: Consumer Bankruptcy Project.

TABLE 17.3. Mean and Total Value of All Claims, Secured Claims, and Exposed Claims, by Secured Creditor for Wage Earners[a,b]

Creditor	All Formally Secured Claims Mean	All Formally Secured Claims N	Secured Portion of Claims Mean	Secured Portion of Claims N	Exposed Portion of Claims Mean	Exposed Portion of Claims N	% of Claims with Exposure
Claim Values—Means							
Bank	$ 7,764	465	$ 6,795	445	$2,766	212	45.6%
Savings and loan	21,210	156	21,269	153	3,205	17	10.9
Credit union	3,646	141	2,961	140	1,310	76	53.9
Finance co.–car	4,745	275	3,460	269	2,241	167	60.7
Finance co.–general	4,763	420	4,260	367	1,720	254	60.5
Private mortgage	20,591	220	20,297	217	6,618	19	8.6
Other	3,287	433	3,004	400	931	238	55.0
Unknown	5,588	11	5,128	11	1,012	5	45.4
Total	7,899	2,121	7,417	2,002	1,927	988	46.6

Creditor	All Formally Secured Claims Total $	Secured Portion of Claims Total $	Secured Portion of Claims %[c]	Exposed Portion of Claims Total $	Exposed Portion of Claims %[c]
Claim Values—Total Dollars					
Bank	$ 3,610,335	$ 3,023,955	83.8%	$ 586,380	16.2%
Savings and loan	3,308,775	3,254,295	98.4	54,480	1.6
Credit union	514,138	414,605	80.6	99,533	19.4
Finance co.–car	1,304,998	930,769	71.3	374,229	28.7
Finance co.–general	2,000,357	1,563,395	78.2	436,962	21.8
Private mortgage	4,530,082	4,404,346	97.2	125,736	2.8
Other	1,423,360	1,201,794	84.4	221,566	15.6
Unknown	61,470	56,408	91.8	5,062	8.2
Total	16,753,515	14,849,567	88.6	1,903,948	11.4

[a]Cases with extreme values on assets, total debt, or income excluded.

[b]Figures based on all debts where both the claim and market value of the collateral are specified. *N*'s refer to debts.

[c]As a percentage of the total claim value in each category.

Source: Consumer Bankruptcy Project.

tor's security interest. In this way we can identify the loans that are nominally secured (yes, the creditor took a security interest) but that are effectively undersecured (no, the value of the collateral will not cover the outstanding loan balance).[5] Even an undersecured loan is much better than an unsecured one, because the debtor has a strong incentive to repay and may do so. But this table shows the worst case scenario for the creditor listed in bankruptcy—the value to be realized from the sale of the collateral if the debtor cannot pay.[6]

Among the secured loans that various creditors took, the savings and loans and private mortgage lenders are the obvious success stories. Savings and loans are listed for $3,300,000 and private mortgage companies for $4,500,000 by the debtors in our sample. But 98.4% of the debt listed by the savings and loans and 97.2% of the debt listed by the mortgage companies is fully secured. While it can be time consuming to deal with trustees in bankruptcy, and every creditor would prefer payment on time to forced resale and repayment, the position of the savings and loans and private mortgage lenders is an enviable one from the perspective of every other creditor listed in bankruptcy.

But the data show that not every creditor is successful in using security interests to avoid the risks of bankruptcy. Table 17.3 shows that even among nominally secured loans, some are more secured than others. For every $100 dollars in credit that car financers extend, for example, only $71 is protected by the value of the collateral at the time of bankruptcy. For credit unions the numbers are somewhat better; $81 of collateral stands behind every $100 of nominally secured debt.

The different success rates in using security interests to avoid bankruptcy losses can be explained in large part by the kinds of collateral different creditors take. Table 17.4 shows the different collateral mixes taken by creditors when they use security interests. The table shows that savings and loans and private mortgage lenders concentrate almost exclusively on home mortgage loans, while other lenders also lend against cars, household goods, boats, and a variety of other collateral. The message from these data are clear: The value of the homes protects the loans against them almost completely, while every other collateral is some protection against risk but is considerably less effective. Cars offer much less protection, being worth only 83% of the loans against them. Household goods are the worst of all, with values less than half the loans made on them.

The long-term creditors with the greatest potential bankruptcy exposure have reduced their exposure the most. As the data in Table 17.5 show, average loans for home mortgages from savings and loans and private mortgage lenders are among the highest per debtor in bankruptcy. Home mortgage lenders frequently make loans extending over 30 years. Even lenders making second mortgages will often offer loans of five years or greater duration. Once the loan has been made, no amount of monitoring of the debtor will change the creditors' exposure. If a debtor becomes unemployed, if a costly illness hits a family member, if other debt burdens overwhelm the debtor, the home mortgage lender risks nonpayment. Yet this lender has reduced that risk to virtually nothing.[7] As a result of the security interest in the home, this loan is transformed from one of the highest risks to one of the lowest risks.

Using the figures on undersecurity, we can get a clear picture of the extent to which various creditors have actually protected themselves through liens. We start with the obviously unsecured debt. Table 17.2 shows that some creditors, such as credit card issuers and stores, never took security interests, whereas some others, such as banks and credit unions, failed to ask for security interests in a significant portion of their loans. When we add the undersecured

TABLE 17.4. Proportion of Creditor's Loans Secured by Various Types of Collateral

	Creditor							
Collateral	Banks	Savings and Loans	Credit Unions	Finance Company	Car Finance Company	Other	Private Mortgage	No Information
Home	22.1%	85.3%	7.8%	15.0%	0.0%	13.9%	87.7%	36.4%
Other real estate	3.0	5.1	1.4	1.3	0.0	3.5	8.6	9.1
Household goods	6.0	0.6	3.5	37.0	0.0	61.4	0.5	9.1
Cars	58.1	4.5	73.8	39.6	100.0	6.7	0.9	9.1
Boats	2.2	0.0	0.7	0.6	0.0	0.2	0.0	18.2
Producer goods[a]	0.9	0.0	1.4	0.1	0.0	1.2	0.0	0.0
Mobile home	5.2	3.8	2.8	3.2	0.0	0.7	1.8	9.1
Cash	0.9	0.0	4.3	0.4	0.0	2.3	0.0	0.0
Potential property[b]	1.1	0.0	0.7	0.6	0.0	4.8	0.0	0.0
No information	0.6	0.6	3.5	2.3	0.0	5.3	0.5	9.1
Total	100.0	100.0	100.0	100.0	100.0	100.0	100.0	100.0
N	(465)	(156)	(141)	(695)	(275)	(443)	(220)	(11)

[a]Includes inventory, business equipment, tools, etc.

[b]Includes interests in businesses, patents, etc.

Source: Consumer Bankruptcy Project.

TABLE 17.5. Mean Debt Owed to Credit Industry Creditors, by Secured and Unsecured Status, for Pure Wage Earners[a] (*N*'s in parentheses)

Creditor	Total	Secured	Unsecured
Stores	$ 2,933	—	$2,933
	(1,026)		(1,026)
Credit cards	2,010	—	2,010
	(463)		(463)
Gas credit	1,664	—	1,664
	(281)		(281)
Banks	8,863	$10,557	4,022
	(716)	(427)	(457)
Credit unions	3,499	4,143	2,358
	(328)	(149)	(225)
Finance co.–cars	5,080	5,080	—
	(296)	(296)	
Finance co.–general	4,768	5,621	2,438
	(807)	(429)	(589)
Private mortgage	22,467	22,467	—
	(215)	(215)	
Savings and loan	24,650	24,650	—
	(160)	(160)	
Other	4,547	4,547	—
	(383)	(383)	
Total	$23,433	$19,042	$7,229
	(1,185)	(1,027)	(1,136)

[a]Cases with extreme values on assets, total debt, or income excluded.

Source: Consumer Bankruptcy Project.

portions of apparently secured debts, we find, for example, that car finance companies actually made 30% of their loans to these bankrupt debtors unsecured. Banks, which appeared to be secured on 72% of their bankruptcy debt, were actually secured for only 62%. Finance companies go from apparently being secured for 67% of their loans to having about half their loans covered by collateral.[8]

These data show that some creditors have used security interests to reduce their bankruptcy risks dramatically. Others have used them to reduce their risks to a lesser extent, and some creditors have not used them at all.

Cutting Losses with Security Interests

The data indicate that creditors could cut their bankruptcy risks by lending only on a secured basis and by taking high-quality security. If every creditor followed the lead of savings and loans and private mortgage companies and made only loans backed up by the promise that they could repossess the debtors' home, the creditors could almost stop worrying about bankruptcy. Of course, if all consumer debt were secured by the value of the home, the debts would more frequently swamp the value of the home, depressing its value as collateral for the subsequent lenders, and far fewer consumer loans would be made. Moreover, if creditors blindly followed the lead suggested by these data, they would miss too many profitable loans.[9] The segmentation of the lending market, as reflected in the bankruptcy listings of secured debt, suggests that creditors have different responses to the risk of bankruptcy losses and that some creditors find there are profits to be made in unsecured loans that outweigh the risks of bankruptcy losses.

Not surprisingly, as Table 17.2 indicated, the creditors who make more loans on an unsecured or undersecured basis are also making smaller loans per debtor.[10] Because these loans are probably short-term credit, the creditors have a greater opportunity to assess bankruptcy risk as the debtors' circumstances change. Possibly they can avoid the debtors most likely to enter bankruptcy. As we noted in Chapter Fifteen, consumer lending decisions involve a substantial element of actuarial analysis, using high volume to spread the small risk of bankruptcy among many thousands of debtors. So long as the overall losses can be held low enough to permit a reasonable profit on the lending activity, the creditor can continue to lend, meeting both the desires of the borrowers and its own profit imperatives.

Most of the debtors' valuable assets, such as homes and cars, are already subject to liens (see Chapter Twelve), leaving little property to secure presently unsecured loans. A lender who insisted on security for all consumer loans would have to forgo a good deal of profitable lending. If all nonhomeowners, for example, were excluded from consumer borrowing, neither borrowers nor lenders would be happy, and a substantial number of good loans would not be made. Profitable activities satisfying both borrower and lender would have been curtailed.

Every creditor who lends against anything other than collateral clearly valued at more than the loan makes another assessment: What is the chance that this debtor will repay the loan? Because different creditors have different exposure—from the amount of the loan, from the value of the collateral, from the term of the loan—they may attend differently to the question of likelihood of repayment. But all except the most secured creditors must assess the risk of nonpayment by separating the can-pay debtors from those more likely to end up in default. Successful creditors are those who can best eliminate the default-prone debtors while making loans to all the likely repayers.

Identifying Bankruptcy Risks

Creditors have long complained that they cannot identify the debtors who are likely to end up in bankruptcy and thus avoid giving them credit. In some respects, our data confirm the creditors' lament. Many of the comparisons we made between debtors in bankruptcy and Americans generally show how similar the two groups are. As we explored in Chapter Five, the debtors who end up in bankruptcy work alongside other Americans, holding the same jobs, working in the same industries, achieving about the same occupational prestige. Chapter Eight confirmed that many similarities also hold up by sex, so that men in bankruptcy bear a striking similarity to men in the general population, and women in bankruptcy and women in the general population are by many measures statistically indistinguishable.

Other indicia that creditors have long used to identify economic stability, and presumably an ability to repay debts, also fail to distinguish the debtors in bankruptcy from other Americans. The data reported in Chapter Seven showed that more than half of the debtors in bankruptcy own homes, and the value of their homes is not sharply out of line with other homeowners. And Chapter Eleven data suggested that today's bankruptcy petitioner is not likely to be a person with a history of bankruptcy.

Even when statistical differences give some clue about the circumstances leading up to the debtors' bankruptcies, they may be poor criteria for sorting out can-pay from can't-pay debtors. Although bankrupt debtors, for example, earned on average one-third less than other Americans, a substantial number nonetheless had incomes equal to those of a large number of other bill-paying Americans and therefore seemed to qualify for at least a modest amount of credit.

Our data confirm that many of the questions creditors currently ask in their credit applications will not be effective to help the creditors sort out which debtors are likely to go into bankruptcy and which are not. Indeed, the data in this book may explain in part why credit industry lobbyists have seized on the notion that the debtors who are in bankruptcy must be slick operators who could repay their debts: From the data the credit industry collects, the bankrupt debtors look like other folks who pay up every month. From that perspective, it is easy to assume that the way to reduce bankruptcy losses is for the bankruptcy system to press the bankrupt debtors harder—even if the creditors do not find it generally profitable to pursue these debtors individually when they are not in bankruptcy.

Better Information

The most important differences we found between bankrupt debtors and Americans generally are not part of the data that creditors routinely collect. To some extent the creditors fail to gather the crucial information and to some extent they get the information, but fail to use it effectively.

Our data show that what most clearly distinguishes debtors in bankruptcy from the rest of the population is their ratio of debts to income. While 95% of the population has a debt/income ratio of less than 0.2,[11] more than 90% of the debtors in bankruptcy had an equivalent debt/income ratio in excess of 0.2. The bankrupt debtors' ratios were not just higher—they were much higher. The mean consumer debt/income ratio for wage-earning debtors in bankruptcy was 2.5, which is more than ten times higher than for all but the worst-off edge of Americans in the general population. Other computations of the debt/income ratio, such as the comparison of mortgage debt to income, showed similar, albeit less dramatic differences between the debtors in bankruptcy and the general population.

The debt/income ratios tag the debtors in bankruptcy as identifiably different from their counterparts who are not in bankruptcy. The tag is not perfect; there are undoubtedly some people with very high debt/income ratios who do not file bankruptcy. But it is a more reliable distinction between the bankrupt debtors and the rest of the general population than any measure currently used by creditors.

Another distinction between debtors in bankruptcy and the general population is the income interruption suggested by sharp swings in income of debtors in the two years before filing. For the debtors in bankruptcy for whom we could compute the difference, more than 40% had experienced shifts of 20% or more between the two calendar years preceding bankruptcy.

Another inference that incomes have dropped significantly for many debtors who end up in bankruptcy comes from the fact that the industry has extended a large amount of credit to debtors whose incomes at the time of bankruptcy were at or below the poverty level. Table 17.6 shows that the various categories of industry creditors had made between 11% and 22% of their loans to debtors who listed income at or below $10,000 by the time of filing. The ranges for lending to debtors with incomes just marginally higher were even more impressive. Creditors made between 27% and 36% of their loans to debtors with incomes below $12,500.

The poverty level in the United States in 1981 was only slightly below $10,000 and our debtors had slightly larger families than average and presumably at least average expenses. Since the poverty level makes no allowance for debt repayment, we assume that few professional industry lenders with access to income information would have decided to extend large quantities of credit to these people. The best explanation consistent with rational lending is that incomes dropped after most creditors had made their lending decisions.

Much of the unsecured debt that our sample carried into bankruptcy must have been incurred during the two-year period prior to bankruptcy. A substantial percentage of that debt—such as that owed to stores and on credit cards—is almost always short term, while other categories of unsecured debt include a significant amount of short-term credit mixed with longer term loans—such as unsecured loans from banks and finance companies. Although we cannot quantify the amount lent in the two years before bankruptcy,[12] it seems apparent that it must be a large part of the unsecured total. On that assumption, a good deal of the unsecured bankruptcy debt was incurred at a time when most of these debtors had terrible debt/income ratios and many had declining incomes as well.[13] As we discussed in Chapter Four, the debtors' incomes two years before bankruptcy were even lower, on average, than in the last year before they filed.

The large debt/income ratios of debtors whose incomes were not declining must have been a product of ever-increasing debt, so that a number of creditors extended credit to them at a time when their debt burdens were already highly

TABLE 17.6. Total Value of Debts and Debt Composition by Debtor's Income and Credit Type (pure wage earners only)[a]

Creditor	Total	N	%[b]	%[c]	Ratio of Exposure[d]
Income ≤ $10,000					
Stores	$ 623,960	254	20.7%	24.8%	0.83
Credit cards	167,052	86	17.9	18.6	0.96
Gas credit	34,743	51	7.4	18.1	0.41
Banks	1,058,880	166	16.7	23.2	0.72
Credit unions	130,578	51	11.4	15.5	0.74
Finance co.–cars	323,108	57	21.5	19.2	1.12
Finance co.–general	692,531	188	18.0	23.3	0.77
Private mortgage	694,348	38	14.4	17.7	0.81
Savings and loan	528,150	26	13.4	16.2	0.83
Other	332,981	88	19.1	23.0	0.83
Total	4,586,271	303	16.5	25.6	0.64
Income ≤ $12,500					
Stores	843,163	366	28.0	35.7	0.78
Credit cards	252,170	130	27.1	28.1	0.96
Gas credit	57,760	80	12.3	28.5	0.43
Banks	1,487,478	235	23.4	32.8	0.71
Credit unions	242,150	79	21.1	24.1	0.88
Finance co.–cars	498,184	91	33.1	30.7	1.08
Finance co.–general	1,053,870	279	27.4	34.6	0.79
Private mortgage	1,100,504	58	22.8	27.0	0.84
Savings and loan	956,877	43	24.3	26.9	0.90
Other	527,794	131	30.3	34.3	0.88
Total	7,020,490	438	25.3	37.0	0.68

[a]Cases with extreme values on assets, total debt, or income excluded.
[b]As a percentage of all debt owed to creditor by pure wage earners.
[c]As a percentage of all pure wage earners who owe debt to creditor.
[d]Ratio of exposure = % of debt/% of debtors.
Source: Consumer Bankruptcy Project.

aberrational when compared to most consumers. The amounts cannot be quantified, but it is apparent that much of the unsecured debt exposed to discharge in our bankruptcy sample was incurred at a time when the debtors were obviously bad credit risks.

Using the Information—Eyes-Open, Eyes-Closed Lending

These data suggest at least two ways for creditors to reduce their bankruptcy exposure. Debtors who are at much higher than average risk for bankruptcy nearly always have extraordinary debt/income ratios by the time of bankruptcy, and they frequently have significant income interruptions within two years preceding their filing. The key to reducing bankruptcy losses by avoiding debtors with extraordinary debt/income ratios or unusually low incomes is to collect more information from potential debtors and to update that information periodically as creditors make new extensions of credit.

Too many creditors fail to ask even on an initial credit application about the debtors' debt burden, which is essential to calculating a current debt/income ratio at the time credit is extended. One way to reduce some exposure to debtors with high debt/income ratios is to ask for the additional information and to exclude loans to debtors with high debt/income ratios. If creditors cut off credit to any debtor when the debtor's consumer debt/income ratio hits 0.2, a substantial portion of their bankruptcy losses could be eliminated. Losses could also be significantly reduced by not making new extensions of credit to debtors with incomes near the poverty level.

Even with additional information, some creditors might not reduce their bankruptcy losses. These creditors make debt consolidation loans ("Can't pay your monthly bills? Come see us for one loan to reduce your payments and pay off everyone.") and other credit decisions after the debtors have entered the prebankruptcy period. These creditors might be called "eyes-open" lenders, the kind who are aware of the high-risk status of the loans they make. These data may make them more aware than they had been of the risks involved in these loans, but if they have determined that the profits outweigh the risks (debt consolidation loans are high-interest loans), our data are not likely to contribute subsequently to reducing their losses.

Other creditors not interested in high-risk lending would have to adjust their procedures for making lending decisions in order to use our findings effectively. Creditors who provide short-term, unsecured "standing" credit, such as revolving charge accounts or bank overdraft privileges, are clear examples of those who may need to amend their practices if they want to reduce risk. They may grant lines of credit to the debtors years before bankruptcy, at a time when the debtors have lower debts or higher incomes. Most of these creditors typically do nothing to update income or credit information after the initial credit decision. The debtor in the year or two before bankruptcy may have lost a job or run up huge bills with other creditors, but if the minimum payments are met, these creditors will usually continue the line of credit and may even raise it at the very time the debtor is collapsing financially. Each charge a creditor approves is a new extension of credit, but many creditors continue to let debtors use their credit lines without any information on the debtors' capacity to repay at the time the credit is actually extended. These "eyes-closed" creditors want to avoid high-risk debtors, but they never check to see if their borrowers have become high risk.

The story told in a popular work of fiction, *Kramer Versus Kramer,* prompted a smile of recognition from more than a few debtors. Mr. Kramer lost his job and was rapidly running out of money, yet he and his son ate "better than ever." They feasted exclusively on delicacies from the gourmet counters at one of New York's finest department stores. The reason? So long as Kramer made a minimal monthly payment on his credit card there, no one would check and he could run up enormous bills—and avoid the neighborhood grocery store, which required cash. Today, when many small convenience stores happily accept the all-purpose bank cards, the basic necessities of life can be charged. The credit system seems almost deliberately designed to permit someone like Mr. Kramer to maintain a lifestyle that his income no longer supports.

Nonetheless, creditors issuing standing credit do not have to keep their eyes closed. As we explained in Chapter Five, our data suggest that many debtors do not file bankruptcy as soon as trouble strikes. There is a substantial period during which creditors could probably reduce bankruptcy exposure by periodically updating income and debt information about their debtors. This process would identify both debtors whose incomes have dropped sharply and debtors whose incomes and debts have swung out of balance. The bankruptcy system already protects creditors against the risk of false answers. Debtors have some incentive to be untruthful in answering simple questionnaires about their circumstances, especially when their circumstances are deteriorating and it may be obvious that bad answers will result in curtailed credit. But if a debtor gives false information about his circumstances and the creditor relies on that information in granting further extensions of credit, the creditor can object to discharge of that debt in bankruptcy. Thus the risk of bankruptcy (as opposed to the more general risk that the debtor simply will not pay) is greatly reduced because bankruptcy withdraws its protection in such circumstances.

Creditors could also reduce their bankruptcy exposure without any debtor cooperation by updating debt information through their own credit services. Creditors have established credit reporting bureaus to compile information on debtors who move, who do or do not pay their creditors on time, who declare bankruptcy, who have judgments entered against them, and so on. What the credit reporting bureaus do not collect or report is the current debt burden carried by each debtor. If the debtor is making minimal payments on time, even to dozens of different credit card issuers and finance companies, most credit reporting agencies today will list that debtor as a good risk—although our data suggest there may be an approaching disaster. It would seem quite feasible to collect relevant data from member creditors about current debt burdens and to signal creditors when new credit approvals or further extensions of credit are high risk. Credit cards could be pulled until a debtor had a long talk with the store's credit manager, just as a stolen credit card can now be taken out of circulation within a matter of hours.

The stronger indicators of risk generated by updated debt and income information would benefit only some of the creditors who run the risk of bankruptcy. Home lenders, for example, have already made long-term single extensions of credit. Learning that the debtor is in trouble will not change the fact that the loan has been made. On the other hand, credit card issuers, stores, and gasoline companies, which make very short-term loans, could use this information profitably. By using relatively more recent information and avoiding new extensions of credit when the risks become unacceptable, they could likely trim a significant portion of their bankruptcy risks. We note the almost perfect symmetry of this position: The long-term lenders could not profit from this information, but they have already almost fully protected themselves through high-quality security interests. The short-term lenders could profit dramatically, and they currently take the biggest real risks in bankruptcy because they have no security protection and virtually no payback in bankruptcy. Such a change, in lending practices would have a disproportionately large impact on reducing the real losses of bankruptcy.

Not Using Available Data

It is clear that creditors do not currently use updated information. Not only do industry reports suggest by silence that such data are not collected or even perceived as important, but the bankruptcy data themselves suggest that the information is not used. If creditors had some inkling that income updates and debt data would be useful in reducing bankruptcy risks, we would expect to see some creditor groups better avoiding the debtors with low incomes or high debt/income ratios. In fact, Table 17.6 shows just the opposite.

Although there is some range between the creditors who make the largest and the smallest percentage of loans to debtors in these lowest income reaches, there are no statistically significant differences. This means that long-term creditors (savings and loans and finance companies, for example) and short-term creditors (credit card issuers and gasoline companies) were indistinguishably caught lending to debtors at or near the poverty level. If creditors were using updated information, we would expect some to better use this information and avoid lowest income debtors. We would also expect short-term and long-term debtors to differ, with the long-term debtors unable to protect themselves and therefore more frequently caught with loans to the lowest income debtors by the time bankruptcy rolls around. In a separate calculation of debt/income ratios, again we find similarity among creditors, with no type of creditor distinguishing high-risk debtors better than any other.[14]

These data suggest that although bankruptcy losses could never be eliminated, they could be sharply reduced with the systematic collection of debt and income data and the repeated review of short-term credit extension decisions. The data suggest that a great deal of bankruptcy loss results from the one-time decision that a debtor is an acceptable credit risk followed by repeated extensions of credit without additional information.

Finally, we note that with more information the creditors may discover other ways to cut losses. Presumably credit markets, like other markets, operate more efficiently with more information. The data developed from the Consumer Bankruptcy Project can help creditors reevaluate their lending practices and formulas. The data comparing the value of security interests and showing customer incomes and debt/income ratios in bankruptcy are completely new. Each creditor in the marketplace has proprietary information about its lending practices and results. The Project data permit it to see how it stacks up against other creditors making those same decisions. If a creditor is doing substantially worse than other creditors in the same industry, the creditor may be able to assess its own process to see how it is not effectively using the information available to avoid high-risk debtors.

The Tension Between Loss Reduction and Mass Lending

Any business, including the business of extending credit, makes cost/benefit decisions. For a creditor to conclude that it makes sense to monitor subsequent lending decisions or to insist on higher down payments, it must decide that the cost is worth the benefit. Both the benefits and the costs in the consumer credit equation bear some analysis.

Actual Losses

We began this chapter with what appeared to be the benefits of reducing bankruptcy risk: $27,768,100 was listed by the 1202 wage-earning debtors in bankruptcy. But that $27,768,100 does not represent a benefit that the creditors could capture by following different practices to reduce their bankruptcy risks. As Table 17.2 shows, nearly two-thirds of the debt listed in bankruptcy is at least nominally secured. Table 17.3 shows that the secured claims, on average, were backed up by collateral worth at least 88% of the outstanding loan. And a debtor will often pay 100% of the value to keep the property. This means that bankruptcy risk is already far below what the listed numbers indicate because some creditors—mostly those with the biggest loans—have already gone a long way toward eliminating their bankruptcy risks. Thus the benefits of reducing bankruptcy exposure are much lower than the gross figures suggest.

Other factors also indicate that the actual bankruptcy losses are lower than the gross amounts listed and therefore potential benefits from improved monitoring of debtors would be reduced. About 20% of the wage-earning debtors in Chapter 7 reaffirmed one or more debts. Although the reaffirmed debt was overwhelmingly from the secured column, these reaffirmations add to the total of debt that was not discharged in bankruptcy. In addition to formal reaffirmations, we found considerable evidence of informal reaffirmations, by which we mean an arrangement where the debtor just keeps paying and the creditor goes along, without a formal agreement. We cannot quantify informal reaffirmations, but we suspect they were at least as prevalent as formal ones. Again, informal reaffirmations were almost entirely of secured debt. The two types of reaffirmation probably contribute to reducing the already small percentage of secured debt that is truly discharged, but probably do not much affect the amounts of unsecured debt that are actually discharged.[15]

Moreover, the current Chapter 13 filings also represent some debt listed but not discharged. Because some debtors attempt repayment in Chapter 13, some creditors have fewer losses than their listed debts indicate.[16] Because even more debtors try Chapter 13 and fail, often slipping from the bankruptcy system altogether without a discharge, again debt listings overstate actual bankruptcy losses.[17]

After all these factors have been considered, the actual benefits to creditors may not be sufficiently great to persuade the credit industry to change its current credit practices. The actual amount of loss each year to consumer creditors cannot be calculated, because our data are imprecise in several respects (as already noted), because we cannot be sure our ten districts are representative of the whole country, and because the Administrative Office of the Courts data are not reliable as to the number of consumers, as opposed to entrepreneurial, bankruptcies. If we ignored all that in a moment of speculation, we could estimate that the exposure in our sample of 1202 wage-earning families is around $8 million, the true unsecured and undersecured debt less 20% for reaffirmations and dismissed cases. A direct extrapolation of that debt over an estimated of 300,000 wage-earner cases a year would yield an industry exposure of about $2 billion in 1981.

Although this is a great deal of money in absolute terms, it is about 0.05% of the $389 billion in consumer debt that was outstanding at the end of 1981. Another way of looking at the potential bankruptcy loss is that if every credit card issuer in 1981 sent a statement once a month to every credit card holder, the postage costs alone would have amounted to more than $1.5 billion—not as much as the speculative bankruptcy loss, but in the same ballpark.[18] Spread over many thousands of industry creditors all over the country, the consumer bankruptcy losses may not be enough to make reformed credit practices seem worthwhile.

The Costs

Balanced against the benefits to be enjoyed if the creditors cut their bankruptcy losses are some potentially large costs. The monitoring we suggest would obviously cost money. Regular updating of debtor income and debts might conveniently be done in connection with annual card renewal, but it would certainly involve some expenditures for printing enclosures and for recording and evaluating the data. It might also have a negative impact on a creditor if competing creditors were not imposing the same requirement. The routine checking of current debt levels and recalculation of debt/income ratios through credit bureaus would be much less expensive and difficult but would still involve some time and expense to modify current practices.

Beyond direct costs, loss reduction based on worsened financial circumstances would necessarily mean a reduction in the amount of credit granted. For an industry creditor this means curtailed sales and revenues. Because no device for identifying high-risk debtors will be perfect, including the more discrete tests we propose, some loans that would have paid will necessarily be eliminated if lending is restricted. This means that along with risk reduction, some profits will be tossed out—a tangible cost of lowering bankruptcy risk.

This point takes on more force when we put it in some specific contexts. In Chapter Fifteen, for example, we observed an interesting phenomenon:

Creditors made highly individualized decisions to extend credit to small businesses, expending substantial resources to make detailed decisions about initial and continuing credit extension. These creditors nonetheless took on much higher risk loans than the consumer lenders (as evidenced by the small business failure rate) and they did so with even less security to back these loans up. In other words, these creditors took highly informed, considered decisions to walk right into the teeth of high-risk lending. And, as we pointed out in that chapter, the high profits of commercial lending may have made these entirely reasonable business decisions.

It is certainly the case that some creditors will continue to make debt consolidation loans and to extend other kinds of eyes-open credit to very bad credit risks, presumably because these are high-interest, high-profit loans, even after losses are considered. The practices of part of the industry were documented shortly before these bankruptcy data were collected. Congress held hearings on the Federal Trade Commission's proposed credit practices rules. The purpose of the hearings was to examine consumer credit industry lending practices, with a particular focus on finance companies. According to the documents and testimony presented, finance companies required detailed financial information from applicants. The information on debts and income was compiled to determine the debtor's monthly cash flow—the amount of the debtor's income less the total of all the minimum monthly payments. (We note parenthetically that finance companies routinely collect sufficient information to calculate debt/income ratios.)

What the finance companies did with the data gives another perspective on the consumer credit system. According to committee testimony, credit applications that showed a cash flow of less than $100 per month were routinely approved, and documented cases showed loans that were approved when the debtor had a margin as small as $13 between the monthly service on his current bills and his income. Indeed, the margins were so thin in the approved loans that the congressional committee found printed instructions appearing just below the net cash flow entry on one company's credit application forms reminding the loan officer to turn down the loan "if the payments planned exceed net cash flow." These lenders kept lending literally to the last available dollar of debtor income. Obviously these creditors are going to continue to lend to high-risk consumers, and they will continue to be listed in some of their debtors' bankruptcy petitions.

Even more conservative lenders regularly take risks because of the profit payoffs. An example is the creditors who finance purchases of their own products. Among the debtors in our sample are two kinds of creditors. The moneylenders make their profits from lending cash and collecting interest as the loans are repaid: banks, savings and loans, and private mortgage companies. Other creditors are financing sellers, using credit to boost the sales of their products, as stores and finance companies do. Financing sellers may make a profit directly from their extensions of credit repaid with interest, but their real concern may be using the availability of cheap credit to boost sales. The captive car finance companies are a bit of both.

Companies such as General Motors Acceptance Corporation (GMAC) and Chrysler Financial do almost no consumer lending except to finance the sale of GM or Chrysler cars and trucks. Traditionally, this finance business has been very profitable, an additional source of revenue over and above profits on car sales. But in recent years the finance affiliates have been used extensively to provide low-interest incentives to buy cars. The low-financing to attract buyers—"2.9% financing for a limited time only"—reflects the role of merchant credit as a device for getting consumers to buy that particular product because of attractive installment terms. The relative emphasis on these two aspects of sales credit—making money on the financing itself versus providing financing to sell the product—differs from industry to industry and from time to time, depending on interest rates and imaginative advertising campaigns, among other things.

The bankruptcy data show how risk decisions can follow the same pattern. The data in Table 17.3 show that although car finance companies always took security interests, their security was collectively among the weakest of all the creditors listed in bankruptcy. They protected only $71 of every $100 made on a secured car loan. Why did the car financers do so badly at the bottom line? Part of the answer is that they make loans on cars, and cars depreciate faster than they roll downhill. Some of these cars had been the victims of benign neglect or fender-benders, but all suffered from the relentless decline in bluebook value by the mere passage of time. These lenders made secured loans knowing that in every case the collateral would be worth less than the debt and that the loan would be "under water" at some point in the life of the loan. Yet car loans that were typically 36- to 48-month loans in 1981 are today often made for 60 months, ensuring an ever-longer period of undersecurity.

The loans could be structured differently. It is a matter of simple mathematics to demand a large enough down payment and large enough payments to match the high depreciation. But such a move would make the initial cost to buy a car higher, presumably curtailing purchases.

These examples suggest that even when the means to cut bankruptcy losses are readily at hand some creditors conclude from their quite sensible cost/benefit analyses that higher bankruptcy risk is simply worth the increased profits from other aspects of the lending process.

Policy Implications

We began Part II by noting that the creditors have been a faceless chorus in bankruptcy debates focused almost entirely on debtors. For example, there have been a number of economic studies of debtors in bankruptcy, but virtually nothing about the kinds of incentives and disincentives to reduce or accept losses that we have just been discussing. We have taken a first step in introducing facts about creditors and their lending practices into the policy debate.

Our data suggest that the key to reducing bankruptcy losses lies in decisions made at the inception of the lending arrangement, not in devices to extract payment from debtors in financial collapse. The data amply show the effect of secured credit in minimizing bankruptcy risk. They also suggest several other avenues, including monitoring debt/income ratios and income interruptions, to reduce bankruptcy risk by making better lending decisions. But this analysis also shows a relatively small bankruptcy risk spread among many creditors. The potential costs of making more restrictive lending decisions means that reasonable creditors may elect not to reduce their bankruptcy risks. In effect, a cost/benefit calculation may indicate that current bankruptcy losses are tolerable for professional industry lenders.

Developments in the consumer credit markets add to our skepticism that loss reduction will prove attractive to large parts of the industry. The *Wall Street Journal* in recent years has run a steady stream of articles on the credit industry. These articles have chronicled ever-rising default rates along with stories about the increases in consumer bankruptcies. Creditor spokespersons have ruefully admitted that the industry has been careless in distributing credit cards and granting credit.

Yet year after year the pages of the *Journal* and the *Federal Reserve Bulletin* reveal that consumer debt has continued to rise to record levels and additional millions of credit cards have been issued.[19] Not only are 60-month car loans on the rise, but so too are three- and four-year unsecured loans solicited on a mass basis. The creditors who are making these loans are as bound for bankruptcy court as if they had asked to be included. The explanation must be as simple as profit and loss, a fact confirmed by an industry analyst who was recently quoted as saying that credit card issuers are so sure that they will suffer high losses from a mass mailing of cards, they charge the resulting unpaid loans to "marketing expense" rather than to bad debt losses.

There will be real social consequences regardless of the course the industry takes in the future. If industry creditors were to restrict lending based on more active monitoring of debtors' financial circumstances, a number of debtors who are now getting credit might be cut off. A family struck by layoff might find itself forced to seek public assistance sooner, because Visa and a bank overdraft facility had been withdrawn. A cushion that currently may permit many people to smooth out the dislocations of temporary job layoffs or extraordinary short-term debt burdens would be curtailed.

On the other hand, our data show that a family which continues to incur debt in the face of income interruption or already high debt burdens is making a high-risk bet that the future will get better. If it does not get better quickly, the increased debt—rather than the initial problem—may be what sinks the debtor. Debtors forced to cut spending sharply when income drops or other debts have risen may feel some immediate pain and may have to face some hard choices to support a family. But that debtor may be better off in the long term without running up high-interest credit. Of course, any debtor in today's system can make a personal decision about these risks. Our point is simply that it is hard to say what net social cost or benefit would result from a tightening of consumer credit practices. Hard-pressed consumers as a group might or might not be better off, just as we have seen that the credit industry might or might not be more profitable if it reduced high-risk lending.

Given the trends of the past two decades, it seems more likely that the industry will continue to accept rising bankruptcy losses in order to maximize revenue and avoid higher monitoring costs. Needless to say, the industry would prefer to lose less in bankruptcy court. Every dollar of loss reduction without added industry cost is another dollar of profit, and corporate managers are quite properly concerned with maximum profits. Thus the industry will no doubt continue to support bankruptcy law changes that might increase marginal repayments at no cost to itself. This is a perfectly sensible position for the industry for the medium term, even if an argument can be made that its long-term interests might be better served by a balanced system that does not generate excessive social costs and risk political backlash.

The long-term social implications of ever-increasing consumer debt and its inevitable concomitant, increased consumer bankruptcies, are not clear. Our data show that in this decade stigma seems to be holding its own as a gatekeeper for bankruptcy, because the great majority of people in bankruptcy are truly desperate. After the enormous increases in filings of the late 1970s and early 1980s, there has been something of a plateau in the last part of the 1980s. On the other hand, we have not had a downturn in the business cycle since the early years of the decade. One has to wonder what level of filings might follow a convergence of harder times with the enormous increase in consumer debt.

The data suggest that relatively few people file more than once, so that most of the consumer bankruptcy filings are new bankrupts. If we come to the point, perhaps before the end of the century, where one American in ten, or even one in five, have been through personal bankruptcy, what might that mean for our society? Aside from the effects of continued increases in business bankruptcy filings by famous and respectable companies and individuals, how much bankruptcy stigma will there be if so many friends and neighbors have been through the process? These may well be questions we will have to address if we have a continued expansion of consumer credit with little attention to reduction of risk.

If the current free-market solution, with debtors and creditors taking their individual chances, leads to serious problems, one alternative would be government regulation of credit. Such regulation exists in a number of other countries. The government could, for example, require the cutting off of credit to debtors when debt/income ratios pass a certain point. One effect would be to eliminate the competitive problem that any one creditor would face in adopting such rules when its competitors had not. Such a system would almost certainly reduce consumer bankruptcy filings to a large extent.

Like any other program of government regulation, such a regime would create its own difficulties. There would be much controversy about the rules for credit restrictions, calls for exemptions, and so on. Close regulation of a four hundred billion dollar credit market serving 250 million people in a multitrillion dollar economy would be awkward and costly. It seems far more likely to us that Americans will take their chances with the free market, enforcing debts without regard to creditor irresponsibility up to the point of granting bankruptcy without regard to debtor irresponsibility. But we think this chapter sounds a faint, but insistent warning. The data show debtors, middle-class people like ourselves, increasingly at risk for a sudden economic collapse. And the credit industry, following its own profit-maximizing decisions, is able to produce higher profits by tolerating the occasional losses engendered by bankruptcy. In effect, we have a consumer credit system in which the risk of individual or even system collapse rises with every increase in debt, and the only check on its growth is the prudence of its borrowers and lenders. The data suggest that borrower and lender prudence may be too weak to match the increasing risks of consumer debt.

Notes

1. U.S. Bureau of the Census, Statistical Abstract of the United States, 1981 (102d ed., Washington: U.S. Government Printing Office, 1981), Table 865, p. 519. Of this total, $315.5 billion was installment credit. In addition, mortgage debt for residential nonfarm, commercial, and farm properties amounted to another $1,452 billion. *Id.*, Table 863, p. 518.

2. The category "residual" is primarily the result of a coding limitation. We were able to code in detail only the first five secured claims for each case, so that the sixth to *n*th claim for each case is reflected only in the total secured debt for that case. In nearly every case, the largest secured debts were listed first, so that it is the smaller debts on which we have limited data. Because we do not have information for these "above five" cases, we cannot break them out by creditor type and must include them in "residual." In our sample of 1202 wage-earner cases, 58 contained more than five secured debts, for a total of 140 undetailed claims that are excluded from our analysis of the secured positions of various types of creditors. These claims totaled approximately $600,000.

3. The "car finance" category consists of all finance company loans secured by cars. Because the captive finance companies do little other lending and the general finance companies rarely lend on cars, the category should be virtually coextensive with the captive automobile lenders.

4. Once again, we must note the uncertainties associated with valuation of the collateral. See Chapter Twelve.

5. For this table, we use only secured loans for which we have complete information both on the amount of the loan balance and the value of the collateral. The reported amounts are slightly smaller than the total debt reports because the dollar values of some debts were listed but the value of the collateral was ambiguously recorded or missing. We eliminated such debts from this calculation. A comparison between the secured columns in Tables 17.2 and 17.3 shows the portion of debt that could not be calculated for each creditor.

Each secured claim has been separately calculated. Thanks to the ingenuity of our programers, multiple claims on the same collateral have been included in the calculation each time. Where there was more than one claim on a particular piece of collateral, the larger claim was assumed to have first priority in the collateral value, the next largest claim the second priority, and so on.

All our figures on secured debt suffer from missing data in two ways. One limitation derives from constraints in coding. We coded only the first five secured debts in detail; any additional secured debts were included in the totals but were not individually coded. See note 2.

The second type of missing data arises because of nonreporting of specified amounts of secured claims and/or of the market value of collateral securing those claims. If either the amount of the claim or the market value of the collateral was not stated, then necessarily we could not include the claim in our detailed analysis of secured debt. Of a total 2777 secured claims that were included within the first five secured debts in a case, 656 (24%) were excluded for lack of a specified claim or market value. The great majority of these claims (613) had a claim value but no market value. These claims are, of course, included in the secured claim totals. We have no reason to think that the missing secured-claims data would alter our results, but we cannot be sure of that.

6. As we discussed in Chapter Twelve, actual recoveries will be less because of selling expenses and the lower prices obtained in forced sales. On the other hand, secured creditors have considerable flexibility in disposing of collateral and may do significantly better in getting close to full value than do bankruptcy trustees.

7. There are always exceptions. For example, when an entire area becomes severely depressed, housing values may plummet and mortgage lenders may be badly hurt.

8. Household goods secured 37% of the general finance company secured loans. Under the Bankruptcy Code, certain household goods liens can be invalidated by the debtor and some of the finance company liens were no doubt of that type. On the other hand, some household goods liens were valid. A further complication is that many, but not all, debtors' lawyers listed a debt as unsecured if it was secured only by an invalid household goods lien. Thus we simply cannot calculate the actual level of shortfall represented by such liens. Because they are such a large part of the secured lending picture for the finance company, no valid computation of their shortfall can be made. The one thing that is certain is that the total shortfall of these creditors is actually greater than Table 17.3 indicates, because of some amount of hidden shortfall on household goods.

9. Prior to development of these data, creditors might not have realized just how valuable a security interest in the debtor's home is to protect against the risks of bankruptcy. In recent years creditors have begun to discern the point, and in several states creditors have started marketing home equity loans that are, in effect, all-purpose credit cards backed up by the promise that the risk of nonpayment will be offset by a lien against the home. But even these lenders regard this as a new lending "product," one for which the creditor can take on larger loans for longer term and perhaps at a lower interest. The home equity loans do not seriously threaten to extinguish unsecured lending. The reason, again, is that too few loans would be profitable, repaid loans.

10. Mean debts owed to each creditor type are presented in the top panel of Table 17.3.

11. See explanation of federal debt income ratios in Chapter Four.

12. The forms require notation of the date the debt was incurred, but most lawyers do not report the data.

13. Some of our debtors may have had bad debt/income ratios at the start of the prebankruptcy period, in which case a short-term creditor was lending into a demonstrably risky situation throughout the period. For those who may have had normal debt/income ratios at the start of the prebankruptcy period, the very high debt/income

ratios reported at the time of bankruptcy must have resulted from a fall in income, a rise in debt, or some combination of the two during those two years. For our "trap-door" debtors whose incomes fell sharply only in the year before bankruptcy, the short-term creditors who lent in the prior year may not have been lending into a bad debt/income ratio. For the larger number of debtors who suffered income volatility in the second year before bankruptcy, debt/income ratios were probably aberrant through a large part of the two-year period. The minority of debtors whose incomes were relatively constant during the prebankruptcy period may have experienced a great increase in debt over the two years or during a relatively short period before bankruptcy. No doubt there are instances of each in our sample, although in our extensive review of the files we did not see much evidence of really short-term debt "run-up," as some creditor groups have alleged. It is worth noting that a run-up of debt just before bankruptcy is a basis for denial of discharge. It was an implicit basis in 1981 and has been an explicit ground since 1984. In summary, a good part of the short-term credit extended to our debtors could have been avoided by updating credit files, and at least a portion of the unavoidable credit could have been blocked from discharge.

14. We constructed federal comparative debt/income ratios owed to each of the unsecured creditor types that are listed in Table 17.2. The ratios range from 0.76 for private mortgage companies and 0.88 for credit unions to 1.64 for automobile finance companies and 1.95 for gasoline credit cards. None of these debt/income ratios differs significantly from the overall debt/income ratio of 1.23. The test was conducted using z-scores with a criterion level of $p = 0.05$.

15. This was a much lower percentage of reaffirmations than was found 25 years earlier, suggesting that the 1978 Code's reform of affirmations [11 U.S.C. §524] worked. D. Stanley and M. Girth, Bankruptcy: Problem, Process, Reform (Washington: Brookings Institution, 1971), p. 60.

16. The total unsecured debt that would have been paid if all our "still-paying" wage-earner cases paid all they had promised would have been $465,800.

17. The total debt listed in dismissed Chapter 13 cases in our sample was $3.1 million, of which $885,800 was unsecured.

18. According to the people who put together the Nilson Report, a credit card newsletter used by numerous industry analysts, 572.2 million credit cards were outstanding in 1981. This number includes bank cards, travel and entertainment cards, and most retail cards, but it excludes most private label cards used in limited areas, such as a card issued by a local pharmacy or local gift shop. If 12 mailings a year were made on each of the 572.2 cards, postage stamps at $.22 each would run $1,510,608,000.00. This leaves out the cost of bills, the envelopes, and the handling to assemble 6,866,400,000 pieces of mail.

19. The Growth of Consumer Debt, Federal Reserve Bulletin, 389 (June 1985). By 1987, the number of cards had grown to 841.1 million. See Chapter One, note 19.

18

Conclusion: Bankruptcy and the Consumer Credit System

Like death, a bankruptcy is a dramatic event. The headline bankruptcies of large and famous corporations and the cumulative bankruptcies of hundreds of thousands of individuals focus attention on bankruptcy as a social problem. Yet bankruptcy is not itself the cause of anything—only the result. This might not be true if bankruptcy had become a routine loophole for clever deadbeats, like a new tax shelter draining millions from the Treasury. Then one might say that bankruptcy was itself a social problem. But our data show that it is not, that it is generally used by people in very serious financial difficulty.

Given that fact, bankruptcy can be correctly understood only in the context of true social problems and the larger social systems that address these problems. Bankruptcy comprises part of an elaborate set of protective measures that soften the stresses of a market economy, from home mortgage insurance to homestead exemptions, from SBA loans to discharge of an entrepreneur. Bankruptcy also comprises part of a large, complex legal system that enforces debts; the essence of bankruptcy law is that it defines the point in that system where the state draws the line on enforcement. Above all, bankruptcy comprises part of an enormous consumer credit system, the relentless growth of which provides current prosperity even while it raises serious questions about our future.

Who Is in Bankruptcy?

Bankrupt debtors are a cross-section of America. There are some important subgroups in bankruptcy, but the data generally show that bankrupt debtors are not an identifiable class. They are not all—or mostly—day laborers and household maids dwelling in squalid apartments on the wrong side of the tracks. More than half are homeowners, and they work at pretty much the same jobs as everyone else. While further research should focus on the special problems of some of the subgroups we have identified, the financial trouble that leads to bankruptcy can be found in any community and no social or economic group is immune from it.

We began with the metaphor of bankruptcy courts as hospitals to treat the financially diseased. The compelling fact about bankruptcy in the 1980s is that a growing number of Americans, now approaching half a million a year, find themselves filing bankruptcy. Faced with a dramatic increase in hospital admissions, researchers would investigate whether the increases were a product of doctors and patients colluding in unnecessary admissions, using hospital beds for people with minor injuries or illnesses. In our analogous investigation of bankruptcy, we found that most people in our sample were very sick financially, weighed down with debts far beyond their capacity to repay. A small group, perhaps 5% of all bankrupt debtors, might be abusing the system. Alternatively, they might have more complicated tales of distress than the numbers in their files reveal. Or they might have been badly advised by lawyers eager to process cases in a high-volume practice, rather like physicians who administer unnecessary treatment.

Finding a small group of potential abusers raises the same question in any system: What should be done to identify and deal with them, and how much cost should be borne to support that effort? But the key finding in our data is that abuse should be dealt with as an aberration, not as the guiding issue in restructuring the system. Overwhelmingly, this system treats those who need it.

Perhaps our most dramatic finding confirms the marginal economic position of American women, especially women heading their own households. This is a finding that is as much about people not in bankruptcy as about bankrupts, because our findings highlight how many other women live on the edge of financial disaster.

Compared with men, women are consistently underpaid throughout the population. The difference between women householders in and out of bankruptcy is to a large extent the availability of supplemental income, over and above a woman's own earnings. Dependence on outside support combined with low income makes women householders extraordinarily vulnerable to financial disruption. A relatively slight dip in income or a small unexpected expense may be enough to throw a family headed by a woman over the financial edge into bankruptcy.

The social ills underlying these findings extend beyond the scope of the bankruptcy laws. But these facts emphasize and particularize the impact of bankruptcy laws on people at the fringes of the middle class. As a group, women householders are so close to financial collapse that they may enter that financial twilight zone of people too broke to go bankrupt. Indeed, the data raise the suspicion that single-filing women are underrepresented in bankruptcy because they are too poor to seek legal help when their bills overwhelm them. Any proposed change in the law that complicates the bankruptcy system, making legal help more expensive, would have a disproportionate impact on single women. Our sample contains men and married couples in equally desperate straits, but the close financial comparisons between women in and out of bankruptcy, combined with the low incomes, assets, and debts for single women in bankruptcy, suggest that women live with special economic vulnerability.

Married women who have chosen a traditional role, staying at home as housewife and mother, appear to be at greater risk for bankruptcy than are those who join the national trend of two-income families. The disproportion of nonworking spouses in bankruptcy is striking and serves, among other things, to discount the stereotype of couples who park the children in day care while working to gather a glut of material possessions. The bankruptcy data sound a different caution: The middle-class wife who does not work may be an endangered species.

Another high-risk group uncovered in the bankruptcy data are the entrepreneurs. Long heralded as the backbone of the capitalist system, their needs were presumably met by the Chamber of Commerce and the Small Business Administration. Many academics have dismissed the financial problems of small business owners, suggesting that they are protected by corporate limited liability so that personal discharge is irrelevant in coping with business debt. Our data thoroughly dispose of that complacent assumption. Many thousands of Americans go into personal bankruptcy each year as the price of an entrepreneurial system that includes a high rate of failure for small businesses.

One discovery in these data is a group of formerly self-employed debtors. These debtors have found a job by the time of filing, but their financial collapse derives from failure of a small business. The 10.4% of the debtors in the bankruptcy sample in business at the time of filing is nearly matched by the 9.6% who are formerly self-employed, combining to make one in five people in bankruptcy a failed entrepreneur.

This group of hidden entrepreneurs enables us to understand the very large role that business debts play in individual bankruptcies. Entrepreneurs are nearly three times more likely to go into bankruptcy than their representation in the labor force. The self-employed and formerly self-employed make up about 20% of our sample, but they account for more than half of all its debt. When those facts are combined with the discovery that business debt is even less fully secured than consumer debt, it is apparent that commercial lending constitutes a very large proportion of total creditor exposure in individual bankruptcies.

This finding significantly recasts the published bankruptcy data. Aggregated statistics about so-called consumer bankruptcies are misleading when one in five involves small business failures and half of all the debt listed is commercial debt. The current business–nonbusiness distinction in the AO statistics is defined by ambiguous criteria and is virtually meaningless. Any analyses that depend on that classification are fatally flawed. Even the little we know about individual bankruptcies may not be reliable.

Other groups in bankruptcy may be more notable for their absence than their presence. A few debtors used bankruptcy to deal with crushing medical debts, a few others seemed unable to resist the lure of their credit cards, and a very few waltzed through the bankruptcy courts more than once. But their numbers were small. There certainly are vivid anecdotes about concluding a catastrophic illness with a bankruptcy, or about wild spending that leaves a trail of plastic cards all the way to bankruptcy court. These anecdotes may be true, and they are certainly noteworthy when they are. But the data indicate that the anecdotes are aberrational. The reality is the far more ordinary story of middle-class people drowning in debt.

Causes of Bankruptcy

Debt

As we said at the outset, it is fundamentally misleading to claim to explain the causes of bankruptcy, as opposed to isolating various factors that contribute to the decision to file a petition in federal court. Yet in one sense the cause of bankruptcy is self-evident. Bankruptcy is caused by debt. If there were no debt, there would be no bankruptcy. This simplistic formulation is not as silly as it seems, because it starts the inquiry with the central proposition that bankruptcy is a function of debt. Our data confirm the perspective, showing that people in bankruptcy are typical Americans in many ways, but they have debts far out of proportion to their incomes.

This central fact emphasizes the distinction between an increase in bankruptcy as a response to financial trouble and an increase in financial trouble itself. Although the recent increases in bankruptcy are striking, they continue a long-term increase throughout the twentieth century. There have been peaks and valleys, but each turn of the wheel has left bankruptcy filings at a higher plateau. During this century the population has increased, but the rate in filings per thousand people has also increased. That same period saw the creation of the massive consumer debt characteristic of the modern economy. The rise in bankruptcy has, in a general sense, been coincident with the rise in consumer debt.[1]

Even more significant has been the increase in consumer debt as a proportion of income. The debt/income ratio for consumers in America has steadily risen throughout the century.[2] Our data show that the most distinguishing characteristic of bankrupt debtors is their high debts in relation to their incomes. The constant increase in debt helps to drive the American economy and therefore the world economy, but it has also made more American consumers candidates for bankruptcy. There is a longstanding debate over consumer debt in the United States, with some arguing that it has become pathologically overextended while others insist that it has remained relatively stable when other factors are considered. The debate is complex and technical. Our findings do not address it, but they do suggest a close connection between rising debt/income ratios and rising numbers of bankruptcies.

Irresponsibility and Volatility

The bankruptcies in our sample seem to stem from two intertwined explanations. One is the increased volatility and instability of economic life, an accelerating change to which both consumers and their creditors have failed to adjust. The other is the irresponsibility of particular debtor–creditor dyads, reflected in credit far beyond any reasonable prospect of repayment. In some cases economic disaster preceded bankruptcy: the failed business, job layoff, or serious medical debt. Other cases offer no apparent explanation for the bankruptcy except that spending outstripped income until the balance was no longer supportable—reflecting debtor and creditor irresponsibility.

We cannot know if increased debtor or creditor irresponsibility has led to increased bankruptcy. Many people believe that it has and they may well be right, although there is a tendency for some people to notice only increased debtor irresponsibility and for others to seem aware only of irresponsible creditor behavior. Our data suggest there is enough irresponsibility to go around.

The analysis of credit card debt, for example, reveals a substantial group (about 15% of the wage earners) who owe more than half a year's income in credit card debt alone. These cases break down into two parts: those who ran up huge debts compared to existing income and those for whom income dropped or was interrupted, making their debts insupportable.

The cases in which a debtor had stable income and managed to amass credit card debts in excess of half a year's income surely represent some clear abuses. But any fingerpointing has to go both ways. Credit card issuers were willing to give out the fifth, sixth, or seventh bank card and to approve charges after debtors already owed short-term debt so large that they could not possibly pay the interest, much less the principal. The consumer credit system currently tolerates debtor irresponsibility because the system is not well organized to police it. Creditors have not organized their information systems to detect and halt credit abuse. Having failed to make fairly inexpensive adjustments to reduce abuse, creditors bear some responsibility for the losses. The explanation may be that maintaining the current state of affairs is cost effective for the industry, even if it produces lending that seems irresponsible as to an individual debtor.

If increased irresponsibility is one piece of the puzzle, increased economic volatility is another. The 1980s have not been the best of times in many parts of the country and in many industries. The post-World War II economy, at least until the devaluation of the dollar by President Nixon in 1971, was relatively stable, although it did not always seem so to those living in that period. Since then the American economy has become more volatile and unstable for many reasons, including its much greater involvement in a largely unregulated global marketplace. At the same time that the volatility has increased, the country has gone deeply into debt, and so have many of its citizens.

The result is that large economic forces that once interested only Federal Reserve officials and commodity traders now directly touch the lives of every American. A family's economic future has become hard to predict, even among those with well-established careers. In our sample are long-time workers for International Harvester, stable employees who found themselves laid off by plant closings. One region of the country is booming while the next is in deep depression—and the roles have shifted within the space of a single decade. Texas and Pennsylvania have changed places as the examples of our boom and bust states during the time it has taken to write this book, and they may change again before someone reads it. Even one area within a state may suffer decline while another area wallows in prosperity.

Income volatility is an important factor in consumer bankruptcy. Nearly half our debtors suffered large income changes in the two years before bankruptcy. The steady income stream on which both debtor and creditor had counted for repayment of a given level of debt was cut off or greatly diminished for part or all of that period. Unfortunately, we have no clearly comparable national statistics on income volatility or its trends. But our data certainly suggest that the increase in bankruptcies is linked to an increase in income interruptions among debtors.

Debtors who save little and charge to the limits of prudence are making a wager with Providence, betting that they can never get sick or be fired, or that they can quickly find new jobs if they lose the ones they have. And their creditors have matched the wager. The twin evils of economic volatility and irresponsibility haunt increasing numbers of debtors and creditors.

Bankruptcy Within a Broader Social Context

Bankruptcy must be understood within a broad range of social support systems. For the entrepreneur, bankruptcy is part of a legal system that helps limit the risk of starting a new business. The SBA guarantees the loan to get the business started, and bankruptcy is there to cushion the blow if it fails. For the homeowner, bankruptcy is part of a set of laws that nurture home ownership, from the FHA financing and a big tax deduction to the ultimate protection of the homestead exemption. For the family facing a catastrophic illness, bankruptcy is an insurer of last resort. For some subset of debtors, bankruptcy probably spells the difference between welfare and continued work. Bankruptcy is not just about debtors and creditors; it is a link in a network of legal structures of far-reaching social significance. To examine bankruptcy laws only within the abstraction of debt discharge, without the context of its other social implications, is to miss a large part of how bankruptcy functions.

Even within the legal system, bankruptcy is only a part of a large and complex legal regime regulating the relationships between debtors and creditors. Federally regulated Truth-in-Lending disclosures start the credit transaction and discharge in bankruptcy may close it. Viewed from the creditors' perspective, the heart of debtor–creditor law is the system of legal enforcement of debt, laws that facilitate repossession, laws that send out the marshall with a summons, laws that seize a debtor's wages or bank account. On that continuum, bankruptcy law defines the point at which the state says "enough" and declines to continue legal action against a debtor, beyond the seizure of nonexempt property or future income permitted under the Bankruptcy Code.

Ultimately bankruptcy has profound political implications, in the largest sense of the word political. Debt is social dynamite and always has been. It lay at the heart of the struggles, often violent ones, between plebians and patricians in the Roman republic. The pressures of debt had much to do with the series of compromises that shaped that republic's political institutions. Even more ancient societies were importantly concerned with the problems of creating a permanent debtor class. One powerful illustration is the biblical jubilee, a release of all debts every seven years. In the modern setting, bankruptcy is one of the safety valves that sophisticated capitalism keeps in place to release the pressures of fear and greed that accompany free market incentives. Every machine must have give in the joints or it will destroy itself, and bankruptcy is part of the give in a free market society.

A 31-year-old unemployed steelworker with a wife and family is a potential social danger. A single mother supporting three children on haphazard support payments and a minimum-wage job at the local diner is another trouble spot. So is the couple holding three jobs between them to keep things together after their card and gift shop goes belly up. If their situations do not move the reader to compassion, they should at least invoke a shrewd wariness. This is the stuff of serious social unrest. Suppose the steelworker, to pay his debts to various gigantic, distant corporations, were condemned to flip hamburgers for the rest of his life, while his family lived at the edge of poverty. His reaction, and those of hundreds of thousands of others, would pose profound social and political problems, especially because the debtors would be likely to believe that the same "big boys" they were paying were the ones responsible for the economic mess in the first place.

To indenture the unemployed steelworker and the others to their creditors would also create a serious problem of externalities. Taxpayers would be forced to assume the burden of supporting their families while the family income satisfied old debts and their attendant high rates of interest. In effect, tax dollars would be subsidizing creditors, many of whom were equally culpable players in the credit game.

The bankruptcy discharge is not the only approach to these problems. American law is by far the most generous in the world in granting discharges to both individuals and businesses. Other countries address in different ways the social problems that are ameliorated in the United States by bankruptcy discharge. For example, in the Netherlands the bankruptcy laws are quite strict, but that fact is balanced by a fairly pervasive regulation of the credit industry, including regulations limiting the amounts of credit that can be granted to consumers. We would guess that the United States credit industry would object most strenuously to this tradeoff. In addition, the apparent toughness of bankruptcy law in other industrial societies is usually balanced by unemployment and social welfare benefits substantially more generous than our own. Taxpayers in those societies have in effect agreed to subsidize the losses of creditors and to accept the externalities just discussed.

Our bankruptcy discharge is a free market solution to the pathologies of borrowing and lending. Creditors are free to extend credit as they like and debtors to accept it. Both face the prospect of bankruptcy if they are foolish or unlucky. The system places the losses on the debtors and creditors who accepted the benefits and took the risks of credit transactions. So understood, bankruptcy is likely to remain the preferred solution for Americans.

The Poverty of Armchair Theories

The findings of the Consumer Bankruptcy Project are fundamentally conservative. In general, bankruptcy serves the sort of people it is supposed to serve. Many of the bankruptcy reforms that have been proposed over the last decade have been based on flawed factual premises. These findings should suggest caution and modesty in changing the bankruptcy system that has evolved over the last century, at least until we gather hard, reliable information about the consumer credit system and its bankruptcy component.

Aside from the false notion that lots of people who can pay are going into bankruptcy, some policymakers and some economists have suggested that the increases in bankruptcy filings were "caused" by the provisions of the 1978 Bankruptcy Code. As we indicated earlier, the studies that attempt to prove this point were based on manipulations of AO data, which are virtually worthless for this purpose. The contention, at best, remains unproven.

Moreover, the assumptions that underlay these contentions are cast into serious doubt by our data. Proposed reforms frequently assume a far more predictable relationship between details of the bankruptcy laws and debtor behavior than actually exists. A principal basis for blaming the Code for increased bankruptcy filings is the notion that the new federal exemptions made bankruptcy "too easy."[3] The data in Chapter Thirteen demonstrate the failure of exemptions to have the predicted effect on bankruptcy decisions. The data strongly suggest that changes in the legal regime may have little effect or may even have effects opposite to those expected.

Many of the flawed proposals for reform originated from simplistic armchair economic models of debtor behavior and the functioning of the bankruptcy system. To create economic models based on historical fact or empirical data is a useful contribution to policymaking debates. It is even useful to create abstract theoretical models to advance the analysis of different aspects of a problem, eventually aiming toward models designed to be tested empirically. It is not useful to rely on untested formal models when writing laws. Bad modeling is worse than useless. Other forms of neoscholasticism may entertain, build academic careers, and teach critical thinking, but bad economic modeling can be positively harmful if its false premises lead lawmakers into legal enactments that affect hundreds of thousands of debtors and creditors every year. To advocate law reforms without a shred of evidence about how the system currently works, who is likely to be affected, and how those effects may reverberate throughout the system is breathtakingly negligent. Bankruptcy policymaking must abandon simplistic models, no matter how superficially attractive they are.

From an economic theorists' point of view, the real puzzle about bankruptcy is why it is so rare. Theorists studying bankruptcy start with the fact that consumer bankruptcy looks like a good deal. A debtor can declare once every six years, wiping out all debts. If there is no penalty, everyone should do it. Despite a decade of greatly increased filings and growing economic volatility, less than 1% of the population went bankrupt. Why do so few do it and then only when their financial situations are dire?

The major economic or financial deterrent to bankruptcy is loss of nonexempt property, a deterrent that many thought had been weakened too much by the 1978 Bankruptcy Code. But our data strongly suggest that exemption changes had little to do with rising bankruptcy filings. Aside from loss of property, the theorist can identify only three deterrents to bankruptcy: lack of information, fear of stigmatization, and a moral commitment to keep promises.

The first deterrent—lack of information—is on its way to obliteration with the recent widespread publicity bankruptcy has enjoyed. There is widespread lawyer advertising: "Having problems with your debts? We can help." Lawyers advertising bankruptcy services in newspapers and on television may contribute to rising filing rates. The Supreme Court decisions permitting widespread lawyer advertising took effect at nearly the same time as the new Bankruptcy Code. Corporate bankruptcies and the personal bankruptcies of celebrities have been extensively publicized. The barrage of information about the availability of bankruptcy surely caused some consumers to decide that bankruptcy, rather than some other response, was the best solution to their financial problems. Although we cannot test this conclusion directly, it was the unanimous view of the judges and other bankruptcy experts we interviewed, and it fits the available data.

Lawyers also became more aware of bankruptcy. The publicity surrounding the adoption of the new Code and the subsequent continuing legal education programs to train lawyers to use it made bankruptcy very visible to a number of lawyers who had never thought much about it before. At the same time, the law schools graduated a lot of hungry young lawyers, and old established law firms changed longstanding policies of "not doing" bankruptcy. Some combination of these factors undoubtedly affected the explosion in consumer bankruptcy filings.

With information about bankruptcy more generally available, the economic theorists are left with only two deterrents standing between us and massive increases in bankruptcy: moral conviction and social pressure. That prospect scares them, because as a group they mistrust variables that seem so ephemeral and only quasi-rational. For that reason, they are inclined to suggest a need for financial deterrents to prevent abuse.

It may be that there has been a general decline in moral values in our society, a decline that includes a reduction in people's commitment to pay debts. It is also possible that there has not been a decline, but rather a change in values. Some of the people in bankruptcy in the 1980s may be those who in the 1940s would have worked three jobs and kept their families at the edge of survival to pay their debts. Many of us have heard from parents and grandparents stories of years of deprivation to pay Depression debts. We have heard about fathers and mothers rarely at home because they held multiple jobs and about families living at the edge of poverty so every spare nickel could go to debt repayment. These stories of sacrifice and heroism are wholly admirable for their moral conviction and strength of character. It is less clear, however, that the present generation would applaud the choices made, as opposed to the strength of commitment to those choices. For example, each reader can make a judgment about the relative virtue of debt payment versus the loss of companionship between parent and child or the lessening of the child's opportunities, educationally and otherwise. These questions are inescapable in a discussion of debt discharge.

Moral values may also have changed in the sense that changes in the credit system may have made moral conviction seem less relevant to those who are heavily indebted. In today's credit market, most creditors are likely to be large, impersonal corporations, rather than Grant Herring down at Herring Hardware. Debtors may feel less compunction about stiffing ITT Financial than they would Mr. Herring, especially if ITT virtually thrust the credit on them ("We have $2,000 waiting for your signature"), while Mr. Herring sold on credit to help out when times were tough.

Whatever changes may have occurred in moral values, we do not doubt that moral conviction continues to play an important part in keeping many people out of bankruptcy. Some shared moral conviction is essential to the functioning of any society and certainly to systems of borrowing and lending. We believe that people generally repay their debts because they believe it is the right thing to do, so that legal enforcement is rarely required. Even among people who have taken the fateful step of filing for bankruptcy, a substantial number reaffirm some of their debts, often for no discernible reason other than their sense of obligation.

It may be that the social stigma of bankruptcy has declined in recent years, in part because of the bankruptcies of so many famous corporations and prominent individuals. The bankruptcies of Johns Manville, Texaco, A.H. Robins, Braniff Airlines, Continental Airlines, Denton Cooley, and John Connally have made for juicy news reports on the airwaves and in print. Although it surely remains true that bankruptcy is not a badge of honor, these examples may help to legitimize a bankruptcy filing for a family that sees itself in hopeless financial trouble.

A more concrete stigma of bankruptcy is denial of future credit, the loss of access to credit for an extended period of time. This specific and highly predictable stigma no doubt offers an important deterrent to bankruptcy. This kind of stigma may also have weakened, however. The example of the Voelkers in Chapter Eleven suggests that at least some debtors are able to get substantial credit following bankruptcy. Credit standards may be generally looser, or a possible increase in the number of lenders of the "E-Z Credit—No Credit Check" variety may be responsible. If so, an important deterrent may have lost some of its effect.

Our data cannot directly support any conclusion about the impact of a stigma in either sense, but they do demonstrate that few people file bankruptcy without crushing debts. We found virtually no debtors who seemed to take bankruptcy on a lark, to deal with relatively minor debts in relation to their incomes. Instead, the debtors we saw were in so much financial trouble we had to wonder how they had stayed out of bankruptcy so long and what it must have been like in the months or years before filing as they dealt with debts that grew mountainous beside an unsteady income. The fact that the debtors in our sample did not choose bankruptcy earlier, given the disastrous state of their affairs, suggests to us that many of them tried longer than was reasonable to avoid discharging their debts. If the economic theorists are correct that moral conviction and stigma are the principal deterrents to bankruptcy, the data suggest that these deterrents work.

The Role of Empirical Data

We began the Consumer Bankruptcy Project because of our realization that so little was known about this important legal and social phenomenon. As our research developed, we discovered how misleading even its gross statistics are, and how little is known about the whole consumer credit system of which bankruptcy is a part. Given the central role of consumer credit to our economic prosperity, it seems to us that it is crucial that we learn much more about its actual functioning.

Doing empirical work is not in all ways rewarding. We are painfully aware that good and careful work will be dismissed as obvious. "Hey, Carol, it says here that these people spent $250,000 and six years of their lives to show that people in bankruptcy are broke!" We have already encountered the frustration of that rejoinder. The critics deftly assume that everything shown was obvious (they just had not thought to mention it before), while all the things one's study does not show were the only important ones. Perhaps it is the only rejoinder to be expected, until scholars take the position that they will not take a new theory very seriously until its adherents advance some data. Until then, the all-embracing theory deduced in the library will always seem to trump a study suffering from the constraints of reality.

In the long run, our hope for empirical support for improvement in the bankruptcy laws must rest on regular gathering of data by the courts on a nationwide basis. No episodic empirical study within realistic funding and personnel limits will be able to cast more than a limited light on these problems.

As other factors force the bankruptcy courts to greater computerization, we can hope that the day of regularly gathered, national data will soon dawn.[4]

Short-Term Reform

The data raise serious questions about the exalted role of Chapter 13 in the bankruptcy system. Originally this alternative was designed for debtors who wanted to try repayment, to attract more people in trouble to use the bankruptcy courts notwithstanding their grave moral reservations about filing bankruptcy. Now it is used to extract higher repayment and to discourage Chapter 7 filings. Thirty-five states and the Congress have adjusted exemption laws to create these incentives. Congress made several other smaller changes in the bankruptcy scheme to make Chapter 13 more attractive. A national campaign to sell judges, attorneys, and ultimately debtors on the benefits of Chapter 13 has been under way since the late 1970s.

The data show that all the legal reform has little of its intended effect, either of generating much repayment or of sorting can-pay debtors from Chapter 7 to Chapter 13. But to say that the bankruptcy reforms have not had their intended effect is not to say they have had no effect. Real live people have filed Chapter 13 in record numbers, with about a third of those in bankruptcy now trying Chapter 13 rather than Chapter 7. These debtors paid money they could ill afford for advice to file bankruptcy in a way that was likely to bring them nothing but grief. Two-thirds of those in Chapter 13 could not make their payments. Some stayed around, struggling for a while, skipping a month then paying a month, until they finally gave up. Some went back to their lawyers and paid another fee for conversion to Chapter 7. Others just drifted from the bankruptcy system, paying filing fees and attorneys' fees, and buying nothing more for their $560 than a month or two spell when the creditors could not call. In short, there are a lot of people in bankruptcy who bought a bill of goods when they filed Chapter 13. These Chapter 13 failures were cheated by a system that made unjustified promises of successful repayments and reestablished creditworthiness, and then left them to founder alone.

Even among the apparent successes in Chapter 13, the data suggest some serious reservations. Most of these people are not paying their debts in full. Many manage repayment by filing plans that pay little more than they would have voluntarily paid in Chapter 7 when they tried to repay to retain collateral and when they agreed to reaffirm a few debts. Among those who pay more, based on the reports of their financial circumstances, we wonder about the level of sacrifice involved and whether the bankruptcy trustee has become a public debt collector, squeezing the last dollar from financially strapped people.

The creditors have not done much better. Although it will take another study to compare directly how much repayment goes on in Chapter 7 and Chapter 13, we are confident that the differences are at best only modest. It is no wonder that creditors generally make little differentiation between debtors who file in Chapter 7 and those who file in Chapter 13. The payment results are too similar. Since the credit industry lobby poured untold sums into pressing for the very reforms that brought them so little return, we wonder if the industry too has been sold a bill of goods.

Aside from the effects on debtors, the drive to push debtors into Chapter 13 has distorted the law itself in important ways. For example, the all-embracing Chapter 13 discharge, which may enable an ax murderer to discharge liability to a victim's family, is a heavy public policy price to pay for a system that does not deliver payment even to ordinary creditors.

We do not take the position that Chapter 13 is always bad. We are certain there are debtors who have repaid and who are rightly proud of their accomplishment. We have nothing but praise for a system that permits them the time and opportunity to pay. Our objection is to the wholesale acceptance of Chapter 13 as the bankruptcy panacea and the consequent formal and informal restructuring of the bankruptcy system to channel people into Chapter 13. This mistake has cost hundreds of thousands of debtors money, time, and heartache and given many of them little but another financial failure.

Conclusion

The findings of the Consumer Bankruptcy Project are both reassuring and troubling. The data suggest that the present bankruptcy system works, at least in the sense that it gives debtors in trouble some chance to start over. It also works in the sense that the debtors who use it are in very serious trouble and are least likely to repay their creditors even without bankruptcy protection. Bankruptcy creates play in the joints to a system of debt enforcement, and it provides a safety valve to avoid the formation of a deeply angered debtor class.

But bad news comes with the good. The data show a bankruptcy system that poorly serves many who seek its protection. They also show the lamentable consequences of debating policy and passing laws using simplistic models and ignoring empirical assumptions that underlie the debate. Moreover, by focusing on the ragged edge of the credit system, the people in deepest financial trouble, the bankruptcy data give some insights into other financial hazards within the credit system. The data show larger economic troubles—women at the edge of economic survival, entrepreneurs at highly disproportionate economic risk, wage earners facing unsteady incomes, creditors extending credit despite overwhelming evidence that the debtor cannot pay.

With better data, with a more modest approach to what bankruptcy laws can accomplish, and realistic assessments of the behavior of debtors and creditors, we look forward to a day when we can write realistic bankruptcy laws that better serve both debtors and creditors. In the short run, we look for changes in the widespread love affair with Chapter 13 among the professionals who do not actually have to live with the budgets and payoff plans. In the long run, we look for a better way to make bankruptcy policy.

Our study is devoted to facts, but we have tried to keep in mind the moral, historical, and social dimensions of bankruptcy. Moral ambiguity is an inescapable part of bankruptcy. Rebirth, renewal, the fresh start—these are ideas as American as the lone wagon setting out for a new frontier. It may not be coincidental that our first effective bankruptcy law was enacted about the time the frontier closed. But broken promises and welshing, being a deadbeat, are not a part of the American ideal. Many Americans might feel that the expansion of bankruptcy—perhaps its growing acceptance and purported de-stigmatization—represents a serious decadence in public morality and social soundness, regardless of the profit-and-loss figures. Others will feel that paying debts is ultimately a moral decision that the law should leave to each individual. Still others will feel that the fresh start is even more of a moral imperative in a world of large and impersonal economic forces. For present purposes, we identify the centrality of the moral questions and call for a shift in the focus of bankruptcy debates.

The fresh start notion has close connections with individualism and a market philosophy. It reflects a basic decision that the costs and benefits of discharge should be—and safely can be—left to the individual debtor. The system rests on a free market philosophy that throws the social and economic risks of credit on creditors and debtors, rather than on society at large.

Whatever we do about bankruptcy must be done with an understanding that our bankruptcy law is distinctively American. Although virtually every market society has a law designed to respond to the crisis of insolvency, American bankruptcy laws are unique in concept, not merely in detail. They rest on the notions of a fresh start and protecting the little guy, ideas some might describe as liberal. But they also differ from the rest of the world in being highly individualistic and in minimizing the role of governmental regulation and subsidy, values generally considered conservative. In one sense, bankruptcy is un-American, because we do not much like to think about failure. But it is peculiarly our own because of its solicitude for the risk-taker. In that sense, bankruptcy is as American as apple pie—and likely to be a permanent, and even growing feature of the economic life of the late twentieth century.

Notes

1. D. Stanley and M. Girth, Bankruptcy: Problem, Process, Reform (Washington: Brookings Institution, 1971), Table 3–1, p. 25; Personal Bankruptcies, Federal Reserve Bulletin 91 (Sept. 1988).

2. The Growth of Consumer Debt, Federal Reserve Bulletin 389 (June 1985).

3. The other provision occasionally cited to prove that bankruptcy had gotten "too easy" was that Chapter 13 1% plans were permitted. Less than 3% of our Chapter 13 cases proposed a 1% payment.

4. T. A. Sullivan, E. Warren, and J. L. Westbrook, The Use of Empirical Data in Formulating Bankruptcy Policy, 50 Law and Contemporary Problems 195 (1987).

APPENDIX

Data and Methods

Debtors: The Unit of Analysis

Most bankruptcy theory assumes that the key variables relate to individual debtors. Our review of earlier literature led us to design a microdata study, that is, a study in which debtors rather than districts are the unit of analysis. Because existing data were inadequate, we had to collect data on the characteristics of bankrupt debtors, their assets, their liabilities, their jobs, their marital status, whether they were homeowners, and so forth. This decision meant we would have to gather an enormous amount of information. We coded over 200 variables for each of 1,529 debtors, generating over 300,000 pieces of information.

The second key decision was to focus on the differences between Chapter 7 and Chapter 13 debtors. The great debate of recent years has been whether too many people who could pay were in bankruptcy and, of those who were, whether too many were taking "the easy way out" in Chapter 7 rather than trying to pay in Chapter 13. If we could describe the financial conditions of those in bankruptcy and report the differences between those who chose each chapter, we could cast considerable light on that debate.

We also decided to collect data about the creditors of the debtors in bankruptcy. No one had ever done that before. Understanding bankruptcy solely through debtors was too Zen-like, the sound of one hand clapping. That no one had investigated creditors before may tell us something interesting about unconscious attitudes toward the bankruptcy process.

Although debtors were the unit of analysis in constructing our data base, we eventually reprogramed the data base to focus on additional analytic units. To construct the variable for attorney specialists in Chapter Thirteen of the book, we reorganized the data base by code numbers assigned to attorneys.

To analyze secured lending, as we do in a number of chapters, we reorganized the data base by collateral type and by lender type.

Geographic Variation: Levels of Analysis

The next issue we had to address was where to collect data. At the risk of stating the obvious, the key to statistical research is variation. The fundamental question for a social scientist is "How does this group differ from that group and what connections are there among the variations?" Many local variations could affect the bankruptcy process for different debtors. Despite an increasingly homogenized and interdependent economy and the development of instantaneous communication, local labor markets and local market conditions affect most consumers, many creditors, and, we suspected, the bankruptcy courts. Moreover, we hypothesized that the local legal culture might develop extrastatutory customs that summary statistics could never reveal. Especially in bankruptcy, experimental efforts and quiet innovations, although unacknowledged, are widespread. For example, repayment plans in the Northern District of Alabama during the 1930s served as a kind of pilot project for the present-day Chapter 13.

The source of variation in bankruptcy had always been assumed to be the states, and most studies had been done with one district assumed to represent the state. The reasoning was that the exemptions are affected by state law. However, the Administrative Office data, for all their infirmities, show that substantial variation exists among judicial districts within the same state. The federal court system, of which the bankruptcy courts are a part, is divided into districts. Although some states have just one district that covers the whole state, most states are divided into two or more federal districts. The AO bankruptcy data showed that the number of filings, the increases in filings, and, above all, the proportion of Chapter 7 cases versus Chapter 13 cases varied greatly among districts *within* each state. Multidistrict studies that select only one district from a state necessarily conflate differences of locality and differences caused by state law, differences that are already apparent even in the limited AO data. That meant we had to study all the districts in a given state to discover variations before examining possible differences among states.

Below the district level, most federal judicial districts are further subdivided into smaller geographic units called divisions. Typically, lawyers file bankruptcy petitions at a courthouse within each division. Thus in the Northern District of Illinois, records are filed in Chicago and in Rockford. In the Central District of Illinois, records are filed in Springfield, Peoria, and Danville. We sampled records from all courthouses where files were kept to yield a complete sample of the district. We traveled to a total of 21 cities. The sample size selected in the divisions was proportionate to the total number of filings in the division.

Because we used all of the divisions and all of the districts within the selected states, it is possible to aggregate our microdata to provide profiles of districts and states.

Sampling

Once we had decided to use debtors' files, we had to draw a sample. There is inevitably a tension between the distinctiveness and the generalizability of microdata. Any individual bankruptcy results from a unique configuration of misfortunes, unforeseen circumstances, uncontrollable economic events, or personal inadequacies. Moreover, idiosyncratic features of the local bar or bench could contribute variation.

The uniqueness argument might suggest a purposive selection procedure: deliberately selecting a group of lawyers with the largest consumer bankruptcy practices; selecting the petitioners with the largest or smallest debts; or selecting a district thought to be "typical." The problem with such a selection procedure is that it would assume that we already knew the important sources of variations among bankruptcy filings, when it is the source of variation that we sought to discover. We could not assume a priori that experienced attorneys or petitioners with relatively unusual debt burdens were most important to study. Nor did we have any basis for assuming that a given district is "typical," because typicality is established after the data are examined, not before they are collected. Because so few systematic data were available, it was not possible to select a characteristic on which to examine debtors without building potential bias into the data collection.

We selected a sample of all bankruptcy petitions filed by individuals. Such a sample of bankruptcy petitions will include some debtors with large debts and some with small debts; creditors and lawyers should be represented in rough approximation to their proportion in the cases. The advantage of the representative sample is that it permits generalization to the larger population.

The aim of sampling is to give every element within the universe (that is, all filings) an equal opportunity to be selected into the sample. Because every court keeps a docket of cases filed during the year, with every case chronologically numbered, we sampled from a list without replacement, a systematic procedure that approximates random sampling. The differences between Chapter 13 and Chapter 7 were of particular interest, and so in four districts with low Chapter 13 filing rates, we drew separate samples of Chapter 13 petitioners to yield at least 50 Chapter 13 cases to analyze.

Another sampling issue that we confronted was whether we could sample debtors from a short time period during 1981 or whether we needed to study debtors from throughout the year. There have been persistent questions about whether consumer bankruptcy is subject to a seasonality bias. Both court clerks and lawyers told us of the post-Christmas "rush" in late January and early February and an analogous back-to-school "rush" in late August. The post-Christmas filings were explained as the effect of the holiday bills arriving; no reason was given for the late summer increase except for the generalization that people thought it happened. We concluded that we should sample throughout the year, in part to check for these variations. When all was said and done, we found there is some seasonality but no post-Christmas rush.[1]

Finally, we had to decide how many cases to analyze. National sample surveys are routinely carried out with fewer than 2500 cases because random sampling (or close approximations to randomness) sufficiently captures the heterogeneity of the population. In this study, we chose a sample size of 1500, or about 150 per district. By several rules of thumb, this is a sufficient number.[2] Our sample size is approximately the same as or larger than the sample sizes in similar studies of economic or financial issues and is larger than those routinely used in national opinion polls.

We estimated the sampling parameters using the data in Table A.1 and the formula $i = Np/n$, where i is the sampling interval, N is the number of cases, p is the proportion eligible, and n is the sample size. The number of cases N was the total cases filed. The proportion eligible p was estimated by subtracting the counts of involuntary, Chapter 11, and other ineligible cases from the total and dividing by the total. We recognized that in a district with many "business 7" cases, the proportion ineligible was always underestimated. This was true because corporate 7's, which were ineligible for our study, were mingled together with the individual "business 7's."

By estimating the relative proportions of Chapter 7 and Chapter 13 filings, we tried to determine whether an ordinary systematic sample of cases would yield the case base of 150 with at least 50 Chapter 13 cases included. Here again, our estimate was off by whatever proportion of "business 7's" were actually corporate bankruptcies. To have our estimates "off" in advance of arriving at the courthouse was no great disaster. Every court had its chronologically ordered docket sheet for 1981, and it was easy to take a random start within the first i cases and to select every ith case thereafter.[3]

Any ineligible case was discarded from the sample, including corporate 7's. To the extent that the proportion p was over- or underestimated because of "business 7's," the interval was either too wide, resulting in too small a sample, or it was too narrow, resulting in many more cases than needed. The former happened only in the Eastern District of Pennsylvania, and there the discrepancy is minor. Our worst example of the latter was in the Southern District of Texas, where a sample designed to produce 150 cases in fact produced 227. This resulted from a quantity p that was too large relative to the actual number of ineligible cases. Put differently, it appears that Houston and environs had many "business 7" cases that were in fact eligible for the sample because they were individual bankruptcies, but which we had assumed were ineligible in the estimation equation.

As Table A.2 shows, sampling fraction varied from district to district as we sought our uniform 150 cases from each district. At least in theory, these data could be weighted to represent the actual filings in the three states of the study. In practice, our sample data are presented unweighted because of the problem in estimating how many Chapter 7 filings in the district are represented by each Chapter 7 in the sample. This problem arises, in turn, from the

TABLE A.1. Nonbusiness Bankruptcy Filings, by Chapter, U.S. and Ten Districts 1980–82 (fiscal years)

	1980[a]		1981		1982	
	Chapter 7	Chapter 13	Chapter 7	Chapter 13	Chapter 7	Chapter 13
Total	*N* (%)[b]	*N* (%)[b]	*N* (%)[b]	*N* (%)[b]	*N* (%)[b]	*N* (%)[b]
U.S.	137,950	44,461	230,404	91,813	217,081	92,689
	(75.5)	(24.3)	(73.6)	(26.2)	(69.7)	(29.8)
Texas	2,169	1,524	4,231	3,245	4,397	3,077
	(58.5)	(41.1)	(56.4)	(43.2)	(58.4)	(40.8)
W.D.	855	1,080	1,142	1,123	1,042	1,025
	(44.1)	(55.8)	(50.2)	(49.4)	(50.0)	(49.2)
E.D.	123	13	282	57	357	53
	(90.4)	(9.6)	(82.7)	(16.7)	(76.9)	(12.9)
S.D.	472	319	1,514	1,330	1,583	1,351
	(59.2)	(40.0)	(53.0)	(46.7)	(53.4)	(45.4)
N.D.	719	112	1,293	735	1,415	648
	(86.2)	(13.4)	(63.6)	(36.1)	(68.3)	(31.3)
Illinois	10,779	4,406	16,188	7,665	14,128	7,853
	(70.8)	(28.9)	(67.8)	(32.1)	(64.1)	(35.6)

N.D.	7,272	3,994	10,890	6,996	9,258	7,186
	(64.5)	(35.4)	(60.8)	(39.1)	(56.1)	(43.6)
C.D.	2,901	314	4,189	480	3,703	505
	(90.1)	(9.8)	(89.7)	(10.3)	(87.9)	(12.0)
S.D.	636	98	1,109	189	1,167	162
	(86.6)	(13.4)	(85.3)	(14.5)	(87.7)	(12.1)
Pennsylvania	2,890	819	6,668	1,898	7,940	3,117
	(77.4)	(21.9)	(77.3)	(22.0)	(71.4)	(28.0)
W.D.	1,168	35	1,742	182	3,654	427
	(96.7)	(2.9)	(92.9)	(6.2)	(89.1)	(10.4)
M.D.	728	9	1,577	46	1,580	96
	(98.1)	(1.2)	(96.9)	(2.8)	(93.9)	(5.6)
E.D.	994	775	2,349	1,670	2,706	2,596
	(55.7)	(43.4)	(58.1)	(41.3)	(50.7)	(48.6)

[a]1980 figures for nine-*month* period ending June 30, 1980.

[b]Percentages may not add to total because of voluntary filings in other chapters.

Source: Administrative Office of the Courts. Annual Reports. 1980, Table F3BC, pp. 559–565; 1981, Table F3B, pp. 555–562; 1982, Table F3B, pp. 402–403.

TABLE A.2. Case Bases and Sampling Fractions, by Chapter, Consumer Bankruptcy Study (full sample)

	Chapter 7		Chapter 13		
District	*N*	Sampling Fraction[a,b]	*N*	Sampling Fraction[a]	Sampling Fraction[c]
Texas					
Western District	75	6.6%	73	6.5%	6.1%
Eastern District	100	35.5	51	89.5	78.5
Southern District	100	6.6	95	7.1	6.8
Northern District	86	6.7	66	9.0	8.2
Illinois					
Northern District	79	0.7	71	1.0	1.0
Southern District	132	11.9	24	12.7	11.2
Central District	99	2.4	46	9.6	8.8
Pennsylvania					
Western District	90	3.3	63	34.6	29.9
Middle District	98	6.2	39	85.0	62.9
Eastern District	79	3.4	63	3.7	3.7
Total	938		591		

[a]As a percentage of nonbusiness cases in this chpater that were filed in the district and tabulated by the AO.
[b]The "true" sampling fraction is unknown because some "business 7's" were eligible for the sample.
[c]As a percentage of nonbusiness 13's plus business 13's.
Source: Consumer Bankruptcy Project.

odd categorization used by the AO in reporting its data. The AO data classify Chapter 7 cases as either "business" or "nonbusiness," but this classification is imperfectly related to the legal classification of "corporate" versus "individual" bankruptcies. To make matters worse, the relationship varied from district to district not only with business conditions, but also with clerical classification practices. Indeed, there were even differences among the divisions within a district. The practice in similar studies of bankruptcy records has been not to weight the data.

Notwithstanding our criticisms of the AO data in Chapter Two, they remain the only systematic data representative of the entire country and published in time series. We did not use the data for calculating rises and falls in bankruptcy filing rates, for dividing debtors according to whether they were businesses or individuals, or for extrapolating the impact of bankruptcy on debtors or creditors throughout the country. Of necessity, however, we used the AO data to build our sampling frame. But we limited our reliance on the AO data to giving us a starting point to determine how to draw our debtor sample.

Despite the legal profession's ideology that each legal case is unique and requires specialized legal services, mass production techniques are sweeping the practice of consumer bankruptcy law. Low-cost, high-volume bankruptcy clinics predicate their approach on the assumption that consumer cases are more similar than different from one another. In somewhat analogous fashion, we proceeded on the assumption that a sample of seemingly unique bankruptcy cases will represent "reality," just as the doctor assumes that a sample of blood will represent the reality of a patient's entire blood supply. At the same time, we sought through ancillary sources of information, such as interviews with judges, to preserve the unique features of specific circumstances or of geographic areas.

Timing

Within the United States the reality of bankruptcy is affected by statutory changes, business cycle changes, and more general changes in the economy and the legal profession. Despite these variations, a study of bankruptcy must refer to some stated period of time and to some definite locale. The problem is to discern the limitations placed on the conclusions by the selection of a study at a particular time and of a particular place.

The universe for our sample consisted of personal bankruptcies filed in three states during 1981. We selected 1981 because the legal community by then had had time to adjust to the dramatic changes in the 1978 Code and the much-discussed rise in bankruptcy was well under way. According to commentators, the 1980s represented the new era of bankruptcy filings. Other researchers had studied the same year, presumably for some of the same reasons.

Although we were analyzing cases filed in 1981, we visited most courts during a period between January 1983 and June 1985. This time lag had the advantage of permitting us to record the progress of most Chapter 13 plans and to note whether 1981 cases had been reopened, perhaps because a creditor had found that a debtor's original filings were not truthful. It also provided time for harassed court staffs to catch up on their backfiling. Nearly every court had its "backstage" area where routine filing had piled up to be accomplished whenever someone had time. This time lag between the filing dates and our trips to the courthouse was the best guarantee that the files we pulled for our sample were as complete as they could be. Storage space is at a premium in every court, but storage was so critical that some courts shipped their completed files off to federal document warehouses as soon as feasible. As a result, in Dallas and Philadelphia we spent a fair amount of time retrieving documents from warehouses as well as from courthouses. Thus studying 1981 cases gave us the benefit of studying cases that were new enough to reflect current bankruptcy filings but old enough to be complete.

Pilot Study

We began our research in the summer of 1982 in the bankruptcy court nearest to us, which was located in San Antonio. This pilot study was designed to test our codebook and to give us a "feel" for the data. The three of us logged over

100 hours apiece in reviewing cases, discussing unexpected findings, and laboring over the arithmetic errors of lawyers and trustees.

A few months later, we flew to El Paso to complete our 150 cases for the Western District of Texas. Again, we did all of the coding and editing of the data sheets ourselves. Our stint with coding convinced us that the codebook was extracting most of the data from the consumers' bankruptcy files. We were confident that we could train law students in its use.

Coding

In January 1983, we began our first training session for 32 law student coders from the University of Houston Law School. Student coders were second- or third-year law students who had to have completed or to have been in the process of completing a course in bankruptcy before becoming eligible for participation in the project. The result was that all the data were coded by someone with at least a basic understanding of bankruptcy law and procedure. Every coder—indeed, every person associated with the project—signed an agreement promising to hold confidential any information acquired about any individual. Although the files we used are public documents, the petitioners, lawyers, and judges had become, for the social scientist, human subjects, and we used normal safeguards for the protection of human subjects. These safeguards included the use of identifying numbers rather than names on all the data tapes prepared, and careful storage, under lock, of any data with identifying information. The names of all debtors and some creditors in this book are pseudonyms.

Law student coders from Houston and then from The University of Texas at Austin underwent an eight-hour training process before they started to code sample cases. To standardize subsequent sessions, we videotaped the original four-hour training presentation, which included a discussion of the purposes of the coding, the procedures to follow in safeguarding and analyzing a case file, and the actual coding procedures to be used. Every student spent an additional four hours practicing coding with two files, one a Chapter 7 and the other a Chapter 13.[4] These practice files were 1982 cases, and thus ineligible for our sample, but they contained a variety of issues and errors for discussion. The practice coding was checked for accuracy and any further questions were answered.

As a safeguard, every case in our sample was coded twice, using different coders, who were then required to reconcile differences. During every coding session, at least two members of our team, a law professor and the demographer, were on call to answer questions and to resolve ambiguities according to a consistent protocol. Our initial coding was done on site, at the courthouses. As soon as we were able to do so, we bought three portable copiers; from then on we copied cases at the courthouses and brought them back to Austin for law student coding.

Some data, especially occupational codes, were coded by sociology graduate students at The University of Texas at Austin. The sociology students also field-edited and cleaned the data. These procedures included developing and using computer programs to check for proper coding ranges, logical inconsistencies, and incomplete or missing codes.

Analysis

The coded data were analyzed on an IBM 3081. Our principal software packages were SPSS-X and SAS. The magnetic tapes containing the data are archived at the Population Research Center, The University of Texas at Austin.

We have consistently used nominal dollar values rather than transformed dollar values. Although the dollar distribution of income, for example, is somewhat skewed, the skew is much smaller than that for the total population. Many economists routinely use the natural logarithm of earnings in the total population because of this departure from normality. We found in our data that the Illinois and Pennsylvania income distributions approximated normality; the Texas distribution departed from normality ($p = 0.02$ when compared to a computer-generated normal distribution). Some recent research indicates, however, that the functional form of earnings has far less influence on results than was previously thought.[5] For this reason, and because earnings were not a dependent variable in our analysis, we used nominal dollars as our consistent metric. Nevertheless, we confirmed our results in Chapter Four using nonparametric tests.

Many of our analyses are not reported in the text. Regression equations done using dichotomous dependent variables were repeated using logistic regression analysis; there were never any differences to report. Analysis of variance was conducted using several types of range tests, and we noted any results that differed.

Interview Data

Others besides the debtor are a part of the bankruptcy system. Lawyers, trustees, and judges are the "supporting actors" in the drama. They have special perspectives born from years of experience with the bankruptcy system and with the debtors and creditors coming through the bankruptcy courts. Although the information they have about the process cannot answer basic questions about the financial condition of the debtors or about which creditors are affected by bankruptcy filings, they can provide useful information about the bankruptcy process and the operation of the bankruptcy courts. We believed that interviewing the lawyers, trustees, and judges could give us important insights about the bankruptcy process and help supplement the understanding we could gain through analysis of the debtors' files.

We ultimately interviewed several different people with different connections to the bankruptcy system, including bankruptcy judges, trustees, lawyers, bankruptcy clerks, and some other court personnel, such as estate administrators. We used a semistructured interview format, and we asked the judges and lawyers to tell us about the bankruptcy process as they saw it. These interviews were scheduled at the convenience of busy professionals, and we promised anonymity to everyone who spoke with us. We made it clear that we wanted neither information that was privileged communication with individual clients nor the details of specific cases.

Our response rate among judges was excellent. Only once were we refused an interview, and even in this case the judge gave us the only time he had, literally while robing for the courtroom. He explained that his docket continued from morning until night, and that he was unable to cooperate because of the press of cases in his large, urban bankruptcy court. Another judge initially refused an interview, but in the process of refusing began to talk about bankruptcy and ultimately gave us a three-hour interview. Most of the judges were brimming with stories, theories, and explanations about the bankruptcy process. Sometimes the interviews lasted for hours, and more than once we raced to the airport after stretching the interview for just one more story. The perspectives of the judges enriched our analysis enormously.

Similarly, the lawyers, trustees, and clerks were amazingly accommodating. They took time off from pressing duties to tell us about the debtors and creditors and about other lawyers and judges and trustees. They reflected on their years in the process, and they suggested avenues of inquiry that we otherwise would not have considered.

Interviews with the judges, lawyers, and others often provided important clues for the unique local variations we discovered. They were also helpful in offering explanations for data we uncovered, often explaining a peculiarity of the community or an unexpected phenomenon they had regularly seen. We are grateful for their help, which enhanced our understanding of the data.

We note, however, that our use of the interview data is limited. As valuable as such informants are, they are one step removed from the "raw data," the petitioners. Judges, attorneys, and other "repeat actors" observe bankruptcy—but not from a detached perspective. Their experience and their involvement become both valuable resources and potential barriers to understanding. The "war stories" told by many of our informants crystallized, in memorable form, many of the points they wanted to make. But war stories, by their very nature, are anecdotes that emphasize a case for something besides its typicality. They may emphasize funny facts, or apparent abuses, or tragic circumstances, but they stick in the memory of a lawyer or judge precisely because they are not "average." Furthermore, experts may unintentionally distort their accounts to align their statements with their beliefs or otherwise to justify themselves. One judge whom we interviewed explained to us that he never permitted debtors to reaffirm a debt (that is, to legally bind themselves to pay the debt despite the declaration of bankruptcy). In our sample of cases from this same court, however, we were unable to find a reaffirmation that this judge had refused to sign! He had a policy of never signing reaffirmations, and he believed that this was his policy. He was not dissembling with us. But, like the dieter who eats dessert "just this once," he took no notice of the many exceptions to his general policy he made from day to day.

Comparative Data and Conceptual Comparisons

Wherever possible, we tried to contrast our data with similar data for the general population. Most of our comparisons were made with the March 1981 Current Population Survey, which was available to us on magnetic tape. Other comparisons were made with published data from the Current Population Survey. We also refer from time to time to consumer surveys conducted by federal agencies and to aggregated data on outstanding debt from the Federal Reserve.

The bankruptcy petitions were not designed for statistical analysis, and social scientists using them for secondary analysis must be wary of the differences in concepts from their use by the Federal Reserve or the U.S. Census Bureau. Where possible, we mention these ambiguities and explain how we resolved them. An example of this is the definition of "family" versus "household," which we mention in Chapter Four. Although both terms have well-understood technical meanings to demographers and to the U.S. Census Bureau, in general use they are likely to be interchangeable. The implicit use of these terms in bankruptcy is more like the general usage. By contrast, national surveys that collect data on "liabilities" are unlikely to make the distinction between secured and unsecured debt. These potential incomparabilities require the concerted efforts of both legal and social science analysts to avoid introducing further error into the analysis.

Notes

1. Our sample should have detected seasonality or other time variations, because we selected every *i*th case filed from the beginning of the year until December 31. Our systematic sample, taking every *i*th case that was filed in the district (where *i* is the sampling interval), should give us an equally good picture of the debtors filing in January and those filing in December, and as good a picture of those filing in Chapter 7 as in Chapter 13. If the characteristics of debtors changed during the course of the year—something that could happen, for example, if Chapter 13's become more popular with the opening of a bankruptcy clinic, as happened in one district we studied—the sample should pick up those differences. In the absence of seasonality, one would expect that about 8% of the cases would be filed in each month. When all filings were considered, there was no post-Christmas rush, although there were some smaller variations.

In Illinois, the statute opting out from the federal exemption took effect on January 1, 1981, and lawyers told us of queues waiting to file bankruptcy cases during the last weeks of 1980. For this reason, our earlier cases from Illinois may be somewhat skewed, but the direction of the bias, if any, is not possible to determine. There were relatively fewer cases filed in January and February in Illinois than there were in Pennsylvania and Texas.

If Chapter 7 only is considered, there was a minor post-Christmas rush in the Western District of Texas, where nearly 21% of the Chapter 7 sample cases had been filed by February 28. Chapter 13 filings in the Northern District of Texas showed a seasonal peak of 22% for the same two months.

The late summer–early fall increase did show up in Chapter 7. Almost 21% of the Texas Chapter 7 cases, 19% of the Illinois cases, and 18% of the Pennsylvania cases were filed in August or September. In both Texas and Illinois, there were also heavier-than-expected filings in July. In Chapter 13, on the other hand, March and April were seasonal peaks in Texas (21% of filings), March was the seasonal peak in Illinois (14.4% of filings), and September through November was the seasonal peak in Pennsylvania (35% of filings). These findings suggest that the putative seasonality of bankruptcy may apply to Chapter 7 but not to Chapter 13, but the inference cannot be sustained based on a single year's data. Although the seasonal effects do not appear to be large, analyzing a full year of data appears to be more prudent than selecting a few months' data, especially if a comparison is to be made between Chapters 7 and 13.

By comparison, the Purdue University study was conducted only during the summer months. The summer months, while a good time for university faculty to conduct research, may be atypical in the bankruptcy courts. From our observations in the summers of 1982, 1983, 1984, and 1985, we noted that bankruptcy courts, much like the rest of the country, experience some irregularities due to summer vacations, especially those of the judges. In addition, lawyers' vacation schedules lead to postponements and rescheduling of hearings. The "back-to-school" rush may instead be the "back-to-work" rush of the legal community. At any rate, it seems likely that interviewing debtors at Section 341 meetings held during the summer months incurs some bias, if only because their lawyers, creditors, and trustee are not on vacation.

2. One rule of thumb is that there should be a least 25 cases in each cell for cross-tabulations of major variables (for example, chapter of filing by district).

3. Cases are numbered sequentially by time of filing, and the unique case numbers begin over again on the first working day after January 1. Periodically, the clerks tabulate data on the number, type, and stage of the bankruptcies within their courts for transmission to the Administrative Office of the Courts. Most of what we know about the secular rise in bankruptcies comes from the Administrative Office's published reports on the number and types of bankruptcies filed, pending, and completed. Although every court we visited keeps its records on a calendar-year basis, the Administrative Office reports its data on a fiscal-year basis. Nevertheless, in each courthouse it was possible for us to sample systematically from the docket.

4. The Chapter 7 forms are nationally standardized as a provision of the Bankruptcy Code. There is no prescribed format for Chapter 13. In our study, we came across four stationers' forms used to file Chapter 13. This is an inconvenience, because the information is differently arranged on different forms, but each form calls for the same type of information.

5. R. Hodson, On the Functional Form of Earnings, 14 Social Science Research 374–394 (December 1985).

List of Tables and Figures

Index

Debt-income ratio, 195, 224n.4, 238, 243, 313. *See also* Medical debt